Collection ...1e

If you want to build a ship, don't drum up people to collect wood and don't assign them tasks and work, but rather teach them to long for the endless immensity of the sea.

—*Antoine De Saint Exupery*

Collection Care

An Illustrated Handbook for the Care and Handling of Cultural Objects

Brent A. Powell

ROWMAN & LITTLEFIELD
Lanham • Boulder • New York • London

Published by Rowman & Littlefield
A wholly owned subsidiary of The Rowman & Littlefield Publishing Group, Inc.
4501 Forbes Boulevard, Suite 200, Lanham, Maryland 20706
www.rowman.com

Unit A, Whitacre Mews, 26–34 Stannary Street, London SE11 4AB, United Kingdom

British Library Cataloguing in Publication Information Available

Library of Congress Cataloging-in-Publication Data
Powell, Brent A.
Collection care : an illustrated handbook for the care and handling of cultural objects /
Brent Powell.
    pages cm
Includes bibliographical references and index.
ISBN 978-1-4422-3881-7 (cloth : alkaline paper) — ISBN 978-1-4422-3882-4
(paperback : alkaline paper) — ISBN 978-1-4422-3883-1 (electronic)
1. Museum conservation methods—Handbooks, manuals, etc. 2. Museums—Collection
management—Handbooks, manuals, etc. 3. Antiquities—Collection and preservation—
Handbooks, manuals, etc. 4. Art objects—Conservation and restoration—Handbooks,
manuals, etc. 5. Cultural property—Protection—Handbooks, manuals, etc. I. Title.
AM141.P66 2015
069'.53—dc23   2015026684

♾ ™ The paper used in this publication meets the minimum requirements of American
National Standard for Information Sciences—Permanence of Paper for Printed Library
Materials, ANSI/NISO Z39.48-1992.

Printed in the United States of America

Contents

Foreword

For responsible professionals entrusted with the preservation of fine art, antiques, and artifacts, the issues can be daunting. Caring for such objects is a complex process, often involving the combined expertise of art handlers, collection managers, conservators, curators, preparators, registrars, technicians, and others. There are many books that address collection care, but they tend to be written by specialists for specialists. Thus, they are inclined to be narrowly focused and too often beyond the grasp of a generalist seeking a broad understanding of collection care. Brent Powell's book is an exception, aimed to educate a wide range of individuals. Anyone who manages a collection, or puts on a pair of gloves to move a small bronze, or packs a large sculpture for shipment overseas should profit from reading *Collection Care: An Illustrated Handbook*.

Powell has extensive experience in collection care, gained by working not only at museums but also at private companies that offer a variety of services, from handling and storage to packing and shipping works, whether the works be antiquities, furniture, or paintings. I first met Powell in 1988, when we worked together on the installation of The Human Figure in Early Greek Art, an exhibition co-organized by the Greek Ministry of Culture and the National Gallery of Art, Washington. After closing in Washington, the exhibition traveled to The Nelson-Atkins Museum of Art, where Powell was then chief preparator. I became enormously impressed with his knowledge and skills as I watched him handle ancient and often fragile marble sculptures, bronzes, painted clay vases, and terra-cotta figures. Some years later, when I joined the steering committee of PACCIN (Preparation, Art Handling, and Collections Care Information Network), a group associated with the American Alliance of Museums, Powell served as the committee's chairperson. There he worked to improve both the availability of information and the educational opportunities for those handling art and artifacts of all types.

For this publication, Powell has assembled an impressive group of contributors, those with exceptional knowledge of and experience in their fields. The book provides a lucid and well-ordered overview of the principles, policies, and technical specifications for proper collection care. It also offers practical recommendations on methods and materials used for the movement, exhibition, storage, and shipping of art and artifacts. The authors have admirably condensed a complex topic into a compact and eminently useful text.

Mervin Richard
Chief of Conservation
National Gallery of Art, Washington, DC

Preface

The responsibility of caring for cultural objects is one that should be looked at as a privilege, not just as a form of employment. The responsibility makes you, as the caretaker, a part of the object's history, as you are entrusted with the task of continuing and improving the conditions for preserving the object for the future caretakers when the responsibility is passed along to them, just as it was to you. The levels of risks do not change except in the political climates in organizational directives of collection care programing. Understanding and promoting the professionalism of your actions, your colleagues within your institution or company create a cohesive and supportive workplace in which to develop and improve the conditions of object care and minimize the avenues of risks that they may encounter.

As museums continue to collect objects of diverse material types, each with its distinct inherent properties, so grows the need to preserve and care for any cultural heritage collection. How to care for these objects is not a simple approach to a few specific requirements but an overarching bridge of understanding many approaches combining cultural, physical, logistical, and technical expertise to which the collection objects will be subjected.

The Collection Care Network (CCN) of the American Institute for Conservation for Historic and Artistic Works (AIC) summarizes the explanation and focus of the collection care profession in the following mission statement excerpted here:

> Collection care, which is sometimes called preventive conservation, involves any actions taken to prevent or delay the deterioration of cultural heritage. The primary goal is to identify and reduce potential hazards to heritage with thoughtful control of their surroundings. The professions most influenced by collections care include conservator-restorers, curators, collection managers, and registrars.

Although preventive conservation is central to our area of interest, we believe the term "care of collections" more accurately describes the holistic, multidisciplined approach that is essential for sustainable, long-term preservation of the cultural heritage. Objects of cultural heritage face threats from a variety of sources on a daily basis, from thieves, vandals, and pests; to pollution, humidity, and temperature; to natural emergencies and physical forces; to all kinds of light. Effects stemming from these issues can be treated and sometimes reversed with aggressive conservation after the damage has occurred. However, many of the sources of danger mentioned above are controllable, and others are at least predictable. Collection care strives to mitigate the occurrence of damage and deterioration through research and the implementation of procedures which enhance the safety of cultural heritage objects and collections. The areas of particular concern with regard to the sources of damage include environmental conditions, object handling, integrated pest management, emergency preparedness, and records management.[1]

My work on this publication commenced in 2006 when, while employed by the National Gallery of Victoria in Melbourne, Australia, I was awarded a Clemenger Family Research Grant to research handling best practices in relation to the collection care of objects at major museums in England and the United States. The secondary focus was to continue my interest in how staffing and training structures were established and supported within the various organizations that I visited. Over the last nine years, I have continued to research and compile information in preparation for this publication.

In my career, I have been extremely fortunate to be involved in management of staff and working with other managers who were dedicated to creating an effective work environment with the highest levels of standards of collection care. I have been fortunate to have traveled as an exhibition courier and to have worked closely with colleagues from other institutions, sharing exhibition responsibilities for numerous types of exhibitions, nationally and globally. Early in my career, I was asked to be a part of the broader museum community by becoming the chair of a newly formed group called PACIN (Packing and Crating Information Network), a task force of the Registrars Committee of the American Association of Museums. This involvement in the larger museum community and outreach dedicated to best practices and collection care programming led me to pursue broader levels of knowledge and networks with colleagues to create and promote museum conference sessions, and organize and conduct independent workshops and courses for best practices in collection care. This fueled my interest in understanding other institutions' policies and procedures and in creating networks of individuals with whom to share information. The basis for the key points of this book has given me the structure for creating this publication.

PURPOSE AND SCOPE

Collection Care: An Illustrated Handbook for the Care and Handling of Cultural Objects is intended to provide the reader with an overview of the basic principles and assessment of collection care procedures, policies, and technical requirements in the museum world today. The content in each chapter addresses the process of planning and the decision-making criteria to assess the potential risks involved and the choice of solutions required in the care of cultural heritage art and artifacts. Different topics are cited with explanations of procedures and policies of collection care best practices, which draw consistency from among the many components found within different collections and organizational structures. Technical subjects address proven handling techniques, materials, equipment, and methodology, along with analysis and problem-solving situations for various object types. The publication provides a reference guide, technical bibliography, and training tools for staff involved in the collection care programming and technical decision making.

This handbook is targeted to give the reader an overview of organizational structures, staff responsibilities, internal relationships, and training to provide a comprehensive understanding of the unity of professionals in a museum or commercial service organization. It is intended to provide individuals who are responsible for collection care practices with the analytical knowledge required for safely handling and caring for collection objects in any organization. The collaboration of these individuals is a key element to creating successful solutions for collection care. The multidisciplinary knowledge of and the choreography among these individuals are paramount for having knowledgeable and committed staff in the museum or commercial company.

The book was written to serve as a reference and assist individuals at any level of employment within the collection care profession, whether within a museum or a commercial company. For individuals just starting their career, the content can act as a framework to learn the various levels of collection care practices and the structural makeup and the relations of other individuals involved within their organization. For individuals who have been involved with the collection care profession for a period of time, the content can serve as a refresher for specific topics or assist in the training and development of staff that they are responsible for managing.

In the industry there are countless sources of collection care information regarding specific object types. This book has been designed to extend past just the specific subjects, by combining the information in a more holistic way for the readers to explore, analyze, and develop successful solutions for their specific collection care needs.

Addressing all this information pertaining to every type of collection care policy and procedure, specific object types, and methods and methodology for materials and equipment to be used would not be possible in a single publication—it would be similar to painting the Golden Gate Bridge in San Francisco: once you were finished painting, you would need to start again— with the new content to be covered and revised information from current research to be shared. The intent of this book is to present the topical assessment of collection care based on which the readers can evaluate and develop their own research outcomes to a successful solution.

The key element in understanding and executing the practices of collection care must be an analytical nature. Many people consider problem solving as simply asking for the "best way" to do something. Knowing "why" it is the best way or the best solution is much more important for the final result. Working in the profession of collection care requires one to be open minded to the process of analyzing a situation in a field that is constantly being researched and developed. Each museum collection is unique in "what" the physical collection encompasses, "how" it was collected, and "where" it is housed or displayed, researched or interpreted. Each object within a collection is different in its material makeup and the inherent properties of its present condition. No one solution fits the collection care requirements of every type of object, so we must approach the assessment as a multidisciplinary understanding and find the best solution for a particular matter.

TERMINOLOGY

Many words or phrases are used in describing the elements of successful collection care information and methodologies. Often, these same words or phrases overlap with others having a similar intended meaning and are used by individuals to emphasize their comprehensive knowledge. Many individuals within the collection care profession use these phrases more as buzz words or in the same way that they seek the quickest and easiest solution, without comprehending the full requirement or understanding the overall activity. These words should not be considered or used lightly. The selected solution for the proper care of any object, whether it is housed for long-term storage or being prepared for traveling display, for mitigating potential pest infestation, for controlling light restrictions, or for a combination of multiple concerns, must be addressed based on research and the knowledge of the collection. The overall knowledge is gained by experience and research and by analyzing questions, which is the creative basis of the nature of our professional responsibility.

Common sense in the museum industry is primarily knowledge gained over a period of time and the methodical approach one takes to seeking a solution. Individuals may have inherited the platform for common sense from their upbringing, personality traits, and communicative temperament. The term "best practices" is another phrase that is often used in a descriptive sense but is not fully understood. Best practices should be standards that are based on proven solutions to risk activities in the past and that are still amenable to development and change. A brief description of the meanings of the common phrases used in best practices for standards presented in this book and by the contributing authors is presented below.

Collection Care: Collection care strategies are based on common sense. Any person working in a museum—whether a registrar, exhibit designer, director, or volunteer—must incorporate preservation principles in all activities that impact the collection. The way money is allocated, staff is trained, equipment purchased, and consultants used impacts the preservation of a collection as much as storage materials and exhibit light levels.[2]

Preventive Conservation: Preventive conservation aims to minimize deterioration of and damage to works of art and, thus, to avoid the need for invasive conservation treatment and ensure that works of art are protected for now and the future. Preventive conservation methods are based on the concept that deterioration of and damage to works of art can be substantially reduced by controlling some of their major causes in the gallery (museum) environment.[3]

Interventive Conservation: Interventive conservation measures are carried out when damage has occurred to collections or unacceptable changes have been observed in them. The aim of these conservation and restoration treatments is to understand and retain the objects' physical integrity as well as their cultural significance.[4]

Best Practices: There is no single "best practice" because the "best" for one is not best for everyone. Every organization is different in some way—different in mission, culture, environment, or technology. What is meant by "best" are those practices that have been shown to produce superior results; that have been selected by a systematic process; and that have been judged as exemplary, good, or successfully demonstrated. Best practices are then adapted to fit a particular organization.[5]

Standards: Standards represent professional consensus on best practices. Standards are developed by knowledgeable practitioners by codifying a reasonable body of practice based on a wide range of experiences.[6]

Museum Industry: The term "museum industry" is a coined phrase that refers to the community, fraternity, or working relations of all organizations practicing in the field of museum-related activities and responsibilities. Examples of these cross-organizational groups include museums of all types, commercial service companies, museum suppliers, insurance companies, and auction houses.

ORGANIZATION

The work begins with an introduction written by Rebecca Fifield and aptly titled "The Context of Collection Care: Elements for Creating an Institutional Preservation Culture." In it, Fifield presents an overarching view of collection care and its purposeful goals. Her viewpoints are insightful and are based on a broad range of professional experience in the fields of collection care, preventive conservation practices, and staff training in collection care responsibilities within institutional and conservation networking groups.

Part I, "Overview and History," features three chapters. The first, "History of Collection Care," explores the history and development of object collection and their relationship to the preservation of objects.

Chapter 2, "Organizational Structures," looks at collection care staff within both museums and commercial service companies. Chapter 3, "Training, Health, and Safety," highlights the best approaches to training collection care staff and building professionalism in management and staff.

Part II, "Guidelines and Principles," provides an overview of the numerous responsibilities in caring for collection objects. Chapter 4 is devoted to aspects of proper collection care principles and guidelines for handling techniques and materials used for the care of two-dimensional objects, while chapter 5 covers three-dimensional objects.

Part III, "Working within Collection Care Environments," is a primer of contemporary collection care. Chapter 6, "Collection Care: The Internal Environment," highlights critical aspects of collection care activities conducted inside the museum. The topics presented include current standards of environmental conditions in relation to the principles and practices involved for storage, display, and workspaces and other areas where collection care activities are undertaken. Chapter 7, "Collection Care: The External Environment," is an in-depth exploration of collection care activities conducted when objects go outside the museum's physical boundaries. Chapter 8, "Working with Materials and Equipment," covers materials used for various handling, packing, and storage techniques and designing or purchasing quality handling equipment commonly used for collection care activities in the industry today.

Importantly, each chapter features one or both of two special types of information. "Case Studies" present special applications of topics within the field today. "Focus On" sections are in-depth technical explorations of essential subtopics within each chapter.

Appendices include a bibliography and reference list covering a wide variety of publications, websites, and articles with pertinent information on collection care.

Collection Care: An Illustrated Handbook for the Care and Handling of Cultural Objects is intended to assist the reader in understanding the pieces of the puzzle so as to be a responsible caretaker of the objects one is entrusted with during one's tenure in the profession. Each puzzle piece combines and connects to the larger and final picture, which must always be kept in sight in order for one to achieve one's desired outcomes and collection care goals. I will consider myself successful in achieving my goals for writing this book if I have helped trigger the analytical thinking process for you to question, analyze, quantify, and then confirm your design to arrive at a successful solution for a collection care responsibility. I hope the connections made will provide you with the ideas to pursue the challenges that you face. Ask the question, not just ponder the possible answers.

NOTES

1. American Institute for Conservation, *Collection Care Network*, accessed November 2014, http://www.conservation-us.org/about-us/our-structure/networks#. VQGJA7k5A2U.

2. Northern States Conservation Center "Collections Care," accessed November 2014, http://www.collectioncare.org/node/178.

3. National Gallery of Australia, "Preventive Conservation," accessed November 2014, http://nga.gov.au/Conservation/prevention/index.cfm.

4. The Horniman Public Museum and Public Park Trust; "Interventive Conservation" accessed November 2014, http://www.horniman.ac.uk/collections/ collections-conservation-and-care-150.

5. American Productivity and Quality Center "Best Practices," accessed November 2014, www.apqc.org/free/terms.htm.

6. Getty Information Institute. "Standards," accessed November 2014, www.getty. edu.

Acknowledgments

I would like to acknowledge the people who have encouraged me in this endeavor and in my career ambitions in the field of collection care. I am fortunate to have had many family members who were teachers, and teachers who instructed me in such aspects as craftsmanship and creative approaches to problem solving and analytical thinking. My upbringing in the agricultural Midwestern region of the United States indoctrinated a work ethic and an understanding of the technical skills required for adapting to the diverse aspects of farming. The challenges encouraged my inquisitive nature in approaching and assessing problems to find solid, creative solutions to various situations.

I offer my thanks and praise to the following individuals for providing the bedrock of my life and their unstinting support in the creation of this publication: my father, Glen, for his patience, problem-solving abilities, and stories; my mother, Evalyn, for her teaching skills, her love for collecting antiques, and her care of them and pride in their ownership; my wife, Kim, for her laughter, love of the big picture and travel, and her support in my career ambitions over the years, and especially this past year; my good friend, confidant, and editor, Christine Droll, who, over the last twenty-five years, has translated the words in my mind to the words on the page so that others can view my thoughts more clearly as I talk in circles; my good friend, confidant and raconteur, John Molini, for the years of growing together in our firm commitment to the importance of being entrusted with the responsibility of caring for cultural objects, making a difference, and leaving our mark for others to learn; and my good friend and conservation mentor, Forrest Bailey, who instilled in me the importance of collection care within the museums' overall operational structure.

To all the many colleagues with whom I have worked over the years, networked, and shared my passion for this profession—we have challenged one another and built strong connections in the workplace and museum community. The flow of the conversation still continues and is vital to achieving our goals. To all of the individuals who attended my conferences, workshops, and session presentations—the rewards of your thoughts and comments made it all worthwhile for me. The challenge to do a good job drives me to improve my teaching skills that much more.

Special thanks go to Mervin Richard for writing the foreword of this book. The professional knowledge of the contributing authors—Rebecca Fifield, who has written the introduction, Geoff Browne (and his technical review), Kurt Christian, Dr. Abby Sue Fisher, Jim Grundy, Kevin Marshall, John Molini, Kim Powell, Mark Slattery, Simm Steel and Nicole Bouchard Tejeiro—has been invaluable for augmenting the content of this publication.

For providing images and background information in the commercial sector of the industry, I thank Kingsley Mundey, managing director, and Simon Hartas of IAS Fine Arts Logistics, Sydney, Australia; John Jacobs, president, and Mark Wamaling, Jim Carey, and Chris Barber of Artex Fine Art Services, Washington, DC; and Bob Crozier, president, and Simon Hornby of Crozier Fine Arts in New York City.

Last but not least, I would like to thank Charles Harmon, executive editor at Rowman & Littlefield Publishing Group in New York, and his staff for their assistance in giving me the proper directives to create this publication. Charles listened to my ideas, answered my questions, and then graciously opened the door to this challenging new opportunity.

Introduction

The Context of Collection Care

Elements for Creating an Institutional Preservation Culture

Rebecca Fifield

Collection care practitioners, be they conservators, technicians, collection managers, or others, often struggle with explaining collection care. Try defining "collection care." Where would you begin? When you describe your professional or organizational role, do you use the term "collection care?"

When we cannot explain our work efficiently, it makes it difficult to convey its importance. All collection care activities aim to mitigate risks posed by the ten agents of deterioration. First outlined in 1987 and published in 1990 by Stefan Michalski and later appended by Robert Waller, the list of the agents of deterioration identifies the forces that cause damage to collections (Textbox I.1).[1] We use careful handling practices and proper support materials to prevent physical damage during handling. We work with environmental engineers to produce a museum climate with a stable temperature and relative humidity. We clean storage spaces regularly and monitor sticky traps to minimize pest activity. These activities are the work of collection care, but considered singly, they do not define collection care. They cannot convey the entire benefit of preventive care that a collection care program provides.

To gain necessary support and maximize collection care functionality, it is crucial that we describe collection care as a system that manages risk mitigation activities, rather than a list of tasks. Museums assess their needs, justify expenditures, and evaluate outcomes for many types of work, from infrastructure to education. Preservation activities must also be managed in a systematic way to use limited resources to the best advantage. Preservation of collections is listed as a responsibility within many museums' mission statements and other core documents, but to make this more than just lip service, preservation programs must be codified.[2] Comprehensive management is required to orchestrate effective application of preventive care methods in order to understand the inputs and outcomes of a collection care system.

Textbox I.1 Agents of Deterioration. *Source*: Canadian Conservation Institute.

- Physical Forces
- Thieves and Vandals
- Dissociation
- Fire
- Water
- Pests
- Pollutants
- Light, Ultraviolet and Infrared
- Incorrect Temperature
- Incorrect Relative Humidity

Beyond the management activities of setting goals, creating procedures, establishing calendars, and evaluating progress, establishing an institutional culture around preventive conservation further facilitates the efficiency and success of collection care work. Components of this approach include the following:

- fostering staff collaboration around collection care;
- setting up policy that supports preventive conservation in all museum activities;
- committing to preventive conservation-friendly design within object environments; and
- sharing the importance of collection care with our visitors.

STAFF COLLABORATION

Collection care is a team effort. Beyond those staff whose job description includes collection care, it is the administration's responsibility to see that all staff understand their role in the preservation of collections. While the Preparator performs calculations to confirm the support that will be needed to protect a crated object during travel, the Finance staff support collection care by disposing of their food waste in central, closed trash cans (to deter infestation) that are emptied each night by the Maintenance staff. The institution's commitment to preservation is mandated by the administration, and performance evaluations assess how all staff fulfill their particular responsibility toward preservation functions.

The museum professional charged with the care of collections wears myriad hats. Unlike professionals whose titles define what they do (doctors, engineers, and lawyers), collection care practitioners have a staggering array of titles and responsibilities. Technicians, Preparators, Registrars, Collection

Managers, Curators, Conservators, Educators, Operations staff, and Administrators may be tasked with activities that promote preservation in various types of institutions. Collection care providers come from diverse training backgrounds. Sixty percent of respondents to the American Institute for Conservation Collection Care Network's Collection Care Staff Survey reported having master's degrees. While many logically reported training in conservation or museum studies, some of the 768 respondents reported backgrounds in foreign languages, architecture, music, and even nursing.[3] This wide array of experiences brings creativity to collection care practice, but it also suggests the need for training to find common ground among the institution's preservation principles.

Collection care training requires institutions to affirm and codify their commitment to professional preventive conservation standards. The best training is that which assumes no status exemptions. An example is a regular training program used to maintain collection-handling privileges at Winterthur Museum, Library, and Garden. All staff that work with collections participate in an initial training program and are assigned an H (may "H"andle) or M (may "M"ove), which is marked on their identification badges. To maintain these privileges, staff, with no exceptions, must take refresher training every three years.

Research design can also build support for preventive conservation systems by requiring staff collaboration. Staff having different perspectives contribute valuable information to collection care planning. For example, the National Trust in the United Kingdom employs multiple segments of staff to investigate the effects of visitors, dust, and other factors on their historic houses, which contributes to their overall risk assessment and management program.[4] R. Robert Waller developed the Cultural Property Risk Analysis Model (CPRAM), which assesses the potential extent of impact and loss of value when various risks affect units of a collection.[5] Compilation of this information requires the participation of conservators, curators, collections managers, facilities managers, security staff, and registrars. Evaluating each risk can lead not only to lively discussions, but also to a better understanding of current issues and challenges faced by each segment of the staff.

COLLECTION CARE POLICY AND PROCEDURES

Establishing collection care policy and procedures that espouse the principles of preventive conservation demonstrates the institution's commitment to professional staff and conservation-approved methods. Many museums insert preservation as a main activity of their institution in their mission statements;

policy indicates how and to what extent the goal of preservation should be carried out. These mandates also need to include frameworks for active management of collection care activities, including evaluation. It is important during straightened times for museums that all departments can demonstrate how their activities support museum goals, and to do so, data are required to report progress.

As collection care actions must take place regularly and repeatedly over centuries for an object to retain its significance, it can be difficult for the museum administrator to understand the resources and the diligence that model collection care requires, without some sort of evaluation model. An interventive conservation treatment upon an object, in which cracks are inpainted, old varnishes are removed and replaced, or missing components are re-crafted, has a great visual impact. The staff and resource contributions of ideally executed collection care are not perceptible over decades without analysis. An object that is examined, dusted, photographed, or crated today to the best professional standards will deteriorate at a reduced rate. Not executing collection care tasks to their full potential will result in the earlier onset of instability and loss.

Collection care is not a luxury. It is not what takes place in between exhibitions and projects with upcoming deadlines. These activities require quantifiable resources in order to achieve satisfactory levels, let alone optimum levels. Particulate removal research (aka "dusting") at National Trust historic houses found that over 75 percent of the housekeeping budget paid for staff time. Increase in visitor attendance directly affected the perception of dustiness among visitors and staff, and it increased the needed staff time to mitigate particulates introduced to the interiors by additional visitors.[6] As collection stewards, it is the administration's responsibility to assess collection care needs beyond the pressures of exhibitions and projects and to consider what prevents deterioration over hundreds of years. The ever-increasing amount of photographic documentation, not as available in the past, will bear future witness to deterioration.

COMMITMENT TO COLLECTION CARE DESIGN

During the creation of collection care policy, the environment in which collection care takes place must be considered. This has generally come to mean innovative climate control systems and low-pollutant finishes, but the significant amount of staff time needed to maintain collection spaces emphasizes that design can help or hinder collection care staff activities. Institutional commitment to collection care-informed design enhances staff efficiency and visitor experience. During a time when museums must work efficiently with fewer staff, it is hardly wise to skimp on exhibition case design that makes it difficult to install art, risking safety of both art and handler.

Design considerations are many, but they can be as simple as eliminating design details on cases that allow dust to collect, raising cabinetry off the floor to facilitate cleaning, not using carpeting in galleries, and eliminating dead spaces that encourage pest activity. The involvement of collection care staff at the initiation of projects can help identify planning mistakes that could prove costly, if not impossible to manage, for decades to come. It is disingenuous to short the construction budget just to let collection care staff deal with it as best they can upon completion, especially when this task is linked to performance evaluations.

Involving the Public

Museums increasingly require that all functions define their role by how they support the visitor experience. Traditionally, collection care has been described as "behind the scenes" and "not sexy," even by the people who believe in its importance. Collection care is of interest to the public. It provides unexpected glimpses of the real workings of a museum, interesting to both adults and children alike. Conservation studios placed within or adjacent to galleries have been extending the discussion of conservation science and the preservation of heritage, as well as demonstrating the equipment, space, expertise, and, most important, the time required for preservation. Institutions are using blogs, social media, and onsite programming to further the understanding and appreciation of collection care and conservation. The United Kingdom is a good place to look for outreach ideas, as many of their cultural institutions receive public support. National Trust properties often perform controlled conservation and collection care activities as an educational program in front of the public. Knole House, a National Trust property, has a conservation team blog that addresses care of clocks, discovery of mummified rats in the attic, and rehousing of photographic collections.[7] A report in 2008 focused on UK collections in storage suggesting controlled and timed public tours. Some ideas might fly in the face of what collection stewards feel is responsible care or a pleasurable experience for visitors, but these contributions help begin discussions on how we can bring the message of collection care to the public.[8] When lamenting the lack of funds for general collection care, it is important to remember that it is difficult to ask for funds when the public is unaware of the role that collection care and conservation play.

Within museums exists a symbiosis between the visitor and collections staff member. The visitor is there to acquire knowledge, be challenged, enjoy beauty, and to gain any number of other personal benefits that might be achieved by attending museums.[9] When they do visit, they are often most moved by the collections that they view. Conservation and collections professionals widely accept the importance of preventive conservation in preserving authenticity and reducing needless damage to collections.[10] Continued diligence in advocating for whole collection care systems and demonstrating their benefits through research are required.

NOTES

1. *Preventive Conservation and Agents of Deterioration* (Ottawa, Ontario: Canadian Conservation Institute, 2014), http://www.cci-icc.gc.ca/resources-ressources/agentsofdeterioration-agentsdedeterioration/index-eng.aspx.

2. *Preservation 101. Introduction to Preservation* (Northeast Document Conservation Center, 2006), http://unfacilitated.preservation101.org/session1/expl_collmgt-mission.asp, accessed 9/14/2014. See also "Developing a Mission Statement," (American Alliance of Museums, 2012), http://www.aam-us.org/docs/continuum/developing-a-mission-statement-final.pdf?sfvrsn=2.

3. AIC CCN Collection Care Staff Survey, 2012, accessed 8/8/2014.

4. Helen Lloyd, P. Brimblecombe, and K. Lithgow, "Economics of Dust," *Studies in Conservation* 52, no. 2 (2007): 138.

5. R. Robert Waller, "Cultural Property Risk Analysis Model: Development and Application to Preventive Conservation at the Canadian Museum of Nature," *Göteborg Studies in Conservation* 13 (2003).

6. Lloyd et al., 135–146.

7. Knole House Conservation Team Blog, http://knoleconservationteam.wordpress.com/, accessed 8/12/2014.

8. Suzanne Keene, *Collections for People* (London: UCL Institute of Archaeology, 2008), http://www.museumsassociation.org/download?id=18411.

9. Samuel Jones, *Culture Shock* (London: Demos, 2010), http://www.demos.co.uk/files/Culture_shock_-_web.pdf?1286815564. 33-42.

10. Preventive conservation is routinely stressed as the primary way of preserving collections. For example, see the American Institute for Conservation of Historic and Artistic Work, Code of Ethics, Item I. I. http://www.conservation-us.org/about-us/core-documents/code-of-ethics#.VBXjsktM8ds, accessed 9/14/2014.

Part I

OVERVIEW AND HISTORY

Chapter 1

History of Collection Care

"The collections are fundamental to all that a museum does in regard to its programming and why it exists as an institution. The primary principal of collection caretakers is the preservation of the collection for future generations to research and admire. Cultural heritage is a fact that the past should not be forgotten and/or destroyed so the future can build on it." Exhibit label for "Afghanistan: Hidden Treasures from the National Museum, Kabul"; Asian Art Museum, San Francisco; October 24, 2008–January 25, 2009.

Introduction to History of Collection Care
History of Collectors
Public Museums
   The Ashnolean
   The British Museum
   The Louvre
   Smithsonian Institution
Development of Collection Care
   Early Approach
   Collection Care Staffing
   Collection Care Management
   Changing Industry
Conclusion

INTRODUCTION TO HISTORY OF COLLECTION CARE

This chapter is an overview of the history of collecting cultural objects with a focus on developing collection care practices and standards. Collectors and museums mentioned in this chapter are selected highlights and only skim the surface of the subject. Why objects were collected can be researched by delving into the history of the collectors and specific provenance of a particular object, or by researching collection or accession records when and where they exist. The following pages will touch on the development of private and museum collection care practices and emphasize the definite marriage between collecting and collection care. For further interest on the history of collectors and museums, please see the bibliography section for this chapter.

The history of collecting can be based on the premise that many objects were intended to be created and used as hierarchical, ceremonial, or educational tools and were often passed along to others within the tribe or group. Some objects were destined only to be buried with the dead to aid them in their spiritual afterlife. Other objects, which were used for utilitarian purposes, have survived because of the quality of the craftsmanship and the environment in which they existed.

The quality of the craftsman's technical ability and the methodologies and materials available at the time allowed these artifacts to survive centuries in many diverse environmental conditions. The care of these objects was in some instances intentional per the maker's or owner's wishes, and in others, consequential, as the climate and the environment in which they survived dictated their longevity. The extent of the craftsman's knowledge about the design and fabrication of these objects is what we base our knowledge of the cultural past on and often on how humans developed and migrated.

The individuals who are responsible for establishing and maintaining the care of collections, both private and public, must state and implement a collection care mission. The inherent properties of a particular object or type of collection guide the direction for proper care of the objects.

Caring for collections is based on specific priorities of how a collection will be handled, stored, displayed, packed, and preserved. This assessment is dictated by the physical aspect of an object: its age, size, weight, material composition, inherent properties, and environmental history.

Attendant upon the physical attributes of an object is its provenance. The history of ownership offers a kind of tracking for the movement and location history of an object throughout its journey from creation to the present time. Provenance can provide luster to an object, which may increase its monetary valuation. Knowing where an object has been could explain physical evidence that calls for conservation treatment. These assessments dictate how an object is to be preserved and cared for.

For the individual collector, the desire to preserve the object and to maintain its cultural heritage is an investment to be developed. The prestige of ownership and monetary investment can be the primary incentive to properly care for and maintain the object. The desire and commitment to protect and preserve an object for its cultural heritage should be the raison d'être of a museum's mission statement.

HISTORY OF COLLECTORS

Throughout history, individuals of wealth or political influence have collected art, artifacts, and natural specimens that often reflect their personal taste and satisfy their desire for possession. During the extension of their imperial dominance, dynasties and kingdoms acquired objects by right of conquest, which, no doubt, added value to their collections. Sometimes these acquisitions were to fill different residences simply with decorative wealth.

One of the largest global collecting periods in history occurred during the fifteenth to eighteenth centuries following the Portuguese, Spanish, and English voyages of exploration to find a sea route to the Far East. Concurrent with that exploration was the interest in and fascination for the flora and fauna of these new lands. Objects of art and artifacts of ceremonial and utilitarian purposes were also highly prized for adding to royal collections—much of which was meant to offset the tremendous expense of sponsoring these enterprises. The following two examples of this European expansion helped to change the cultural history and scientific research of this period and have established some major collections that are still in existence today.

Ferdinand and Isabelle, the fifteenth-century king and queen of Spain, collected artworks from Europe and the New World over the course of their imperial expansion. Many of the artworks from neighboring countries were acquired and brought to Spain to establish the royal collection. Throughout this and the next three centuries of Spanish dominance, the artworks acquired helped to form the collection now housed in the Museo Del Prado in Madrid.

During the Spanish empire's ascendancy, many artworks were acquired through the negotiations undertaken by Spanish ambassadors and viceroys in art centers, especially those in Italy. Artists were commissioned by the Spanish Court or were subjects of the Spanish Crown who were hired to paint or sculpt works that were added to the monarchs' collections. This approach of collecting was conducted in a similar fashion throughout Europe during this time.

Joseph Banks, an English naturalist, explorer, and botanist, noted for his promotion of natural sciences in 1768 traveled on an expedition supported by the British Royal Society led by Captain James Cook. The expectation and mission was to explore the uncharted lands of the South Pacific and visit South America, Tahiti, New Zealand, Australia, and Java. The three-year expedition afforded Banks notable recognition through his collection of many previously unknown specimens of flora and fauna and by his scientific documentation of the overall voyage. Many future voyages of discovery were approved and carried out under his supervision.

The objects collected were quickly recognized in the European science community as new findings and sources for advanced scientific study.

The preservation of these objects has helped to establish many collection care principles which are used even today.

Such interest in collecting and preserving objects was not unique to the monarchy or empire. Wealthy private individuals also sought to establish collections to enhance or glorify their reputations. These collections were often termed "cabinet of curiosities" and were designed to cultivate an individual style or an encyclopedic group of objects. Collectors often considered this grouping or collection as an interpretation of the "whole" of the knowledge of a particular area or subject.

Cabinets of curiosities (also known as Kunstkabinett, Kunstkammer, Wunderkammer, Cabinets of Wonder, and wonder-rooms) were encyclopedic collections of objects whose categories were yet to be defined in Renaissance Europe. Modern terminology would categorize the objects included as belonging to natural history (sometimes faked), geology, ethnography, archaeology, religious or historical relics, works of art (including cabinet paintings), and antiquities. "The Kunstkammer was regarded as a microcosm or theater of the world, and a memory theater. The Kunstkammer conveyed symbolically the patron's control of the world through its indoor, microscopic reproduction." Of Charles I of England's collection, Peter Thomas states succinctly, "The *Kunstkabinett* itself was a form of propaganda." Besides the most famous, best documented cabinets of rulers and aristocrats, there were collections formed by members of the merchant class and early practitioners of science in Europe, which were precursors to museums.[1] (2)

Some of the most famously described seventeenth-century cabinets were those of Ole Worm, known as Olaus Wormius (1588–1654). These seventeenth-century cabinets were filled with preserved animals, horns, tusks, skeletons, and minerals, as well as other interesting man-made objects: sculptures wondrously old, wondrously fine, or wondrously small; clockwork automata; and ethnographic specimens from exotic locations. Often they would contain a mix of fact and fiction. The specimens displayed were often collected during exploring expeditions and trading voyages.

PUBLIC MUSEUMS[2] (3)

The establishment of museums, institutions dedicated to housing collections, became the next extension to the vast collecting growth begun by European exploration. The purpose of these institutions was to bring the collection of objects into one location and to make them available for scholarly research and for public delectation. With the identification of a clear role for museums in society, there gradually developed the study of museology. The following four museums are highlighted as major examples.

The Ashmolean

The Ashmolean is the oldest public museum in Britain and the first purpose-built public museum in the world. It was a gift from Elias Ashmole who mandated that a building be erected to house his collection. The University of Oxford was the first corporate body to receive such a gift, and it carried out Ashmole's wishes when the Ashmolean Museum opened in 1683.

The British Museum

The eighteenth century saw the flowering of the Enlightenment and the quest for encyclopedic knowledge, as well as a growing taste for the exotic. These influences, encouraged by increasing world exploration—by trade centered on northwestern Europe and by developing industrialization—are evident in the opening of two of Europe's outstanding museums: the British Museum, in London, in 1759, and the Louvre, in Paris, in 1793. The British Museum was formed as the result of the government's acceptance of responsibility to preserve and maintain three collections "not only for the inspection and entertainment of the learned and the curious, but for the general use and benefit of the public." These were housed at Montagu House, in Bloomsbury, specially purchased for this purpose. The collections had been made by Sir Robert Cotton, Robert Harley, First Earl of Oxford, and Sir Hans Sloane. The Cotton and Harley collections were composed mainly of manuscripts. The Sloane collection, however, included specimens of natural history from Jamaica and classical, ethnographic, numismatic, and art material, as well as the cabinet of William Courten, comprising some 100,000 items in all.

The Louvre

It was a matter of public concern in France that the royal collections were inaccessible to the populace, and eventually a selection of paintings was exhibited at the Luxembourg Palace in 1750 by Louis XV. Continuing pressure, including Diderot's proposal of a national museum, led to arrangements for more of the royal collection to be displayed to the public in the Grande Galerie of the Louvre palace. However, when the Grande Galerie was opened to the public in 1793, it was by decree of the Revolutionary government rather than royal mandate, and it was called the Central Museum of the Arts. There were many difficulties, and the museum was not fully accessible until 1801. The collection at the Louvre grew rapidly, not least because the National Convention instructed Napoleon to appropriate works of art during his European campaigns; as a result many royal and noble collections were transported to Paris to be shown at what became known as the Musée

Napoléon. The return to its owners of this looted material was required by the
Congress of Vienna in 1815. Nevertheless, the Napoleonic episode awakened
a new interest in art and provided the impetus that made a number of collections available to the public.

Smithsonian Institution

The Smithsonian Institution, in Washington, DC, came into existence through
the remarkable bequest of nearly one-half million dollars from James Smith-
son, an Englishman. He wished to see established in the United States an
institution "for the increase and diffusion of knowledge among men." In
1846 the U.S. Congress accepted his bequest and passed legislation establishing the Smithsonian as an institution charged with representing "all objects
of art and curious research . . . natural history, plants, [and] geological and
mineralogical specimens" belonging to the United States. The U.S. National
Museum opened in 1858 as part of the Smithsonian's scientific program and
formed the first of its many museums, most of which stand along the Mall in
Washington, DC.

Nineteenth Century

It was during the second half of the nineteenth century that museums began
to proliferate in Europe; civic pride and the free education movement were
among the causes of this development. About 100 opened in Britain in the
fifteen years before 1887, while fifty museums were established in Germany
in the five years from 1875 to 1880. This was also a period of innovation. The
Liverpool Museums in England, for example, began circulating specimens to
schools for educational purposes; panoramas and habitat groups were used
to facilitate interpretation. As gas lighting, and then electric lighting, became
available, museums extended their hours into the evenings to provide service
to those unable to visit during the day.

   Museums in the later part of the nineteenth century developed around
the world with a proliferation that was smaller, yet similar, to that of their
European counterparts. Major cities throughout the world built museums,
which were often named to represent the popularity and pride of their cultural
heritage and governmental status. The majority were built to house objects of
cultural or natural history and established as royal or the people's collections.

Twentieth Century

The first half of the twentieth century saw the profound social consequences
of two world wars, the Russian Revolution of 1917, and periods of economic
recession. In the industrialized world, new types of museums appeared.
Some nations made conscious attempts to preserve and display structures and

customs of their more recent past: the open-air museums at Arnhem in The Netherlands (the Open Air Museum, opened in 1912) and in Cardiff, Wales (the Welsh Folk Museum, opened in 1947). The preservation and restoration of buildings or entire settlements in situ also began; particularly well known is Colonial Williamsburg, founded in Virginia in 1926. A new type of science museum also emerged in which static displays of scientific instruments and equipment were replaced with demonstrations of the applications of science.

The years immediately following World War II were a period of remarkable achievement for museums. This was reflected both in international and national policy and in the individual museums as they responded to a rapidly changing, better-educated society. Museums became an educational facility, a source of leisure activity, and a medium of communication. Their strength lay in the notion that they were repositories of the "real thing," which—unlike the surrounding world of plastics, reproduced images, and a deteriorating natural and human environment—could inspire and invoke a sense of wonder, reality, stability, and even nostalgia.

Contemporary museum development has been much influenced by changing policies in public sector finance. In many countries, the contribution of public funds to museums has remained static or has fallen, so that museums' governing bodies and directors have had to seek funding from alternative sources. This has not only affected the way museums are organized but also accentuated the need for marketing and fund-raising expertise.

Many buildings of historical significance have been adapted to house museums. Among these are the Orsay Museum, formerly a major railroad station in Paris, which was reopened in 1986 as a national museum of the nineteenth century, and the Tate Gallery of the North at Liverpool (1988), an art museum housed in a warehouse in the Albert Dock, by the River Mersey.

Currently, existing museums continue to grow with the social and economic changes being placed upon them. New museums both large and small continue to be created and are shaped through economic support, mainly from private and, less so, from government sources. This change is being seen not only in wealthy industrialized nations but also in the nonindustrial countries around the world, where the main focus is still to acknowledge their pride of cultural history and craftsmanship of the objects, which reflect their native heritage.

DEVELOPMENT OF COLLECTION CARE

The desire and commitment to protect and preserve art and artifacts for the future of human cultural heritage is the basis of many museums' mission statements.

The collections are fundamental to all that a museum does in regard to its programming and why it exists as an institution. The primary principle of collection caretakers is the preservation of the collection for future generations to research and admire. Cultural heritage is a fact that the past should not be forgotten and/or destroyed so the future can build on it.

Anonymous

Early Approach

Historically, museums displayed and handled their objects in a "static" manner. Collections would be installed for display and often would remain unchanged for an indefinite length of time. Some objects, like large sculptures, were mounted in place with the idea that this is where they would reside for a long or more permanent time period. These were the practices, and, depending on the object's material, a safe and practical standard of care of the object.

Objects composed of light-sensitive materials such as paper or textile fiber often had their life expectancy reduced dramatically because of extended display. Often, the object was placed in direct daylight or in extremely bright incandescent light, which hastened its deterioration. This type of damage creates a bleaching of the image and fiber and often destroys the object as the fibrous structure becomes brittle. Learning what the best collection care approach for an object was, was often through trial and error with regard to a particular display or storage environment.

In the early museum organizational structure, there were few staff who were fully dedicated to the care of collections. The responsibility of collection care was addressed in a collaborative approach by the director, researcher, or curator; librarian or keeper; volunteers; and if the collection staff was large or financially viable, a restorer. The physical handling was often conducted by the tradesmen whose primary positions were as carpenters, painters, and maintenance staff or ground crews.

Technologies used for preserving collections were first introduced with the use of alcohol as a preservative to maintain various natural specimens for future study and research. At the same time, the printing press and the advantage of multiple documentation recordings created a broad, efficient approach to tracking and logically recording content.[3] (4)

The position of the librarian, documentations clerk, keeper and, eventually, the registrar gained importance as the recorded history, changing research and documentation of location, and logistical requirements affected the object. This corollary and additional information about an object was available and could better inform a person about how the object should be handled, displayed, or stored.

A restorer, keeper, or, eventually, conservator was often charged with the knowledge of how to care for the collection. These positions increased in professional status as research was conducted into the materials and the environmental effects on the objects during display, storage, and handling.

The major part of the physical handling was often conducted by tradesmen such as carpenters, painters, and maintenance or ground crews. The dedication and individual talents of these staff developed their particular responsibility and handling expertise. As museums grew, depending on collection type, these individuals developed the required knowledge, and new positions were created for this dedicated responsibility. The quality of care given to the collection was based on these individuals' dedication and on the commitment of the management to the overall mission of the museum.

Over the last century, museum collections have become increasingly more active in their uses, or "less" static. Collections are actively researched by scholars as increasing public interest and approach to museum missions has been directed to public outreach and education. In the permanent collection displays of museums, themed displays rotate within the collection and give the curator the opportunity to work with and show different objects within the collection. These themed collection rotations offer the visitor another insight into the curator's research and the museums' number of similar objects or depths of the collection. These rotations entice visitors with a new experience upon their return to the museum.

The advantage of collection care for objects during such rotations is that the collection, especially light-sensitive objects, can be removed to storage and be allowed "to rest" from the rigors of the display conditions. As with all museums, a high percentage of the collection is housed in storerooms; thus, rotation opportunities allow objects to be inspected for current inherent makeup, cleaned, and potentially restored to make the object suitable for display. The collection object being prepared for display may be handled extensively and with a risk of damage, but the advantage is that the object will be examined, possibly restored, or assuredly in a better physical condition and appearance than in its previous history.

With the increase in scholarly research of collections, the evolution of the specialized themed exhibition developed. During the last century, the themed exhibition has grown in interest to not only be displayed at the originating institution but also to be lent to other institutions or venues. Over the last fifty-plus years, the technical research into how exhibitions can be properly packed, crated, and transported has evolved into an ever-growing and changing segment of the museum industry.

Individuals in the field of conservation have studied extensively how objects fare when included in traveling exhibitions. The research focuses on the rigors of transport to which objects would be exposed under varying environmental conditions: shock and vibration, temperature and humidity variations, and handling techniques and equipment.

Handling of objects during the rigors of transport has created an entirely new focus and new positions specializing in guiding and implementing these new requirements. Successful commercial vendors must now offer services of proper packing and safe transportation of these objects. Obtaining government indemnity for insuring these objects during the exhibition travel requires that these collection care activities are conducted by highly knowledgeable staff. The understanding of the risk to the current inherent properties of an object in relation to the object's being transported is a challenge. The potential improvement of the object itself can again be taken into account in its being properly restored, conserved, cleaned, and mounted so that it can withstand these rigors.

Collection Care Staffing

As with all museums, the quality of object care is based solely on the dedication of the collections care staff and the knowledge they have gained in the areas of employment for which they are responsible. This same summation can be accounted for within the commercial sector of the industry as companies are built and survive on their staff's professionalism in providing proper collection care while at the same time providing services to the client. Private collectors also must educate the staff they employ on the best practices to ensure that their collections are cared for and maintained for their investment. The knowledge and support of collection care staff is solely dependent upon the management whose responsibility it is to implement the organizational mission.

Over the last century, there has been emphasis on specialized education and supporting the professionalism of staff needed to properly care for the collection objects. The evolution of the keepers, restorers, carpenters, painters, general maintenance, and groundskeepers' staff changed when institutional management agreed to develop full-time positions to specifically care for the evolving collection care programming needs. The chapter titled "Organizational Structures" will offer an enumeration of these positions, which will be presented in greater detail. Changes in three positions of collection care professionals are highlighted in the following paragraphs.

Conservators were full-time employees or individuals in private practice periodically hired to oversee and assess the condition of the collection or to conserve specific objects targeted for future display. Institutional missions then adopted the theory of "preventive conservation" whose focus is to protect the collection for future generations any time objects are handled, displayed, lent, stored, and researched within the institutional confines or jurisdiction. The principles of preventive conservation target the mitigation of deterioration of objects caused by exposure to light, temperature and humidity, pollutants, and pests, thus avoiding the need for invasive conservation treatment and ensuring that works of art are preserved for the future.

The position of Registrar was constructed from the various titles such as keeper, librarian, or documentation clerk who was responsible for documenting the object's collection history and internal movement and location. As this position evolved, new designated areas of need were added to the basics of ascribing numbers and locations: documenting packing and shipping details, inspections of incoming and outgoing condition of objects, insurance regulations and acquisition reports for review of curatorial and administrative staff, to name a few. The continual updating and development of museum policies and regulations from the collection's being in demand also created ongoing reviews and current lending and insurance policies. Each institution has specific responsibilities and documentation needs for which some positions are created.

Previously, the staff assigned to assist with the installation and handling of objects comprised the technical staff such as carpenters, painters, general maintenance, and groundskeepers. As museums developed more active collection programming with collection rotations and themed exhibitions, the need increased to develop staff positions dedicated to doing this work. These new technical personnel are commonly termed Preparators with the distinction often being designated by title, indicating the specialty of the position: installation, storage or packing preparator. Staff positions can be based on the technical distinction of particular job responsibilities, and the persons may be titled as Technician to the specialty or area he or she is associated with. More information regarding all of these positions will be addressed in the chapters on organization and training in this book.

Collection Care Management

The management of collection care staff within museums, by commercial service companies or private collectors, has the obligation to hire, train, and provide professional mentorship to all staff under its employ. This sort of support for the staff should be viewed as an investment in ensuring proper care of the collection objects and preserving cultural history. With the support and training of the collection care staff, the directives of the institutional mission regarding preventive conservation can become a reality. Throughout history, staff with a professional attitude has held the care and understanding of safely handling objects first and foremost, above all other considerations.

In the private and commercial sector, the individuals who hire and manage the staff to implement collection care responsibilities need to promote museum practices and standards. This level of support is achieved by hiring and educating staff by implementing the discipline of preventive conservation. The majority of private collectors cannot hire full-time staff and depend upon the commercial service providers and private consultants. Insurance companies often have dedicated branches within their organization comprising individuals who manage the policy coverage of collection objects. These individuals are educated, or have a previous background, in the field of collection care and offer the insured collectors direction and advice to fit their collection type.

Commercial Service Companies

Commercial service companies within the museum industry follow a staffing pattern similar to that of museums, depending on the size and type of services provided. Depending on the overall directives of the company, most offer specialized services and are confined to just a few areas of expertise distinguished by its available client base. These areas of expertise commonly include display installation, transport, packing, crating, photography, storage, mount-making, and rigging and construction of display cases and walls.

The majority of commercial providers offer a range of services for regional museums and private collectors in the areas of installation, handling, transport, and, sometimes, storage. Larger commercial providers offer specialty services for handling, packing, transporting, freight forwarding, and supervision of loans and exhibitions for domestic and international museums. Multidisciplinary providers can sometimes offer management of museum collection relocation with the ability to manage all aspects of the relocation under a company's broad structure. The professional knowledge of collection care practices and principles within a commercial company's directives and staff training provides the museum and private client the highest quality of services.

Changing Industry

In the present day, collection care techniques, materials, equipment, and training within the industry are constantly changing due to research and product development. In all museums, multidisciplinary commercial service companies, or private collections of any object type or scale, understanding the collection care practices and principles is essential. The management and staff must stay abreast of the newest research and training within the industry. The history of collection care is based solely on devising and implementing best practices for preserving objects for future generations.

CONCLUSION

To conclude, this chapter first offers an overview of how objects have been collected and the individuals or groups who dictated or directed their collection. The collectors highlighted are just an example of the overall history of collecting. Second, the history of collection care has always gone hand in hand with the primary purpose of collecting, which is to preserve the integrity of the object for monetary investment or cultural heritage—or both. The chapters that follow will explore the basics of collection care and the principles and policies currently in use.

NOTES

1. *Wikipedia*, s.v. "Cabinet of Curiosities," accessed June 2014, http://en.wikipedia.org/wiki/Cabinet_of_curiosities.

2. Encyclopedia Britannica Online, s.v. "The First Public Museums," by Geoffrey D. Lewis, accessed June 2014, http://www.britannica.com/EBchecked/topic/398827/history-of-museums/76513/Public-collections.

3. Rebecca Buck, "Order from Chaos, a History of the Museum Worker," presentation at the Association of Registrars and Collection Services, Chicago, Illinois, 2013.

Chapter 2

Organizational Structures

Management is doing things right; leadership is doing the right things.

—Peter Drucker

COLLECTION CARE STAFF ORGANIZATIONAL STRUCTURES

The intent of this chapter is to give the reader a background to the type of staff positions found within institutions and commercial sectors regarding the collection care responsibilities and how these staff members operate within the overall management of an organization. The type and scope of a collection dictate the staff required to manage, and care for, the objects. Most structural situations are built and positions created for particular functions as the collection grows. Each organization varies in its type of collection growth as does its staff to support that growth, and it is difficult to define a single organizational structure that would fit for all collections.

Although positions and titles may vary among institutions, a standardization of jobs and duties has been established over the years as the profession has taken shape. As new requirements present themselves, new positions and titles are created.

As part of the 2006 Clemenger Grant for researching best practices of object handling that I received from the National Gallery of Victoria, my main area of focus was research on the organizational structures of institutions and businesses dedicated to collection handling and the management positions and divisions within which they were placed. The goal was to propose a restructure of the Art Services department, which I managed at the National Gallery of Victoria. Over the many years of my career as a manager of preparation staff, I have pursued my interest to continually build the professional standards of the staff so as to enhance the professionalism of individuals working in the technical side of the museum industry. To do this, one must understand the management support and the role of these positions within a particular structure. The management of the collection care individuals in an institution, commercial service provider, or private collector should be approached as a business investment program. The professional growth of individuals having collection care responsibilities requires the support of the administration to provide opportunities for career advancement.

Providing the funds for continuing education and job training as well as attending conferences or professional gatherings all contribute to maintaining a high level of skill and talent in the workforce. The monetary investment helps to build a professional attitude in the staff, which in turn generates an effective and efficient collection care environment, culminating in the overall best practices mission of the organization.

Museum Management Structures

The following information is based on my research of the most common types of organizational structures of management and collection care staff positions in art museums. Nonetheless, I expect that much of this information will also offer observations and comments on the basic management of staff in historical and scientific institutions. To describe the different structures of these types of museums here would require a volume dedicated to this subject because of the huge diversity in collections, staff positions, and structural makeup within these types of organizations.

Director: A museum director is responsible for all business matters and cultural activities presented and maintained in the institution. The director oversees all museum operations, reports to the board of trustees, cultivates patrons, and implements successful public programming.

Assistant Director or Deputy Director: The position of assistant or deputy director follows suit and supplements many of the main responsibilities of the director. Often, the direct management of specific departments or divisions falls under the responsibility of this position. Divisional management is often based on departments that are related to each other in the coordinated functions such as collections, exhibition programming, public programming, and facility management. Specific noncollection departments may include human resources, finance, information technology, and security.

Director of Collections (or other applicable title): This position has the responsibility of maintaining and preserving the collection. It often includes the departments of conservation, registration, preparation, storage, exhibition programming, and design.

Director of Exhibitions: This position is responsible for planning and implementing major outreach programming through exhibitions. It works very closely with departments responsible for collections as well as with noncollection departments such as education and fundraising.

Director of Collection Services, Sciences, or Keeper of Collections: This title is typically used for the highest level manager who works within a historical or science museum. The collection care departments that report to this type of position vary in titles and description based solely on their development at that particular institution. Examples would be specific departments at a historical museum: Anthropology, Palaeontology, Mammals and Vertebrates, etc.

Curator: The primary role of a curator is to develop a collection through acquisition and research of objects. Working with the education and design staff, the curator leads the interpretation and physical display of the collection for the benefit of the public. Depending on the size of the museum, the curator will focus on a specialized area of the collection based on the type or cultural grouping of the objects. In smaller museums, a curator may be responsible for all aspects of the collection and programming. In volunteer-based museums, such as local historical societies, a curator may be the only paid staff member.

Design: The designer and curator work closely together from the initial concept phases through to the final display. The designer has the task of making the entire exhibition visually intriguing by using the objects as the visual highlights in the contextual flow of the curator's vision. The designer's ideas will be coordinated with the functions of the collection care staff to guarantee the protection of the object and to fulfill any contractual agreements if the objects are on loan for the display from another museum or collector.

Other management positions in an institution that support collection care programming and are based on the business aspects of operating an institution are titles that may include Chief Operating Officer, Chief Financial Officer, Chief Information Officer, Director of Development, Director of Education, Director of Facilities, Director of Security, and Director of Human Resources.

In my career, I have worked primarily in large art museums and commercial fine-arts service companies. I have always been fascinated with how a particular institution is structured not only in the overall management but specifically in the staffing for positions responsible for collection care.

The following paragraphs attempt to give the reader a listing of specific positions commonly found in both large and small museums as well as in a commercial, fine-arts service company. The goal is to create a better understanding of how collection care staffing works within, and how all these responsibilities relate to the overall mission of, an organization.

All institutions or companies vary in how they were established and are managed; no one structure matches another in type and description. I continue to collect and read job descriptions and have found many similarities, despite the fact that there are always some specifics that dictate a unique way of accounting and reporting. Job titles are often good markers that indicate collection type, size of institution, and organizational hierarchy.

Collection Care Staff: Large Art Museums

In large museum collections, the amount of work required to care for a specific collection and for collection programming often requires dedicated divisions, departments, or individual staff. The type of work and responsibilities of these individuals vary widely and are based on the museum's collecting policies and programming. Some of the world's larger museums have established divisions specified by the curatorial, historical, or scientific type of collections for which they are responsible. Collection care staff positions are created and work within a specific department, which has the expertise to serve the needs of the collection or programming.

Depending on the skill level and scheduled commitments, some staff may be shared among divisions or within the multiple departments in a division. Such examples of this could be the Metropolitan Museum of Art, which has staff dedicated to its arms and armaments collection, or the Victoria and Albert Museum, which has departments focused on furniture and textiles. Such hierarchies operate in larger divisions of curatorial or collection care expertise. And all can be brought together when large numbers of staff are required to do a specific activity—for example, a large or difficult installation of a display or exhibition. Specialized technical skill such as heavy rigging of large objects may be placed under an organization's facility staff or commercial specialist, but the responsibility may be shared under the auspices of conservation when the objects are being rigged and moved.

In large art museums, the responsibility of care, handling, movement, and display of collection objects is placed under the guidelines of conservation, registration, and preparation departments. The specialized work can involve individuals whose expertise is required to oversee a specific type of object. Listed below are some common examples of specialized staffing responsibilities with respect to art-based museum collection:

Conservation Department

Conservation departments comprise multidisciplinary staff defined by the collection programming and the types of objects that the museum's collection policy supports. Conservators are responsible for the examination, physical analysis, and treatment of cultural, historic, and artistic objects. Professional conservators rely on their training and knowledge in the technical research of material science. They also research an object's historical and cultural provenance to ensure the object's structural originality and proper visual preservation for future generations.

The following is a list of the multidisciplinary areas that can be commonly found within a conservation department at large art institutions. I will not go into detail about each of the specialized fields of discipline, but rather group the typical material type under the department in which these disciplines can be found. For further information and research on these specialized disciplines, please consult the bibliography section and website links provided.

- Paintings: oil; acrylic; tempera; painting on canvas, panel, mural, and contemporary media.
- Works on paper: drawings; photographs; manuscripts; books; contemporary media; and Asian paintings, screens, scrolls, and albums.
- 3-D objects: metal, ceramics, wood, stone, glass, composites, furniture, textiles, and contemporary, monumental outdoor sculpture and masonry.
- Textiles: costumes, uniforms, embroideries, tapestries, carpets, blankets, curtains, flags, banners, and furniture upholstery including ethnographic, archeological, and contemporary media.
- Framing: standard framing of matted or mounted objects, painting frame restoration, contemporary media, and specialty display construction.

Specialized discipline roles: mount making, exhibition, and permanent-collection exhibit display rotation, preventive conservation and treatment, condition reporting for incoming and outgoing loans, environmental monitoring, and internal and external cleaning and maintenance.

Registration Department

Registration staff are responsible for all documentation of historical provenance and inventory of objects in the museum collection. They are responsible for ensuring that the museum's collection policies are updated and implemented for all objects in the collection. The following are key highlights of the registrars' responsibilities. Depending upon the amount of programming activity, staff often undertake multiple tasks to accommodate a very busy roster of commitments.

- Documentation and record keeping: maintaining record-management systems to document and record all procedures and policies required of the museum.
- Acquisitions: documentation, assigning numbers, and tracking new objects in the collection as acquired.
- Deaccessions: recording the removal of objects that have been deemed redundant to the collection, documenting all aspects of the museum's policies for the legal conditions in the verification of the objects.
- Loans: maintaining all documentation and tracking of objects that are lent between museums for loan periods or exhibition display; managing all loan, courier, insurance, and transport agreements required by other institutions or outside service contractors.
- Exhibitions: working with the curator; exhibition manager; design, conservation, and preparation staff in all phases of objects chosen for exhibition or loan by creating a separate documentation numbering and tracking system; managing all loan, courier, insurance, and transport agreements required by other institutions or outside service contractors.
- Storage: maintaining and managing all documentation, movement records, and collection activities within storage facilities; working with facility managers and outside contractors to maintain and monitor building environments.
- Packing and shipping: maintaining all documentation, insurance, packing, and transport arrangements of objects being moved from the museum facilities to other locations for storage, loan, or exhibition programming.
- Transport security: maintaining all documentation of specialized security requirements of loans or exhibition programming; courier, insurance, and commercial transport arrangements, and contractual requirements.
- Risk management: working with other collection care departments to create and implement collection and risk management policies including disaster management and mitigation procedures.

Collection Manager

Collection manager is another title that is separate but often related to a registrar's position and is sometimes used in large art museums and those with a focus on history and natural history whose diverse collections require experienced assessment to properly sort, catalog, and store artifacts. Collection managers work collaboratively with registrars, who are document-oriented and responsible for risk management of the collection. The roles of collection managers and registrars are two distinct collection roles that are often combined into one in small to mid-size cultural institutions.

Collection managers are responsible for the long-term preservation of collections. They oversee the physical care of objects and are the hands-on problem-solving components of a collections team. A collection manager may oversee the registrar, archivist, curator, photographer, or other collection professionals, and may assume the responsibilities of these roles in their absence within an organization.

Preparation Department

Preparation is the most overarching and commonly used title for the technical staff responsible for handling objects for collection care activities. Depending on the job distribution in the museum, other titles can include art handler, technician, specialist, and coordinator, or with the addition of the name of the technical service responsibility, for example, installation specialist or installation technician. Preparation staff in large museums are required to handle artwork on a daily basis as dictated by the collection policy. As the preparation profession continues to develop, so, too, do specific responsibilities, and they tend to vary more than do staff structures involving the conservation or registration departments.

- Exhibition installation: receiving, unpacking, and installing objects for display—technical requirements such as lighting, electrical, or computer display needs are often the bailiwick of facilities or IT departments; labels and signage are installed by design or facilities staff—handling of objects from storage or conservation when objects are ready for display; working with the curator and the designer on layout and installation, based on requirements indicated by conservators or previous installations; returning objects to storage when de-installed from display.
- Ongoing handling: moving objects as related to storage projects, research, conservation treatment, or photography within an ongoing schedule.
- Packing, crating, and transit: designing and fabricating packing and crating for objects based on the inherent properties of the object and the transit arrangements of the loan.
- Storage: maintaining and managing collection activities within storage such as research, conservation and display, and internal movement within facilities.

Other areas include mount making, display lighting, matting and framing, cleaning objects and displays, and video; video and touch screen display maintenance can be conducted within the management of a preparation department. Such areas of lighting, carpentry, and painting often fall under the purview of facility or design departments, but preparation staff often execute these technical activities as well.

Collection Care Staff: Small Museums

Within a small museum, collection staff may have a specific job title or responsibility, but the majority are required to take on a variety of different responsibilities. This "wearing of different hats" occurs because the workload is not as great as in large institutions, which necessitates a more focused approach. The structure of these multidisciplinary positions is dependent upon the collections and the associated programming.

The individual's knowledge and professional commitment are essential in doing the job effectively. In working with these colleagues, I find that although they can be daunted by the amount of work, they gain a unique dedication to, and a broader understanding of, their institution and its programming.

In small museums, sometimes many staff, including the director and curator, can be actively involved in handling the collection objects when acquisition and programming require extra support. Facility or maintenance staff may also be called upon to assist in handling collections for a particular activity. Many small museums depend on casual or part-time technical staff as well.

Volunteers, under the supervision of collection care staff, who are dedicated and trained, can make a valuable addition to the work required of collection care. Management support of individual professional development for full-time staff and overall staff training of part-time or volunteer staff is essential to create an efficient and effective team in a smaller institution. More information on training programs and opportunities will be supplied in chapter 3 of this book.

The following is a descriptive list of staff responsibilities commonly found in a small art museum's collection care staff. As with any museum, large or small, the collection care staff is built by the direction of the museum's collection growth. Many positions are created and built by a particular individual's talent or professional ambition, which complements the institution's overall mission to acquire a collection and develop and implement programming. No one single management structure can be used for all museums.

Conservation Department

Many small museums do not have full-time staff dedicated to maintaining a conservation department. When an object to be treated is beyond the knowledge of the staff, the treatment can be hired out to a contract conservator who has the particular training or experience with the object's physical disposition. Often, these outside contractors are planned and budgeted with targeted funding. Grants make up much of the financing, in which selected objects, timeframes, and outcomes are extensively detailed and exhaustively enumerated. Specific projects or ongoing programming activities that cannot be implemented within the full-time staff schedules can be created through museum internships, which are beneficial for young or outside contract conservators to gain experience and build their professional portfolios.

Registration Department

The necessary documentation and record keeping of collections of any size mandate that these tasks be undertaken by a staff member, regardless of the number of hats he or she must wear. If the responsibilities outlined in registration departments of large institutions cannot be undertaken by the staff of a small museum, experienced part-time staff can be hired or trained to fill the need when it occurs. Larger or ongoing projects may require hiring a contract registrar consultant to fill the void in case of a particular project need.

Work related to a special exhibition can be budgeted in the overall exhibition costs. Financing for specific staff can also be sought through grants in a fashion similar to that for conservation needs, but there are fewer funding support organizations. Specific projects or ongoing programming activities that cannot be implemented within the full-time staff schedules can also be created through museum internships.

Preparation Department

Preparation departments in small art museums undertake similar responsibilities as listed for larger museums. Like their counterparts in the registration department, the individuals need to be multidisciplinary in their work activities. Exhibition display is perhaps the main area that differentiates the small museum from its larger counterpart. The need to design and construct display furniture such as cases, plinths, and decorative accents is undertaken by these staff members as part of the overall display or exhibition rotation. The primary reason for the additional responsibility is usually the cost constraints of having these activities contracted to private service vendors or the absence of a facility department with experienced staff that could undertake these activities. Since the preparation staff have the technical experience to do their related collection care activities, it follows that these individuals do this work, especially if they have a strong knowledge of craftsmanship in wood and metal. When exhibitions are installed, often these same staff are required to construct, install, and paint walls and plinths in the galleries awaiting the placement of objects for display. Mount making and lighting requirements are also often added to the preparation staff's responsibilities. These individuals are required to have additional specialized backgrounds or training to understand the technical requirements of these activities.

Preparators and facility staff members work directly with the exhibition designer to create, build, and schedule exhibition display needs. The reverse process in the dismantling of an exhibition takes place at the close of the exhibitions, with casework and other materials tossed or recycled to be used in a future exhibition. During these exhibition changeovers, casual or part-time staff are hired who are experienced in the technical requirements for both constructing displays and installing artworks under the supervision of full-time collection staff members. Funding for these positions is usually factored into the exhibition budget. For specific projects, extra staff are accounted for within the general budget or with grants.

In both large and small institutions, support for training and professional development of collection care staff is essential. Management must budget and promote these educational activities as part of the ongoing programming for collection care and conservation policies. The investment in training and professional development is easily justified when the risk management is shown to be effective, thus leading to lower annual insurance premiums. Establishment of a positive working environment for collection care staff and their work with other museum staff ensures that the objects will be cared for properly and the collection activities will be carried out successfully. The types of training available within the museum community will be explored in greater detail in chapter 3.

Historical Museums

Historical museums follow a similar pattern as do art museums in their collection growth and staffing. Each museum collection is different, and the staffing needs are even more diverse when one considers the type of objects collected. To undertake an explanation of historical organization structures would be a task that would continue to evolve as it was researched and constructed. Art museums are more defined in the variations of object types. Most art museums have fewer objects compared to historical, natural history, or science museums. Depending on the type of collection, historical or science museums can have total object counts in hundreds of thousands, even several millions, as certain collections have multiples of collection grouping, or their actual physical size is extremely small.

For example, medical collections may have a huge volume of specimen slides, which are collected, researched, and referenced. A historical museum can have coins or stamps, which are small but are sufficient in number to make the object count quite large.

Throughout my career, I have worked primarily within the fine-arts museum and service industry. As I have worked with museum colleagues from historical, natural history, or science museums, I am always interested to hear their stories of the type of objects that they encounter on a daily basis. Though there are differences in the type and number of objects, the issue of collection care still follows the same principles of best practices in preventive conservation. The collection care practices and policies are necessary for the way the objects are handled, stored, and displayed; the environment in which they are kept; and the materials used to protect them. Regardless of the nature of the collection, all objects are equally important to the cultural heritage, and their care and preservation should be maintained.

As with the comparison between a registrar and collection manager of art and historical institutions, the difference in museum types and their collections predicts the type of staffing needed. The diversity of collections for any museum requires the recruitment and retention of specialized staff who will properly care for the objects and enhance the attendant programs.

Commercial Service Companies

Within the museum industry, commercial service companies are created and built to address the collection care needs that an institution, private business, or private collection cannot afford to undertake under its own organizational structure. Companies offer different services and hire appropriate staff, based on the needs of their clients. Most companies were originally built by individuals who had previous experience in the collection care field or educational interest in art, history, science, or other cultural heritage studies. Some companies expanded into the specialized collection care industry as it was a natural outgrowth of the other services that they offered. An example is household moving or removal companies expanding and training staff to undertake the more specialized service of handling high-value art, antiques, and artifacts.

While companies offer services to historical or science museums, I will present and compare only those that also offer services to art museums. The following is a list of four kinds of services offered by commercial companies to fine-arts organizations.

Transport Services

Most museums, large or small, do not have the staff, facility, or equipment required to transport objects when they are required for collection activities. Museums with multiple buildings to facilitate storage or display of their collection may have a small truck, van, or other vehicle to transport objects between sites. Over the years, the quality and level of specially designed vehicles have been developed and offer the best protection in regard to handling the rigors to which objects are exposed such as shock, vibration, and climate variation. Owning, operating, and maintaining these vehicles is not cost effective when compared to hiring this same service from a local service provider.

Many commercial companies provide local, regional, and interstate transport services, depending on the type and number of trucks and the licensed, qualified staff to operate the vehicles and to handle specialized cargo. Vehicles can be built and equipped to monitor internal environments of temperature and humidity and to reduce shock and vibration, and they can be outfitted with handling equipment and specialized support structures to reduce the possibility of damage to objects during transit.

Many large service companies offer regularly scheduled transport over regional and interstate routes or shuttled interchanged service. Scheduled transport offers the clients within the routing locations a service that reduces costs as multiple clients employ the same service. A client can request that the shipment be transported in an exclusive-use vehicle in which the client's objects are the only cargo. The cost for this service may be higher, but it does offer the advantage that the objects are given full and undivided attention during transit. This type of service moves multiple clients to use this on an ongoing basis because the cost of staffing, maintaining, and operating the vehicles is high, and profits are a challenge to maintain.

Storage Services

Collections—whether privately held by a museum, an individual, or a business—are not always on display. Proper storage during these times is necessary for the care and maintenance of the works of art. Facilities that provide long-term storage allowing for temperature and humidity control, premises secured against theft and damage, and confidentiality will have many interested clients. Larger companies may provide related services such as inventory management, photography, viewing rooms when the collection is required to be inspected, minor conservation treatment, and the basic handling documentation of objects coming into, and going out of, the storage facility.

Installation Services

Most fine-arts service providers offer some level of installation services for display in institutions, commercial galleries, or private collectors' homes. The amount and type of work they can undertake is dictated by the knowledge of the staff they have in their employ and the service proficiency that can be maintained within their organization. These installation services commonly include handling of two-dimensional framed and unframed works, three-dimensional objects with or without mounts, furniture, textiles, and small sculptures. In the institutions, service staff are additional personnel supervised by the registrar or preparation manager on staff to assist the installation. In the commercial galleries and private collectors' homes, installation staff are directed by the client as the client usually does not have full-time, knowledgeable staff. In many European museums, the installation of exhibitions or rotations is hired out completely to the specialized service company and its teams of dedicated staff.

Packing and Crating Services

Over the last fifty-plus years, the uptick in the purchase, sale, or loan of artworks among institutions for exhibitions touring multiple venues has led to the development of new research and technical breakthroughs in properly protecting objects during handling and transport. Museums, commercial galleries, and private collectors have become active participants in these activities. To mitigate the risk to their collections, this technical knowledge is specialized and often cannot be maintained within an institutional or private collectors' capacity. Commercial service providers have stepped up the task of developing the staff and expertise to offer their clients. Most companies offer some level of packing and crating for their client base that is similar in scope to their transport services. Larger companies can offer multiple levels of technical designs required of packing and crating, from single, one-time shipments to museum-level traveling exhibitions.

Multiple Services

Offering the technical services of transport, storage, installation, and packing and crating creates, in some companies, a complete and full-service provider. The company's organizational structure is dependent upon the profitability of successfully meeting a client's needs. The people hired and trained by a company have to be competent and professional when undertaking all projects. A well-choreographed team that fulfills a client's request is akin to the way in which a museum's staff executes programs and exhibitions for its public.

Other services often found within a company's organizational structure are created and developed by the technical expertise of the staff employed and the clients' needs.

- The transport service can be extended to another related, trusted company to use its vehicle to offer effective routing to move objects.
- International transport for air and sea shipments requires staff with knowledge of the rules and regulations that must be followed for interstate and international transit.

- Rigging of large objects requires a highly trained staff who understand the technical aspects of handling the objects and the equipment and methods to use during the rigging process.
- Fabrication of display casework and furniture requires staff to have a high level of knowledge of cabinetry design and related material construction skills.
- Mount making for three-dimensional objects is a specialized skill that requires knowledge and understanding of an object's material composition and its inherent properties, and the skill of working with fabrication materials such as metals and plastics.
- Matting and framing of two-dimensional objects requires knowledge of archival methods and materials, technical equipment, and framing design and fabrication.
- Photographic services are necessary for the visual documentation of inventory, condition reporting, packing and crating, and recording movement of objects within the storage facilities.
- Special project teams are often created in some larger companies for managing and executing large or complicated projects such as museum relocation moves, transporting and installation of traveling exhibitions, unique packing and crating, and specialized large-object installations or relocations.

The ability to manage and maintain a profitable company is reliant on offering high-quality service, which leads to repeat business and to new business through a satisfied clientele. A management structure that promotes recruitment and retention of a competent and professional staff which sees to the needs of its clients is the recipe for success.

Private Collector Structures

Private collectors often hire dedicated staff to manage their collecting activities. These activities can include the arrangements for purchasing, insurance, transport, and installation and storage of the collection where it is displayed, oftentimes in residences or office environments. The collector's manager, depending on the size and activities related to the collection, may be one individual who manages all activities by developing working relations with various service providers and, in some instances, is supported by the collection staff within a museum where the collector may be part of the museum board or a wealthy benefactor.

The organizational structures I have presented are highlights of staffing scenarios one can commonly find within fine-arts museums and the commercial service sectors. The type of collection dictates the type of staffing required to manage and maintain the preservation and care activities required of that particular collection. The methods and methodologies related to the staff training and technical skills will be explored in further detail in subsequent chapters of this book. For further research, the bibliography and appendix of this book will offer the reader additional resources.

ORGANIZATIONAL CHARTS

The organizational charts of any institution or commercial company are an effective structural tool to give management and all staff members the knowledge of how the entire group of individuals operates within the whole structure. Understanding the structure gives staff and outside stakeholders a clear vision of how the mechanics of the organization functions and who different staff members report to or are responsible for managing.

The organizational chart for each situation or company will be different and is defined by how it has developed over time. Organizational charts are or can be fluid in development or change but rigid as required to explain one's operational structure. The structure should be used and maintained by all management staff and made available for all staff in employee handbooks and by institutional updates. The benefit of keeping the organizational chart a part of the employee's knowledge is that it creates the visual structure of the group or team and the importance of the various players to the whole.

The internet is an excellent source to find examples of museum organizational charts for all types and sizes of institutions. This is also an excellent source for seeing how different staff are titled to their positions in relation to the whole. The Association of Art Museum Directors publishes a salary survey based on the professional levels of positions within the United States. It is an informative document that shows the differences in position titles in relation to the size of an institutional collection type. The internet also offers other possibilities, but conducting one's own research among one's colleagues from other museums may offer infinitely more knowledge as it can be built for direct questions about specific topics.

Commercial companies can benefit in the same manner as their museum counterparts by developing their structural charts as the company grows or by changing the formats of the services they provide. Human resource managers can best build the organizational charts as they are the most knowledgeable regarding the structural arrangements with the commercial sectors of the specific industry.

CONCLUSION

Building, maintaining, and operating an organization of specialized staff who are entrusted with the handling and care of valuable or irreplaceable cultural objects is not an easy undertaking. The knowledge and skill levels of all involved in the organizational structure must be commensurate with the level of commitment that their responsibilities entail in relationship to the whole organization's overarching mission of preserving and caring for objects. Investing in the importance of the mission and all the individual contributions creates a work atmosphere that then is the best that can be provided for the support and implementation of quality collection care policies and practices. Supporting the staff in creating and maintaining this atmosphere will continue to yield the dividends of sharing and passing on the knowledge to future generations, much like the preservation of the cultural objects for which they are responsible for future generations.

CASE STUDY: COMPARING APPROACHES—
THE MUSEUM AND THE TRANSPORT AGENT

by Jim Grundy

What are the similarities and differences between the museum and commercial sector approaches? To try to answer this question, I will draw on my experience working in London at Tate from 1983 to 2006 and at Gander & White Shipping from 2006 to the present.

I started at the Tate Gallery as an Art Handling Technician at the beginning of what was to become a period of huge change and expansion. I became a team leader working across all areas of installation, packing, and storage involving major exhibitions and a rolling program of collection re-displays. As Head of Art Handling from 1993, I was responsible for staff management, training, handling procedures, and the technical delivery of the Tate program.

I joined Gander & White to help build and expand the company's museum business. This has included upgrading existing warehouses and fitting out new warehouses to museum standards. It has also involved developing security, handling, and environmental procedures to the level that museums require as clients.

From an art-handling perspective, the key area where the two worlds meet is at the museum loading bay. It is the point where mutual understanding and respect are brought sharply into focus. It can be a place of tension and misunderstanding if both sides do not appreciate each other's pressures. Working on both sides of the loading dock has been fascinating and has given me an insight into the two ways of working.

Similarities, General Points

We are handling the same works of art and want to leave them in the same condition that we found them. Fundamentally, the equipment and handling techniques are equivalent. When you walk around a museum and an art shipper's warehouse, you are likely to see similar equipment in both. It is more cost effective to purchase pallet trucks, skates, forklift trucks, and racking from industrial suppliers. When items are crated for loan, they could travel through air cargo handling. Crates are therefore designed to accommodate this type of handling where the forklift is the main method of lifting and moving. This requires all cargo to be standardized as much as possible.

Procedures for documenting changes of location or works being handed in or out are broadly aimed at achieving the same goals, namely knowing where everything is and keeping control. Whatever computerized collection management or manual paper-based system is used, the accuracy of the information is reliant on art handlers in both sectors being meticulous about documenting their actions.

Staffing

It is a very team-oriented environment, and art handlers on both sides learn to rely on each other and often form close bonds. Some enjoy working with the same team members for long periods in familiar surroundings. This can improve efficiency, but in both sectors managers have to consider the skills and experience of the whole team in order to continually develop and improve them across the whole department for the long term. There are also fundamental similarities in team structure. To operate successfully, a core art handling team comprises two or three technicians. One technician will be the team leader who is responsible for the safe completion of the job on time. This applies equally to a commercial transport team collecting and delivering works of art and a museum team receiving them. Time pressures also exist equally for museum and transport agents' teams. Each team leader is likely to be thinking ahead about the team's sequence of work and will be calculating the impact of an unexpected delay. They are both working under the pressure of deadlines.

Training

There are also many similarities in the approach to training and skills. Classroom-style training is appropriate for some situations such as health and safety certificates and equipment licenses. For art handling, I have found the most successful approach to be on-the-job training supplemented with written guidelines. Newly recruited art handlers at Tate and Gander & White are not sent immediately on a training course but join a team and are gradually assimilated. It is time consuming to build the confidence of a new team member who will need support and guidance from colleagues. The best way to learn art handling is by working alongside colleagues who are committed to sharing skills and knowledge. However, written procedures and techniques are helpful in giving new recruits an insight into the wide range of activities that art handlers are involved in, and you are more likely to maintain consistency across all the teams working in the organization.

Art Handling Manuals

I have contributed to two separate publications aimed at providing guidelines. In 1993 I collaborated with Bruce McAllister, my predecessor as Head of Art Handling, and Roy Perry, Head of Conservation, to produce the Tate Gallery Art Handling Manual. The aim was to cover every aspect of the subject, and it was evident to me that there are so many unique handling situations that it is very difficult to avoid the guidelines' becoming complex and difficult to use as a training aid. In 2009 we set ourselves the task at Gander & White of condensing our own version of the guidelines into a collection of single pages describing each skill and identifying the key points and risks involved. Gander & White Standards included an easily accessible list of basic dos and don'ts for each skill. The aim was to produce a quick-reference training aid and establish clearly defined standards. We still listed and described 95 separate skills, and this highlights the wide-ranging and varied nature of the role. The risk for all publications about art handling is that they may end up on a shelf after the huge amount of effort by the authors. It is a useful process for clarifying a museum's procedures, but it is a challenge to make them relevant to busy art handling teams out in the museum or on the warehouse floor. A competent art handler needs to develop a complex mix of awareness and attitude, technical skills, experience, and communication skills. One important thing to note is that nobody knows everything about art handling.

Differences, General Points

Museum teams of art handlers know their collection and the particular access issues in their buildings. There are likely to be detailed method statements created from previous installations, and art handlers have the support and expertise of conservators to help with advice during packing, moving, and collection care. The information about wall construction and floor-loading enable teams to tailor equipment, materials, and techniques to the site. Also, prior to acquisition, research is usually carried out and instructions will often be provided to help teams to plan installations. By contrast, the transport agent's teams rely on information provided by clients. The project manager will ask pertinent questions during the quoting stage, and this often highlights the need for a site visit, but clients may not necessarily be museum professionals. This means that art handlers are sometimes in situations where they have to adapt to unexpected problems such as stairs, low doorways, awkward turns, heavier-than-expected items, and parking problems. They are more exposed and often have to solve problems without support.

Packing Specifications

Another difference I have noticed is that a museum will have developed its packing standards over many years. Every museum art handler will be familiar with the museum's methods, and you would not expect to specify materials and techniques every time. There is likely to be a well-rehearsed way in which they pack every object with shorthand ways of specifying. For instance, the standard "soft wrap" at Tate was referred to as "jiffy" corners and polythene seal. Jiffy is the name of one manufacturer of many different types of foam, and the type referred to was a perforated, laminated polyethylene foam roll often known as Cell-Aire. This can lead to confusion, especially as the person specifying the method may not be a conservator or art handler. For a transport agent's art handlers, there are many different packing specifications, depending on the client's requirements. In the course of a day, there may be collections and deliveries from private clients, commercial galleries, antique dealers, and museums. In different situations, "soft wrap" can be interpreted as bubble or tissue wrap, fully card wrapped, or Cell-Aire wrapped. Each packing method has to be appropriate to the expectations and budget of the client.

Recruitment

Recruitment processes can be very different between a large publicly funded museum and a transport agent. In the publicly funded sector, the process of advertising a vacant post, the deadline for applications, then the sifting and shortlisting of applicants, followed by the formal panel and interview procedure can be a major commitment of time for a manager. In contrast, the process in the commercial sector can be much quicker, and prospective candidates can be interviewed and made an offer within a week. In my experience, I would not say that one way is better than the other. To be a college graduate or an artist, or to have the ability to write an outstanding application is not, at the end of the day, the main criterion for a successful art handler. In each scenario, the manager is primarily looking for evidence of technical, team working, and communication skills, and the ability to deliver under pressure of deadlines.

Conclusion

There are some myths about the differences between the two approaches that I think are outdated. "Museums are too slow, are always in meetings, and have rigid procedures to follow." This was not my experience at Tate. "Art transport agents are just removals companies. Their handlers don't appreciate art or understand conservation issues." Likewise, this is not my experience at Gander & White. In recent years I think the two worlds have converged, and crossover, collaboration, and mutual appreciation have increased. Museum couriers, who travel onboard vehicles, witness the work ethic and professional approach of the commercial art handling teams first hand. Similarly, it is not uncommon for art handlers to move jobs between both sectors. With the increase in the use of, and the continual improvement to, mobile phone technology, everyone can be kept up to date as works of art travel the world. This has all contributed to the increase in trust.

Finally, back to the museum loading bay, mentioned earlier as a place of potential tension. This is a particular issue when heavy or large items are involved because of the risk of injury. When delivering, the transport team will have already handled the object and will be aware of any problems. This will enable them to advise the museum team about the best way to offload. When the transport team is collecting, the museum team will have that experience of the object. In addition, each team will have different issues to consider such as lack of space in the receiving bay, the order in which crates are brought on and off the loading bay, or the even the distribution of weight in the vehicle. Problems occur when one side thinks it knows best and takes control without listening. When it works well, each side brings particular expertise and skills, which are shared.

Jim Grundy
Director of Art Operations
Gander & White Shipping
London, England

Chapter 3

Training, Health, and Safety

No method nor discipline can supersede the necessity of being forever on the alert. What is a course of history, or philosophy, or poetry, or the most admirable routine of life, compared with the discipline of looking always at what is to be seen? Will you be a reader, a student merely, or a seer?

—Henry David Thoreau

INTRODUCTION

The importance of training collection care staff in any institution or company is paramount to creating an effective, efficient, and successful operation. Professional development of staff should be part of its yearly employment benefits and be supported and budgeted for competitive salaries and other benefit-package amenities. The benefits outweigh the time, expense, and potential risk to the collection in comparison to not establishing, implementing, and revising an ongoing program for your staff. The following section will present several types of training opportunities which can be managed within the organizational structure for both internal offerings and external programs, which have proved successful in my experience and research.

COLLECTION CARE DIVISIONS

Collection care professionals are individuals who are responsible for executing the various policies, protocols, and techniques to perform these activities, and they are the key components in a successful organizational structure at any institution or business. The structure of support for these individuals is based on the decision-making factors guiding the management team who oversee their positions and performance. The specific positions have been developed by the needs of the organization built within the overall structure. Both creating and maintaining staff positions are dependent upon the quality of knowledge that the individual possesses when hired, his development while employed, and the support provided through training during his career at the organization.

In all business structures, training staff to understand the organizational policy and procedures is extremely essential. The field of collection care is a unique profession because a uniform standard in policies and procedures is relatively new within the overall museum industry. The understanding of the levels of standards and polices is knowledge that is not easily gained except through "on-the-job" experience. The knowledge gained within an individual organization is similar to the uniqueness and diversity of its collection, and so it cannot often be compared directly to that acquired in another organization with respect to approach and principles.

People often state that a good staff member should possess the qualities based on just "simple common sense." If you possess this intuitive sense and apply it in your approach to your job, it can be very effective and productive, but that sense is only a small part of the overall attributes that one must possess. Others that are beneficial are attention to detail, tactile sensibilities, assessment analysis, quality communication skills, patience, and diplomatic

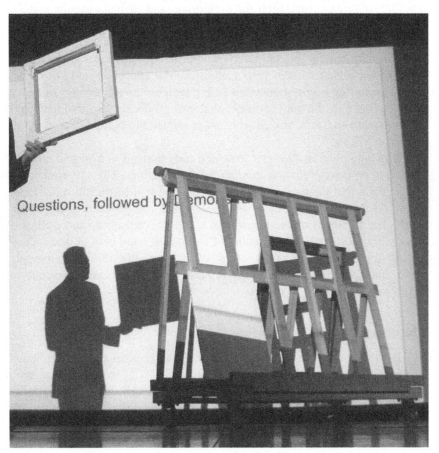

Figure 3.1   PACCIN Art Handling Workshop Wadsworth Athenaeum. *Source:* Author.

forethought, among others. We will explore these in more detail in the chapters on handling 2-D and 3-D collection objects.

Since collection care standards and principles are still relatively new, the development and implementation of training programs is essential for educating new as well as long-time staff. The purpose of this chapter is to reference the various training programs for professional development available for management to support and for individual staff to pursue to increase their collection care knowledge.

TRAINING OPPORTUNITIES

Professional development for collection care staff should be an ongoing part of the staff benefits within a museum or commercial organization. The level of commitment required for preserving, and maintaining the care of, cultural objects in an institution or for a commercial service client is paramount to the existence of both organizational structures. The time and commitment required for training staff should be recognized by management as an essential part of staff responsibilities. The education and knowledge gained regarding proper collection care practices should be approached as an investment in the staff member that can produce a professional work environment and can be shared with and promoted through other staff within the organization.

All training programs require dedicated commitments of time and financial support in both nonprofit and commercial organizations. This investment will outlast the initial financial outlay of support and will be transferred through the workforce on a daily basis as the standards and procedures are undertaken. The highlight of the investment is that the efficiency and quality of work will reflect back on the quality of the overall mission of collection care for the objects and their preservation. When developing training programs, senior management must be an active participant throughout the process to ensure support as well as success.

Museums: Internal or "In-House" Training

Depending on the size of the museum and the number of staff dedicated to caring for the collection, you can find various approaches to training programs. Some museums have extensive programs which are supported by the senior management and reflect the management's dedication to the professional development of the collection care staff. Other museums are still developing programs as the support of professional development is an element in competition with other financial and scheduling issues within the institution. As stated previously, ongoing management support is essential to providing the best professional knowledge for newly hired as well as senior staff levels within an institution. The following examples will explain some of the different types and potential combinations of training programs that are commonly found within museums. Some of these same programs can be developed within the commercial service companies, but I will use museum programs for these examples.

Collection care staff are those within the departments of conservation, registration, and preparation, and in some instances, they may be curatorial staff. Some of these staff members handle the collection objects more frequently than others because of their daily job responsibilities. For example, in large museums, the preparation staff handle objects the most as their daily responsibilities are focused on the movement of objects for the majority of collection care activities. Preparators are responsible for ensuring the safe handling of objects while packing and unpacking and installing and de-installing them for display, exhibition, and preparation for transit—whether on a cart from storage to gallery or in a crate across the continent.

Conservators must understand the inherent properties of the object and the ways and means to properly handle a specific object. Registrars handle objects when they are required for daily or specialized activities such as inventories or documenting and overseeing the handling requirements for loans or other legal dictates. Curators handle the objects the least in large museums as other staff are dedicated to this focused responsibility. Because specific collections are under the curators' domain, and as they should have access to the physical collection, they need to be a part of training programs. This will give them a stronger understanding of the best practices and, hence, the staff responsibilities for handling objects.

On-the-Job Training

"On-the-Job training" is the most common approach to training on a daily basis. The managers of collection care staff in any department should promote and set the tone for the atmosphere in which daily activities are conducted. The communication structure of the activities must be clearly stated and monitored as they are undertaken with the collection object. The coordination of all players involved, whether within one department or among several departments, will be successful if all of them understand the activity to be undertaken. This approach to communication and choreography will ensure the ongoing and dedicated effectiveness of the policies and procedures required for all activities related to collection care programming.

On-the-job training can be focused by establishing daily meetings when the schedule is discussed before activities are undertaken. A working scheduling

Figure 3.2   Staff Choreography / On-the-Job Training. *Source*: Wamaling, Artex FAS.

calendar, often depicted on a whiteboard or on an updated computer-based calendar, should be made available for the staff to see the activities during an individual or group discussion. These same scheduling calendars will be used as a reference during the workday as the schedule develops or, more often, changes. Creating and maintaining an effective scheduling calendar is essential and should correlate succinctly with all activity or tracking documents.

Procedural and Handling Manuals

Creating a manual, usually titled "procedural" or sometimes called a handling manual, should be an ongoing training component within an institution's collection care program. The purpose of this manual is to create a document that will contain, and be, a reference to the policies, procedures, and technical aspects of caring for collection objects. Manuals need to be developed by a collaborative effort of individuals representing the various collection care departments and teams. As with all training programs, the creating of the manual will need to be undertaken with the support of senior management in committing staff time and expense to produce and maintain the documents.

Manuals should include all collection care policy documents so that the user can reference information regarding specific procedures. These documents will inform the reader of methods that have been established for the collection care operations within a specific department or among related departments. Policy documents can reflect basic movement and inventory forms, numbering and labeling of objects, case and key numbers for display and storage locations. If there are sensitive statements or sections within the policy documents, they should be redacted to maintain privacy. These manuals are to be used by a variety of levels of collection care staff and should be written and edited in an appropriate manner.

Manuals are necessary in that they provide procedures and technical information for physically working within a specific institution. These documents should include information regarding the procedures, and the environmental and logistical requirements of certain areas where collection objects will be handled, stored, and displayed. Maps of rooms and hallways with dimensions for doorways, elevators, and turning radius are necessary when planning movement activities. Each building is different and has been configured over the years to accommodate growth and change, so it is important that this information is researched and clearly documented.

Manuals can be used to explain proper handling techniques for specific object and collection types. Research of the institution's collection for this content will give the collection staff a clear understanding of the attributes of the objects within each collection and curatorial division. Documenting this information creates the understanding of how to develop, support, and conduct policies and procedures for the larger overview of the collection. This information is essential for handling all levels of training and can be made detachable for training purposes; it should be easily reviewed and updated as new techniques, material, and handling equipment are researched and acquired.

A section may also be included to identify and list objects that require special attention before movement is undertaken. Categories can include sizes, weights, treatment reports, mounting or installation instructions, handling specifications, packing notes, and staff notification, or the supervision required. This section is extremely beneficial to the reader as much of this information maybe the only record in existence to interpret difficult or delicate object requirements. Staff memory or the overall institutional memory cannot compare to taking the time to record accurate accounts of how an object and its history is to be considered.

Each institution varies in what content it believes is needed to be placed in a manual. The examples noted above are the most common, but each institution should build content to include what works best for its ongoing reference and training needs. Additional sections may include the following:

- Emergency response and recovery plan; This is often placed in a separate manual as it encompasses the entire museum staff and facility. Related documents specific to collection care areas can be added to a procedural manual.

- Special exhibition procedures: These documents can be tailored to the most common procedures involved within special exhibitions. Examples could be the requirements of truck and dock handling, courier requirements, and loan or insurance issues.
- Other site locations: Examples could entail such additions as outdoor sculpture or display gardens, government houses, related historical houses or facilities, and storage facilities. Each institution is specifically unique in its external collection areas.
- Appendices: This is the place for institutional documents, such as object movement forms, job descriptions, training agendas, and environmental requirements such as light levels, temperature and humidity, and basic security allowances.

STAFF TRAINING EXAMPLES

Departmental Training Teams

In any institution or business, the best scenario is to have someone who can be a dedicated staff trainer. This person would coordinate with departmental supervisors and representatives, training programs, and schedules regarding all daily responsibilities and activities. If a dedicated individual cannot be supported to manage the overall program, a group with representation from all collection care departments should be established.

The successful outcome of any training program is based on the requirement that the various departments are involved in the overall development of the program. This structure requires that departmental supervisors and appointed representatives are available to attend planning and development meetings and that they then share the information with their staff. Individual training programs can be developed for each department, but most programs are developed and conducted for a multidisciplinary group. Topics in collection care training programs are cross-departmental in context with those of all staff groups.

Scheduled meetings need to be established for review of, and for updating, content, and for developing new and refresher training programs. Senior management needs to be kept abreast of these meetings and must be required to attend some development meetings along with individual training programs in order to be confident of overall program goals and outcomes. Budgets need to have an accounting figure placed into the division or departmental budget to support internal training supplies and tools such as printing, training videos, reference books, publications, and webinar purchases.

The human resources department will need to be involved in the development and structure of all training programs, and it should review and support any issues related to equal opportunity and occupational health and safety compliance requirements which must be addressed. Operation of heavy equipment and the use of certain materials in handling, storage, and tracking require specific practices that are maintained for the health and safety of individuals and for facility protection. Some training may require that a license or certificate be obtained before an individual is allowed to operate a certain piece of equipment or that he or she must be fitted with protective gear. Examples of equipment and protective gear that require special training include forklifts, scissor lifts, and respiratory fitting and training. By law, the individual must carry this proof of training with him or her at all times and must keep it current with continued testing or training—all of which must be budgeted as well. The specialized training must be made available to all staff members who wish to undertake it, but it cannot be made mandatory. Some staff may feel uncomfortable or will be unsuitable to work with such specialized equipment.

The security department and the facilities department are two other groups who will need to be made aware of the collection care policy and procedure training. They can review the documents that are produced to make sure that they comply with the security and facility regulations and standards for which they are responsible. Examples of working with a security department would be allowing access to specific rooms, keys, codes, and specific displays to educate the public regarding egress routes or potential bodily injury. Examples of working with a facility department would be fire safety in workstations, proper storage of pressurized gas containers and hazardous material, and the correct disposal procedures. These examples are only a few to give the general idea of what may be required. For more information, speak directly with the representatives of these two departments of your institution.

The following are examples of training for new and full-time collection care employees. Each institution will vary in its requirements for staff training, but these examples are key components in developing and maintaining successful programs for staff professional development.

Training for New Employees

In the hiring process for a new employee position at any level, seeking individuals with previous experience is a key factor. Training should be conducted as part of the induction of the individual within the first week of his arrival. Time needs to be taken to give the new hire an overview of the facility, and an introduction to department collection care managers and staff, as well as the security and facility managers. A review of the procedure manual and a copy given to the individual is an essential aspect of his initial training. Staff members should be assigned to work directly with the new employee for a period of time as he/she learns the departmental responsibilities. The human resources department should devote time for the induction process with an explanation of the organizational structure and present an employee handbook of all benefits and rules.

In the instance of a new employee to an entry-level position, the department manager should designate a member of his staff to be a mentor to the new hire for an initial period of time. When a mid-level or substantially experienced individual begins work, senior staff members within the department should work with the new person for immediate on-the-job training. If senior staff members are dedicated to a certain section of the department, time should be scheduled for the new staff member to work with each of the senior staff to give him or her a solid introduction into the working structures within the department.

Part-Time, Temporary, or Casual Staff Training

Many institutions and service companies rely on employing part-time, temporary, or casual staff members. These staff members are usually hired to fill staffing needs for a specific or termed project such as a special exhibition, building renovation, or collections relocation. These staff members can become a group of employees to be used on an "on call" basis if an organization has multiple projects which are scheduled over different times within the calendar year. These individuals are often seeking part-time employment to supplement their "other" career as artists, craftsmen, musicians, or students.

In the hiring process for these temporary positions, seeking individuals with previous experience is not common but can be a key factor. The human resources department will need to be involved in all hiring and training programs because of the distinctly different employment regulations pertaining to this staffing level status. Advertising, job description, and training programs need to be clearly written and presented as to the limits of responsibility and reporting structure within the department and organization.

Training should be conducted as part of the induction of the individuals being hired for part-time employment. A dedicated meeting prior to commencement of work needs to be planned to give the individuals an overview of the project, their responsibilities, reporting structures, and an introduction to department collection care managers and their responsibilities. As work commences, the manager of the department needs to instruct these workers as to the specific work required of them. Full-time department staff will need to be assigned to supervise these individuals during the daily work schedule.

REFRESHER TRAINING FOR EXISTING STAFF

Collection care procedures, policies, and technical knowledge change with the advancement of research within the profession. As this information is gained and adjusted to accommodate the particular institution and its staff, time should be allocated for its dissemination to the staff. Having a forum in which there can be comments, suggestions, and answers to questions is an effective use of the workday. Posting the information in a staff email or on the bulletin board is not an approach that guarantees any continuity other than the basic act of passing information along to the staff members. The following are a few examples of ways that can be developed for making successful communications, sharing of information, and guaranteeing that the information is clearly presented to the employee.

Departmental Staff Meetings

Staff meetings should be scheduled on a weekly or biweekly basis. Most of the meetings would usually pertain to communicating the current or upcoming workflow and schedule. Because these meetings are conducted on a regular basis, it is a good forum to openly report and discuss new information that is of interest. Information can be as basic as topics found within a new internet posting, a website link, creative solutions of any recent activity, and new procedural forms, materials, equipment, or tools. If the information is deemed to be of interest to all departments, it can be scheduled for reporting in a multidepartment meeting. For the manager and moderator of this meeting, it may be difficult at first to develop this venue of sharing ideas, but persistence will pay off eventually to the point where staff will appreciate the effort and participate more fully.

Division or Multidepartment Meetings

A collection care division should have a monthly or a bimonthly meeting, which all staff within the division are required to attend. This meeting, like the departmental meetings, pertains to the current or upcoming workflow schedule. The division head should set an agenda to include additional information such as divisional updates in matters related to the overall group, a summary of senior management directives, and budgetary planning and updates. Though the details of this information should be shared by the division head with departmental managers on a continual basis, it is important to have an overview presented by the division head to the entire group.

The second part of this meeting can include individual department managers' reports of current activities within the department. This is an excellent opportunity to share with the entire group any new procedural, policy, or technical information that has been discussed in the weekly staff meetings. This method can be used to present larger subjects in greater detail as part of ongoing training. The topics should be discussed prior to the division managers' meeting so that staff members can prepare their presentations for the time allocated on the agenda. This is also an excellent opportunity for staff members to employ their communication skills. Examples could include a report of a current departmental project, attendance at a conference, or courier travel, or research into new material or techniques. Such communication should be developed and promoted as an opportunity for all individuals within the division, and supported for personal and team professional development.

Training Sessions

A training program should be developed on an annual basis that is focused on giving a refresher course to all full-time staff. This program should be focused on giving all levels of staff an update on development, changes, and additions to the procedure manuals, new technical research, and materials and equipment that have been added over the previous year. This "refresher" training, in its approach, yields a positive outcome in that it reminds even the most senior staff of the importance of the ongoing responsibilities of the division. It will keep all staff focused on the need of best practices while reacquainting them with certain procedures, policies, or technical topics that they seldom undertake but need to be mindful of.

All collection care staff members in the division should be required to attend these meetings.

The presenters need to be encouraged and supported by each department manager to present a specific subject. The presentations each year should be shared among the staff to give different individuals an opportunity to research and develop new additions to the overall agenda. Depending on the size of attendance, this program may need to be conducted over a sequenced period of time to keep presenters and participants focused on its outcome. Human resources, security, and facility departments may want to be involved to present any new updates in those divisions that affect collection care activities.

Larger meetings of this type are often the hardest to conduct because of the commitment of time within the schedule. Senior staff may see it as a waste of time as it is knowledge they already have. The development and commitment of support by senior management is essential as the professionalism of the division is seen as that of a focused group. Some organizations have developed these programs to include other departments to give these staff members a better understanding of the overall museum mission. Examples of additional attendees can include volunteers, docents, security guards, and individuals who usually interact with the visiting public regarding the front-of-the-house responsibilities.

Presentations for Museum Staff and Public

On occasion, a particular department or individual has been involved in a project, travel, or professional conference that can be the topic for presentation to other museum staff and members of the public. One benefit of this is that it spotlights the collection care profession before a greater audience within and outside of the museum. Promoting the professionalism of collection care acknowledges the mission and responsibilities within the museum. This knowledge will help support future research and attendance of external programs, which will then be brought back to educate the entire division.

Presenting and sharing information is a basic factor in the professional development of support and training of collection care staff. Examples of collection care presentations that would be of interest are topics such as conservation treatments; recent exhibition highlights; unique handling, installation, or rigging projects; travel reports of couriers; research studies and highlights of conferences attended by staff.

MENTORING

Mentoring is a difficult subject to address as there is no one comparison that can be drawn from within an organization or individual's career. Mentoring is solely dependent on the commitment of supervisory staff and on having an effective leader, teacher, and communicator of all that he does in his job. Mentoring is a relationship between two people—the "mentor" and the "mentee." This relationship that is built over time allows a mentor to pass on valuable skills, knowledge, and insights to the mentee to help him develop his career.

Mentoring should be developed between senior staff and younger or new staff. In the manufacturing world, apprenticeship is a common, long-time practice used as an effective tool to teach the technical attributes of a trade or craft such as that of a carpenter or electrician. Today there are programs offered to the business world in which mentors are trained to work alongside particular staff members to assist them in their growth. The quality of a strong relationship still depends on the factor of the personal skills of the mentor to motivate the mentee to seek the professional development of his or her career.

CASE STUDY: MENTORING AND THE
COLLECTION CARE PROFESSION

by Kurt Christian

In thinking about the topic of mentorship, I found myself surveying my own past and those who have mentored me as well as those whom I have mentored. In this essay, I will focus on my experiences as a preparator working in art museums, and I will focus in particular on one specific experience that both challenged and shaped my career. While thinking about mentoring experiences, I recalled things that I hadn't really given much thought to in a very long time. Some of these recollections made me laugh, some made me smile, and some made me cringe with embarrassment. Throughout my career, I have had, and continue to have, people around me who have been significant in helping me learn from my experiences, regardless of whether those experiences happened to be positive or negative. But there have been a handful of colleagues who have really taken time to help me understand things in ways that have had a profound effect on how I think. Mentorship requires both an openness and a willingness to learn, as well as some kind of connection between two people. As is the case in any relationship, mentorship also requires time and nurturing.

Collection care professionals, especially preparators and art handlers, have a lot in common. They tend to be artists or musicians, and they are almost always highly skilled craftsmen who, by the very nature of the behind-the-scenes work that they do, are usually calm and low-key in nature. These individuals routinely handle important, priceless, and irreplaceable cultural artifacts in high-stress environments for a relatively low financial compensation and in spite of infrequent acknowledgment from their supervisors.

Joshua Rosenblatt, my friend and former boss, was quoted in the *New York Times* as saying that art handling was often like "threading a needle all day."[1] There aren't many of us who have set out to become preparators or art handlers, but we have, rather, fallen into this work while pursuing a means to support ourselves as we make our art. The collection care profession is still a young one, and until very recently, collection care jobs at many institutions came under the facilities or building operations departments. Many professionals in our field haven't had computers, email addresses, business cards, professional development, or even a dialogue with their own peers at other institutions. Because of these factors, many preparators have little interest in the work that they do all day and may not even acknowledge it as their career, even if they have been doing the work at a high level for many years. Perhaps it is due to some of these issues and circumstances that it often seems like we are our own worst advocates, and incidentally, we are quite often very difficult candidates to mentor.

CHANGE IN EMPLOYMENT

Several years ago I stepped into a new role in a new city, where I found extremely low morale among the staff. The museum had recently reorganized its staffing structure, which upset the majority of the staff members on my team. It was necessary to make some pretty big changes, but large-scale changes do not happen quickly. The first priority was to gain an understanding of the new environment and the individuals who were a part of it. Fortunately, the head of the department understood and supported the change that needed to happen in order to turn things around. It was a long-term commitment and a slow, often contentious process; many staff members found it difficult to adapt. The changes took seven years to implement and involved a lot of turnover and conflict, but, ultimately, they were successful. The turnover mostly happened naturally as people accepted other jobs, moved, or went back to school, and though it was difficult and stressful at first, it allowed me to form a new team with a new attitude.

Most importantly, the supervisor who was supportive in making this change became one of the most important mentors I have had in my career. This individual gave critical insight, supported decisions, and provided much-needed challenges throughout it all. This mentor is still one of the first people I call when I need advice, and that is a great resource to have. This supervisor consistently supported the changes needed at the museum, and those actions exemplify the role of a personal mentor. Trust and belief in this relationship was paramount, as mentorship really is a two-way street.

CHANGE IN STAFF STRUCTURE

Prior to enacting any change, some homework was necessary. The first step was to reach out to peers at museums of a similar size and in the same region. The purpose of contacting colleagues at similar institutions was to obtain information about their staff structures and pay grades, which helped to determine whether those statistics at my own institution were close to average. The response received from these peers was remarkably open and extremely helpful, and helped create important friendships and alliances. Research also involved purchasing all of the relevant museum salary surveys to offer a better understanding of what had been established as the norm for the profession and institutions in the region. This information was essential to have before pursuing a significant structural change.

The first couple of steps to make actual changes were fairly easy and included the following:

- Obtaining additional computers and personal email addresses for the staff, which improved both communication and morale as the staff had been addressed more as a group, not as individuals, up until this point.
- Evaluating job descriptions, including my own as manager, was very difficult as there needed to be a change in the current structure, which consisted of a head preparator with six art handlers, undifferentiated by level or specialty. The ultimate goal was to build a hierarchy. My previous experience was from an institution with a tiered hierarchy, which seemed to work effectively because it gave individuals the potential of upward mobility. The new change was a very difficult and time-consuming endeavor. Ultimately, two new positions were created and all of the old job descriptions changed, along with the job titles.
- Additionally, business cards for the staff were acquired. This may sound small, but it was actually a big step at the time and improved the overall professional morale.

In the end, the changes weren't everything that was initially desired, but what was accomplished was definitely something that was worth the fight, even though it took several years to achieve.

CHANGE IN METHODS AND METHODOLOGIES

In the beginning, there was quite a bit that could be done fairly quickly because the department had a healthy budget. It was a priority to acquire a range of new tools and equipment and to introduce new packing and crating materials and methodologies. Certain staff members resisted change, and the group was splintered at times. Staff who embraced the change were ostracized to some degree by the others, which is a normal but unpleasant part of any group dynamic. As a manager, there were definitely periods spent questioning the directive of making all of the change. Continuing to make changes with so much resistance was exhausting to say the least, but as staff shifted and grew, so did their attitudes, and along with that shift came acceptance. As positions opened up, the job requirements were re-tooled to require a higher entry level of experience.

Four new employees who were hired for these new positions and requirements all had previous museum experience. Slowly, things really did start to change for the better. One individual was a very skilled preparator who helped to rebuild and refurbish the painting trucks and object carts, as well as to design and build new and more adaptive versions. It was rewarding to see these improvements becoming contagious, and soon three people were making really incredible and inventive adaptations in the equipment we used to transport art through the museum.

A very positive change was receiving support from the museum to send the preparator staff on courier trips both nationally and internationally. This afforded staff valuable knowledge of art handling personnel and practices outside of their own museum, while acknowledging them as skilled, trusted, and important stewards of a collection. Staff members were encouraged to exchange business cards on these trips and to connect with colleagues at the institutions that they were visiting.

The preparators developed more collaborative and cooperative relationships with the museum's registration and conservation departments because of the improved staff professionalism and a stronger understanding of the responsibilities that were required of them. Developing and strengthening cross-departmental relationships was something that needed to happen, but starting within the team was the first step. The individuals of the staff began to operate more fluidly as a team and became active participants in the planning and assessment of the collections care programming.

MANAGEMENT ON AN INDIVIDUAL BASIS

In the course of rebuilding the team of preparators, I was able to learn the specific artistic interests of the staff and assign projects that allowed individuals to work more closely in those areas, whether that was textiles, contemporary art, or fabrication, which gave staff members a sense of ownership and pride in their work. Talking with staff about the objects being dealt with on an artistic level is important, especially since objects are what bring most preparators to the job in the first place. Encouraging professional development whenever possible is equally important, whether it is through a webinar, an online course, or a conference. Budgeting appropriately to send at least one person per year to a class or conference is helpful. The purpose of building these opportunities was to encourage staff engagement in, and enthusiasm for, their profession.

One of the best and cheapest ways to encourage development and enthusiasm was to coordinate with a colleague at another institution to find a day when I could send my senior preparator to shadow him and his staff. This museum was only a few hours away by train, and it was an institution with a similar size and type of collection. For the cost of a train ticket and a one-night hotel stay, this was a helpful experience for my senior preparator, and one that had a real impact on how he viewed his own profession. This preparator grew to become a valued and indispensable staff member, and ultimately became my successor.

THE CIRCLE OF MENTORSHIP

My own networking with colleagues at other institutions has always been a tremendously positive experience for me as these are the people who share ideas with me. I cannot count how many late-night calls I have had with these colleagues who have helped me solve issues and work through problems. What we do is not only important but very special, and sometimes we need to remind ourselves of that. It is strange to me that people do not want to see different approaches, or that they dislike change, as it keeps me awake, challenged, and engaged. My own mentors have taught me invaluable trade skills, critically challenged me, and led by example in their work ethic, diplomacy, and leadership. The lessons of my own mentors will be passed along by me and others and will make a valuable contribution to the collections care field.

After seven years of putting together a wonderful and diverse team with a great and supportive supervisor, I left to start over again at another institution. I am proud of my accomplishments at my previous job, but there are still things I could have added to my list of achievements. Such is work, and life, and I am sure my successor will continue the work that my supervisor and I started together.

Kurt Christian
Chief Preparator
Preparation and Installation Department
Carnegie Museum of Art
Pittsburgh, Pennsylvania

INTERNSHIPS

Internships offer an individual on-the-job training to develop his/her professional career. They benefit a particular department by adding an employee who will assist in the departmental activities or project that is being undertaken. Intern positions are often factored into the annual department, or project-based, programming schedule and budget. Some intern positions are unpaid, depending on project schedule, but both unpaid and paid positions are targeted for a temporary period.

The quality of an internship program should be based on a specific activity to allow both the individual and the organization the benefit of the best combination of success. Individuals benefit by gaining knowledge that only work experience within an organization can offer. It also offers the individual the opportunity to get acquainted with the career path that he may be considering or redirecting his professional ambitions. A benefit for the employer is that if a position is made available, the intern may become a viable candidate for it. Some institutions that are affiliated with a university have developed work-study programs to offer paid employment that could lead to a future career. Commercial service companies can develop intern or work-study programs which offer a similar opportunity to the person seeking an educational and employment opportunity.

Noncollection Staff Training

In most museums, there are a number of individuals, paid or unpaid, who are the public face of the institution and are crucial to the viewing and under-standing of the collection. These individuals need to have some level of collection care training so that they understand the principles of why collec-tion care and preventive conservation are important. The level of training is based on the size and type of institution and is primarily about the principles and policies of the museum rather than the actual procedures and technical knowledge.

These individuals are primarily docents, educational instructors, and security guard staff. These staff members are oftentimes referred to as the "face of the museum" as the public are in direct contact with them on a regular basis. They are an excellent conduit to give the public a glimpse into the importance of collection care and to support the direction of preventive measures when the collection is being viewed. It is a symbiotic relationship in that it creates public awareness and interest in the mission of a museum while assisting the museum in protecting the collection made vulnerable by public access.

EXTERNAL TRAINING

During the last thirty years, there has been a significant increase in external training opportunities for collection care staff. Though these opportunities have increased in number, many are not available in various museums. Programs available are limited by number of attendees, budgetary costs for attendance, and the small number of topics presented on any specific subject. As the need for professional development grows, the support for these programs will con-tinue to develop and be made available to more museums and their collection care staff. The following are several external programs that are available, with additional contact information listed in the bibliography section under training.

Networking with or Visiting Other Institutions

One of the most cost-effective and least time-consuming training opportunities is having staff visit their colleagues in another institution in the same city or region. This can be done effectively by having staff contact their colleagues at another institution to arrange a visit to view and discuss their facilities or particular areas of interest. This type of exchange can be reciprocal for both museums. The costs of this program are minimal as travel and housing costs can be eliminated or managed on a minimum financial outlay. Time allocated to conduct these visits is mutually determined for each person's schedule, and visits can be conducted in the course of a few hours on a single day. The major benefits are that the employees are able to see other institutional programs, learn from this exchange, and gain valuable contacts for the future. Staff members can compare their achievements or discover possibilities for change within their area of responsibility at their own institution.

The long-term benefit to all museums involved is that it builds good relations within the local museum community. Single or multiple networks formed are invaluable to the expertise that can be gained by all. Oftentimes, this networking develops into specific training programs developed by staff and conducted within the region or by promoting external groups or individuals to come to the region to conduct a particular training program. Many times, commercial service companies are involved in these community programs as it enhances their staff training opportunities and develops their understanding of their clients' needs. Some programs can be as simple as organizing an after-work gathering to meet for drinks or a meal as a social networking opportunity.

Sessions and Workshops

One of the best multilayered training opportunities is to have collection care staff attend museum-based conferences or annual meetings. The conference setting allows the attendee to choose from a broad range of sessions over several days of presentations. The attendee will benefit from sessions of direct topical interest, learn more about a related subject, or gain new knowledge from aspects that are not directly related to his current area of expertise within the museum industry. Conferences are usually developed, and sessions are selected to correspond to the significance of a particular theme. The diversity of topics for the overall conference based on the target theme creates an excellent opportunity for the attendee to better understand the work of the museum community. No one attendee can attend all of the sessions, but each should be encouraged to look at a variety of topics while creating his attendance list.

A list of museum-based conferences is provided in the bibliography section under training opportunities. These conferences are usually held on an annual basis in different cities, which allows attendees the possible advantage of reduced travel expenses. The dates and locations are scheduled two years in advance, which assists managers in budget planning for their professional development projections for the fiscal year. Many such conferences offer supplemental budget assistance in the form of reduced fees for early registration, reduced rates at hotels, and special travel stipends offered to attendees in a competitive format.

One of the best-focused training opportunities is having collection care staff attend workshops. Many workshops are developed and designed by specific museum organizations on a current topic of interest. The initial planning for a workshop takes into account a desired regional location and timing to accommodate the host organization and participating institutions. If a workshop is offered on a popular topic, the same organizational structure and content can be duplicated at other venues and times in a touring format, which requires less effort in the development stages.

Most workshop formats are conducted in lecture-style presentations with time allotted for question-and-answer sessions between the audience and the presenters. Depending on attendance size, facility adaptability, and overall time allotted for the workshop program, "hands-on" components can be added to allow attendees to work with the technical concepts, build to designs, and use materials, all while under the direction and supervision of the presenter or organizers.

Some workshops are developed, designed, and coordinated in a joint partnership by two organizations; the topics are of interest to each membership or professional constituency. These types of workshops can also be developed in association with a larger museum conference and scheduled prior to, during, or immediately after the conference dates at the same location at which the larger conference is being held. A list of museum-based workshops and the organizations that develop and conduct them is listed in the bibliography section under training opportunities. Some of these workshops are scheduled for one, two, or more days, depending on the topic of interest and location. A few workshops are conducted through a university or academic affiliation, which may offer accredited hours that can be used toward certain levels of professional education programs.

Webinars

A webinar is a Web-based presentation, lecture, workshop, or seminar that is transmitted over the Web using video-conferencing software. The webinar format is an excellent way to conduct training for multiple attendees at

Figure 3.3   Preparator Conference 3 Campbell Center 2013. *Source*: Author.

various locations at a designated time. The benefit is that the participants
can be several staff members gathered to view the same presentation in one
location while never leaving the confines of their work environment. This
training opportunity creates an efficient, cost-saving program by eliminating travel costs and minimizing disruption of work schedules. The program
format is conducted by a designated group of individuals, comprising speakers, moderator, and technical assistance to produce the program on the Web.
Those in attendance only need a computer with speakers and a keyboard
and a designated person to share written text with the presenters and other
attendees in the group.

Most webinars are structured, maintained, and produced by the larger
museum organizations because of the technical costs, registration, and marketing required for reaching out to potential attendees. This same format can
also be structured through online host sites for a minimal fee, for small groups
of individuals needing to communicate or be trained on a specific subject
while remaining at their different locations.

Although the obvious drawback of the webinar format is that interaction
is mediated by computer peripherals, the overall benefit is advantageous for
networking opportunities because of the large number of attendees and the
concomitant sharing of the participants' registration lists.

Private Consultants "Training within Institutions"

Private consultants can offer training programs in three formats. The first is by offering a workshop or course on a specific subject at the trainer's working studio or facility. Workshops are conducted at this location to which attendees will travel, where they will be taught, and where they will work within the confines of the designated facility. This format offers the consistency of space and equipment and other necessities required of the trainer to conduct the course. This format greatly assists in reducing preparation time and expense by having the correct equipment and material at hand on a repeated basis.

The second type of workshop or course conducted by a consultant is to provide training at a designated facility. This format allows the trainer to travel to the site at a particular museum or facility to which the participants from various museums around the city, state, or region can travel to attend. This format reduces the costs of travel-related expense for the attendees but will increase the trainer's costs substantially in terms of travel, housing, and related preparation expenses. These additional costs are minimal in comparison to the overall reduction of attendee expense. The facility required to conduct this training will need to be associated with an existing museum or facility that has the space for attendees and the required equipment on site or easily obtainable for the proposed training.

The third format of training by a consultant is when an organization requires the training to be specifically developed for its institution, facility, and staff. The consultant will work with the management of the departments involved prior to the actual training, by developing and creating a program that covers the specific needs. These programs will be the result of meetings with managers, research of current policies and procedures, interviews with staff, and observation of the physical operations of the facility. The result is a training program that is tailored to the organization's specific structure and collection base. Depending on the amount of support for the program from senior management and financial support for the trainer, the selected outcomes such as policy and procedural documents, working manuals, and staff professional development can be quickly established. This is a valuable aid for creating a training program as it allows it to be developed in a shorter, more focused period of time, without disruption to staff work. A concise, solid training program can be built upon this foundation by having staff assigned to updating and conducting the ongoing training programs.

Collection Care Training Programs

There are collection care training programs offered by various museum-based organizations in both the public and private sectors. The type of programs offered are generally developed to a specific subject and created based on the presenter's area of expertise. Many public-based programs offer a certificate of completion or credited points to be used in a degree of higher education. To describe the various programs offered would be difficult as each has subtle differences in the overall program approach. A listing of many of the organizations which offer collection care courses, workshops, and degree programs are listed in the reference section of the publication under the heading of "Staff Training." In this same section are listed many of the museum studies programs among which many include some solid collection care training.

Commercial Service Company Training

Commercial service companies offer training to their staff and design the programs specifically to fit their operational structure and the client base that they serve. Each company's training program focuses on the various highlights of its services, which include logistical transport and regulatory management, storage facility and maintenance, collection relocation, and technical expertise in all activities offered to its clients. Depending on staff disciplines, number of individuals, and potentially multiple locations of their operations, training programs are built internally to ensure that policies, procedures, and standards of operational knowledge are effectively understood across the company's structure.

A company's commitment to staff professional development is a strong reflection on its overall approach to customer service. The development of training programs is often managed by a designated staff member to develop all programs in a combined effort by the departmental managers for their specific areas. Scheduling time to conduct such training is often a difficult task as service commitments can be sporadic in scheduling compared to the known structured schedules in an institution. Time committed to training is also dictated by loss of income as staff are taken out of the daily workflow. Staff time and commitment for training programs have to be efficiently scheduled and viewed as an investment in knowledge, which will yield improved staff performance, work efficiency, high-quality standards, and, ultimately, successful customer-service relations.

Museum-organized training programs are excellent opportunities for commercial staff to attend and learn about current standards and practices of collection care. The attendance of these programs and, in many instances, individuals being asked to present information on a specific topic is an excellent professional development opportunity. The largest benefit in attending such programs is bridging the knowledge gap between the commercial service expertise and the museum expertise. It also helps the museums to have a better understanding, as clients, of the service that the companies have to

Figure 3.4 Artex FAS Client Training. *Source*: Carey, Artex FAS.

Figure 3.5 Artex FAS Rigging Training. *Source*: Carey, Artex FAS.

offer. Many companies offer training programs to their clients both in the institution and in the private sector, which are structured to address a specific operational or technical subject.

As each company is distinctly different in organizational structure and service, it is difficult to list all of the potential training programs that are developed. For direct information, you can contact a company to see what it offers in client relations regarding internal and external training. The following article helps to understand how a successful training program is structured within the commercial sector of the museum industry.

CASE STUDY: TRAINING AT CROZIER

by Nicole Bouchard Tejeiro

At Crozier Fine Arts, a leading provider of art handling, warehousing, and logistics, training has evolved greatly over the last decade. In the early 2000s, while Crozier had a reputation of quality handling and a low incidence of damage, training of new art handlers depended greatly on the techniques and time investment of individual crew chiefs and the managers under whom they worked. At the same time, the company was experiencing a period of growth and sought to put safeguards in place that would ensure continued quality of service for their clients.

Starting in 2005, Crozier embarked on a mission to develop and implement a training program that would ultimately become a process underlying the company's culture. Starting with a council of leading art handlers at the company—most with more than a decade of experience—Crozier's team discussed techniques, materials, and best practices for an extensive list of activities and factors. The findings of this study were documented in an "operating manual," a guide that managers could access whenever needed.

Next, a smaller team chosen for leadership, coaching, and communication skills developed a curriculum that took this manual and put it into an active presentation, covering each of several critical areas. The outline included ethics and principles, documentation, roles and responsibilities, safety, wrapping, packing, installation, storage, and client contact.

Crozier's training team delivered sessions in a seminar-plus-practicum format presenting topics in a morning session and then applying them in an afternoon hands-on session. This required the team to procure or create sample "artworks" that would expose trainees to a wide array of challenges: oversized paintings, glazed flatworks, hinged works on paper, odd-shaped mirrors in ornate frames, and sculptures made of atypical materials. The team prepared and presented material, hardware, crating, and packaging samples. This hands-on experiential element was discovered to be crucial to staff learning.

The following is an example of how Crozier approaches one topic: training staff on wrapping an artwork:

1. *Start with the big picture.* There are a few questions that are critical, no matter what the work to be wrapped is: What are the distinguishing characteristics of the piece? Is it framed, glazed, or mounted? What elements of the work are vulnerable? Where is the piece traveling to and by what method? The answers to these questions determine the materials and approaches to use.
2. *Get down to technical details.* The discussion shifts to specific examples, starting with the types of works that are most frequently encountered. At Crozier, we see many flatworks under glazing of some kind. What if the piece is under treated glass or plexiglass like Den Glass or UF3 or UV plexiglass? Then it should be wrapped with an archival primary layer to guard against discoloration as a result of reaction with polyethylene. Treated glazing should not be taped as the tape will damage the treatment.
3. *Put the new knowledge to work immediately.* Here, the wrapping training turns to execution. Art handlers are shown how to lay out, measure, score, cut, and fold materials to make a safe, neat soft-pack for a flatwork. This is shown through demonstration and then through practice. Each art handler wraps a sample work, which is then inspected and graded by the instructors. This takes place during the practicum of the training.

Realizing that mastery of a few key skills at one time was more effective than an intense overload of all practices in one shot, Crozier created separate, more advanced modules for experienced staff. These modules cover handling oversized works, rolling, folding, and complex installation challenges. Valuable concepts such as crew leadership, communication, and client management principles are also addressed.

The same general approach is used for advanced modules such as folding a large painting:

1. *Again, looking at the big picture.* Folding a work can be risky. Art handlers are asked to determine if this is the best course of action. Must the work be folded? Has it been folded before? Can it be folded safely? And because keeping a work folded over the long term is not advised, when will the work be able to be unfolded?
2. *Details again, and preparation.* Folding keys for wet paintings and brackets must be made in advance. Or, a sonotube may need to be prepared with

archival materials to keep the folded work from creasing in place of the folding keys. Tools for removing canvas tacks or staples must be on hand. A clean workspace for the folding activity must be made ready on site; will that entail moving furniture or bringing in work tables?

3. *Practice, practice, practice.* With all the preparations covered, the art handlers receive a demonstration outlining the steps for a safe and successful fold, and then they execute one in the classroom with a sample work.

To make the advanced modules both challenging and fun, training staff would hang bells from various locations of the classroom ceiling and then ask art handlers to navigate a very large example work into the room and place it on the far wall, without ringing any of the bells. This simulates the situation of moving a piece in a home with hanging chandeliers or other works.

In addition to technical skills, it is important that Crozier's senior art handlers and managers have a firm grasp of how to effectively lead a team on site or in the warehouse in sometimes time-restricted or otherwise challenging situations. Training sessions also discuss how to guide and correct junior art handlers, how to respond to a client's complaint on site, and how to troubleshoot project challenges working in collaboration with client representatives back at headquarters.

But a singular training session alone does not suffice. To reinforce the program, the training staff issues reminder bulletins and updates on specific topics. Taking a page from other professions where technical skills require update and refresh, all employees are provided annual recurrent training to continue to hone their abilities. What is more, since art handling and the art world is highly dynamic, the mantra "communication, awareness, and forward thinking" is repeated throughout the program. It is these three principles that drive judicious decisions in unknown territory.

Parallel to the training, Crozier sought to retain a culture of personal responsibility at the art handler level, keeping the organizational structure as flat as practicable. By allowing art handlers and project managers access to the training resources and their internal team of experts, everyone was charged with, and empowered to act on, the mission to protect artwork above all else. Through thoughtful planning and preparation, the training and materials set clear expectations for large concepts—like professional ethics—to small details—like hanging-hardware choice. And yet, the program is never a finished work. As new materials and techniques are introduced in our field, and as fresh challenges such as new artistic media or regulatory requirements arise, the program must continue to evolve, and so it does at Crozier.

The payback: Across industries, most companies struggle to maintain quality as volume increases, and in the past this had been the downfall of larger art-service companies. Yet, over the period that Crozier implemented its training program as head counts continually grew, the art handling staff not only maintained but also actually improved their claims record. This has been the result of a documented standard to which managers can hold staff accountable. And each art handler has a clear understanding of the correct approach, empowering him or her to make prudent decisions in the field.

Nicole Bouchard Tejeiro
Director Corporate Strategic Projects
Crozier Fine Arts
New York, New York

OCCUPATIONAL HEALTH AND SAFETY TRAINING

How does this subject pertain to the care of collection objects in the workplace? The answer is simple: the health and well-being of all staff members working with the collection need to be maintained as the highest priority for a safe work environment, which will translate into the efficient, proper, and safe handling of the collection object. Today, within the museum industry, the unique attributes of individuals and their responsibilities to undertake collection care functions have created a training challenge both in the institution and in the commercial sectors.

Government regulations require that training be undertaken in the workplace, but programs are often generic in most of their content as they are developed to cover a wide audience and the required legislation. These programs are invaluable and need to be supported, maintained, and conducted with a serious commitment. The human resources department, building facility department, and security managers are the keepers of this information, and collection care managers should work with these departments under their guidance and supervision. Occupational Health and Safety (OH&S) training is a cross-departmental effort within both the institution and commercial organizations.

The challenge in creating and developing a program that is targeted specifically to benefit collection care staff is as specialized as the objects entrusted to them to handle and protect. Many of the required training regulations and programs are basic to common, physical actions in the public workplace. Examples of these are proper lifting techniques, visual and respiratory protection, and weight and measure restrictions for walking, sitting, and standing within the daily workplace environment. These examples may be basic but they need to be complied with on a daily basis and in the development of overall training.

The repetitive physical nature of activities in the collection care environment presents ergonomic challenges to understanding and developing proper lifting techniques. While lifting activities and associated techniques among the collection handling staff are not necessarily of a repetitive nature on a daily basis, there are projects that demand such activity over a set period of time (an exhibition installation or a collections move). If a person is handling the same type and size of object, then there can be a repetitive physical movement that should be understood and proper training given to reduce physical risk. The greater percentage of work activities are associated with the type and size of object and vary dramatically as handling requests for movement and type of object are seldom the same during an average day.

To compensate for the variables of these physical activities, proper lifting techniques and ergonomic training should be developed by researching the most common lifting scenarios undertaken as part of the department's responsibilities. Specialists in the field of OH&S, physical therapy, and ergonomics should be brought in to better evaluate what your staff is subjected to on a regular basis. The experts can help develop a program that is specific to your daily work environment and to the ways to properly train and monitor staff during these activities. A common lifting activity found in most museums and service companies is the lifting of heavy crates during transport or when unpacking and packing them. Case lifters and wheeled supports are just two examples of equipment that, when employed and properly used, greatly reduce workplace injuries. Crate rollers convert from a roller assistance to support tables, which is ergonomically a more proper working height during unpacking and packing activities. Case lifters have been adapted within the general warehousing practice of lifting heavy industrial components, and wheeled supports come in a variety of low support dollies to lift and move crates easily during transport handling.

CREATING A PROGRAM AND STANDARD PROCEDURES

Creating a health and safety program is an organization-wide endeavor that needs to have the full support of the senior management and the division and department managers.

In the book *Health and Safety for Museum Professionals* (2012), Michael McCann states the following:

The major objectives of an effective safety, health and environmental management program are to prevent injuries and illness to museum staff, volunteers, students, and members of the public visiting the museum; to prevent loss to property and collection; and to reduce adverse environmental impact through its operations. Museum management accomplishes these objectives by establishing a proactive safety culture distinguished by top management commitment, supervisory control over risks, and employee compliance and cooperation.[2]

The ultimate goal of a safety and health program is to reduce or eliminate occupational injuries and illness. However, this by itself is insufficient. To provide a proper framework, there is a need to develop clear and measurable objectives. These objectives then become a basis for assigning activities, allocating staff and funds, communicating information about the program, and evaluating the effectiveness of the program. On this basis, the well-defined goals of a museum safety and health program are to (a) recognize hazards within the institution, (b) evaluate these hazards, and (c) reduce the hazards to the extent possible.[3] (2)

Developing a program specifically for the collection care departments should coincide with and be an extension of the institution's overall health and safety program. The collection care staff members who are assigned to be a part of the institutional health and safety group should investigate and develop objectives that are specific to each department's operations. These same staff members should attend and receive advanced training on specific subjects such as hazardous materials handling, respiratory protection, and fire safety, and participate in the organization's emergency planning programs. The goal should be to establish and implement proper health and safety objectives for all staff in the work environment.

New employees should be given training by the organization's health and safety committee and provided any documents that they can take with them to review and reference as policy and procedures in the future. Existing staff should attend an annual refresher presentation in which all aspects of the program can be reviewed so that they are reminded of the importance of the programs and introduced to any new policy or procedures.

Health and safety documents should be written to address the specific policy and procedures that the collection care staff need to practice daily within each of the work environments. These documents should be placed in a manual and given to all staff so that they can review and reference them as needed. This manual should be developed and structured so that it can be easily updated as policies change and the new elements should be added to the appropriate section. Other documents from the organization's overall health and safety programs that are pertinent to daily activities should be added to the manual. The combined manual should be made available in a designated, accessible location of the workstations as needed.

Each organization will be different in the amount and type of documents it may develop and place in the manual. Some of the documents that should be considered for inclusion in the manual are as follows:

- evacuation route maps per building level with fire alarms/extinguisher locations marked;
- individual room/area evacuation maps;
- emergency contacts: fire department, ambulance services, hospitals, with directions to local facilities;
- emergency contacts within the organization: security, human resources, facility management, department managers, and staff designated as health and safety monitors;
- fire alarm and extinguisher locations and proper usage diagrams;
- general first-aid kit locations with content lists;
- eye wash stations and hazard spill kit locations, and proper use diagrams;
- lists of hazardous materials and proper storage locations;
- manual tools with descriptive use and safety precautions;
- manual equipment with descriptive use and safety precautions;
- power equipment with descriptive use and safety precautions;
- heavy mobile equipment with descriptive use and safety precautions;
- handling techniques to prevent physical risk to individuals;
- handling techniques in specific areas involving distinctive characteristics of rooms, hallways, elevators, stairs, and loading docks; and
- other documents to be created for particular departments with regard to precautionary conditions.

Examples of Specific Documents

Common Museum Back Disorders and Risk Factors

Descriptive examples of repetitive or prolonged activities to reduce potential disorders:

- repeated bending over at the waist as a focal point for the lift;
- twisting from the waist during the lifting action;
- repeated initial lifting action from below the knees;
- repeated lifting from above the waist to above the shoulders;
- lifting or moving objects of excessive weight;
- lifting or moving objects of asymmetric size;
- frequency of movement within the work action;
- duration of time that one is working and the physical pace of the actions;
- stability of load when lifting or handling during movement;

- reaching motions over distances to lift and retrieve;
- height of workstations; and
- prolonged standing and/or sitting with poor posture

Safe lifting of equipment and techniques:

- Assess the object to be handled, noting its inherent properties; damage; loose parts; or fragile surfaces.
- Carry one object at a time, and use both hands.
- Avoid holding objects by extended parts or appendages; hold the main structure only.
- Use object carts or other object-handling devices whenever possible to avoid carrying and the risk of physical injury during movement.
- Avoid carrying a heavy object by hand for any distance.
- Use lifting equipment with a combination of support structures to avoid physical injury.
- Determine the weight limitations before lifting heavy objects.
- Seek out advice and/or assistance before lifting heavy objects.
- Bend at the knees and use your legs to lift, keeping your back straight.
- Grip the object from the bottom, and note asymmetrical shape in weight location.
- Agree to coordination of lifting motion when two or more individuals are undertaking the lift.
- Know the location to which the object is to be moved.
- Make sure the path is clear and that you have assistance with holding a cart or dolly.
- Avoid stairs, and avoid walking backward.

Working as a team when lifting heavy objects:

- Appoint a designated leader to discuss the procedure so that all individuals are in agreement before the move.
- Appoint a spotter who is not handling the object so that he can be aware of other potential obstacles the movers may encounter.
- Avoid unnecessary talking, and be attentive to the leader's discussions and directives.

Example explanation for a specific task:

Subject: Weight Assessment

- If uncertain of how heavy an object is, do a quick test by lifting the object slightly, then putting it back on the surface.

- This test motion will allow you to determine if you need assistance or not.
- When two or more people are going to lift an object, you can still do the same test as above, by having everyone lift the object up and then place it back on the surface.

This avoids someone on the team losing his part of the load in the middle of a move.

Examples of Specific Equipment and Procedures

Proper Care and Use:

The mobile ladder stand or ladder stand platform manufacturer is required to provide maintenance instructions with each unit. These instructions must address visual inspection procedures, general maintenance, and proper tightening directions for threaded fasteners. Users are required to read and understand the instructions before they are allowed to employ a mobile ladder stand or ladder stand platform. As an alternative, employers must instruct employees on the proper use of the units prior to allowing their use.

Upon receipt following shipping and prior to each period of use, each mobile ladder stand or ladder stand platform unit must be visually inspected for damage, such as unusual wear, deterioration, or corrosion. Any loose bolts, nuts, or connections must be tightened. All threaded fasteners must be equipped with locking hardware. It is the owner's responsibility to comply with the manufacturer's maintenance instructions to maintain the quality and serviceability of the unit.

Units that are damaged or weakened are not to be used until repairs are completed. Units that are damaged subsequent to their receipt and/or are worn beyond repair must be removed from service and destroyed.

General Operational Notes:

- General maintenance of a mobile ladder stand or platform includes cleaning, lubrication, painting, and the replacement of on-product labels and markings as well as wheels, casters, and rubber pads.
- Climbing a damaged ladder stand or ladder stand platform is not permitted.
- Ladder stands and ladder stand platforms must never be moved while they are occupied.
- Units must not be loaded beyond their rated load capacity.
- Materials and/or equipment must not be stored on the steps or platform of a unit.
- Additional height must not be gained by the addition of any type of extension or object placed upon the unit.

- Users must remove foreign materials, such as mud or grease, from their shoes prior to climbing or mounting.
- Handrails, when provided, should be used while ascending or descending. The user must face the steps while ascending or descending except when the slope of the steps is 50 degrees or less above the horizontal.
- When electrical lines are present, proper safety measures to avoid contact with energized conductors, insulated or uninsulated, must be taken to avoid electrical shock or electrocution.
- Occupied units must not be placed in front of a door unless the door is secured in an open position, locked, attended, or barricaded.
- Overreaching while on a unit can cause instability and result in a fall. Always place the unit in close proximity to the work. Descend from the unit and relocate it to avoid overreaching.
- Use ladder stands and ladder stand platforms only on level surfaces. They are not to be used on uneven or sloping surfaces.
- Access to or egress from a step or platform from any other elevated surface is prohibited unless the unit has been positively secured against movement.
- Users are not permitted to stand on components of the unit other than the steps or platform.[4]

Personal Safety Recommendation Documents

Personal safety recommendation documents can be written to give the employees the specifics of a particular activity and the safety measures of which they should be aware. These can be written to cover single activities or to cover multihazard work environments. They can also be written to describe the manner in which a particular piece of protective gear or equipment should be used; examples are steel-toed shoes, protective eyewear, and/or respirator masks.

The example presented here is to give an overall graphic description of protective measures when working in a multihazard work environment.

Dismantling Exhibitions:

- Wear steel-toed leather boots. These will protect your feet from injury from falling heavy wooden, glass, or other materials during dismantling.
- Wear canvas gloves, which will protect your hands from injury caused by sharp edges or splintering of wood, glass, metal, or other materials during dismantling.
- Wear protective eyewear, which will protect your eyes from flying debris and dust.
- Wear hearing protectors when working with tools and equipment that produce high decibel levels of noise during use.

- Discuss and plan dismantling of large walls, caseworks, plinths, or other display structures to ensure that you have enough assistance and to understand the choreography with all involved in the dismantling process.
- Maintain a debris-free work environment to eliminate trip hazards, slippery surfaces, or objects falling when working around and through paths.
- Have proper lighting installed to increase your ability to see the space and the work around you. Do not simply use the gallery lights that were used for the previous display.
- Dismantling of electrical components that are installed into the circuitry of the room should be undertaken by trained electricians.
- Dismantle display furniture to reduce the overall weight or secure multiple components which are being saved for future use before moving to an off-site location.
- Reduce rubbish to manageable pieces before moving to the dumpster, which will help prevent injuries caused by glass or wood breaking or falling.
- Use proper moving and handling equipment for all activities to help prevent injuries resulting from object shifting during movement and to minimize or reduce back and muscle strain.
- Other precautionary measures can be added depending upon the work activities.

Supplemental resources are listed at the end of this chapter.

CONCLUSION

Collection care staff deserve and require to be trained in the best practices currently prescribed within the industry. The investment in time, money, and continuing the education process throughout a career will yield returns in that another generation will benefit from the fruits of your knowledge and labor.

Every museum, from the small county historical society run by volunteers to the major metropolitan fine-arts museum with a multimillion dollar endowment, has one thing in common: a collection that needs constant care.

Anyone who works in a museum knows that, despite everyone's best intentions, collections often receive less than ideal treatment. Everyone cares about his or her collection, but not everyone has the specialized knowledge, skills, and training to provide absolutely the best treatment. Some know just a little, such as the importance of acid-free storage material. Some know more, such as how to construct storage mounts. All too many know too little and have not updated their skills in recent years.

Responsibility for updating those skills, for properly caring for a collection, falls on everyone associated with a museum. If collection care is left solely to the curator, the registrar, or even the conservator, the collection is in danger. Collection care must begin at the top, with the director. If the director is committed to caring for the collection, that commitment will permeate every aspect of the institution and every staff member, volunteer, and patron.[5]

Additional References

The best book for health and safety information for you is *Health and Safety for Museum Professionals*. It is the "bible" of reference resources regarding health and safety for any person working in museum collection care departments. It is an excellent resource for all departments within the museum and can be easily adapted for use within the commercial service industry. *Health and Safety for Museum Professionals*. New York, Society for the Preservation of Natural History Collections, 2010.

The American Institute for Conservation of Historic and Artistic Works (AIC) and the Society for the Preservation of Natural History Collections have joined forces on the ultimate reference book for museum professionals: *Health and Safety for Museum Professionals*, edited by Catharine Hawks, Michael McCann, Kathyrn Makos, Lisa Goldberg, David Hinkamp, Dennis Ertel, and Patricia Silence. The nineteen chapters are written by top specialists in their field. This hardcover book is nearly 650 pages with an extended bibliography, an appendix, and highlighted articles per chapter. This comprehensive volume is treated in three parts:

Part 1: Principles of Safety and Health—fire protection, occupational hazards, and waste management.
Part 2: Specific Hazards—particulates, chemical hazards, and toxins; physical, mechanical, and electrical hazards; and radiation.
Part 3: Museum Work—facilities management, emergency salvage, collections management, fieldwork, conservation and restoration, and exhibit protection and maintenance.

Another good reference is a slide presentation, which covers the various basic components of body mechanics, *Risks of Manual Material Handling* 2012 by Dhananjai Borwankar; Canadian Center for Occupational Health and Safety, Website Link: http://www.slideshare.net/CCOHS/mmh-risks

NOTES

1. Carol Bergman, "Making It Work; No Klutzes Need Apply," *New York Times*, August 22, 1999, accessed January 21, 2015, http://www.nytimes.com/1999/08/22/nyregion/making-it-work-no-klutzes-need-apply.html.

2. Michael McCann, *Health and Safety for Museum Professionals* (New York: Society for the Preservation of Natural History Collections, 2010), pp. 23.

3. Ibid., pp. 23.

4. ANSI-ASC A14.7-2006, American National Standard for Mobile Ladder Stands and Mobile Ladder Stand Platforms.

5. Alten, Helen, "It Takes a Staff to Care for a Collection," *Northern States Conservation Center Collection Caretaker* 1, Summer 1997: Accessed August 2014.

BIBLIOGRAPHY

Bergman, Carol. "Making It Work; No Klutzes Need Apply." *New York Times*, August 22, 1999. Accessed January 21, 2015. http://www.nytimes.com/1999/08/22/nyregion/making-it-work-no-klutzes-need-apply.html.

Part II

GUIDELINES AND PRINCIPLES

Chapter 4

Two-Dimensional Objects
Common Procedures and Practices

Behold thy portrait!—day by day,
I've seen its features die;
First the moustachios go away,
Then off the whiskers fly.
That nose I loved to gaze upon,
That bold and manly brow,
Are vanish'd, fled, completely gone—
Alas! Where are they now?

This anonymous poet describes the disappointment of watching an image fade, less than ten years after the invention of photography. But these lines could have been written about photographs from any era—including the digital photography of recent years. Concerns about permanence and stability have always been part of the history of photography. Understanding the environmental and handling stipulations for photographs will slow their deterioration and enhance their stability and longevity.[1]

Introduction
    Risk Evaluation
    Monetary Value of an Object
Common Two-Dimensional Handling Precautions
    Unframed Works on Paper
    Matted Works on Paper
    Framed Works on Paper
    Paintings: Framed or Unframed
Asian Works on Paper
    Hand Scrolls
    Hanging Scrolls (paintings)
    Album Leaves

INTRODUCTION

Risk Evaluation

This chapter and the one that follows will provide the reader a reference for common approaches to the procedures and practices of handling art and artifacts. Every initial discussion before an object is handled, displayed, or stored needs to address the potential risks that may be encountered and the

Figure 4.1   Handling Framed Painting, Two Staff Members. *Source*: Carey, Artex FAS.

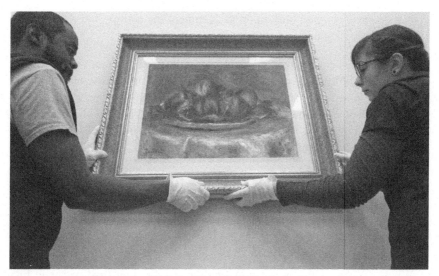

Figure 4.2 Handling Framed Painting, Two Staff Members. *Source*: Carey, Artex FAS.

best solution for that problem. The assessment cannot always be perfect and often is not. Many factors dictate the outcome.

This process of evaluating the best solution to a particular scenario entails outlining a step-by-step plan. Enumerating the details in a chronological order and putting the proper resources—both human and equipment—to the task are crucial to a successful transfer of an object or a collection. The following categories should be addressed.

Who: All individuals involved in the process of executing the activities required need to be informed and accounted for. Understanding the responsibilities and selecting the individuals to implement the move will guarantee the best outcome.

What: Know the type and number of objects to be moved. The inherent properties of the objects will dictate the staffing, materials, equipment, and route best suited for the transit.

When: Drawing up a timeline with defined start and end dates is necessary when coordinating all activities attendant upon the relocation of a collection. It is crucial that a plan be developed with specific steps to be undertaken. Timing and action must work in concert throughout the process.

Where: The space and environment are two factors to be considered when anticipating moving a collection. From the original location to its final destination, an object or an entire collection must pass through a physical space.

How: How this movement is successfully achieved depends on the people and the equipment employed when carrying out the plan. The final outcome can be reviewed and built upon to document the actions and reference for the specific plan or other future moves.

These factors should be considered for collection care activities, whether for a simple object move or for the relocation of an entire collection. The subject matter may change with the size and level of the project to be undertaken, but the evaluation process remains the same. The checklist is a mental process, which can be intuitive, but it should be reviewed, especially in the coordinated decision-making efforts of multidisciplinary staff projects.

- Who: Who will be handling or how many people are needed for the move?
- What: What are the object's inherent properties, and how does this dictate the materials or equipment needed?
- When: When is the best time to undertake this activity, what is the duration of time required, and how does this affect, and is coordinated into, the overall work schedule?
- Where: Where is the object now, and what is its logistical path and final location?
- How: How is the final solution to be implemented and understood by all involved?

This knowledge is obtained through on-the-job training, by asking questions, and by creating the thought process that one must assess before one commits to action. Over years of experience, some of the factors should become second nature and can even be termed common sense. People often state that a quality staff member should possess the qualities based on just "simple common sense." If you have this intuitive sense and apply it to your job, it can be very effective and productive, but that simple sense is only a small part of the overall attributes and knowledge that one must be able to possess, definitely not the only one.

"Thinking outside the box" is another phrase you often hear when discussing assessment of the object and the procedure that will best fit the solution. Take the time to ask yourself another question, or step out of your daily comfort zone to how you typically may arrive at another solution.

The insightful approach one must maintain is focused on the attention one constantly gives to the assessment of one's work. Sometimes this focus is called "being in the zone" or having an "internal radar." In the world of sports, a player is often termed "in the zone" when he/she is focused and is performing to his best level. This same focus, when performing collection care activities in regard to best practices, should be to evaluate your activities, understand the components of your actions, and be aware of the surroundings in which you are undertaking these actions. Your sensibilities must be a combination of many attributes: attention to detail, tactile sensibilities, good communication skills, patience, and tact, to name a few.

Procedures and practices for handling two-dimensional objects must take into consideration the most basic property of such an object: its physical nature of a two-dimensional plane or flat structure in space. The movement of this plane must be supported and dealt with in a linear fashion with no flexing or with minimal deflection of the flat plane surface. Handling a glass sheet is a good example in that support must be maintained so that the flat plane does not flex to the point of cracking, bending, or breaking.

If the plane is not rigid or is more pliable than a sheet of glass, then the movement of the flexible plane can also be a stress factor if the movement goes against the object's normal structure. Such an example would be a sheet of paper falling off from a table top and then catching itself on a lower surface that suddenly shifts the plane in another direction and leads to creasing or tearing.

Monetary Value of an Object

Knowing the monetary value of an object can be a double-edged sword when considering how an object is to be handled. For example, a chair can be mistaken as being replaceable because it is a mass-produced, conventional object used every day. Stating that the chair is irreplaceable will alter the perceived value to the handler, thus giving the matter of how it should be handled a greater importance.

An object of high value or extreme rarity should be made known to the handler to ensure that it is cared for properly. However, the high value of an object and the focused attention surrounding the object can create an air of tension for the handlers, which may decrease their attention to the overall procedure. Therefore, an experienced staff member should be assigned to handle high-value objects in these situations.

The best collection care policy is to create a work environment where the staff are instructed that regardless of their monetary value, all objects must be respected and handled in the best possible manner. Whether an object is valued at $5.00 or $5,000.000.00, it is the responsibility and mission of the staff to focus on the best possible handling procedure.

COMMON TWO-DIMENSIONAL HANDLING PRECAUTIONS

Precautions for handling two-dimensional objects require observation and understanding of the structural elements of these objects. Many of the procedures and techniques for handling two-dimensional objects share a similar approach, whether the objects are framed, unframed, or without any support structure. The following are examples of procedures and techniques for handling two-dimensional objects. Many of these examples may apply to several object types but are listed in this format so that the particular aspects are specifically addressed.

Unframed Works on Paper

Works on paper (flat works as opposed to bound or mounted) are extremely vulnerable when not housed within a framed structure, which gives support and protection to the sheet and surface image. This section will explore the procedures and techniques of works on paper, in both an unmounted state and a supported or mounted state.

All types of paper-based objects are inherently fragile and are easily damaged by improper handling, excessive exposure to light, extreme levels and fluctuations of temperature and humidity, pollutants from airborne transmission, or contact with handling or packing materials. These conditions can potentially affect these works at different levels of exposure and should be constantly monitored to reduce these potential damaging effects.

Paper-based objects often found in collections include the following types: prints in various media, drawings in various media including pastels or other un-fixed media, photographs, documents, and contemporary media.

Other categories of works on paper include a broad range of object types such as Asian paintings, hanging scrolls, hand scrolls, album leaves, maps, and manuscripts. Parchment, vellum, papyrus, and fibrous paper are some of the support material for the ink, charcoal, water color, pastels, or gouache that are the media. This chapter explores only the more common categories. Listed in the bibliography section are numerous links to explore in greater detail the handling of other two-dimensional objects.

Handling Basics:

- Handle works on paper with clean, washed hands for best tactile sensibility. Wash hands often and avoid handling other items or objects, which will transfer dirt and oils.
- Nitrile or latex (antistatic and powder-free) gloves offer the next best protection when handling works on paper. Keep gloves clean and change them frequently. Following removal of gloves, wash hands as they will be subjected to additional perspiration during use.
- Workspace on the table or bench needs to be maintained and clean at all times. Work on an acid-free support board or sheeting material that can be removed and replaced easily when dirty.
- Keep all tools and materials for handling/treatment of the object away from the workspace, but within easy reach. Liquids, if present, need to be housed on a tray to prevent overflow spills spreading over to the object.

- Do not cough or sneeze over the work on paper. Remove rings, watches, bracelets, necklaces, and lanyards or other apparel that may snag the paper during handling.
- Use wooden pencils, not ink pens or felt markers, to make necessary marks or inscriptions. Inscribing objects should be done on a hard surface to avoid pressing into the surface and thus embossing the marking, which would be visible from the other side. Heavy pressure could puncture the paper sheet.
- Eliminate the potential risk of air movement around the workspace. Quick bursts of air, whether from quick gestural movements or the operation of fans and ventilation systems, can lift a loose sheet of paper up and off the workplace surface and into harm's way.
- When not working on a paper sheet, place an acid-free cover over the work to prevent risk of air movement and excessive light exposure. Include a "warning note" that there is an object residing underneath.
- When lifting the paper sheet from the work surface, do not use finger tips or finger nails to lift paper edges, as doing so could lead to scuffing or folding of the edge of the paper.
- Lift the paper sheet from the work surface with a micro spatula or a folded triangle of acid-free paper by gently sliding it under the corner edge of the paper.
- Handle the paper sheet with the image facing you and in your line of sight.
- Small objects: Lift the paper by its opposite corners with a spatula; then grip it between the fingers and lift it up in a coordinated motion to keep the paper from folding or creasing. The paper will be maintained in this curved shape if the hands are kept in a choreographed sequence to each other in distance and during transition of movement. It is advisable to place any large object onto a transport support for ease of handling.
- Large or oddly shaped paper sheets may need to be handled by other pickup points or additional staff to maintain a safe lifting motion. It is advisable to place these uncommon sizes or shapes immediately onto a transport support for ease of handling.
- A paper sheet can be easily handled by placing it on a rigid support such as a Gaterfoam board. An acid-free corrugated board or thick mat board (4 mm +) can be used, but one must be aware of the support flexibility under the weight or size of the object being handled.
- A protective acid-free cover sheet should be placed on top of the work during handling on a support board to reduce the possibility of the air movement lifting the work up and off the board.
- A paper sheet can also be placed in an acid-free folder with an interleaving cover, which will stabilize it for handling and storage.
- Any object with interleaving within a folder should not have the covering shifted on the surface of the work. Lift interleaving material in the same fashion as moving a paper sheet, up and away from the object's surface.

- Interleaving material needs to be clean and flat and should not have any creases, tears, or folds, which can cause pressure or marking, thus damaging the image surface.
- Be cautious when stacking folders while housing objects. Folders can shift easily and should not be shuffled when lifting them apart.

Supportive protective enclosures include acid- and lignin-free folders, mats, and document boxes (all available alkaline buffered or with neutral pH); and polyester film sleeves that are stiff enough to adequately support the paper(s) within. Alkaline buffered storage materials provide a desirable neutralizing effect on acids that are inherent in works on paper, especially as paper ages, but be aware that some media found on paper objects may be sensitive to alkaline pH. Polyester film has the benefit of being clear, but does not contain an alkaline buffer and with little friction readily produces an electrostatic charge that can lift powdery media such as pastel, charcoal, pencil, and flaking paint.[2]

Matted Works on Paper

Handling Basics:

- Handle matted works on paper with clean washed hands for best tactile sensibility. Wash hands often and avoid handling other items or objects, which will transfer dirt and oils.
- Nitrile or latex (antistatic and powder-free) gloves offer the next best protection when handling works on paper. Keep gloves clean and change them frequently. Following removal of gloves, wash hands as they will be subjected to additional sweating during use.
- Matted works should be moved flat, but when handling them vertically, move them with hinged side up. Moving a matted work on its side will put excess stress on the hinges.
- Handle matted works with image facing you and in your line of sight.
- Matted works can be stacked but in stacks of the same size. When supported or stored in an archival box, the matted works should be of the same size, so that the stack will not shift when the box is tilted during handling.
- Eliminate potential risk of air movement around the workspace. Quick bursts of air, whether from quick gestural movement or operation of fans and ventilation systems, can lift up a hinged paper image and damage the paper or the hinges.
- When lifting a hinged-mat window or a hinged image sheet from the mat back support, do not use finger tips or fingernails to lift edges to avoid scuffing the surface.

- Lift matted window or paper image with a micro spatula or a folded triangle of acid-free paper by gently sliding it under the corner edge of the material to be lifted.
- Small objects: Lift the matted work with a spatula, then grip it between the fingers in a coordinated motion to keep the mat from flexing. In contrast to unmatted sheets, the mat will help maintain the flat shape if hands are kept in sequence to each other in distance and transition of movement.
- Large or oddly shaped matted objects may require additional staff to maintain a safe lifting motion. It is advisable to place these uncommon sizes or shapes immediately onto a transport support for ease in handling.
- When not working on a matted object, place an acid-free cover over the work to prevent risk of additional light exposure. Include a "warning note" that there is an object residing underneath.
- A matted object should have an interleaving sheet placed between the mat window and the hinged paper.
- Never remove interleaving material by pulling it out of a closed mat. When the mat is open, lift up the interleaving and off the image so as not to drag it across the surface.
- Interleaving protection within a mat should not shift on the surface of the work. Lift the interleaving material in the same fashion as moving a paper sheet: up and away from the object's surface.
- Interleaving material needs to be clean, flat, and without any creases, tears, or folds, which can cause pressure or marking, thus damaging the image surface.
- Matted work can also be placed in acid-free folders with interleaving, which will stabilize it for handling and storage.
- If a paper sheet comes unhinged from the mat, move it to a flat, safe position and report the damage to a knowledgeable person to repair.

Contemporary works on paper can often challenge all common procedures and techniques when being handled and displayed. Extensive assessment and research need to be undertaken to ensure the safety of the object.

Framed Works on Paper

Handling Basics:

- Works on paper when framed are most commonly protected by a type of clear glazing, glass, or plexiglass. Some contemporary types of glazing offer UV filtering and antistatic and antireflective capabilities.
- Works on paper are commonly supported by a windowed mat or are hinged, both mounted to a support backing before being fitted into the frame.

- The interior of the frame allows adequate spacing between the support mount and the glazing so that the image on the mounted paper does not come into contact at any point with the glazing.
- No pressure should be placed on the frame's glazed surface that would allow the glazing to be scratched, marred, or flexed and to break inward toward the image.
- Before handling, note how well the work on paper is secured within its frame such as with loose strainers, hardware, locking plates, keys, or glazing points.
- Before handling, check the structural components of the frames such as miter joints, decorative elements of ornate frames, and hanging hardware, and make sure that they are secure and stable.
- Always use both hands when handling framed work; do not lift it by the top of the frame, stretcher support, or hanging hardware such as D-rings, eye hooks, or wire.
- Always handle and transport the work in the display orientation so as to not put undue pressure on the mounting hinges of the work.
- Before handling, determine the size and weight of the framed work to ensure that you have enough staff to move the object and proper equipment for transport.
- When picking up a small, framed work, place one hand under it to support the bottom and one hand on the side in the structural position to balance the weight.
- Small-framed works (categorized as having dimensions of, on average, *less* than 36 × 36 inches or 100 x 100cm in height and width) can commonly be handled by one person, depending on the combined weight of object, matting support, and frame weight.
- Do not carry framed works for any distance so as to avoid tripping over obstacles. Use a padded cart.
- Keep the workspace environment clean and free of tools, materials, or equipment on the floor to avoid trip hazards in pathways.
- Before handling a large-framed work (categorized as having dimensions of, on average, *more* than 36 × 36 inches or 100 × 100cm in height and width), determine its size and weight to ensure that you have the appropriate number of staff to handle the object and proper equipment for transport.
- When handling large-framed works, be aware of the support given above the horizontal center so as to minimize the weight of the top half and to prevent cantilevering as the object is moved.
- Many large-framed works on paper can be extremely heavy because of the weight of the glazing and the accompanying structural support; handle them accordingly, with more staff or proper equipment.
- Be aware of the top and bottom edge of a framed work when moving it to ensure that it does not come in contact with ceiling elements (lights and exit signs) or floor elements (door stops, door sills, and elevator jams).

- A spotter (staff member to accompany but not handle) should be assigned to observe possible hazards all along the pathway during transport. The spotter will be the voice to direct the movement as well as alert other staff or public that the move is being undertaken.
- Be sure frame carts are large enough to accommodate the framed work. The vertical supports of the transport structure should have telescoping extensions to increase the capability to support tall frames.
- Two staff members are required to safely move a loaded transport cart, each supporting and directing one end of the cart through the journey.
- Avoid multiple stacking of framed works whenever possible. When stacking, add pads or sheeted barrier support between frames.
- When stacking, do not lean or stack one framed work on another to avoid pressure being placed on the face of the first framed work.
- When stacking multiple paintings, keep the number to a minimum (five or less, depending on size and weight) to reduce the weight and to ensure that the paintings are properly supported. Make sure that the structural frame components are overlapping or supporting the other work's frame.
- Cardboard sheets or foam core sheets with larger dimensions than the framed dimensions should be placed between stacked objects to ensure structural support.
- Stacking of framed objects should be in a sequence of proper "face to face" and then proper "back to back" with the sheeted support over each object.
- Framed works can be placed into a collar or travel frame for extra protection when being stacked or handled.
- Place framed works on pads or blocks when standing them on the floor, leaning toward the wall. Blocks sized at a minimum of 2″ (H) × 4″ × 12″ and made of high-density foam or padded wood will cover most precautionary measures such as support, frame protection, or flooding.
- Ornate frames may need additional support to protect decorative elements, when they are placed on the floor or on a transport cart.
- Works such as drawings with pastels or charcoal images should travel flat, with face up, to minimize material loss of pigment. Consultation with conservation staff is important in assessing the condition.

Paintings: Framed or Unframed

Handling Basics:

- Do not touch the surface directly with the hands or any foreign objects when handling.
- Do not grip an unbacked painting by its stretcher frame as fingers or knuckles may push into the back side of the canvas.

- An unframed canvas requires special attention when the uncovered edge of the painting is being handled. Grip the painting by the exterior edge of the face of the painting without placing pressure directly on the front plane of the paint surface.
- Before handling, determine the size and weight of the painting so as to ensure that you have enough staff to safely lift and handle it, and the proper equipment for transport of the object.
- Always use both hands when handling any painting; do not lift it by the top of the frame, stretcher support, or hanging hardware such as D-rings, eye hooks, or wire.
- Handle paintings keeping the face of the painting in your sight to avoid its coming into contact with other objects, including your body.
- When two people are handling a large painting, they should lift it in a coordinated cross-grip direction (handler on left uses left hand on top, handler on right uses right hand on top). This will ensure that the painting is lifted or tilted while they are moving in unison, without placing tension on one or both of the handlers.
- Handle and transport paintings in display orientation unless a combination of size or handling equipment requires the painting to be laid on one of its proper vertical sides to ensure safe handling along the path.
- Small paintings (categorized as having dimensions of, on average, *less* than 36 × 36 inches or 100 × 100cm in height and width) can be handled by one person, depending on the painting and frame weight.
- When picking up a small painting (framed or unframed), place one hand under it to support the bottom and one hand on the side in the structural position to balance the weight. Carry only one painting at a time.
- Do not carry paintings for any distance so as to avoid tripping over obstacles. Use a padded frame or painting cart.
- Keep the workspace environment clean and free of tools, materials or equipment on the floor to avoid trip hazards in pathways.
- Before handling a large painting (categorized as having dimensions of, on average, *more* than 36 × 36 inches or 100 × 100cm in height and width), determine the size and weight to ensure that you have the appropriate number of staff to handle the object, and proper equipment for transport.
- When handling large paintings, be aware of the support given above the horizontal center to minimize the weight of the top half and to prevent cantilevering as the work is being moved. A common procedure is to handle the work with both hands on the sides of the painting, with one hand gripping the painting above the center.
- Be aware of the top and bottom edges when moving a large painting to ensure that it does not come into contact with ceiling elements (lights and exit signs) or floor elements (door stops, door sills, and elevator jams).

- A spotter (staff member to accompany but not handle) should be assigned to observe possible hazards along the pathway during transport. The spotter will be the voice to direct the movement as well as to alert other staff that the move is being undertaken.
- Be sure painting carts are large enough to accommodate the framed work. The vertical supports of the transport structure should have telescoping extensions to increase the capability to support tall frames.
- Two staff members are required to safely move a loaded painting transport cart, each supporting and directing one end of the cart through the journey.
- Avoid multiple stacking of paintings (framed or unframed) whenever possible.
- When stacking, do not lean or stack one framed work into another, to avoid pressure being placed on the face of the first framed work.
- When stacking multiple paintings, keep the number to a minimum (five or less, depending on the size and weight) to reduce weight and to ensure that the paintings are properly supported.
- When stacking multiple paintings, make sure that the structural elements (stretcher frame or decorative frame) are overlapping so to support the other paintings' frames.
- Cardboard sheets or foam core sheets with larger dimensions than the frame dimensions should be placed between stacked objects to ensure structural support.
- Stacking of framed objects should be in a sequence of proper "face to face" and then proper "back to back," with the sheeted support over each object.
- Unframed paintings should be wrapped or, preferably, placed into a collar or travel frame to protect the painting surface when it is being stored, stacked, or handled.
- Framed paintings give additional support and protection to the actual painting surface and structure. Ornate frames may need the additional protection of decorative or gilded elements when they are being placed on the floor or on a cart.
- Before handling, note how well the painting is secured within its frame by checking the components such as miter joints, decorative elements of ornate frames and loose hanging hardware, making sure that they are secure and stable.
- In the case of large ornate frames that are extremely heavy, it may be advisable to remove the painting from the frame first and handle it separately to avoid any damage to the painting while handling the size and weight of the frame to the prescribed location.
- Place framed works on pads or blocks when standing them on the floor, leaning toward the wall. Blocks sized at a minimum of 2″ (H) × 4″ × 12″ and made of high-density foam or padded wood will cover most precautionary measures such as support, frame protection, or flooding.

- Ornate frames may need additional support to protect decorative elements when placed on the floor or on a transport cart.
- Paintings on wood or panels should have additional support when being handled to avoid flexing of the surface. If the painting is small, then it should be transported face up on a rolling table.

ASIAN WORKS ON PAPER

Asian works on paper and silk are different from traditional Western works on paper. The procedures and techniques in regard to handling and display should be researched and assessed with trained conservators and collection care specialists who are familiar with the unique differences. The physical properties of Asian works on paper—rice paper, inks, and water color on silk or other textiles—necessitate special handling and storage, because of the inherent fragility of the mediums. These works are vulnerable to pollutants, damaging light exposure, and chemical degradation, which they can encounter in any museum environment.

Careful handling, storage, and display will minimize most physical damage. Maintaining a clean, pest-free, and stable environment within a range of 50–60 percent RH and 60–70°F will help check chemical degradation. Because screens and scrolls are permanently damaged by overexposure to light, a rotation cycle of six months on display at approximately five foot candles followed by five years in storage is maintained at the Freer/Sackler Galleries.[3]

The procedures and techniques listed here are used for object types found in most collections. There have been many changes in how these objects are displayed and stored, but the great majority are still being handled in the traditional fashion and style used over the centuries. Many different preservation systems, from mounting the rolled works flat onto a support board to affixing the images directly to a wall with magnetic strip mounts, have been adopted in the Western world. The delicate nature of these objects continues to challenge collection care specialists to find alternative ways of preserving these works.

A good display mount is a critical factor in protecting delicate art. Artwork often needs to be displayed on gallery walls without a traditional frame, for a number of reasons. Asian paintings were seldom designed for European-style frames, while many costumes are simply too bulky. Displaying such works has traditionally required hidden pins, stitching, or paper hinges, but a new generation of super-strong rare earth magnets offers a new option.

These reusable magnets serve as gentle clamps, pressing the artwork against a padded sheet of steel hidden inside a backing board. The pressure can be adjusted by adding more magnets or padding, and the artwork need not be altered by pins, sewing, or other attachments. These reusable mounts can be quickly installed, saving time and money.[4]

Handling Basics:

Listed in the reference section of the book are links to some excellent videos and sites that will provide further explanation of proven handling techniques for Asian works of art.

- When handling Asian works, use cleanly washed hands for best tactile sensibility. Wash hands frequently and avoid handling other items or objects, which will transfer dirt and oils.
- Nitrile or latex (antistatic and powder-free) gloves offer the next best protection when handling works on paper. Keep gloves clean and change them frequently. Following removal of gloves, wash your hands as they will be subjected to additional perspiration during use.
- Handle only one object at a time, no matter what the size, using both hands. Handle rolled objects by the outer edge of scrolls/paintings to reduce pressure on the center of the roll where the image resides. When untying a scroll/painting, place a hand under the center of the object to support and secure its balance.
- Workspace on a table or bench needs to be clean and maintained as such at all times. Work on an acid-free sheeting material that can be removed and replaced easily when dirty.
- Use only clean padded weights to hold the work in position when unrolling for inspection. Never touch the surface of the artwork unless support is needed, and then use clean padded weights only.
- Keep all tools and material for handling/treatment away from the workspace on which the paper is lying, but within easy reach. Liquids, if present, need to be housed on a tray to prevent overflow spills spreading over to the object.
- Do not cough or sneeze over the work on paper. Remove rings, watches, bracelets, necklaces, and lanyards, or other apparel that may snag, abrade, or stain the paper during handling.
- Use wooden pencils, not ink or felt markers, to make necessary marks or inscriptions. Mechanical pencils are not recommended as the lead will easily break when pressure is applied.

Hand Scrolls

- When unrolling or rolling scrolls, use a flat, clean surface that will allow plenty of length if you need to open a long section for inspection or treatment.

- Scrolls are typically stored in a wooden box, which is part of the history of the object and often contains provenance information. Tilt the box on its side to gently roll the scroll out into your hand and onto the work surface.
- If wrapped, unwrap carefully, fold and replace material back into the box for future use.
- Two pairs of clean padded weights must be positioned at each end of the potential rolling space. Additional clean padded weights need to be available in the immediate vicinity for use if needed.
- Untie cord on scroll, remove cord protective paper if used, and place two weights on the beginning edge (outside edge) of the scroll. Roll out the remaining section to a short distance and place weighted pads on that end next to the roll to keep it from rolling back onto the exposed scroll.
- Wrap the tie cord in tissue or soft cotton fabric so that it covers and supports the tie. The beginning section can then be rolled up gently, and the rolled shape will be maintained for the rest of the unrolling process.
- The process of unrolling will continue by unrolling the main section of the scroll, padding it off with weights, then rolling up the beginning section, and padding it off with weights; the process can be repeated as needed.
- When rerolling, repeat the unrolling process in reverse. The main section of the scroll will need to be rolled straight without telescoping in and out on the edges. If telescoping occurs, stop, unroll, and straighten the roll, then continue rerolling.
- Always use both hands and only apply slight tension on the roll. When rolling is complete, do not stand the scroll on end to correct any unevenness, or roll it tighter through a twisting motion. Any excess tension of twisting the roll will put pressure on, or abrade, the image in the center of the scroll.
- Do not tighten the cord excessively. Replace the protective strip of paper rolled around the scroll and placed under the tying cord.
- Replace the covering material, if previously used, around the scroll and gently roll it back into its storage box, tilt the box upright, and secure the lid.

Hanging Scrolls (Paintings)

- When unrolling hanging scrolls use a flat, clean surface that will allow plenty of length to open the entire roll if needed for inspection or treatment.
- Scrolls are typically stored in a wooden box, which is part of the history of the object and often contains provenance information. Tilt the box on its side to gently roll the scroll out into your hand and onto the work surface.
- If wrapped, unwrap carefully and fold and replace the material back in the box for future use.

- Two pairs of clean padded weights must be positioned at each end of the potential rolling space. Additional clean padded weights need to be available in the immediate vicinity for use if needed.
- Untie scroll cord and remove cord paper protection covering if present. Inspect the hanging cord and top support bar for existing condition. Inspect the knobs on scroll ends to make sure that they are secure. Some Japanese hanging scrolls will have hanging strips (*futai*), which will need to be unfolded and inspected.
- Roll the top section out and place padded weights next to the top support bar. It is recommended to unroll the scroll completely for inspection or treatment.
- After inspection or treatment is complete, reverse the process, roll evenly, and do not allow the roll to telescope in or out. If telescoping occurs, stop, unroll and straighten the scroll, then resume rerolling. Do not stand the scroll on end to correct any unevenness or twist to tighten.
- When installing hanging scrolls, unroll the top section on a flat surface to examine the hanging hardware, and unfold hangings strips (*futai*) if present. Unroll only a small portion of the mount; do not unroll fully exposing the image.
- Cradle the partially unrolled hanging scroll in one hand and with the other hand, grip the center of the hanging cord with slight tension; proceed to the display wall.
- At the wall, another staff member will pick up the hanging cord in the center with his hand or a "hanging stick" (*yahazu*), while the original handler continues to use both hands to cradle the roll. Lift the cord and scroll up to where the cord can be hung and centered on the wall hook.
- With the rolled scroll cradled from beneath with both hands, the scroll is unrolled, moving down the wall until it is fully opened. When fully opened, adjust its level by moving the hanging cord.
- Large, wide, or heavy scrolls should be handled by two people, one on each side of the roll, and in sequence to create a smooth even tension.
- Two hanging hooks can be used on the wall to displace weight on the cord and to stabilize, overall, the level of the open hanging scroll. Some cord attachments on the top bar can allow the cord to be hooked in two level hook locations.
- To de-install follow the handling procedure of installing in reverse, slowly rolling each end of the scroll up, against the wall, with slight tension placed on the cord engaged on the hook.

Album Leaves

- Album leaves are generally stored within their original box or in an archival storage box. As with matted Western works, the archival box should be of a bespoke size so that the album does not shift inside when being handled.

- Open the box and unwrap the contents carefully; fold and replace materials back into the box for future use.
- To view the album, work on a clean, archival-sheeted surface. Make sure that there are support boards for handling loose album leaves and multiple support boards to support hinged pages.
- Inspect the album for damage to the cover, hinge, and edges of interior leaves before opening.
- In all steps, be careful when handling the leaves because the hinged portion can be extremely delicate. If hinges are damaged or there are loose leaves, do not slide the facing sheets against each other. Turn each leaf and stack loose leaves evenly; do not straighten them after they are stacked or closed.
- Open the album by handling the cover with one hand and supporting the hinge with the other.
- Each page should be opened by using a spatula and handled in the same manner as the cover. Large leaves may require both hands on a leaf when lifting, or two people working in unison to ensure a safe lift.
- Place support pads under the hinged cover to level the album as the leaves are turned and opened. Adjust the level of the stack as needed to prevent undue pressure being placed on the hinge.
- If leaves are not attached to the hinge, remove and place them on a support board and create a separate stack as required.
- If the album has interleaving sheets, remove them by lifting them up and off the image. Do not pull interleaving out between leaves or across the surface of the image.
- When closing the album, follow the same process as when opening the album.

Folding Screens

Folding screens should be handled and moved completely closed with two tying strips, one near the upper third and the other near the bottom third of the vertical height. This procedure ensures that the screen is handled as a solid unit, reducing pressure on the long attachment hinges between the screen panels.

- When moving a closed screen in a workplace, keep the screen upright and do not leave it standing on the closed bottom edge unaccompanied or leaned up against the wall.
- When moving a closed screen for a long distance, use a transport cart, by tying it upright to the cart or laying it flat on a rolling table on either side of the exterior panel.
- When handling a closed screen, pick it up with one hand on each side of the folded edge near the center, gripping it with pressure toward each hand.

- Measure your placement of the screen on the surface where it is to be viewed or displayed. Calculate a minimum of ninety degrees to each panel section (front, then back) when opened.
- During opening, have the face of the screen open toward you. Open the screen by holding the top edges or outer edges of the screen only. The initial opening will start at the center with the two halves being opened to ninety degrees.
- During the opening/closing process of the folding, the screens should not touch the hinges in the area of the face of the painting. Handle only the lacquer or wood frame, the back side of hinges, and if required, the surrounding silk borders of the mount at all times. Be extremely cautious when working near the painted face of the screen.
- When opening the first half section, put one hand on the upper-front corner of the frame to support the hinges of the screen. Put the other hand on the upper-back edge of the screen holding the panels together. Rock the panels slightly forward and slowly swing the outer panels of that half of the screen to the 90-degree position.
- When opening, do not drag the bottom edge across the base or floor. Gently rock the screen back and forth so that the panel that is being opened does not allow pressure to be placed on the bottom edge.
- Open the remaining panels of the first half section of the screen, one at a time, using the same procedure, and opening them to 90 degrees.
- It is recommended that two staff members always work together to open a screen, one supporting the screen section that has not been opened, while the other staff member opens the other half of the screen panels to 90 degrees. The person assisting must not exert any pressure downward while holding the unopened half, but work in unison with the member who is gently rocking the screen back and forth while opening the other half of the panels.
- Attention to these details is extremely important. The coordination of the opening of the screen is crucial to maintain the overall stability before it is fully opened. If movement is not done in a fluid, coordinated motion, it can put stress on the delicate hinges, which will easily tear, breaking their support.
- Adjusting the screen to the desired display position should be continued using the same process of coordinated effort while making the final placement.
- To close a screen properly, the process is reversed.

Thangkas

The Himalayan thangka is another form of Asian painting whose handling procedures are very similar to those of a hanging scroll. The main difference is that the embroidered mounts may be quite ornate, and there is often a traditional silk curtain that hangs down and over the object when it is not being displayed or viewed. The decorative element traditionally provided a teaching cover that would be unveiled or opened when the lesson was being taught. It also offered protection from light, candle soot, incense smoke, and other pollutants while the thangka was closed.

Often these works are mounted or displayed with the curtain arranged in its proper fashion, above the image in a traditional decorative tying practice. Many Western mountings have taken the thangka from its traditional rolled storage and mounted it open on a support board or installed open within a shadow box with the curtain tied into a more permanent display configuration. The mounting, embroidery, curtained silks, and the actual painting surface itself are extremely delicate in whatever type of handling scenario that may be encountered.

PHOTOGRAPHIC WORKS ON PAPER

Photographic works on paper are objects of an extraordinarily diverse combination of materials and technical methods. It is of great importance that one must first know the materials and processes of the photograph. To understand how to properly care for a photographic object or collection, one must research or contact a specialist.

Photographs are images formed by the action of radiation, usually light, upon a sensitive surface. While often thought of as a single technique, photography is many hundreds of related chemical processes known by a wide variety of processes and trade names.[5]

Photographic techniques are relatively new to the realm of collection care procedures. Photography encompasses not just paper materials but also includes the related categories of negatives, transparencies, film, and, more recently, digitized processes such as inkjet printing.

Photographic materials are especially subject to environmental conditions, more so than other works on paper. Chemical reactions between medium and support are more volatile and are subject to more rapid change than traditional paper-based works. Pest infestation and mold growth can become active in photographic material when humidity and temperature fluctuate or remain at high levels for a period of time.

Handling Basics:

• Handling procedures can mirror the same techniques as with traditional works on paper: clean work surfaces, handling on support boards, matted and/or framed to reduce damage from handling.

- Use wooden pencils, not ink pens or felt markers, to make necessary marks or inscriptions. Inscribing objects should be done on a hard surface to avoid pressing into the surface and thus embossing the marking that would be visible from the other side. Heavy pressure could puncture the paper sheet.
- Exhibition handling and display techniques follow a process similar to that for matted, framed, and glazed works. Some exceptions are contemporary works that are displayed without any protective support or glazing but by being pinned or affixed to the wall by magnets.

Handling and storage materials are crucial when caring for and protecting photographic objects. The following points provide a good explanation of the materials used in the storage practices for photographs:

- Proper storage provides physical support and protection for fragile objects, acting as a barrier between a photograph and the potentially unstable environment.
- Appropriate storage materials prevent environmental issues and other factors of deterioration from affecting collection materials.
- Storage enclosures must be nonreactive to photographic chemicals, meaning that all materials must be stable and approved for archival use.
- In the past, a great deal of damage was done through the use of reactive storage materials: acidic paper sleeves made of ground wood pulp, dry rubber bands, rusting paper clips, pressure-sensitive tapes, and staining adhesives such as rubber cement or animal glue which cause damage that is irreversible.
- Prints and negatives are especially sensitive to the stains and surface damage caused by these inappropriate materials.

Storage Enclosures

When purchasing enclosures, there are two standards to follow, which guarantee the stability of the material. The International Organization for Standardization (ISO) specifies the physical and chemical requirements for enclosure formats, papers, plastics, adhesives, and printing inks, as detailed in ISO 18902:2013. Consumers should contact their suppliers to check if their products meet these requirements.

The Photograph Activity Test (PAT) involves a test to detect harmful chemicals in an enclosure and another to detect staining reactions between enclosures and the gelatin layer of a photograph. Check for the PAT logo, which is established in ISO 18916:2007. See http://www.iso.org/iso/home. htm for more details on these and other international standards.[6]

Either paper or plastic enclosures may be used to house photographic materials. There are many types of both available from archival supply vendors, but keep in mind their different characteristics.

- Paper enclosures are opaque, which protects the item from light exposure but may increase handling because the item must be removed to be seen.
- Archival paper is porous and stable, which protects the items from changes in environmental levels, and prevents any accumulation of moisture or gases.
- Choosing between buffered and unbuffered paper is less important than previously thought; both types of paper can pass the Photographic Activity Test (PAT) and selection depends on your usage.
- Avoid Kraft paper or glassine paper, which has high acidic levels.
- Plastic enclosures should be made of uncoated polyester, polypropylene, or polyethylene. Other plastics may have components or coatings that off-gas and weaken as they deteriorate, damaging photographs and other archival materials.
- Always avoid polyvinylchloride (PVC), as it is very unstable.
- Plastic should not be used to store nitrate film, or older safety film, negatives.[7]

OTHER WORKS ON PAPER

There are many other types of paper-based objects which are commonly found in collections. Generally, most of these objects can be handled using similar procedures and techniques described in this chapter. If you have works on paper that pose additional questions as to how they should be properly handled or be cared for, you must do extra research before risking potential damage to the object. Contact a paper conservator and supply him or her with the work or an image and description of the present condition of the object and state the concerns you have in your collection environment. The following are a few examples of object types that one may encounter and the basics that are common to handling requirements:

Documents

- These objects come in many sizes, shapes, and materials. Often, they are made of very acidic materials and should be handled and stored by placing them into separate archival sleeves or containers to protect the acidity migrating to another object.
- Handle such objects and store them in archival materials that best support their structure and condition. Common solutions are to use a closed envelope, or to keep the objects flat in a box or on a support board when being handled.

- If they are folded, it may be advisable to unfold, handle, and store the paper in a new relaxed, flattened state. To properly flatten the paper, one should seek advice from a conservator.
- If a piece is too large to store flat, consider rolling it onto a large-diameter acid-free tube. Cover the tube with archival paper or cloth, and tie with cotton tape to secure. Handle tube by each end, and support it in the center where the image is located.

Manuscripts and Parchment

- These are often works that were made to reflect a special event and often will contain a painted or water color image. This image may be a composite of multiple materials.
- These objects should be handled and stored flat in shallow drawers or acid-free boxes. If stacked within these housings, add interleaving sheets to prevent them from rubbing the image surface.
- Use archival materials and store in the method that best supports their structure and condition. This may require their being mounted and placed into frames for best protection.

If a piece is too large to store flat, consider rolling it onto a large-diameter acid-free tube. Cover the tube with archival paper or cloth, and tie with cotton tape to secure. Handle tube by each end, and support it in the center where the image is located.

Maps

- Maps should be handled and stored flat in shallow drawers or acid-free boxes. If stacked within these housings, add interleaving sheets to prevent them from rubbing the image surface.
- Image surface can be made of many different types of mediums, which need to be protected so they remain bound to the paper in a secure manner.
- If folded, it may be advisable to unfold the paper, and handle and store it in a new relaxed, flattened state. Repeated unfolding will eventually damage or tear the paper fibers.
- If rolled, it may be advisable to unroll, handle, and store the paper in a new relaxed flattened state. Rolling causes increased surface damage to the pigments on the surface as the paper flexes when being rolled and unrolled.

If a piece is too large to store flat, consider rolling it onto a large-diameter acid-free tube. Cover the tube with archival paper or cloth, and tie with cotton tape to secure. Handle the tube by each end, and support it in the center where the image is located.

Semipaper Objects

Ancient paper objects are scrolls or scripts made of plant-based materials, such as papyrus, silks, and tapa, which are called semipapers. These materials were constructed by methods related to their fibrous properties. Unlike cotton or wood-based fibers, which are pulped and made into a slurry, these objects were made from materials that were present in the regional fauna of the environment where they thrived. To understand how to care and protect these materials, a specialist conservator should be contacted.

Books

Books are a set of bound paper sheets. Because of the variety of sizes, shapes, and binding material and methods, as well as the age of materials and the methods used at the time, details of the best practices for this material have been amply covered in other publications about library and archive collections. However, I would be remiss not to mention this type of collection. Because special collections are often under the purview of collection care staff, the following is a basic description of the common rules for handling. In the reference section of this book, there is a list of excellent resources for further research.

Handling Basics:

- Handle and store books by placing them in custom-made boxes so that when housed, they do not shift. This will reduce the pressure on and potential damage to the cover and bound pages.
- Wrapping the books will also help protect the surface of the cover and the pages within.
- Basic handling rules are to secure the book to remain closed, lay it flat to transport, and not to stack.
- To display, lay flat or upright between supports; do not lean a book as it will transfer stress to the bound hinge.
- When storing unwrapped or in boxes, smaller books should be stored upright between supports; do not allow them to lean as this will transfer stress to the bound hinge.
- When handling or storing large books, lay flat so the book can support its structure. Make sure that the transport surface or shelf surface is large enough to support the overall book surface.
- When storing, allow air circulation around the exposed book so that it does not come into contact with the wall or a surface that may transfer excess temperature or humidity.

- Books can be stacked on their sides but only in a manner that evenly displaces the weight. Stack a few books only temporarily as the stack may shift.
- Do not leave acidic markers or other items in books. If related to the book, remove them and store in a separate enclosure.
- If books have mounted paper examples such as prints, maps, or illustrations, add an interleaving sheet to prevent the page, when turned, from shifting on its mount.

CONCLUSION

Understanding the risks associated with handling two-dimensional objects is essential primarily because of the fragile nature of the materials structured in the single, flat, dimensional plane of each object's existence. Even a large piece of flat steel plating is vulnerable to flexing, bending, and breaking under the same forces of nature, leading eventually to its demise. Two-dimensional objects come in many different types of materials, shapes, and sizes and each should be assessed for specific risks for proper collection care. Though many policies and procedures may be different for specific objects, the basic facts related to collection care make the assessment of risk a more manageable undertaking than for three-dimensional object scenarios. Though less problematic on many accounts, questions as to the level of risk should be addressed with a conservator or collection care specialist in the objects' material collection base.

FOCUS ON: THE U.S. NATIONAL PARK SERVICE MUSEUM HANDBOOKS: THE EVOLUTION OF A MUSEUM MANUAL

by Dr. Abby Sue Fisher

The National Park Service (NPS) *Museum Handbook*, which is available online, is one of the most comprehensive resources for the preservation and protection of museum collections in the United States. It has been seventy-three years in the making, has three parts with thirty-eight appendices, and it continues to grow and be revised.[8]

The primary readership of this handbook comprises stewards of federal museum collections; however, much of the handbook is applicable for use in any museum collection repository, large or small. It is written to be applicable to a diverse range of professional disciplines including history, ethnography, art, archives, archeology, geology, biology, and paleontology.

Today there are 405 NPS sites, 273 permanent and temporary employees in museum positions, and an additional 402 nonmuseum professionals working with museum collections. Currently, over 380 parks have museum collections. The *Museum Handbook* is intended to provide guidance to all these professionals.[9]

Museum work in the NPS had been going on for years before anyone was given the official title of "curator." Curatorship was the province of superintendents, naturalists, rangers, archeologists, and even maintenance workers. Park museums did not grow from one source, or any central authority. In fact, they got their start even before the creation of the NPS in 1916.

The first museums were developed independently at Yosemite and Yellowstone National Parks early in the twentieth century. Park staff had two primary goals that remain fundamental to the NPS today: to preserve and protect park resources and to serve park visitors. Visitors were eager to learn about their new national parks, and rangers responded in part by identifying, collecting, labeling, and exhibiting collections.

Collections began to grow exponentially without formal guidelines or professional training. This set a precedent and influenced museum development in other parks for many years. Early exhibits were typically overcrowded with collections that were on display primarily to be seen by visitors. Little attention was given to long-term preservation and protection. Without a museum manual or the benefit of formal training, early NPS museums followed the Code of Ethics and standards initiated by the American Association of Museums (AAM), which was created in 1906.

In 1921, Chauncey Hamlin became vice president (and later president) of AAM. He established and chaired the AAM Committee on Museums in National Parks. The committee focused on establishing small natural history museums in a number of the larger parks. Through their efforts, the AAM obtained a $70,000 grant in 1924 from the Laura Spelman Rockefeller Memorial to build and equip a permanent museum in Yosemite. This set the stage for other permanent museums to follow.[10]

An official Museum Division was established in Washington in 1935. By 1940, the service developed policies for defining the appropriate scope of park museums, and for the first time established a required system for documenting museum collections. NPS museums continued to grow prior to World War II, with parallel developments in museum policy and procedures moving the NPS toward professional standards. The general maintenance and operation of museums was still left to superintendents who managed the parks, and to the archeologists, historians, and naturalists who interpreted the collections.

Yosemite naturalist Carl Russell knew that superintendents and other nonmuseum professionals badly needed a ready reference to help them carry out

Figure 4.3 NPS Field School. *Source*: Courtesy of the Yosemite National Park Archives, Museum and Library.

Figure 4.4   NPS Yosimite Museum. *Source*: Courtesy of the Yosemite National Park
Archives, Museum and Library.

their part-time but critical museum tasks. He gave this assignment to Ned
J. Burns, former Chief of the Museum Division in Washington. Burns had
a breadth of practical museum knowledge and wrote the *Field Manual for
Museums* in 1941, which was edited by Ralph Lewis.[11]

The *Manual* went out of print during World War II just as many changes
were occurring in the museum world. Object conservation became a field
of specialization, and the NPS was developing new exhibits to serve the
public, all of which increased the need for a comprehensive museum manual
for the parks.[12] With museum operations in full swing, several discoveries
were made starting in 1940 that would change the tide of the NPS Museum
Management Program.

Interior Department investigators discovered that valuable museum collections lacked accountability in several parks. This fact was brought to the
attention of Congress, which promoted a servicewide survey of the status of
park museum records between 1939 and 1940, which revealed that few, if
any, parks had kept these records to a satisfactory standard.[13] Existing records
were often incomplete and backlogs of unrecorded material had accumulated.
As a result, upper management directed the NPS to plan and execute a huge
project that would bring the servicewide museum collection records up to date
by June 1960. This instigated the execution of the first *Museum Records Handbook*, written in 1957, and the recognition that it was time to rewrite the *Field
Manual for Museums*, which was the precursor to the NPS *Museum Handbook*.

With funds supplied by this cataloging project, the regional offices recruited curators to supervise museum programs in the field. For the first time, professionally trained curators were available to assist field personnel in localized regions throughout the nation. A host of NPS curators, exhibit designers, naturalists, administrators, registrars, and other resource professionals, including Ralph Lewis and Newell Joyner, compiled the original NPS *Museum Handbook* between 1959 and 1969.

The format was intended for a three-ring binder so that pages could be replaced for easy updates. Each revision had a cover sheet with directions on which pages to discard and where to insert the new pages. These early typed volumes laid the basic foundation and format for the current NPS *Museum Handbooks*. The *Museum Handbooks* contained information about the day-to-day operations of museums and were meant to provide curatorial standards and serve as a reference for museum workers everywhere, regardless of their professional backgrounds. Original release No. 3, dated February 26, 1969, contains the following sections that were indicative of the priorities at the time:

- Part I Museum Collections (release 1, July 1967)
- Part II Museum Records (November 1959–1966)
- Part III Furnished Historic Structure Museums (1968–1969)
- Part IV Exhibit Maintenance and Replacement (October 1968)

Today the NPS *Museum Handbook* consists of three parts. They maintain the original format of being hole-punched to fit in three-ring binders to readily accommodate updates.

MANEUVERING THROUGH THE NPS *MUSEUM HANDBOOK*

The standard practice of updating relevant sections of the NPS *Museum Handbook* has continued to the present. Updates include chapters on biological infestations, museum collection storage, health and safety updates, and disaster preparedness, legal issues, and other topics. As before, hard copies of these updates were distributed to the field to insert in the handbooks. Starting in 1996, the updates were made available online for NPS staff and the public on the NPS Museum Management Program website.

Part I (Museum Collections) includes an extensive introduction and overview of museum management and strategic planning for collection growth, and chapters on handling, storage, conservation treatment, environment, security, and fire protection, to name a few. The twenty-one appendices for this part have grown to such an extent that they require a separate binder.

Each appendix provides comprehensive information on the curatorial care of specific collection types such as textiles, leather, wood, glass-ceramics-stone, metal and paper, with emphasis on agents of deterioration, preventive conservation, and specific environmental concerns.

Part II (Museum Records) covers all aspects of museum documentation, including accessioning, cataloging, inventory, and loans. The volume is full of official forms, from deed of gift, to incoming and outgoing loan forms, as well as sample templates and flow charts that guide you through the deaccessioning process.

Part III (Museum Collection Use) covers some challenging topics such as legal issues, intellectual property and copyright, publications, and reproductions. Each chapter and appendix has its own selected references and, in most cases, a list of resources.

An interesting aspect of the *Museum Handbook* is that the chapters are written in what is referred to as "Plain Language." Each chapter is set up in a question-answer format, asking simple questions and providing the reader with a response. Plain Language was an initiative under the Clinton administration to use methods of presenting information that are easy to understand. While the question-answer format is simple and certainly easy to understand, it is problematic if you don't know what question to ask, or if your question is not one of those found in the table of contents. Complicating this format was the fact that the hundreds of pages in the three parts were not indexed. The online PDF of the *Museum Handbook* is currently being indexed, and users can do word searches, which greatly improves maneuverability.

NPS *CONSERVE-O-GRAMS TECHNICAL LEAFLET SERIES*

An additional resource available online is the NPS-produced *Conserve-O-Gram* series. These two- to three-page leaflets cover preservation, security, fire, and curatorial safety, agents of deterioration, storage, disaster recovery, and archival and digital collections, as well as material-specific collections. First distributed in 1975, today there are 173 *Conserve-O-Grams* available and they are still being produced. Many *Conserve-O-Grams* are being updated with many new leaflets added by NPS staff and other museum professionals who are invited to make suggestions and contributions. Author guidelines and information are available online.[14]

A RESOURCE FOR OTHER MUSEUM PROFESSIONALS

The NPS *Museum Handbook* and *Conserve-O-Grams* are unique in that their audience supports a servicewide program, or a system of museum management across the National Park Service, which is at the same time being made widely available to other museum professionals in the United States and internationally.

The evolution of the NPS *Museum Handbook* mirrors the changes and complexity the museum profession has experienced over the past sixty-six years. Early on, in the absence of their own guidelines, the NPS took the lead from AAM and borrowed expertise from other museums.

Over time, NPS museum professionals responded to the need and created a bureau-specific *Museum Handbook* that has grown in scope to address a variety of museum disciplines and management issues. The NPS *Museum Handbook* and *Conserve-O-Grams* are widely respected in the field of historic preservation, and are used as textbooks in many museum studies programs, and also to introduce interns and volunteers to the program. The interdisciplinary nature of the materials addressed in the handbooks demonstrates how a collaborative effort is essential for producing such a comprehensive reference.

Dr. Abby Sue Fisher
Chief, Division of Cultural Resources
United States National Park Service at Golden Gate
National Recreation Area
San Francisco, California.

NOTES

1. *Punch*, vol. 12, 1847, p. 143. *Preservation Leaflets; Photographs; 5.3 Care of Photographs*, (Andover, MA: Northeast Document Conservation Center, 2014) .

2. Library of Congress, "Preservation: Care, Handling, and Storage of Works on Paper," *Proper Storage of Works on Paper*, http://www.loc.gov/preservation/care/paper.html, accessed August 2014.

3. *Painting Conservation, The Freer/Sackler Gallery of Art*, (Washington, DC: National Museums of Asian Art at the Smithsonian Institution), http://www.asia.si.edu/, accessed August 2014.

4. *Preservation Conservation: Magnet Mounts*, (San Francisco: Asian Art Museum), http://www.asianart.org/collections/magnet-mounts, accessed August 2014.

5. "The Nature of Photographic Materials, Appendix R; Curatorial Care of Photographic Collections B"; *Museum Handbook Part I*, (Washington, DC: Department of the Interior, National Park Service, 1996) .

6. ISO 18902:2013 Imaging materials-Processed imaging materials-Albums, framing and storage materials: http://www.iso.org/iso/home.htm, accessed August 2014.

7. *Preservation Leaflets; Photographs; 5.3 Care of Photographs*, (Andover, MA: Northeast Document Conservation Center, 2014) .

8. *Museum Handbook*, (Washington, DC: Department of the Interior, National Park Service), http://www.nps.gov/museum/publications/handbook.html.

9. Federal employment data taken from the United States Office of Personnel Management in 2013.

10. Ralph Lewis, *Curatorship in the National Park Service, 1904–1982* (Washington, DC: Department of the Interior, National Park Service, 1993), 31, http://www.nps.gov/parkhistory/online_books/curatorship/index.html.

11. Ned J. Burns, *National Park Service Field Manual for Museums* (Washington, DC: United States Government Printing Office, 1941).

12. Lewis, *Curatorship in the National Park Service*, 335.

13. Ibid., 96.

14. National Park Service Conserve-O-Grams, http://www.nps.gov/museum/publications/conserveogram/cons_toc.html.

Chapter 5

Three-Dimensional Objects
Procedures and Practices

Conservation embodies minimizing change and maximizing longevity.[1]

INTRODUCTION

Risk Evaluation

The preceding chapter and this chapter will provide the reader a reference for common approaches to the procedures and practices of handling art and artifacts. Every initial discussion before an object is handled, displayed, or stored needs to address the potential risks that may be encountered and the best solutions for those problems. The assessment cannot always be perfect and often is not. Many factors dictate the outcome.

In the preceding chapter, we discussed how the process of evaluating the best solution to a particular scenario entails outlining a step-by-step plan. The reference checklist can be made again to the categories of risk assessment: Who, What, When, Where and How. The checklist is a mental process, which can be intuitive, but it should be reviewed, especially in the coordinated decision-making efforts of multidisciplinary staff projects.

This knowledge of the mental checklist is obtained by on-the-job training, asking questions, and creating the thought process that one must assess before one commits to action. As previously discussed, with years of experience some of the factors should become second nature and can even be termed "common sense" or "thinking outside of the box." After years of experience, this intuitive nature is essential, but still risk assessment checklists must be reviewed to ensure that one does not become complacent but stays abreast to cover all aspects of the checklist for the evaluation process.

The insightful approach one must maintain is focused on the attention one constantly gives to the assessment of one's work. Sometimes this focus is called "being in the zone" or having an "internal radar." In the world of sports, a player is often termed "in the zone" when he/she is focused on performing to his best level. This same focus, when performing collection care activities in regard to best practices, should be on evaluating your activities, understanding the components of your actions, and being aware of the surroundings in which you are undertaking these actions. Your sensibilities must be a combination of many attributes: attention to detail, tactile sensibilities, good communication skills, patience, and tact, to name a few.

Monetary Value of an Object

Knowing the monetary value of an object can be a double-edged sword when considering how an object is to be handled. For example, a chair can be mistaken as being replaceable because it is a mass-produced, conventional object used every day. Stating that the chair is irreplaceable will alter the perceived

Figure 5.1 Furniture Handling. *Source*: 2015 Museum of Fine Arts, Boston.

value to the handler, thus giving the matter of how it should be handled a greater importance.

An object of high value or extreme rarity should be made known to the handler to ensure that it is cared for properly. However, the high value of

Figure 5.2   Sculpture Movement. *Source*: Author.

an object and the focused attention surrounding the object can create an air of tension for the handlers, which may decrease their attention to the overall procedure. Therefore, an experienced staff member should be assigned to handle high-value objects in these situations.

The best collection care policy is to create a work environment where staff are instructed that regardless of their monetary value, all objects must be respected and handled in the best possible manner. Whether an object is valued at $5.00 or at $5,000.000.00 dollars, it is the responsibility and mission of the staff to focus on the best possible handling procedure.

COMMON HANDLING PRECAUTIONS FOR THREE-DIMENSIONAL OBJECTS

Three-dimensional space is a geometric three-parameter model of the physical universe (without considering time) in which all known matter exists. These three dimensions can be labeled by a combination of three, chosen from the terms length, width, height, depth, and breadth. Any three directions can be chosen, provided that they do not all lie in the same plane.

Figure 5.3   Custom Mount. *Source*: Author.

Common procedures and practices for handling three-dimensional objects requires an understanding of some basic concepts. Compared to two-dimensional objects, moving objects that contain a third dimension offer a multitude of different approaches.

In two-dimensional space, you are dealing with a planar projection of space that is measured by height and length. Three-dimensional space embodies the two dimensions of length and width plus the depth of physical space. The additional criterion challenges the process of evaluating the movement of the object.

Understanding the Physical Space of an Object/Training Exercise

The following is a basic training exercise that I use when talking about the physical difference between two- and three-dimensional space and how it relates to handling objects. It is simple and may seem so in its explanation, but the point of the exercise is to bridge the balance of your visual understanding with the physical space of an object by interpreting your body as an actual object to be moved. The goal is to have the student understand the physical space that an object occupies in space and what an object will encounter from its physical space outward.

Many call this concept "building from the object outward." To visually express dimension, have a person stand vertically erect with both arms and hands out to each side of his erect body, horizontally level in space. The body represents a flat plane from fingertip to fingertip to create the first plane (width). From the top of the head to the base of the foot is the second plane (length).

To visually express the additional third dimension, the person must maintain the original position while moving one arm and hand directly out in front of the body, horizontally at a 90-degree angle to the original flat plane (two-dimensional) position. The arm and hand create the third dimension (depth). As the figure now moves in this formation, a three-dimensional space is created. The options of moving this figure with the additional dimension of depth increase the limitations compared to the two-dimensional space.

As one moves a single flat plane through space, it can be taken in, around, and through space by tilting and turning. With a three-dimensional object, the extra dimensional element creates additional complications to the movement.

A practical tool to explain the physical nature of the previous exercise is to have students handle mockups of both two- and three-dimensional objects. The first mockup involves two people moving a sheet of foam core board (1.5m × 1.5m) up or down a staircase. At the stair landing, if the turn cannot be made with the board being kept vertically upright at that point, the flat plane may be tilted and turned to allow the turn on the stairwell landing. This exercise shows how the two-dimensional plane has several options as its only limitations are length and width.

Now conduct this movement with the addition of a third dimension. Construct a box to the same dimensions with the additional dimension of depth.

The mockup now embodies three dimensions (1.5m × 1.5m × 1m to 1.5m). Handling this box on the stairway and landing will emphasize the restrictions that one will encounter and the limitations that are created by adding the third dimension of depth to the exercise.

This exercise presents the logistical perspective of the physical space an object may encounter. Assessing the limitations in the movement of objects is the primary factor in practicing proper handling techniques. When conducting these exercises, examples of actual objects should be discussed in comparison to collection objects that these students may handle in their work experience. The size of the mockup may vary depending upon the size of the stairwell to be used for the exercise. To reduce the weight of the board, foam core (15mm) is recommended as it is rigid enough to maintain the shape, yet light enough to make it easy to handle to demonstrate the transitional movement. Working with additional mockups of varying shapes and sizes that mimic collection objects would be beneficial in planning a move.

Precautions for handling three-dimensional objects require specific observation and understanding the structural elements of these objects. Many of the procedures and techniques for handling three-dimensional objects share a similar approach but are extremely diverse in their material makeup compared to two-dimensional objects. The following are examples of procedures and techniques one should employ when handling three-dimensional objects.

Handling Gloves

The proper glove to be used in handling three-dimensional objects can vary considerably depending on the object's inherent properties and current condition.

- The primary purpose of using gloves is to protect the object from contaminants that could be transferred through the skin of the hand. Hands can transfer the body's oils and salts along with dirt, moisture, and other contaminants that they may have come into contact with. These contaminants often include salts, urea, and other acidic chemicals, which can be harmful to the object's surface.
- The same pair of gloves should never be worn when handling multiple types of materials or noncollection objects in your work environment. It is extremely easy in the work environment to leave your gloves on as you handle other materials such as packing crates, installation hardware, tools, and equipment related to handling the object.
- The practice of removing or replacing your gloves between the steps of any handling process is important. Once the gloves are dirty, you may do more

harm than good in preventive protection. Replacing gloves is inexpensive in comparison to conservation treatment.

- Nitrile and latex gloves need to be thrown away after being used, because when you wear them in the reverse, the previous interior of the gloves will have residue from the oils of your hand, retained from the previous use.
- There is a large range of gloves that is available in the market today. Gloves should be immediately accessible and in sizes suited to the staff.

The choice of gloves depends on the type of object, the tactile sensitivity when handling an object, and personal preference.

Type of object: The object's material makeup and surface can be extremely reactive to certain contaminants. Examples of such materials include metal objects, which are easily susceptible to oils and dirt that create chemical reactions between the combined materials. Organic materials are highly absorbent to oils and dirt and can easily retain the contaminants that are transferred to them. Glass objects are more resistant to oil and dirt, but their surface is extremely smooth and can be stained over a period of time.

Tactile sensitivity: Being able to feel the object's surface, weight, and shape is essential when securely handling objects. Feeling the tactile components of the surface can dictate the type of gloves to be used in that it does not abrade or mar the surface. There are many glove types that offer additional gripping capabilities with a rubber surface of dots or ridges. Although these gloves give additional support to the contacted surface, the grip design can be directly transferred to the surface, even when the gloves are used in a new, clean state. In some instances, especially in the case of extremely delicate objects, it is recommended to handle an object with clean, dry hands to ensure that complete tactile sensitivity is achieved.

Personal preference: One must consider the object to be handled and the choice of gloves first and foremost. Your personal preference is subject to how you feel that you can best handle the object, how the glove reacts to your skin, and what is readily available. Some individuals are sensitive to nitrile and latex and can have allergic reactions or excessive excretion of moisture through sweat. Objects that have been subjected to hazardous materials or contain such materials will require the use of gloves, which should be chosen foremost for personal protection over object protection. In some instances, personal preference may be handling the object with clean, dry hands and washing them often during handling.

The types of gloves we use in collection care for handling different objects can be compared with those used in the medical and scientific industry. Many gloves and materials have been developed to be tactile-sensitive, acid-free, and antistatic, and with no production residue such as powders, binders, or coloring agents, which can be easily transferable. The U.S. National Park

Service offers a good explanation of the types of gloves, their advantages and disadvantages, and the object types to be handled. Other listings will be provided in the reference section of this book.

The most popular, diverse, and commonly recommended gloves used today are the nitrile, powder-free gloves. The qualities that these gloves have offer many advantages: they are disposable, safe for a wide array of objects, do not deposit residue, are chemically stable, do not degrade or discolor quickly, provide an impermeable barrier between object and human skin, give a clear indication of tears and breaks, allow a firm grip on smooth or slippery objects, have a low risk of allergic reaction, are the best choice for a wide spectrum of chemicals because of their good solvent resistance to many chemicals, are good for solvents, oils, greases, hydrocarbons and some acids and bases, and have a good resistance to abrasions.[2]

GENERAL HANDLING GUIDELINES FOR THREE-DIMENSIONAL OBJECTS

When looking at the guidelines for handling three-dimensional objects, first look at the similar procedures and practices that are relevant to most objects. This approach provides a clear analytical assessment that takes into account the diversity that one may encounter in the collection care of three-dimensional objects.

The second set of guidelines will focus on specific objects and their inherent properties. The object material and its physical makeup and design dictate how it should be handled and cared for. The variety of these factors preclude generalized guidelines. Each object's needs should be addressed and analyzed before starting to best define how the object should be handled.

Every movement of a three-dimensional object is unique because of the physical space of height, length, depth, and weight that it embodies.

Handling Guidelines:

- Handling the object as little as possible while ensuring its safety is the goal of any movement.
- Never handle objects in haste. Proper handling techniques are safer for the object than any deadline, no matter the urgency.
- Remove any personal jewelry, watches, rings, belt buckles, ID tags or lanyards, and other items that may fall out from the pockets of shirts or sweaters.
- Never eat or drink in the workspace or when handling objects.
- Use pencils, not ink pens or felt markers, when working around objects.

- Use the proper gloves that are suitable for the object's material type and surface to eliminate damage.
- Prepare and maintain clean work surfaces where the object may be placed during the handling process. If liquid materials are needed for treatment, keep them in a tray that is large enough to contain the liquid if spilled.
- Always maintain a clean workspace, with pathways free of excess tools, cords, or other items, which may create possible trip hazards.
- Determine the best pathway through which the object will be moved by checking the size of doorways, door hardware, floor plates, ductwork, and other potential obstacles that may be encountered. A spotter should be assigned to move through multiple areas to detect any potential obstacles.
- Consider support boards, boxes, or trays for handling the support structure instead of handling the object itself. Handling a simplified structural shape is safer for support and easier to handle in comparison to handling the object itself.
- Consider proper support materials that accompany the object at all times when it is being handled and when it is being placed into a temporary or long-term storage location.
- Never layer objects on top of each other when wrapped or when support materials are used.
- Move one item at a time when directly handling by hand. Multiple objects can be handled on a cart or in a tray only if they are properly separated, supported, and secured for transport.
- Never shift or drag an object on any type of surface; always lift it and place it onto a support board, tray, or equipment surface, no matter how heavy it is. An object can be placed on a support board, and the board can then be slid onto a storage shelf.
- When removing an object from support material or wrappings, double-check to see if all parts of the object are present. Do not dispose of support material without checking for possible remnants of the object.
- Never transfer an object from one person to another without using the support material as the intermediary. Transfer the object by placing it onto a support surface first, and then allow the other individual to pick it up and support it for the exchange.
- Do not carry an object by hand for any distance so as to reduce the potential risk of tripping. Use the proper mechanical equipment based on the size and weight of the object, and make sure that it can be properly supported and secured for transport.
- All handling equipment should be operated by trained personnel. This is important for the most basic of equipment, and without exception for heavy, motorized equipment, which will require that individuals be instructed and licensed by accredited trainers.

- When accessing an object by using a step ladder or stool, remove the object and hand it directly to another individual to receive it. In this instance, the hand-to-hand exchange is less of a risk factor than a single individual handling the object while descending the ladder's steps.
- When storing an object for an indefinite period of time, locate, support, and secure it so that it is not in harm's way. Cover it to protect it from the elements, but always label with a warning sign to indicate its presence. Locate it so that it is easily retrievable when another individual is preparing to move it in the future.
- Discuss, analyze, and secure additional help when moving large, heavy objects. Never handle large objects in haste so as to prevent personal injury and potential damage to the object.

Initial Examination/Prior to Handling

The initial examination is crucial for the planning and choice of the proper procedure and practice that is best for handling the object.

- The material composition of the object needs to be determined to choose the appropriate handling gloves and support material.
- Ascertain if any documentation that has been created from previous handling requirements or notes detailing the inherent nature of the object exist.
- Measure the object. Do not rely on previous notes as to size or weight.
- The weight of small objects can be determined by a simple test of lifting the object off the surface and returning it back to its original location.
- Look inside an object when possible to see if any additional material is placed within that would increase the overall weight or shift the weight of the object when handling.
- The weight of a large object can be determined by putting it on a support platform that can then be placed upon a scale. Weight can also be determined by calculating the object's material type and dimensions.
- Observe the object's overall inherent properties and structural makeup regarding old repairs or structural weakness. Do not test or probe these conditions as it may damage the structural integrity.
- Determine the stability of the surface to ascertain if it is in a friable state, which could cause the surface to be removed, smudged, cracked, or flaked when being handled.
- Examine the object's structure to take into account the handling of any loose parts such as lids, ties, or other separable components. Be prepared to remove loose parts and note their existence by tagging or numbering them in relation to the whole object.

- Examine the object's structure to take account of any appendages or projecting elements. Observe if these areas have had previous damage or repairs. These will include such types as arms, spouts, handles, decorations, or others that may be at risk when handling.
- Many objects may comprise multiple components, which may be made up of different materials and attached in unique ways. These aspects will need to be accounted for in the overall assessment of handling, displaying, or storing the object.

General Guidelines during Handling

- Remove any loose components from objects to ensure that they do not fall off during the handling movement. Keep components with the main object and track them so as to prevent their being separated from the main body.
- Objects that have a hinged component should be padded with tissue to reduce abrasion and tied to the main body to ensure the component does not open during the handling movement. The amount of tissue used should be kept to a minimum so as to relieve pressure on the hinge by torqueing and bending of the hinge structure.
- When lifting an object all by yourself, lift the object with both hands, one underneath the object and one on the side or in a location to gain the best support, while not putting pressure on sensitive areas such as handles, spouts, or decorations. Do not use your body as a support structure.
- Discuss and choreograph handling movements that involve two or more individuals before the movement starts. One individual should be designated as the lead to supervise and direct the object move. An additional person should be designated as a spotter for multiple-staffed or complicated moves.
- Do not grip an object by the lip or upper structural portions for lifting or to stabilize a movement. This is an extremely vulnerable point on any object because of the pressure that is applied to support the accompanying weight of the object.
- Use a support board, tray, or box to move an object whenever possible. The board, tray, or box gives the handler a more simplified structure to support and handle, and it eliminates the direct handling of the actual object.
- Do not overload a tray to avoid creating an imbalance of weight because of object placement or because of the combined weight of all the objects on a tray. Be conscious that individuals of varying strength will encounter this weight during the next handling.
- Bring the transport equipment close to the work area where the object is located. Place equipment so that the movement is unencumbered when transferring the object onto the transport equipment.

- All transport equipment should be clean and free of tools or other work-related paraphernalia, which may come into contact with the object during the movement.
- An object should be secured to the equipment with padded support materials. Putting multiple objects on transport equipment must be kept to a minimum. Separate objects by padded supports or dividers so that objects do not shift during movement.
- Before transporting, secure the object in its most stable position on the equipment. Depending on the size and shape of the object, this position should reflect its standard display configuration.
- Be conscious as to how you secure and support an object during the movement to the location where it will temporarily reside, so that another individual will easily be able to determine how to lift and handle the object for the next segment of the movement. This is especially important when moving large or heavy objects, which may require instructions or rigging straps for proper lifting and handling.
- Objects should be moved without display mounts unless it is determined that their removal poses additional handling risks to the object and that the mount presents no risk when the object is secured on the transport equipment or when placed in storage.
- Objects attached to display bases should, in most instances, be removed before handling and transport. The contact point of the object to the base is a vulnerable area subject to stress if the weight of the object is not properly supported or allowed to flex during handling.
- Use a minimum of two people when moving an object on transport equipment. One individual should be in control of maneuvering the equipment and the other can assist with maneuvering when needed, open and secure doors, operate elevators, and act as a spotter to observe potential obstacles.
- Large-object movement will require extensive discussion to choreograph handling that involves two or more individuals before a movement starts. One individual should be designated as the lead to supervise the team and direct the move. For multiple-staff and complicated moves, an additional individual should be assigned as a spotter to observe potential obstacles.
- Unleveled or multiple-level transfer points encountered on floor surfaces should have flat transfer boards laid to cover and create a smoother transition of the equipment being moved over the conditioned area. An example would be the transitions from the hallway floor over to the recessed elevator door and interior carriage deck. The transfer boards will level and reduce the potential shock transmitted to wheeled equipment as they transfer from hallway to interior of elevator.

- On arriving at the final location, secure the transport equipment in a safe place where it will not be easily moved by others working in the immediate area.
- Do not leave the object on the transport equipment for an extended period of time. Install or move the object to its final location as soon as you can after movement, unless this is the safest solution for storage till a final location is determined.

GUIDELINES FOR HANDLING/OBJECT MATERIAL TYPES

Ceramics

Ceramics are one of the most common objects of cultural heritage that have survived for millennia and can be dated to prehistoric times. They were made to serve as both functional, utilitarian objects and highly decorative objects, and represent and record many aspects of historical activities.

Ceramic objects are made of various types of clay or combinations of clays, and when combined with water can be shaped to a malleable consistency. Once shaped and dried, the objects are placed into an open fire (pit) or closed fire containment (kiln), and heated to a degree where the molecular structure of the clay becomes vitreous.

Assessing ceramic objects before they are moved is extremely important. This list of observations includes variants in material makeup, structural strengths of particular appendages and surface decorations, and condition of previous treatment or repairs.

Ceramic objects that are fired at a low temperature (earthenware up to 1150°C) are not structurally very hard and can be very porous in the final processed state. These objects, due to their softer structural makeup, are vulnerable to breakage by significant impact and often have been broken or repaired.

Low-fired ceramic objects can be glazed but are commonly unglazed and decorated with a clay-based slip material, which, when fired, becomes a part of the object's surface. Surface decorations can be friable and easily damaged by improper handling or material brushing against the surface. Surfaces are very susceptible to being stained by moisture because of the porous surface makeup.

Ceramics that are fired at a high temperature (stoneware and porcelain: around 1200–1300°C) are much harder and less porous in the final state. Though having a harder structural makeup than the low-fired earthenware, these objects are vulnerable to chipping or breakage by minimum levels of impact with a harder substance and often have been broken or repaired.

High-fired ceramic objects can be designed and glazed with multiple types of surface decoration and glazing processes. This means that the objects' surface should be thoroughly inspected before handling. The strength of high-fired clays allows delicate decorations to be designed, glazed, and attached to the surface of an object, making it susceptible to breakage with minimal impact. Often, these decorative components have been broken or repaired. Glazed surfaces create a coating, which allows liquids to be stored.

Although handles have been designed for the use of picking up, holding, or carrying the object, do not lift the object by appendages such as handles or spouts, no matter how it was meant to be used prior to its becoming a collection object. Handle objects singly using both hands for short distances only. Lift and carry with support underneath the object and support on the side, but not in an area of decoration or surface stability. Do not lift or support by the lip of an open vessel.

Do not stack during transport or storage to avoid surfaces coming in contact with each other, which may cause an increase in weight or affect the surface decoration or associated appendages.

Multiple handling can be done with the use of a divided and padded tray to prevent potential impact with the other objects. Weight in similar sized ceramics can easily vary. Do not overload a tray to avoid creating an imbalance of weight by object placement or by the overall combined weight of all the objects on a tray. Be conscious that individuals of varying strength will encounter this weight during handling.

Glass

The earliest man-made glass objects, mainly nontransparent glass beads, are thought to date back to around 3500 BCE, and have been found in Egypt and Eastern Mesopotamia. In the third millennium, in central Mesopotamia, the basic raw materials of glass were used principally to produce glazes on pots and vases. Glass objects, like ceramic objects, were made to serve as functional, utilitarian objects and as highly decorative objects, representing and recording many aspects of historical activities.

Glass has various uses as a full construction material or as a surface adaptation such as a glaze or enamel. The basic process of making glass is combining silica, calcium, and alkali and heating these elements to the molten state. The temperature provides the designated level of heat to transform them into a molecular structure for the type of glass and construction process desired. Glass in its finished state can be either transparent or fully opaque with the addition of colorants of metallic oxides to the original composition or during the molten stage of heating process.

Glass is extremely fragile in its structural makeup, so potential risks should be assessed carefully before handling. Glass is very stable in regard to environmental changes, and it reacts to fluctuations of temperature and humidity. Glass with a manufactured edge or when broken can be very sharp. How it is handled and the type of gloves to be worn will need to be considered to prevent bodily injury or the object's edges snagging, chipping, or cracking as pressure is encountered.

Glass objects are extremely diverse in their design of decorative or utilitarian function. Glass components are often a composite material included in structural and decorative makeup within other objects such as jewelry, furniture, windows, and sculptural and electronic objects.

For general handling precautions, one should follow the same assessment and procedures listed under ceramics. If there is a question regarding a certain object to be handled, consult a conservator to understand the proper procedure that is best for that object.

Two types of glass objects that have unique properties and need additional assessment for proper handling procedures are mirrors and stained glass. For specific information regarding proper handling of such objects, one must contact a trained specialist.

Mirrors

Framed mirrors should be handled in a similar manner as framed, two-dimensional works. The size, weight, and structural support of the mirror glass may require additional handlers, and during transport, it must be tied to the cart to secure it.

Unframed mirrors should travel on the longest edge to create the best structural support. If the mirror needs to be handled flat, it first needs a support board made and attached in its vertical state so that as it is being handled, the flat plane of glass will be supported to take the change.

If a mirror does not have a protective covering on the back side of the glass, precautions need to be taken to protect this delicate surface from being scratched and to avoid damaging the reflecting properties.

Mirrors mounted as a part of a furniture design should be removed and handled as a separate component to reduce the risk of damage. If the mirrored elements are small, they can remain if they are judged to be well attached. Consideration should be given to how these areas are supported and padded to protect them from being affected by other objects or materials during handling.

Stained-Glass Windows

Stained glass has many different attributes in its composite construction and must be handled in a very specific manner. A detailed assessment must be undertaken by a specially trained person who will also guide all handlers in handling the glass in its constructed state and in removing or handling panels during dismantling.

Panels within the window frame are composed of multiple pieces of glass sheets commonly secured to each other by lead or other metals such as zinc or copper. These combined pieces of glass are then attached to framing supports commonly constructed of wood or metal. This construction creates a potentially flexible surface that, depending on age and strength of the support, can disengage and fall apart. Extra support of this structure is essential during handling.

During handling or transport, the window should be oriented in an upright position and supported by a sandwich pack (two padded panels secured on each side of the window) or a full-crate to support the frame and internal glass during movement. Only if the window is properly supported can it be laid flat for transport if required.

Materials for support and padding should be used in such a way that they will not snag or abrade surfaces, absorb moisture, or off-gas to other materials with which they come in contact.

Due to the combined size and weight of the transport support, glass, and frame structure, additional handlers and equipment will need to be accounted for to securely move the window.

Metals

Objects made of metal ores were historically created for utilitarian purposes and manipulated into useful tools or shapes. The Bronze Age (3500 BCE ±) saw the use of such ores melted and molded into forms or cast into usable shapes. The varieties of objects made are endless and continue to be developed as creative needs are excited by new processes.

Metals—gold, silver, copper alloy, pewter, and iron, to name just a few— are produced from ores that are found in nature and are processed, or smelted, from a stable mineral state to a less stable metallic state. Almost every metal material you will encounter will be an alloy—a mixture of more than one metal. Metals are mixed to achieve certain qualities like color, strength, or corrosion resistance. Metals are also often layered together, as in the case of silver plated on a base metal substrate or tin plated on an iron substrate.

Metal objects are subject to damage by the environment in which they reside. Noble metals like gold and silver corrode less readily than baser metals like iron, tin, and lead. Gold, for example, is inert and does not corrode. Silver can suffer from sulfide-related tarnish and can corrode under very aggressive conditions such as in archaeological contexts. Other metals, such as copper alloys, corrode more readily; base metals such as iron corrode very easily. Because metal is electrically active, galvanic corrosion can occur when two metals are in direct contact with each other. The base metal will contribute electrons to the noble metal creating an electric circuit. This causes preservation of the noble metal and corrosion of the base metal. [3]

Metals are susceptible to mishandling. Guidelines should be written and staff trained in procedures for handling specific metals that are commonly found in collections.

Gloves and handling materials that are clean and nonacidic should be used to eliminate the transfer of oils, salts, acids, dirt, and moisture to the metallic surfaces. Careless handling can also lead to scratching, denting, bending, or breaking of metal artifacts. It is best not to overestimate the strength and resiliency of metal pieces; they are often weaker or more brittle than one anticipates. Extra caution in handling can prevent serious damage that can be expensive to repair.

When handling smaller, metal objects, one should follow the same assessment and general procedures and practices listed under ceramics. If there is a question regarding a certain object to be handled, consult a conservator to understand the proper procedure for that object.

For larger metal objects, one should reference the different sections of this book regarding handling and lifting equipment and rigging. A conservator or rigging specialist should be consulted for handling large objects because of the variants of weight and structural support required for the movement of the object to a particular location.

A controlled environment is one of the most important elements in the preservation of your metal objects. Excessive humidity is a leading contributor to the corrosion of metal. It is important to keep the relative humidity below 55% in areas where you store or display these objects. You can use dehumidifiers and air conditioning to limit the amount of moisture in the air. Avoid storing your items in the basement, where the relative humidity is often far too high. Bronze and iron artifacts from an archaeological site should ideally be kept at an even lower relative humidity, below 40%. Dust can attract moisture to any object, which should be kept clean and covered during all handling and storage scenarios.

The best handling guidelines for caring for metal objects is to know what types of metals are in your collection, maintain the correct environment for temperature and humidity, and protect them from pollutants. Having a metal conservator on staff, or accessible when questions arise regarding handling concerns, is highly recommended.

Wood

Humans have used wood in many different fashions throughout history and for many different needs. It is a material that has always existed in the abundance of tree varieties found on the planet in various locations and climatic conditions. The material when cut, shaped, and dried is used for fuel, tools, weapons, shelter, and transport.

Few cultural artifacts made of wood survive. Fluctuating environmental conditions, pest infestation, fungal growth, and destruction by war or political/religious divisions all contribute to the relatively few historical objects made of this material.

Wood is naturally very durable; in moderate, sheltered environments it can last for thousands of years without substantial change. Biological deterioration is found principally in the form of insect infestation and fungi. While this activity can result in the complete destruction of an object, it pales by comparison to the use and abuse by humans. And in contrast to human intervention, biological deterioration can be a preventable form of damage.[4]

The stability of the environment in which a wooden object is handled, stored, and displayed is crucial to its care and preservation. The changes that affect the biological decay of this organic material involve the following components: changes of temperature and humidity, light exposure, and pest infestation. These biological effects can be encountered at all levels of handling, from temporary movements through long-term storage, and should be accounted for in the proper procedures and practices.

Wood is a hygroscopic material, which means the amount of moisture in the wood easily fluctuates when subjected to changes of temperature and humidity. The condition of joinery in furniture can be seen and felt by the untrained individual during the seasonal changes, often between summer (warm/humid) and winter (dry/cold). A trained specialist can assess the correct environmental conditions required for specific wooden objects. An extreme example of an object's requiring specific environmental conditions would be of wooden objects discovered in a late-nineteenth-century paddle-wheel boat that sank and was buried in a river sandbar in the midwest United States. The wooden objects on the paddleboat were submerged in water for decades, and when retrieved required a high-humidity environment for the best level of continual care. Dramatic changes in humidity levels may destroy a piece if there are rapid changes within the hygroscopic structure. A specialist can see the indicators of past and present progressions and make recommendations to correct the environment so that it can be stabilized for the object's future preservation.

Light exposure can have long-term deleterious effects on the surface of the object. Light damage is determined by the intensity and color of light multiplied by the length of cumulative time to which the object is exposed. Damage from ultraviolet light (daylight) is the most common and the most invasive and causes the wood to fade and surfaces to discolor to irreversible levels. Long-term exposure can break down the wood surface and internal structure to the point where the fibrous layers become brittle and the damage is irreversible.

Because light exposure has a cumulative effect, wooden objects should be covered to reduce exposure to light in the temporary display or long-term storage. Covering objects will also prevent dirt and other pollutants coming into contact with the surface, which could attract moisture and potential pests.

Pest Management

Depending on the type of wood, the object can be exposed to wood-boring insects. If the temperature and humidity levels are high, the conditions for wood-eating insects are enhanced by providing ample supplements of food (wood) and water for their existence. Active infestation can be noted by the dust (frass) that is created by the boring of tunnels for their nesting and food consumption. These tunnels can degrade the integral strength of the wood; therefore, close observation and assessment of the particular area before handling is crucial. New pest activity is primarily noted by the color of the fras or holes in the wood, which will appear as fresh cuts.

If there is suspected activity, the object will need to be isolated, sealed in plastic, and fumigated. Fumigation processes deplete oxygen and water and introduce chemicals or freezing temperature to eliminate any remaining, live insects. All fumigation techniques require the understanding of how the process will penetrate and affect the hygroscopic structure of the object. To be effective, it must be administered over a designated period of time so as to minimize the damage to the wood structure, yet effectively terminate the type of insect residing in the object.

Mold and fungus can also cause damage to wooden objects if they are kept in an area where humidity levels are sustained above 70% for extended periods of time. These conditions are commonly found in basements, attics, or other storage areas in the museum where the surroundings have no controlled environmental system. Wrapping or sealing wooden objects in plastic can possibly create a micro environment subjected to increased temperature and humidity, which will retain moisture and potentially lead to the growth of mold and fungi.

Ethnographic Objects and Furniture

Ethnographic artifacts and furniture are good examples of two types of objects, whose care and handling practices will establish guidelines for wooden objects in general.

Since wooden objects tend to be utilitarian in nature and can be compared to one's own daily household items, one has to remember that these are collection objects and should be treated as such. Just because they are made of a common, abundant material does not mean that they are replaceable or repairable. Most damage is sustained by the carelessness of the individual when handling the object. An object's surface, for example a table top, is not a place to put your tools when working with the collection.

If questions arise, a conservator or specialist in the particular material and object type should be consulted. The trained specialist can differentiate between object types, their inherent properties, and the structural and environmental requirements that dictate the care and handling practices required for wooden objects.

Ethnographic Objects

Ethnographic objects represent the heritage of specific cultures, traditionally based in the more tribal social organizations, both historical and contemporary. These objects are made from a variety of woods and are constructed for daily, domestic needs or for ceremonial rituals particular to the culture.

Ethnographic objects are made from local, natural materials such as wood, feathers, plant fiber, leather, shell, ivory, and bone in combination with each other or singly.

Wood is often the support on which a combination of materials will be attached, applied, or carved. A thorough inspection must be conducted to understand how to support and handle these objects. Carved surfaces or shapes of wooden objects often become extremely brittle because of the soft wood used and the simplistic methods by which they were produced. Fiber and leather, often used as ties, may become extremely brittle with age and should be supported so as not to flex with the environmental variation of the materials to which they are attached.

Often, the materials used in combination become corrosive to each other and cause deterioration of the attachment or related surface areas. Decorated surfaces are made of plant pigments or soil oxides, used to stain or paint on the wooden surface. The surface decoration is susceptible to abrasion and flaking and can easily stain handling gloves and support materials, which should be used only once to ensure that contamination does not occur when handling or supporting other structures.

Decorated surfaces can be made of oils or tars, which may be sticky or become runny with changes in heat and humidity. The porous makeup of wood retains these materials deep within the surface, and they are unseen upon initial inspection.

Often, objects will have past exposure to mold or insect infestation and may be structurally weak in certain areas. Inspect for new signs of infestation and treat in an appropriate manner. Mounts should be made for delicate objects to support the fragile structure of the wood and any combination of materials with the object.

Because of the hygroscopic nature of a wooden object, minimizing fluctuations in temperature and humidity must always be considered when creating a mount. The mount should support, but not restrict, the movement of the wooden structure. Paintings on tree bark need to be supported in a planar manner, which will allow them to flex to even minimal environmental changes. This is accomplished using mounting plates that grip in all directions, yet allow adequate space for the object to swell and contract in the same support clip.

Ethnographic objects are susceptible to dirt and other pollutants and may also contain residue from their previous use, such as smoke or food. Assessing what is dirt, dust, or surface decoration can be difficult. A conservator experienced in ethnographic objects should be consulted if assessment questions arise.

Furniture

Furniture is a common type of object used on a daily basis in our everyday lives. As such, these common, everyday objects are seldom considered special or valuable beyond their utilitarian purpose. However, furniture as collection objects must not be thought of in the same way. Crossing the threshold of a museum's doorway immediately places the table, chair, or stool in a higher realm, and the care and respect due to all collection objects is now accorded to them. Being aware of the object's uniqueness and preserving it for the future is now paramount. A table top in a display may have related items placed upon it, which will need to be buffered to protect the surface. This same table top should not be used as a place to lay tools. Educating the museum staff on best practices and continually reminding them about their importance should be an ongoing process.

When furniture is on display, barriers and cautionary signage must be placed visibly to instruct the public and to protect the objects. Too often there is evidence of a visitor's touching, moving, sitting upon, or handling a piece of furniture as if it were in a department store. Curators and exhibit designers are often at odds with collection care staff because unobstructed display—no barriers, pedestals, or signage—may be aesthetically more pleasing, but it can contribute to the public's disregard of and ignorance about the uniqueness of the object.

The design and quality of construction is the first and foremost aspect in assessing how to properly handle and care for the furniture. Assessing the structural components and their present condition will dictate the initial stages of your handling procedures.

Note if there has been previous repair or there are areas of previous infestation, which may be structurally unsound for support in handling and bracing.

Note if components such as decorations, handles, knobs, upholstery, or other materials are securely attached to the piece. Note if components are removable. Common examples are decorations, drawers, doors, chair seats, or mirrors, and marble or glass tops. Some objects may have been constructed in sections, yet will be interlocked in the final orientation. Depending on the specifics, these items may need to be removed to avoid their becoming dislodged and to reduce overall weight for ease of movement.

Some components of furniture design have movable or hinged parts in the form of adjustments to a chair back or seat or table leaves, which are not easily removed; their movement must be contained when handling. Contemporary wooden object designs often require detailed assessment and specific solutions for securing these adjustable components before they are moved.

In some instances, these removable components may need to remain as part of the object's overall structure, supplying additional support during movement. Components such as drawers and doors will need to be closed and secured by padding and tying with cotton twill, plastic stretch, or other archival banding.

Marble tops, glass tops, mirrors, or doors should be considered for removal as their susceptibility to the potential flexing of the wooden structure can damage them during movement. If the glass component is not removed, be aware of the potential damage that can be caused by its coming into contact with moving equipment. Marble tops should be transported and stored on their edge and in a secure fashion so that they do not topple over. Glass or marble sheets are best placed directly on a support board and secured in the initial process of removing them from the object. Attached handles or hanging decorations, if not easily removed, will need to be padded and tied so as not to abrade the surface through vibration during the move.

Understanding where the strongest lifting areas on a piece of furniture are varies with the object. Usually the primary lowest horizontal element is the strongest, such as the seat rail of a chair, the apron section of a table top, or the base support rail of a cabinet. Do not slide or shift furniture on its legs, feet, or base as it may cause splintering, gouging, chipping, or breaking, or create pressure points in related structural components. Always lift vertically up and onto the next surface to which it will come in contact. Using proper equipment to handle and transport furniture is essential. Creating a mobile platform to support the object will ensure that the risks are greatly minimized during its movement.

The legs or feet of furniture bases are often weak areas of support when placing them onto a mobile platform. Bracing may need to be added to lift the object up and off these static supports so that they do not incur damage from excess weight or shock. A table may need bracing to lift and support the table apron and top, leaving the legs free of any support.

When transporting an object, know the route through which you will be moving to ensure that all potential obstacles are minimized. Multiple staff will be needed to open doors and operate elevators. One individual should be assigned to supervise the movement and one assigned as a "spotter" to watch for potential physical obstacles. This includes human "onlookers" viewing the overall spectacle.

If objects are covered or padded, be aware of what is covered and being protected. Gripping or holding onto padded areas may transfer undue pressure to the object beneath the padded surface.

Any handling or transport where there may be fluctuations in environmental conditions may require additional wrapping of the object or the use of climate-controlled trucks to reduce these changes.

Stone

The history of stone as a medium for creating objects for utilitarian, decorative, or spiritual purposes or for documenting records dates back to the prehistoric ages and offers the earliest form of our cultural heritage. Because of the durability of this material, many objects have survived the rigors of time and environmental changes. Early relief carvings were created by a process of abrading softer stone by using a harder stone. The development of metal tools allowed stone to be carved in the round, and stone objects in collections range from the utilitarian to architectural, sculptural, and ornamental, and vary in size and shape, from decorative beads to architectural columns.

The extent and range of carvings is matched by the variety of stones from which they are made. Limestone and sandstone are the principal materials, but within each of these categories, there is a substantial variation in both appearance and behavior. Many other stones such as granite, marble, and alabaster have also been used depending on their geography, availability, and cost.[5]

Handling stone objects and caring for them require a diverse knowledge in regard to the type of stone and its physical and inherent properties, both internal and external. The quality of stone used will dictate the object's structural stability in relation to its natural fissure layers or cracks, which are vulnerable to weight shift, shock, and vibration during handling. Assessing the use of proper handling equipment and materials is dictated by the individual object in relation to the logistics of the movement.

The object's surface is vulnerable to pollutants such as smoke, vehicle emissions, dirt, oils, and salts, which react with moisture to cause corrosive decay to the porous nature of the stone. Mold and fungi growth are common to environmental decay. This is seen on outdoor sculpture or architectural elements that are subjected to a highly humid environment. Vandalism accounts for much damage to stone objects placed in outdoor public areas. Most decay is cumulative and can be restricted through regular inspection and cleaning.

Handling guidelines for stone objects are diverse because of the type of stone and the inherent properties of a particular object. Consulting a conservator or specialist will assist in the determination of how to move an object safely.

Seeking advice from a stone conservator or hiring a rigging specialist is essential when moving large, heavy objects. The expertise required is not common in most museum staffing and handling equipment inventory.

The size and shape of stone objects could be problematic because of the weight of the particular type of stone and its structural makeup. The weight of the stone is a primary factor in selecting the method of lifting and transporting the object, and the load-bearing restrictions for the ultimate placement must be determined. Assessing the correct weight is crucial.

If an object can be weighed easily, do so, and record that information for future reference. If no scales are available, try doing a basic lift test on a stable surface. For large objects that cannot be placed on a scale, one can work with dimensional formulas for specific types of stone to estimate the weight.

The surface of stone can be polished to different levels or maintained in its quarried state. The porous surface of stone should be protected by using handling gloves, which create a secure tactile contact for lifting support. Oil, salts, and moisture from bare hands can leave residues, which can, over time, stain the surface.

Smaller objects need to be padded and separated when placed in multiple trays or on top of a handling cart. Surfaces can be scratched or chipped on impact with other objects. All handling materials need to be clean so as not to transfer dirt to the object's surface.

Tilting objects onto an edge of the base or foot can place undue pressure and cause the stone to chip and crack under the weight shift.

Painted, gilded, or other applied mediums on surfaces need to be protected when pressure or support materials are applied to the surface. Many painted surfaces do not adhere securely to the porous surfaces and, over time, lift and become loose.

Handling and rigging materials need to be clean and should be used in combinations with a padded barrier placed under strapping to prevent abrasion to the stone surface. The strapping configuration needs to be closely reckoned to guarantee that the barrier paper does not slip when straps are pulled taut under the progressive lifted weight of the object.

Lifting equipment should be used to minimize handling and protect the handlers from potential physical injury. Hydraulic lift tables and vertical platform lifters are versatile in their height, weight, and mobility.

All stone objects, especially large objects with heavy weight restrictions, should be handled as minimally as possible. Design and construction of handling equipment need to be developed so that the object is handled by the support structure until it needs to be moved from that support. These supports can be made to accommodate long-term storage and transport, and may even be adapted for display without moving the object from the original support.

Mounts required for display should be considered for removal unless they offer additional stability during movement. Many mounts are attached to the stone object by pins, screws, or pressure plates. The area of the attachment can create undue pressure as weight is shifted during handling and may cause those areas to chip or crack.

Planning a move with the requisite handling equipment and materials is essential to safely moving any stone object. Evaluating a safe pathway for an object's movement must take into consideration the object's weight and structural configuration in relation to the proper equipment and handling techniques. With large objects, load-bearing restrictions and calculations need to be confirmed to ensure safe conditions for both staff and building floors, elevators, and surfaces.

Textiles

As with the abundant material and objects made from wood, textiles are made from naturally abundant fibrous materials. With the advancement of mechanical technology to bind and weave different types of fibers, various textiles have been created for a multitude of needs: clothing, blankets, rugs, and upholstery. Like furniture, textiles are common and used in our daily lives. Caring for textiles of cultural heritage requires a specialized understanding of the proper handling procedures and practices for their care. The use of the washing machine is not a common cleaning process to bridge similarities when handling and preserving textiles.

The environmental conditions to which textiles are exposed are numerous and highly detailed for the specific material type and construction technique. The following is a brief summary of the conditions from the website of The Textile Museum in Washington, DC.

Environmental Control

One of the greatest threats to textiles is light. The worst damage is caused by ultraviolet (UV) radiation from natural daylight and from fluorescent light bulbs. However, while the UV rays causes damage most rapidly, the entire light spectrum causes textile dyes to fade and the fibers to become brittle. This includes plain incandescent interior lighting. There is some protection in keeping window shades pulled down or shutters closed during the sunniest times of the day. UV-filtering materials or films can be placed over windows and fluorescent bulbs and used in the glass or Plexiglas® when framing textiles. Perhaps the most important rule of thumb for care is to use or display your textile for limited periods of time. Ideally, rotation should be done seasonally—display your textile for four months, and then allow it to "rest" in proper storage for the remainder of the year. This method of care allows several different textiles to be exhibited, while extending the lifetime of each one.

High temperatures, excessive heat, and high humidity accelerate the deterioration of textiles and provide a conducive climate for insects, mold, and mildew. If mold and mildew are caught early enough (before staining has set), the textile should be moved to a more stable environment, and a conservator should be contacted immediately.

Ideally, a climate of 65–70°F and 50–55% relative humidity is best. However, the maintenance of an environment with as little fluctuation as possible is most important. Temperatures can be controlled with central heating and air-conditioning systems. These can be supplemented with window air units or space heaters for individual rooms. Humidity can be modified with humidifiers or dehumidifiers. Fans and a constant flow of air can also be helpful in preventing mold and mildew. Textiles that are found wet from a leak or high humidity should be immediately dried with a fan.

Air pollution is also an enemy of textiles. Sulfur dioxide fumes from automobiles and industries affect some dyes. However, dirt and dust will probably be the greatest problem with your collection. Dust particles act like small knives, cutting into fibers as the textiles expand and contract in response to changes in relative humidity. A regular schedule of inspection and vacuuming is necessary to maintain your collection. Further, textiles brought into your home for the first time should be inspected and isolated before they come in contact with other pieces in your collection. This allows you to ensure that you have not brought any insect pests into your home. For more information on pest control, see The Textile Museum publication, *Pest Busters*.[6] For further information, consult a textile conservator, and refer to other informational links listed in the reference section of this book.

Handling procedures for textiles are many because of the diversity of the types of fabric used and the functional design of the objects made. The flexibility and fluid nature of textiles when handling them can be compared directly to similar attributes described for two-dimensional works on paper. Many of the basic handling principles can be compared to procedures and practices for handling paper in the sheeted form for support and transport.

Never wear loose, open clothing, or jewelry, lanyards, rings, watches, and belt buckles, which may snag the textile during handling. Many conservators recommend that handlers wear aprons that tie in the back to prevent buttons on clothing snagging the fabric of the textile.

Never lift the object by gripping an edge or multiple edges and pulling it up, thus supporting the full weight of the object. Unlike paper, the textile does not keep a semirigid tension but flexes in the motion, which may cause damage in the form of stress on the fibers.

The flat work surface for handling textiles needs to be big enough to accommodate the object when fully opened into a flat, relaxed position. Creating a support board large enough to handle the object once opened will enable the handler to move it easily and freely.

The object should be placed on a clean, archival support surface. The board or sheeting material covering the table should be white in color to observe any trace residues of dirt, insects, or loose fibers that may have fallen from the object. The white surface also acts as a reflective light source when working upon the fine detail of the fabrics.

Gloves can be used, but often many conservators prefer using clean hands because of the finer tactile sense that is needed for handling the delicacy of the fabric. Handling objects with previous fumigation residue, commonly arsenic, needs to be addressed by using nitrile and latex gloves to protect the handler. Inspections and testing should be done to determine if the object contains traces of arsenic or any other form of fumigation treatment.

Archival support boards and trays should be covered to reduce exposure to light and dirt accumulations within the work when it is not being worked on or is in the storage environment for temporary storage.

Lidded archival boxes can act as secure structural handling devices and long-term storage containers. When handling objects within closed boxes, be aware to not tilt the box, allowing the object to slide within. After handling the boxed object, inspect and readjust before leaving it in the box for any length of time.

Often, objects may need to be stacked within a box or tray. When stacking, place the heaviest objects on the bottom and use acid-free paper or tissue to create a barrier between the stacked objects.

When working with small objects, they can be easily turned over by sandwiching the objects between two sheets of corrugated board and securing them, then turning them over and placing them back onto the work surface. Depending on their size, assistance of another handler may be required to ensure that the objects remain secure between the boards.

If a sandwiched support-board method is too large for safe handling, a small object can also be rolled onto a tube. The object is then transferred by reverse rolling it off the tube so that the other side is exposed.

Rolling textiles onto support tubes for transport or storage can be an extremely safe method of securing and protecting the object, and it reduces the space required for the object's size. The tube should be of a diameter that allows the fabric to create an arc that does not adversely crease, stretch, or break the fibers under the pressure of the object's wrapped layers.

The tube should be of a heavy thickness so that, once the object is wrapped, it does not bend under the weight of the object. Archival tubes should be used when possible. An acidic paper or plastic tube can be used as long as there is a proper barrier seal between the tube and the object when rolled.

When rolled, the tube should extend past the edge of the object to allow the tube to be handled on each end without having to touch the wrapped object. The object should be tied to the tube to ensure that it does not unroll. Ties should not be tightened, so as not to add pressure on the rolled object.

The basic rules for rolling various textile structural configurations are as follows:

To roll a textile, place it face up on a flat, clean surface. Smooth out bulges or creases and straighten the top, bottom, and edges. Place the tube parallel to either the warp or the weft threads. Interleave rolled textiles with acid-free tissue paper or prewashed cotton sheeting. Roll the flat textile onto the tube with the right side inward. Roll pieces with a raised texture such as pile carpets, velvets, or embroideries with the right side outward. For velvet and other fabrics with a pile, roll in the direction of the pile. If there are fringes, cut acid-free tissue to the width of the fringe and fold in half over the fringe. Once rolled, cover with muslin, cotton sheeting, or acid-free tissue and loosely secure with twill tapes. The roll should not support its own weight; to avoid this, provide support for the ends of the roll by using a hanging system or polyethylene foam blocks with corresponding carved recesses.[7]

Covering the final roll with cotton muslin or linen will protect the roll from dirt and light, but still allow it to have sufficient air flow so as not to trap moisture, which could occur if plastic sheeting is used.

Rolled tubes should be handled horizontally by holding the exposed end of the loaded tube. Never carry the rolled tube in the center so as not to place pressure on the object; do not handle vertically so as to prevent the object from sliding off the tube.

Sheeted textiles or costumes can be placed onto a support board for handling. If the size of the costume is larger than the manageable size of the support, the excess can be folded back onto the object with rolled tissue placed into the folds to support it from bending or creasing on the adjoining area.

Costumes can be hung on padded hangers if they are sound in their upper shoulder areas and not too heavy in the sections that make up the remaining parts of the garment as they will be hanging freely.

Sheeted textiles can be hung onto a padded roll or a hanger's horizontal section as long as the weight of the object is not too heavy on the area over the padded support.

Sheeted textiles or costumes can also be moved by laying them on top of a sheet of fabric that will create a cradle, which then can be handled by lifting on the edge of the cradle support and without touching the object. This method should be followed for short movements only as tension must also be kept on the cradle to ensure that the object does not slide off if the cradle is allowed to flex too dramatically.

Large textiles such as carpets or rugs can be rolled onto tubes but may need to have additional support built within the tube to carry the weight of the overall object. Often, a steel pipe or aluminum insert can be placed inside the tube to make it rigid and adapt it to be a part of the attaching support when hanging it on storage racks. Never store rolled textiles of any size directly on the floor at any time.

Many large textiles such as tapestries are hung on the wall for display. The mounting system is often constructed of Velcro strips, which are sewn and affixed on fabric support and then attached to the actual work. When hanging, the hook and nap of the Velcro are adjoined, and the work is hung with a minimum stress on the supported edge of the tapestry.

Some textiles can be mounted on a solid support board, which will then allow the object to be handled and displayed vertically. The backing, which supports the weight and size of the work, is attached to the board by stitching the object directly to the archival covering placed on the board. The mounted textile can be placed into a wooden travel frame or collar and covered for ease in handling and safe storage.

The primary rule for the best procedures and practices in handling textiles of any size is to handle them as minimally as possible. Using support boards, trays, or boxes for small objects and rolling larger objects onto tubes or mounting to support them presents safe and effective handling designs without having to handle the object multiple times. The combination of minimal handling and maintenance of the proper environmental conditions is the best care practice for long-term preservation of these delicate objects.

Contemporary Objects/Plastics and Electronic Materials

Within the last 200 years, new, man-made materials used for the industrial development of the Western world have been used in objects of cultural heritage as well. The uses of materials found in contemporary objects vary from the utilitarian such as furniture, appliances, and even automobiles, to the purely nonfunctional, which are created and crafted in ways that elicit wonder, humor, or illusion.

Plastics

Plastics are the more common materials found in contemporary objects. Plastic is a generic term covering all types of synthetic materials. These different types of materials may differ dramatically from each other with respect to their care requirements. It is, therefore, most important to try to identify the type of plastic from which the object is manufactured.

Plastics are commonly classified on the basis of their origin from natural types such as amber, horn, wax, shellac, or rubber. Semisynthetics are chemically modified natural materials like hardened rubbers and man-made synthetics such as phenol formaldehyde (Bakelite), polyvinyl chloride (PVC), polymethyl methacrylate (Perspex, Lucite), polyethylene (Polythene), and many others.

A conservator specialized in this field can help to identify the material and the manufacturing process used in making the object. This will help you to catalog and document your items and give you direction as to how best to keep them in good condition.

Creating the best environmental conditions for handling and caring for these objects requires knowledge of their chemical makeup and understanding the factors and forces that can cause deterioration.

All light sources, especially ultraviolet light, can cause discoloration and eventual deterioration of the plastics. Reduce light levels when objects are on display and cover them in temporary handling situations.

Temperature should be maintained below 70°F. Cellulose nitrate-based film may deteriorate and disintegrate at room temperature. Cellulose nitrate film stock can be combustible and should be isolated and stored in an environment of 40° F ±.

Cellulose nitrate-based material can potentially create hazardous storage conditions. Objects need to be stored separately and visually monitored. Individuals working in the facility where these materials are stored must know the location of this material and be apprised regarding what to do in emergency situations, such as fires, earthquakes, or hurricanes.

Relative humidity needs to be monitored and maintained within the standard museum requirements, 50–55% ±. Some plastics may require cooler conditions, but if humidity levels are too high, all plastics can degrade rapidly.

Never store plastic objects in sealed environments for long periods or even for temporary periods of time when handling. The plastic will off-gas as it ages, and it needs to be stored in a well-maintained, ventilated space. Plastics are affected by their own off-gassing, and deterioration will accelerate in a closed environment. If off-gassing is extreme, then the object should be stored in a separate location and not in close proximity to other objects.

The surfaces of plastic objects are susceptible to all common pollutants and can be easily stained by moisture or oils. Plastics in contact with other plastics can adhere to each other if temperature levels are high.

Do not store or handle objects by stacking them on top of each other. This can cause physical distortions of bowing, denting, or slumping, and damage to the object will be permanent.

When handling objects, use clean hands or, preferably, cotton gloves. Nitrile or latex gloves can be used but may cause a reaction between two plastic-based materials under certain conditions. When handling cellulose nitrate film or plastics that are off-gassing from deterioration, it is advisable to wear respiration protection. Handling precautions are dictated by the type of plastics being handled and the inherent properties of the object. Consulting an objects conservator is advised if there are questions regarding the type of material and its handling requirements.

Electronic Materials

Many contemporary objects can contain electronic materials such as circuit boards, cathode-ray tubes, electrical wiring, or dry-cell batteries. Many objects must have some of these elements removed as they may be harmful to the preservation of the main object. If the components remain attached, they must be dealt with as a composite design in the handling and care of the overall object.

Oftentimes, the electronic components are necessary for the object to function when displayed. Contemporary artworks may have lights, sound, or movable components, which are a part of the design and function.

All electronic components need to be maintained, and understanding how they are used in the installation is mandatory. A maintenance schedule will need to be established, and any repair work needs to be conducted by a qualified person.

Heat build-up in the electronically powered objects can affect other objects within the display. Power cords may become trip hazards if exposed and must be hidden if it is required to transverse a walkway to a power source. Some power sources may need to be upgraded to a higher voltage or amperage level or may require adapters to convert power standards from different countries and their UL ratings.

Motors, belts, chains, or other movable components may contain oils, grease, or graphite, which must be monitored and not allowed to come in contact with other objects on or off display. Handling must be undertaken only when the power source has been disconnected. When lifting and moving the object, one must be aware of all movable components.

Seeking assistance and advice from trained and licensed experts is required for all such objects. The components need to be inspected for deterioration caused by age or misuse and may need to be upgraded to meet new safety standards.

CONCLUSION

The care and preservation of three-dimensional objects is a diverse challenge. Many of the techniques for handling, storing, and display are similar to those for other objects found in the collection, but each object material type may have specific requirements and should be assessed per each handling scenario. Researching for the proper approach and finding a conservator or specialist to give a knowledgeable answer may take time, but the investment is crucial. Collection care has no scheduled end date, it is a continual process.

FOCUS ON: RIGGING SAFETY IS NO ACCIDENT

by Kevin Marshall

Moving an art object is often simply a matter of assembling a group of people, surrounding the artwork, and lifting the object from one place to another. However, when the artwork is unusually large, heavy, fragile, restored, rare, an irreplaceable piece of cultural heritage, or any combination of the above, some type of rigging is needed.

The importance of safe rigging cannot be overstated, and the critical nature of rigging and moving loads makes it imperative that everyone involved with these practices proceeds with care and adequate training. A rigger's task is to determine the best possible method of lifting the object, considering all the potential risks to the object. The rigger is responsible for all operations below the hook. The rigger is the person in charge, who devises and supervises the process used to pick up the object, to move it, and place it down again safely. Rigging may be as simple as placing a sling or slings around or under an object and securing the slings to a lifting device to achieve a successful, well-balanced lift. At the other extreme, rigging may involve applying extensive engineering, removing walls and floors, navigating steps and restricted areas, avoiding obstacles, closing streets, and using a wide range of equipment and slings.

The top priority in rigging and moving any object must always be preventing personal injury and avoiding damage to the object. It is important to "plan your work and work your plan." If all parties involved in the rigging and movement of artwork plan, coordinate, and communicate, they will successfully minimize potential risks to people and property. The use of slings and rigging is subject to certain hazards that cannot be mitigated by engineered features, but if safety, common sense, and qualified experienced users are employed, the results of any lifting operation should be successful. Like any operation, training for the use of specific equipment is the first step.

Every operation presents its own challenge. The sheer physicality and added challenge of moving large objects when equipment and rigging are employed are big deals, and everyone involved should come away with a good story.

The hoisting triangle consists of three elements for any lifting operation: the selection of the lifting equipment, the operation of the lifting equipment, and the rigging of the load and the attachment to the lifting equipment.

Planning and selecting the appropriate equipment for moving and installing each object requires a careful consideration of the object's size and weight, inherent properties of the object, obstacles and potential hazards in the path of movement, and access to the final location for the object's placement. Many objects are best moved by or in consultation with professional crane or rigging companies because there are very few rigging companies exclusively working with art. In selecting the right crane company and rigging crew, it is important to ask if they have experience handling art objects. If the answer is no, this does not necessarily rule them out as a contractor. Rigging large, complex objects is rigging large, complex objects; the difference is attitude and awareness of the object to be moved. It is as necessary for you as the steward of the art objects to educate and inform them about the objects to be moved as it is for the rigging company to educate and inform you. They should provide the necessary and requisite permits. The object being moved, the method, and the equipment used to move the object will determine the size of crew required.

CHOOSING THE RIGHT EQUIPMENT

Mobile cranes are heavy lifting equipment usually used in the outdoor environment where uneven terrain, landscaping, elevated walls, expansive reach, and other obstacles prevent site access. Cranes can move more weight in more directions than other types of equipment and are available in a wide range of sizes and load capacities. Setup time is often faster with cranes than with other types of equipment. A crane is an extremely useful piece of equipment that can meet a wide variety of applications. The limitations of carry-deck and overhead cranes are that they require space for operation and have restricted use in tight spaces. Mini crawler cranes offer versatility, maneuverability, and lifting capacity in a compact design. They are self-propelled on crawler treads and can fit through doorways for use indoors in confined working spaces.

Telehandler forklifts are straight-reach boom, all-wheel drive steering forklifts with excellent maneuverability over rough terrain and are usually used outdoors.

Forklifts are very useful in tight spaces indoors or outdoors. An electric-powered riding or a walkie-style forklift is a good choice for indoor use. Lifting hooks and boom attachments are available for forklifts, making them more versatile for lifting.

Gantry cranes are available in a variety of fixed, portable, and adjustable sizes with varying load capacities. Gantries are good choices for site installations with restricted access indoors or outdoors. A benefit of a gantry as opposed to a forklift is its ability to lift heavy loads without adding the extra weight of the forklift to the floor load. Gantries can easily be configured with multiple chainfall hoists for lifting.

Gantries can require more setup time and usually must be moved between sites in sections for assembly. Ratcheting lever or puller hoists can also be used in place of a chainfall when headroom is limited.

Other common lifting equipment for lesser loads are manually operated portable crank lifts, hydraulic lifting tables, rol-a-lifts, and pallet jacks. Common rigging hardware includes screw-pin shackles and center-pull hoist rings.

Slings are possibly the most useful tools for rigging and lifting. The most common sling types for lifting art objects are synthetic round or continuous loops. Polyester round slings are made of polyester core yarn covered by a seamless, tubular polyester or nylon cover. Round slings are exceptionally supple and conform firmly to uneven shapes during lifting. Synthetic nylon web flat slings are available in a variety of eye-to-eye and continuous loop configurations. It is helpful to have a variety of sizes and lengths as well as types of slings for different applications rated for a range of load capacities. The colors of slings and covers are not color-fast in general and can transfer to the surface of objects, especially marble. Slings should be wrapped in protective covers like Tyvek, or they can be produced with white nylon or polyester covers to prevent transfer. Slings carry their loads in three primary sling hitches. The three types are vertical, basket, and choker. Slings have the greatest workload limit when used in a basket hitch. The vertical hitch workload limit is 50% of the basket hitch. The synthetic choker hitch workload limit is a maximum of 80% of the vertical hitch workload limit.

Vertical Hitch

One end is on the hook, while the other end is attached directly to the load. Use a tagline to prevent load rotation. The vertical hitch is a method of

Figure 5.4   Rigging Diagram 1 / Vertical Hitch. *Source*: Kevin Marshall.

supporting the load by a single vertical leg of the sling. The angle of the lift is 90 degrees. A vertical hitch should be used only for lifting items with lifting eyebolts.

Basket Hitch

The basket hitch cradles the load with both eyes attached overhead. It is usually used in conjunction with a second sling to stabilize the load and prevent the load from tilting and slipping out of the sling. It cannot be used on a load that cannot be balanced.

Choker Hitch

The choker hitch passes around the load and through one loop forming a noose on one end, with the other loop of a continuous round sling placed on the lifting hook tightening the choke as the load is lifted. Load control is

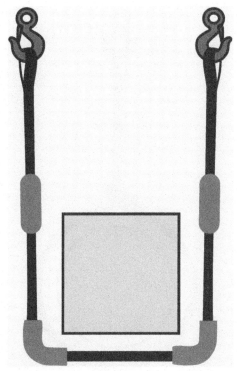

Figure 5.5   Rigging Diagram 2 / Basket Hitch. *Source*: Kevin Marshall.

limited with only one sling rigged in a choker hitch. The choke point should be on the sling body, not on the sling eye, fitting, base of the eye, splice, or tag.

Turning a Load

Turning a load with a choker hitch requires the stirrup of the choker to face the direction of the lift.

Sling-to-Load Angle

The sling-to-load angle is the angle formed between a horizontal line and the sling. Increased tension on the sling is magnified by any change from the vertical when the sling legs are used at angles less than 90 degrees, resulting in reduced workload limits. As the sling-to-load angle decreases, the tension on the sling increases.

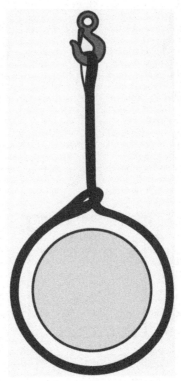

Figure 5.6   Rigging Diagram 3 / Choker Hitch. *Source*: Kevin Marshall.

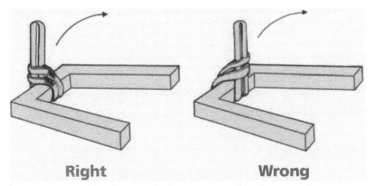

Figure 5.7   Rigging Diagram 4 / Turning the Load. *Source*: Kevin Marshall.

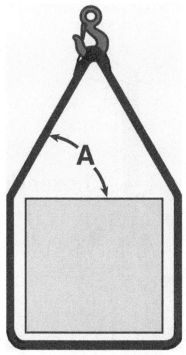

Figure 5.8   Rigging Diagram 5 / Sling-to-Load Angle. *Source*: Kevin Marshall.

Choker Hitch Angle

When a sling is used in a choker hitch and the choker hitch angle is less than 120 degrees, the choker workload limits are reduced.

EQUIPMENT AND SAFETY CHECKLIST

First Considerations

- Plan and evaluate the move.
- Identify the crew and maintain communication continually during movement.
- Thoroughly inspect all equipment before each use to ensure it is in good working order.
- Maintain a safe operating radius with clearance of surrounding structures, power lines, and other hazards.

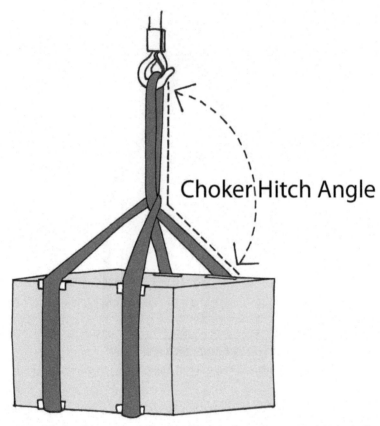

Figure 5.9   Rigging Diagram 6 / Chocker Hitch Angle 1. *Source*: Kevin Marshall.

- Keep a clear path for load movement, with a contingency plan and an alternate setdown area for the object.

Rigging Factors
- Know your limitations; do not forget the law of gravity.
- The center of gravity is vital to achieve load control; it is the balance point of the object.
- Inspect slings before each use for damage that could result in failure.
- Record the weight, dimensions, and the center of gravity of the object.
- Consider the inherent properties of the object and its surfaces and the object's susceptibility to crushing or compression. Use adequate protection and cushioning between the rigging and object to prevent damage to the object or rigging.

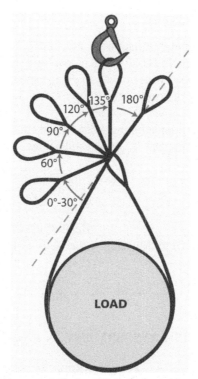

Figure 5.10   Rigging Diagram 7 / Choker Hitch Angle 2. *Source*: Kevin Marshall.

- Secure or remove loose components before moving begins.
- Select slings appropriate to the size and weight of the object, and ensure that a proper lifting angle tension is maintained.
- Choose suitable sling hitches to maintain center of gravity and load control.
- Secure all connections between slings, shackles, and hooks to ensure attachment point integrity and maintain positive sling-to-load engagement.
- Position rigging crew as required.
- Make sure the lifting point is directly above the object's center of gravity before the load is lifted.
- Perform test lifts to ensure the load is well balanced. Unbalanced usually means asymmetry or something with a high center of gravity.

Environmental Conditions

- Check for wind and weather conditions that could adversely affect equipment and movement of objects.
- Assess the stability of the ground or resting place for the object.
- Be aware of all site conditions.

Personnel Considerations

- Know the location and destination for movement.
- Identify an escape path. Never let personnel get under or between a suspended or moving load with no way to escape should the load fail.
- Keep the area clear of spectators for their safety and the safety of the rigging crew.
- Maintain clear communication between riggers and equipment operators.
- Take the time to develop a safe, successful lifting plan, regardless of schedule pressure.
- There is always enough time to do the job right the second time.

Kevin Marshall
Head of the Preparations Department
The J. Paul Getty Museum at the Getty Center and the Getty Villa
Los Angeles, California

FOCUS ON: RISK ASSESSMENT IN PACKING DESIGN

by John Molini

In the late 1980s, while traveling with the Anselm Kiefer exhibition, I was fortunate to meet and spend some time with the Head of Packing at the Philadelphia Museum of Art, the esteemed Timothy "Blues is the name, packin's the game" Farley who imparted these nuggets of wisdom: work from the object out, the materials are only as good as the application, and the application is only as good as the information. At a time when packing materials and methodology were still being hotly debated, these "nuggets" were a welcome relief in their soundness, logic, and simplicity.

The design of the packing and the application of materials should be informed by a knowledge of the materials, experience, and a risk assessment based on the condition of the object and any external conditions regarding transport and destination that may affect safety. Choosing materials for the right reasons, applying them as part of a common sense design, and working from the object out help keep it simple.

There are no set standards that dictate the size, weight, or "complexity" of an object. Working from the object out starts with assessing risk due to its present condition, where applicable, its treatment history, and its inherent strength. While its condition informs the choice of material, the design type, and placement of padding and the amount of cushioning, it should not produce a packing panic, as in "too much ain't enough." Overreacting can be avoided by concentrating on the positive: where an item can be touched. Too often concentrating on the negative, where it can't be touched, usually results in packing oneself into the proverbial corner, producing a situation where the packing actually increases the risk to the object.

Keep in mind that the materials we employ are most effective when applied in a simple and logical manner. Cushioning curves and manufacturer's specs work best when partnered with common sense. Choosing the right materials and using them accordingly is important, but an often overlooked risk reducer is incorporating easy access to the object in the design of the packing.

While pads act as lock-and-loads, they also act as guides and keys. Bottom pads bear the load while the side, back, and front pads act as locks and need to be applied to ensure a proper fit: snug but not too tight, which is essential to controlling shock and vibration. Properly spaced pads help guide one's hands to safe touch zones and guide the object in and out when removing and replacing, thus keying the object in place. If internal packing requires moving parts, such as braces or foam yokes, keep them to a minimum and make them user friendly. Any images, registration marks, or instructions should be easy to understand and easy to find. Think and design with the understanding that the condition of an object is informative not restrictive, with the mind-set that the object, padding, and access are all connected. Keep in mind that packing is an extension of art handling. The easier it is to handle the packing, soft or hard, the safer it is for those doing the handling, making everything safer for the contents.

Risk assessment does not end with the condition of the object. Nor does risk dissipate once a packing solution is agreed upon. As we work from the object out, assessing risk needs to include external conditions related to transport and destination.

When it comes to trucks, not all are created equal. Some are longer, some are shorter, a few are higher, most have a standard width of 8 feet, and lift gates vary in size. Some are sprinter vans outfitted with air ride and climate control but perhaps without a lift gate. Many trucks are designated as "exclusives"; these are dedicated to a specific loan or an exhibition. Employing this mode of transit minimizes the amount of handling, because once the cargo is loaded it stays until it reaches its destination for off-loading. More than likely there will a courier accompanying the shipment.

Other trucks operate as shuttles. Fine-art shuttles, similar to FedEx and UPS, provide affordable transport because they deal in bulk, crisscrossing the country, picking up and delivering both soft-packed and crated items, shifting the load accordingly at each stop, be it a gallery, a museum, a residence, or a cargo hub. While one can request "last on first off" to minimize the amount of handling, that request's being met is dependent on many factors: your location related to the destination, size of your package, and the shuttle's schedule.

In the last ten to fifteen years, what can be shipped by air where, when, and how has changed. Internationally and domestically, there are fewer cargo flights. Domestically, the number of standard passenger flights moving smaller-sized freight directly to major cities has been reduced due to industry trends, passenger capacity, fuel economy, and the type of aircraft available.

Whether objects are transported by air or ground, there are circumstances and situations that directly affect the type of packing choices required to mitigate risk by providing simple, efficient handling and protection solutions. Doubling feet or skids to easily accommodate forklifts, pallet jacks, and J-bars, spacing feet to allow easy placement of dollies, a sufficient number of handles to assist with manual lifting, and not wrapping crates are some simple ways to address risk associated with handling during transport. Shipping via a shuttle?? Like FedEx and UPS, it is about bulk and shifting loads and more handling, so pack accordingly and to the situation.

The final piece of risk assessment is the destination. Facility reports not only provide information about security and light levels, but should also address staff, equipment, and access: docks, doors, hallways, and elevators. Not all venues were originally designed to accept everything, in some cases, especially not artworks.

Packing and handling solutions should be based on a risk assessment that includes the physical particularities of a destination. Even if the packing has reached its destination safely and is in the door, the potential for risk does not end. There is still the process of unpacking, when an object is vulnerable. The safekeeping of the contents rests in the hands of those who are at the other end, unpacking and handling the object.

Having to reach into a crate to remove a large, heavy 3-D object, even on a handling slide, can be risky for the object and those doing the removing. It is better to remove the crate from the object as opposed to removing the object from the crate.

Paintings normally ride on their sides to reduce the height of a crate, or in some cases packed as side loaders, which requires laying the crate on its back to unpack. Up to a certain size, that method works quite well. However, once a certain height and weight are reached, laying a crate on its side puts the handlers and the contents at risk. Besides overcoming the laws of physics as related to weight and gravity, there is still the matter of removing a large lid, usually two pieces of plywood seamed, and carrying it over the face of the work. A safer alternative is packing the work in a travel frame that goes in an end loader, a design where one side is the lid, which allows the large heavy crate to stay upright while handling a much lighter travel frame.

As you can see, there is more to the process of proper risk assessment and arriving at a good packing solution than the condition of WHAT is being considered for loan and WHERE it is going. The process needs to include external conditions: HOW it is going, WHO will be doing the handling during transport and WHO will be responsible for receiving, unpacking, and repacking WHAT it is that we are all entrusted to protect. Protect the art and those who handle it.

John Molini
Manager of Packing and Crating
The Art Institute of Chicago
Chicago, Illinois

NOTES

1. Konstanze Bachmann, *Conservation Concerns: A Guide for Collectors and Curators* (Washington, DC: Smithsonian Books, 1992).

2. The NPS Conserve-O-Gram 1/12, *How to Select Gloves: An Overview for Collections Staff*, http://www.nps.gov/museum/publications/conserveogram/01-12.pdf.

3. *How to Protect Your Metal Objects, Caring for Your Treasures, Metal Objects* (Washington, DC: American Institute for Conservation of Historic and Artistic Works, 2014), http://www.conservation-us.org/about-conservation/caring-for-your-treasures/metal-objects#.VPp-VcIcTIU.

4. *Biological Deterioration & Damage to Furniture & Wooden Objects* (Washington, DC: Smithsonian Museum Conservation Institute, 2014), http://www.si.edu/mci/english/learn_more/taking_care/biodetwood.html.

5. "Care and Conservation of Carved Stone," *Conservation Registrar* (Paris, France: International Council of Museums, The Institute of Conservation, 2014), http://www.conservationregister.com/PIcon-Stone.asp.

6. *Environmental Control; Learning Resources/Care and Cleaning of Textiles* (Washington, DC: The Textile Museum, George Washington University, 2014), http://museum.gwu.edu/environmental-control.

7. *How to Care for Textiles: Handling, Storage, and Display* (Ottawa, Ontario: Canadian Conservation Institute, 2014), http://www.cci-icc.gc.ca/resources-ressources/objectscollectionsobjets/textiles/423-eng.aspx.

Part III

WORKING WITHIN COLLECTION CARE ENVIRONMENTS

Chapter 6

Collection Care

The Internal Environment

INTRODUCTION

There are many factors that involve sound collection care practices within a museum or in the commercial service industry. The focal point of the next two chapters is to present the physical locations where collection objects reside or are used with the purpose of interpreting cultural heritage programs. The content of these chapters will discuss the various environments to which the collection can be subjected.

I will use the overarching term "environment" for the location in which the collection objects are cared for. Using two distinct categories, internal environment and external environment, I will discuss services commonly performed in these environments, with the proviso that each museum is unique in how it is designed, built, and staffed. The internal environment is tailored to the museum's specific collection care requirements. Where and by whom collection care activities are undertaken will inform the spaces and programming in the institution.

This chapter will explore the various locations, facilities, activities, and physical requirements for best practices for collection care in the internal environment. The internal environment is where the object resides in storage or on display or in the additional working spaces such as conservation or imaging services studios and other preparatory spaces. This assessment is sometimes termed "working in the building envelope" with the specific locations termed "the box within a box" or "the room within a room."

The following chapter will explore the various locations, facilities, activities, and physical requirements for best practices for collection care in the external environment, broadly defined as spaces where activities such as packing and transport and offsite facilities for storage or display occur.

The physical environment refers to the climatic conditions where the object resides such as temperature, humidity, lighting, and contaminants (dust or pests). Whether in the storeroom of the internal environment or in the temporary spaces of the external environment, objects require varying sets of standards and practices to maintain their optimal condition.

Figure 6.1   Internal Gallery Space. *Source*: Author.

Figure 6.2 Internal Public Space. *Source*: Author.

CONTROLLING AND MAINTAINING THE PHYSICAL CLIMATE CONDITIONS WITHIN THE ENVIRONMENTS

The challenges of maintaining a proper and secure climatic environment for the collection can be difficult because of the type of collection, the spaces allotted specifically for the collection, and the various kinds of programming that may be required for the objects. The facility maintenance staff working with collection care staff must be able to control and maintain the desired temperature, humidity, and light levels at all times, whether in a storeroom or for programming in spaces used on a temporary basis in collection care activities.

Figure 6.3 Internal Storage Space. *Source*: Author.

Standards have been established over the last half-century for different material types and their care for long-term preservation. Because of new research and findings, conservators have challenged these standards and are currently re-evaluating them to adjust and reduce some of the strict levels that were previously required.

The research goals, application, and monitoring of these standards are based on best practices targeted for preventive conservation and the ability of institutions and staff to work within these standards. For further reading on this evolving subject, a list of articles and links are listed in the reference section under "Environmental Topics."

STANDARDS FOR ENVIRONMENTAL MEASURES

Current Research and Changes

The following two excerpts will offer a general discussion of the history, research, and standards that are focused on monitoring and maintaining the temperature and humidity requirements within the museum. For more information and topical papers, the resource section of the book has listed various details and links to this discussion.

In recent years, there has been increasing concern regarding current practices for maintaining climatic conditions for objects—not only those imposed by institutions in international loan agreements, but also, more generally, those for collections on long-term display and in storage. These concerns reflect a general awareness of the imperative of environmental and financial sustainability as well as the need to take into account new understanding about collection requirements and advances in thinking about approaches to environmental control.

At least since the mid-1970s, many museums have regarded a relatively narrow set of environmental parameters, 70°± 4°F (20°± 2°C) and 50 ± 3% RH, as providing the optimum conditions for the preservation of their collections. Although never actually prescribed as a standard by a professional body, this range has, nonetheless, served as a de facto standard and has become a common and—until fairly recently—generally unquestioned specification for loan agreements between institutions. However, this somewhat narrow range has proved difficult for collecting institutions to meet consistently for a number of reasons, including those relating to the vagaries of climate, the capabilities of climate control systems, and the availability of the human and financial resources necessary for maintaining tight controls. Managing climatic conditions within this narrowly defined range is also highly dependent on continued access to reliable and relatively low-cost energy sources, a situation that can no longer be taken for granted. As a result, museums, libraries, and archives are now engaged in a reconsideration of their specifications for collection environments, taking into account the growing imperative of both environmental and economic sustainability.[1]

In September 2014, at the IIC (International Institute for Conservation of Historic and Artistic Works) congress in Hong Kong and the ICOM-CC (International Council of Museums Committee for Conservation) conference in Melbourne, delegates discussed and agreed on a new position for environmental guidelines. The position supports accepting interim guidelines as standards, including those by AICCM (Australian Institute for the Conservation of Cultural Material).

The AICCM recommended Interim Temperature and Relative Humidity Guidelines for acceptable storage and display conditions of general collection material:

Temperature—between 15–25°C with allowable fluctuations of ± 4°C per 24 hours, relative humidity—between 45–55% with an allowable fluctuation of ± 5% per 24 hours. Where storage and display environments experience seasonal drift, RH change is to be managed gradually across a wider range limited to 40–60%. Temperature and relative humidity parameters for preservation of cultural materials will differ according to their material, construction, and condition, but stable conditions maintained within the above parameters are generally acceptable for most objects.

AIC Interim Guidelines endorsed by the Association of Art Museum Directors:

For the majority of cultural materials, a set point in the range of 45–55% relative humidity with an allowable drift of ± 5%, yielding a total annual range of 40% minimum to 60% maximum and a temperature range of 59–77°F (15–25°C), is acceptable.[2]

Basic Environmental Condition Guidelines

I have included the following environmental guideline requirements as a reference to the current standards that the majority of collection care individuals have previously, and most likely still are, committed to maintaining and operating within the internal environment.

Temperature General Levels

• General Levels: 18–22°C or 70°F ± 2°F is a general level recommended to be maintained, yet this standard has been challenged in recent years.
• Conservators should be consulted and research conducted to understand what is needed for specific collections needs. For more information refer to the reference list under "Environmental Topics."
• Temperature levels and ranges may need to be maintained at different levels for specific material types. For example, ceramics are stable at a range of temperatures, whereas organic materials are less so with fluctuations in

relative humidity. Certain film- and polyester-based materials need to be kept in colder or, in some instances, at freezing temperatures for maintaining their stability.

- Maintaining temperature levels will also reduce the effects of fluctuations in relative humidity, thus offering a more stable environment for objects.
- Temperature fluctuations can be transmitted by sunlight and climatic conditions through the exterior envelope of the building, altering the internal conditions within the building.
- Mechanical equipment within the building can radiate heat and create temperature fluctuations and variables to internal conditions if not monitored and properly maintained.

Relative Humidity (RH) General Levels

General levels in the past were targeted at 50% ± 5% RH for collection objects. Current and continuing research now calls this standard into question. Relative humidity may be defined as the proportion of the amount of water vapor in a given quality of air compared to the maximum amount of water vapor that the air can hold at the same temperature, expressed as a percentage. As air temperature increases, so does its capacity to hold moisture. Therefore as temperature goes up, the RH goes down, and vice versa. The two measurements generally are considered together. Research by the Image Permanence Institute (IPI) indicates that heat and moisture are the primary controlling factors in almost every form of decay. The best or most suitable range of RH for any object and its material makeup is a level where direct change is minimized.[3] Conservators should be consulted and research conducted to understand what is needed for specific collections needs.

Mechanical/General Set Points

The target value of temperature or relative humidity (RH) that a mechanical system is designed to maintain over time is known as the "set point." However, even the best mechanical systems will produce values that fluctuate above and below the given set point.

The term "set point" can be used in two ways:

- to refer to the setting of the thermostat or humidistat over a short period of time (hours, days) and
- to refer to the average annual setting of the thermostat and humidistat (because the set points may be adjusted over the year for various reasons, such as energy saving).

Note that the "set point" is often defined by museums as 50% RH with the temperature between 15 and 25°C, although it can also be based on the historic averages. In practice, it may be defined by factors such as the needs of the collection, the performance of the building plus the HVAC system, and the climatic variation in temperature. On the other hand, class of control is defined by the degree of fluctuation in temperature and RH. And it is fluctuation rather than the set point that we now strive to control because fluctuation presents the main threat to most artifacts and class of control defines the allowable degree of fluctuation.[4]

Monitoring Temperature and Relative Humidity (RH)

Temperature and humidity are closely related in the relationship of cause and effect for the decay in objects. The need to monitor and maintain records is essential in managing the best conditions for collection preservation.

The recording hygrothermograph is one of the most common devices used by museums today to measure temperature and RH. You may see these in discreet locations throughout the museum galleries. The charts on the drum hold a one-week record of readings made by a sensor of human or synthetic hair (for humidity) and a bimetallic strip (for temperature). Each sensor is attached to a separate pen, which in turn moves up or down in response to a change in humidity or temperature. Because of the sensitive nature of the mechanism, the hygrothermograph requires frequent calibration. One device used in calibration because of its reliability is called the psychrometer.

A psychrometer consists of two ordinary thermometers. The dry bulb simply reads air temperature. The wet bulb has a fabric sleeve fitted over the mercury bulb, which is wetted with distilled water. Swinging this instrument around will move air past the wet bulb, cooling it by evaporation of water and thus giving a lower temperature reading than the dry bulb (provided the air is not fully saturated with moisture). The difference between the temperature of the wet bulb and dry bulb is calculated, and RH is determined from a chart called a hygrometric table.

A few other devices used to measure temperature and RH levels in the museum environment are as follows:

- Dial Hygrometer—this device can be hung on a wall or mounted on a shelf. It measures temperature and humidity within 3 degrees.
- Data Logger—this device can record, display, and download temperature and humidity information to a computer for analysis and tracking.
- Analog Thermohygrometer—this device is placed discreetly in exhibit cases to monitor temperature and humidity levels.
- Temp/Humidity Cards—these cards record temperature/humidity levels by indicating a change in color, from blue (drier) to pink (wetter).

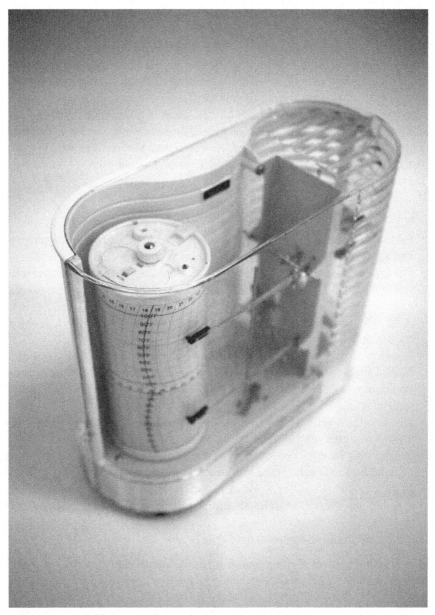

Figure 6.4 Hydrothermograph in Storage. *Source*: Carey, Artex FAS.

Light Levels

Light is part of the energy spectrum and is composed of wavelengths of varying lengths. Energy wavelengths just shorter than visible light are in

Chapter 6

the ultraviolet (UV) end of the spectrum and just longer wavelengths are at the opposite end of the spectrum in the infrared (IR) region. The visible region of light is between ultraviolet and infrared. Ultraviolet and infrared radiation are invisible to humans. Shorter wavelength UV radiation is the most damaging, although visible and infrared (heat) radiation are also harmful. Various light sources contain different percentages of UV, visible, and infrared light. Daylight contains all three. Fluorescent lights usually combine UV and visible light energy. Tungsten lights usually combine visible and infrared light energy. Newer bulbs vary in the wavelengths they emit. Some halogen lights emit enormous quantities of ultraviolet radiation.[5]

Lighting General Levels

- Eliminate UV and IR wavelengths before relying on lux (fc) measurements and applying a policy of lux-hour conditions.
- The type and intensity of collection display lighting and exposure over time (lux hours) can result in cumulative damage and therefore require continual monitoring.
- Adhere to maximum lux levels and lux hours according to individual object specifications.
- Rotating display period of objects allows the object the suggested minimal time of lux hour exposure per year. For example, textiles can be on display for six months, and then off display for 24 months before they are returned to display.
- Display lights activated by motion sensors to turn on/off for viewing may allow for higher lux (fc) levels if lux hours are significantly reduced.
- When being handled outside display hours, objects should be kept covered or returned to closed storage to reduce exposure.
- Light levels in storage or work areas need to be kept to a humanly safe and sensible minimum, and lights should be turned off when not in use.

Visible Radiation—Recommended Light Levels

The acceptable level of illumination is based on the relative risk of an object to light damage. Many museums categorize collections into four groups.

- High sensitivity: 50 lux (5 fc): Formerly, all paper, photographic materials, textiles, many organic, natural history specimens, and some unstable plastics and modern paints were placed in this category. Many museums use this light level as a categorical condition for loans of these materials.
- Moderate Sensitivity: 100 lux (10 fc): Since not all paper, textiles, and photographic materials are extremely sensitive, some museums have been able

to reclassify select materials such as dyed wood into this category, although some wood dyes can be highly sensitive. Professional advice is essential when determining the appropriateness of using this category.

- Low Sensitivity: 200 lux (20 fc): Oils and acrylic paintings are usually placed in this category along with undyed organic materials such as leather, wood, and ivory.
- Insensitive: 300 lux (30 fc) or more: Objects that are not sensitive to light do not require lux or lux-hour limitations. The 300 lux value is based on the importance of balancing the relative intensity of illumination of all surfaces within the field of vision to no more than a 6:1 ratio. Objects lit above 300 lux may make objects lit at 50 lux look underilluminated. Conversely, light levels may be increased to above 300 lux to balance an object against a day-lit background.[6]

Monitoring Light Levels

- Monitoring light levels is a task that should be done each time an object is placed on display and being lit by the lighting designer or technician for best possible public viewing.
- Light levels should be monitored on a scheduled basis during the display period to observe if previously set levels have been altered because of changes in building conditions or energy fluctuations.
- All exhausted lamps must be replaced with equivalent lamps. New light readings may also be made as the fixture may have been moved out of the context of its previous angle or setting.
- Light-sensitive objects being researched, treated, or inspected may require monitoring of light levels or lux hours, and protective covers should be placed on them when they are not being viewed.
- Light meters and other monitoring equipment resources will be listed in the equipment section of the book. References to technical information and other topical sources can be found in the reference section of this book.

Pests/General Guidelines

To address the subject of pests within a museum, one must understand that the subject is vast and requires specific research to understand and fully develop an approach for preventive care of objects that may be affected by pests. A conservator or pest-management specialist should be contacted or employed to conduct an analysis and recommend preventive measures or treatment to protect collection objects from pests in your specific internal environment. The following content will highlight the major points and give an overview of the subject.

Museum Integrated Pest Management

Integrated pest management (IPM) is developed from research and standards created for accessing, monitoring, and managing environmental information regarding pests and how to prevent damage to the organic materials. Museum environments need to be constantly monitored and managed to prevent pests getting into the building, and especially in the locations where collections are stored or displayed. The key components of an IPM program include monitoring, identification, evaluation, inspection, habitat modification, good housekeeping, education, and treatment.

Monitoring

- The monitoring of pests within the museum is a program that needs to be developed and maintained on a daily basis.
- A watchful eye for evidence of pests or the means to reduce their potential habitat within the building is an ongoing policy that all museum staff should be educated about and that they must adhere to.
- One designated person from the facility maintenance staff and another from the collection care staff should be assigned to work together and establish a scheduled program of monitoring pest activities.
- Noninvasive action can include setting sticky traps and recording data of the type of pest caught and implementing an invasive program if needed.
- Dispensing fumigants to kill pests must be administered in an effective way so as not to harm the staff or come into contact with the objects.
- Monitoring activities should be recorded for date, time, and location of monitoring device.
- Record keeping and accountability should reflect seasonal weather changes outside the building and internal building activities or renovations to best expedite future deterrents of pest activity.

Identification/Evaluation

- Identification and evaluation of the type of pests commonly found in the external environment of your building will assist in deterring and eliminating their access to the internal environment of the building.
- Identification and evaluation of the type of pests that your specific collection may attract will need to be cross-referenced to the pests that are commonly found in the external environment.
- Identification and evaluation should be noted directly to habitat and food source to create the related link of pest and life cycle in order to eliminate all passive deterrents.
- Continued evaluation of current practices and ongoing research in pest management within the museum industry is crucial.

Inspection

- Incoming packages, crates, or unwrapped objects should be inspected in a separate room or space prior to being placed among the other collection objects.
- Upon object inspection, if pests are found, the object needs to be fully segregated and sealed in plastic to eliminate any possible migration of the pests before a fumigation process can be determined and implemented.
- Objects coming in from interstate or other countries may be required to be considered for fumigation prior to entry into the receiving state or country.

Habitat Modification

- A primary deterrent for pests is eliminating their access to the internal environments of the building.
- Education in controlling human food sources and waste can help eliminate potential habitats with a food source for pests.
- Education in controlling access to potential organic materials, such as the objects themselves or the materials in which they are handled or housed, is essential.
- Controlling the temperature, levels of humidity, air circulation, and excessive moisture content within the internal environment is important as these are factors conducive for pests to thrive.

Good Housekeeping/Education

Educating all staff members about good housekeeping practices is a museum-wide endeavor to eliminate habitats suitable for pests to survive. Maintaining a pest-free environment is a never-ending task. Educating staff about maintaining good housekeeping should be as common and intuitive as understanding and following the building's emergency evacuation procedures.

Treatment Action

Treatment action comes in many forms, but knowledge of the correct form of treatment to eradicate the pests is essential. Seek expertise from a conservator or pest-management specialists to ensure the correct choice of treatment.

- Chemical pesticides work well for immediate action and are commonly used, but they should only be an alternative to passive, less invasive methods.
- Before using any chemical product, research its chemical properties, application processes, and the ongoing risks to staff handling the objects, and the potential effects it could have in direct contact with the object.

- History has proved that long-term residues such as arsenic, methyl bromide, and other fumigants can remain in the object many years after their being used as a treatment method.
- Hazards of using invasive and noninvasive treatments need to be fully understood, and training staff in how to use them and protect themselves during treatment is essential.
- Passive or nonchemical treatments include freezing or creating sealed environments, which are modified for periods sufficient to destroy a pest life cycle. The modification of the sealed environment includes decreasing oxygen and increasing carbon dioxide levels, and the introduction of inert gases.

Goals of Pest Management

- Proactive pest management can provide a positive work environment that allows all staff to be informed about and to assist in the efforts to reduce the effects of pests on the collection.
- Quality pest management will reduce the high costs of treating pest infestations and the conservation treatment or repair of objects previously affected by mold or pest infestation.
- Quality pest management will reduce the potential risk of staff being exposed to or affected by harmful chemicals, molds, or allergies, which can cause long-term health problems.
- Quality pest management will mitigate the third largest risk to organic collection objects. (Handling and light exposure are the first and second, respectively.)

Pollutants/General Guidelines

Air pollution occurs from contaminants produced outside and inside museums. Common pollutants include dirt, which includes sharp silica crystals, grease, ash, and soot from industrial smoke; sulfur dioxide, hydrogen sulfide, and nitrogen dioxide from industrial pollution; formaldehyde and formic and acetic acid from a wide variety of construction materials; ozone from photocopy machines and printers; and a wide variety of other materials that can damage museum collections.

Air pollutants are divided into two types:

- particulate pollutants (e.g., dirt, dust, soot, ash, molds, and fibers) and
- gaseous pollutants (e.g., sulfur dioxide, hydrogen sulfide, nitrogen dioxide, formaldehyde, ozone, formic and acetic acids).[7]

Particulate Pollutants

- Airborne particulates are made up of a variety of substances, the most common being dust, dirt, skin cells, fibers, soot, mold, and pollen.
- These particulate substances come from external elements found in nature as well as from man-made sources, and can be produced and transferred within the internal environment by machines and humans.
- Some particulates coming from a natural base, such as mold, pollen, and skin cells, can be easy food sources for pests.
- Some particulates such as silica can be abrasive and even more damaging when mixed with moisture and other solids.
- As particulates accumulate, they can attract moisture and gaseous pollutants, which in combination can cause corrosion, staining, and acidic reactions, depending on the combination and the base materials with which they come in contact.
- Particulates are measured in microns (1/1,000,000 of a meter). Knowing the particulate size is important when you are determining the size of air filters to use in a building.[8]

Gaseous Pollutants

Gaseous pollutants are reactive chemicals that can attack museum objects. These pollutants come from both indoor and outdoor sources. Outdoor pollutants are brought indoors through a structure's HVAC system or open windows. There are three main types of outdoor pollution.

- sulfur dioxide (SO_2), and hydrogen sulfide (H_2SO) produced by burning fossil fuels, sulfur-bearing coal, and other organic materials;
- nitrogen oxide (NO) and nitrogen dioxide (NO_2) produced by any kind of combustion, such as car exhaust, as well as deteriorating nitrocellulose film negatives and objects; and
- ozone (O_3), produced in the upper atmosphere by sunlight reacting with pollutants in the atmosphere and indoors by electric or light equipment, such as photocopy machines, printers, and some air filtering equipment.

When sulfur and nitrogen compounds combine with moisture and other contaminants in the air, sulfuric acid or nitric acid is produced. This acid then causes deterioration in a wide variety of objects. Ozone reacts directly with the objects causing deterioration.[9]

Other Common Pollutants

- Human interaction with objects poses the threat of contamination by the transmission of oils, moisture, and other dirt via the hands.

- Collection care staff should be trained in the proper use of protective gloves when handling different types of object material.
- When on display, objects are threatened by the potential touching, intentional or otherwise, of viewers and their interaction with the object. Guard staff, signage, and other educational attempts by museum staff are used do deter this interaction.
- Vandalism can be directed to an object by making a specific statement or by a simple act of affection or humor. Human contact with an object can affect its inherent condition and if this is not inspected or treated in a timely manner, it may cause permanent damage.
- Improper display, storage, or handling procedures often create an opportunity for pollutants to come into contact with an object. Most of the time, this stems from neglect or disrespect or from an untrained individual moving an object.

Monitoring and Maintaining a Pollutant-Free Environment

The primary response to potential damage from pollutants is the minimization or elimination of contact, either by creating a physical barrier between the object and pollutants or by chemically altering the rate of deterioration through increased exposure to reactive compounds.[10]

Air Filtration

For museums, it is important to remove as much dust as possible. The use of a filter with a relatively high efficiency is best for this purpose. A dust-spot rating of 90–95%, which is capable of stopping particles as fine as tobacco smoke, is preferred; certainly efficiency should be no less than a minimum of 80–90%. The American and European ratings of these levels of filtration are MERV 13/EU 7 at 80–85% and MERV 14/EU 8 at 90–95%, respectively.

The removal of gaseous pollutants requires special filters containing a medium that absorbs or chemically breaks down the targeted gases. The use of gas phase filtration is not widespread in museums because of the initial costs involved in such systems. Retrofitting existing systems is very expensive because of the high maintenance costs and the scale of required filtering materials when depleted. The decision to install such a system needs to take into account the quality of the outside air, since protection from a highly polluted environment could justify such an investment in air treatment.[11]

Dust Control/Collection Care Cleaning

Maintaining a quality air filtration system is the primary method of control of dust and particulates found within all collection areas of a museum.

The filters cannot collect a high percentage of particulates because these are directly deposited by human and mechanical means within the spaces.

Humans produce skin cells, which actively fall from the body by physical movement and become airborne. Clothing carries particulates and expels this dust along with various fibers within the composition of the fabric. Shoes bring dust and dirt into the space, and with the wear and tear on carpeting caused by foot traffic, even the carpet fibers can become airborne and may be dispersed. A prime location to observe the level of dust accumulation is the top of a vitrine or a flat deck surface. Even during a major exhibition, where cleaning is done by the staff on a daily basis, a person can see how quickly these human-based particulates are produced and how they accumulate.

Education in the merits of good housekeeping is essential to minimize the damage caused by air pollutants to collection objects within a museum. Research into the preventive conservation and proactive care practice of regular dusting and cleaning of objects continues to be conducted in the collection care profession. The time and effort spent in training designated staff to keep objects clean yields the benefits of having more visually appealing displays as well as of reducing the related costs of treatment to clean and repair damage resulting from negligent housekeeping.

Development of a regularly scheduled cleaning program is essential. Many large museums often hire and train designated staff to do these activities because the scale of the work is huge and the need is dictated by the collection type. Some museums approach this responsibility as a cross-departmental staffing requirement, working with a schedule and reporting structure to guarantee efficiency and coverage of particular objects or collection types.

Cleaning programs primarily target the objects that are on open display. Similar cleaning programs should be established and scheduled for storerooms and other spaces where objects may reside for extended periods of time. Maintaining a clean work environment where any collection activity is performed should be an ongoing practice for all members of the collection care staff. One of the advantages of having a regular cleaning program is that the collection is observed in a purposeful manner, on a regular basis, and by means of which damage to, or changes in, the objects can be noted.

Pollutants and Microclimates

As with the overall internal environment of the building, interior rooms or zones to control the conditions in which the objects reside can be designed. This box within a box (room within a room) concept can be determined in a similar fashion for storerooms as they can be designed as a storage cabinet or display case.

Figure 6.5   Cleaning Maintenance. *Source*: 2015 Museum of Fine Arts, Boston.

When one is creating these microclimates, consideration of the type of materials to be used to construct these spaces must be researched. These units represent another layer of protection from the external conditions, and knowledge of their structural makeup and effectiveness in controlling infiltration and fluctuations is essential.

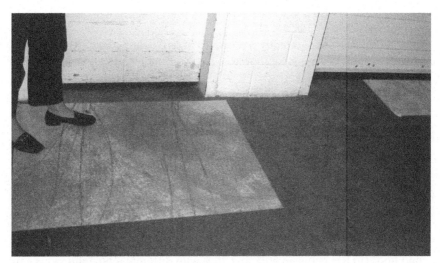

Figure 6.6 Dirt Sticky Mat. *Source*: Author.

The preparation of microclimates needs to be focused on the use of appropriate materials and a technically effective design for specific objects. Commercial manufacturers who specialize in producing these units are an excellent source of information as their product is based on the continual research with the conservation community that continues to establish standards for objects to be protected within a particular microclimate. The object itself can become a detrimental force if the material off-gasses or exhibits a negative reaction to the space created for it.

More information will be presented in this chapter under the sections regarding storage cabinets and display cases. The resource section of this book will list resource links and papers related to this broad technical subject.

Basic Environmental Condition Guidelines

Preventive Conservation and Agents of Deterioration is a resource link provided by The Canadian Conservation Institute. It provides guidelines and information on general care for heritage collections based on the principles of preventive conservation and risk management. This resource identifies ten primary threats specific to heritage environments and encourages their prevention at the collections level, first, by avoiding, blocking, and detecting possible damage, and then by responding and treating damage. This integrated approach to conservation has also led to developments in risk assessment.[12]

Biological Damage

The biological threat directly related to relative humidity (RH) is mold growth. Mold is always undesirable in a collection. It causes irreversible and often devastating damage.

Mold spores are naturally present in the air around us, and it is impossible to eliminate them. However, it is only when the mold spores have sufficient nutrients, time, and moisture that they grow into destructive mold. As suitable nutrients are readily available in almost any environment, the route to controlling mold is controlling moisture. Without moisture, mold spores cannot grow.

The safe RH boundary usually cited to prevent mold growth is 65%. Below the safe RH boundary, mold will not grow at any temperature. In contrast, mold is very likely to grow at high RH. For example, at 85% RH, mold will probably appear in less than a week. Establishing what happens in borderline conditions (in RH between 60% and 70% with different temperatures) is a bit more challenging.

Chemical Damage

Chemical damage is caused by chemical reactions taking place within a material. The key reactions are hydrolysis and oxidation, which account for most natural aging processes.

Hydrolysis is a reaction between a substance and water that results in the chemical breakdown of the original substance and the formation of one or more new substances.

Oxidation is a reaction between a substance and oxygen, often resulting in physical breakdown.

Both temperature and RH affect chemical processes:

- Heat speeds up any chemical reaction (the rule of thumb is that the rate of reaction approximately doubles for every 5°C increase in temperature).
- RH is significant because some reactions require moisture before they can take place.

Mechanical Damage

Extremes of temperature or RH make many objects vulnerable to mechanical damage. For example, materials that become stiff or brittle when cold are more likely to break at low temperatures. Luckily, extremes are usually easy to avoid, except in rare cases such as sudden failure of an environmental control system. It is fluctuations in temperature or RH that cause the most mechanical damage. Unfortunately, these are less easily controlled and not as well understood.

The explanation for the dangers of fluctuations lies in the basic mechanical properties of materials:

- Inorganic and organic materials (e.g., metal, stone, paint, and wood) respond to temperature changes by expanding when hot and contracting when cold.
- Organic materials, which are hygroscopic, respond to changes in RH by shrinking when RH drops and swelling when RH climbs.[13]

THE FACILITY AND MECHANICAL REALITIES

The Rooms within the Internal Environment

The first understanding of the environmental conditions and how to maintain them is gained by understanding the facility's overall attributes and the specific room or rooms where the collection objects are to be stored or worked with. This knowledge and the choice of rooms designated for collections will inform the decisions to maintain the proper conditions for care of the objects within that environment. This assessment is sometimes termed "working with the design of the building envelope" and then with a methodical approach of the "box within a box" or the "room within a room."

The location of a building must take into account the function of the building—in the case of a museum, a repository for a collection of objects and their display and preservation. Factors contributing to its design and fabrication are the geologic stability and the ability to withstand climatic forces such as wind, rain, heat, earthquakes, landslides, and floods.

The location will also be influenced by the access to basic utilities, which include electricity, gas, water, sewage, and emergency services such as fire, ambulance, and police response if required. The spaces within this envelope are also subject to the ability to control and maintain the temperature and relative humidity.

Rooms immediately adjacent to outside walls will be more greatly affected by the exterior elements and changes than the rooms placed completely within the interior, which will be less subjected to the effects of temperature and humidity fluctuations in the outside environment.

The further the physical location of an interior room to the exterior opening of a building, the greater the reduction of the effects of the air exchange from the outside elements and levels of temperature and humidity. Controlling fluctuations of humidity can be difficult and will require infrastructure that is expensive and not easily adaptable to other facility configurations.

Entry points to an interior room are also advantageous in reducing outside elements such as pests, contaminants, and general security access. It does entail objects being handled for greater distances when required to leave the internal environment, but this can be easily managed with accommodating equipment and training practices.

Basement-Level Rooms

- Potential Benefits: excellent floor-loading capabilities, a potentially high-buffered environment, greater security, and better ability to control light exposure.
- Potential Drawbacks: flooding from ground water or interior plumbing and drains, no direct access to or from the exterior, requiring stairs, lifts, or ramps to access the rooms.

Ground-Level Rooms

- Potential Benefits: excellent access because of level grade, less danger from flooding, floor-loading capabilities if built on slab and increasingly better support than upper levels.
- Potential Drawbacks: less secure because of ease of access, conditions affected by exterior climatic conditions, heavy public use of nearby spaces.

Upper-Level Rooms

- Potential Benefits: limited danger from flooding, buffered environments, greater security control, reduced public access.
- Potential Drawbacks: floor-loading capabilities are greatly reduced, access limited to stairways and elevators, risks of roof-top leaks.

Control Strategies/Mitigating Shock and Vibration

An effective preservation strategy involves setting up control measures to counteract the action of potentially damaging forces. The general strategies for basic-, medium-, and high-level control are summarized below. They also incorporate priority issues for force control, which are also listed below in approximately decreasing order:

- earthquake (stabilization of buildings, hardware, and objects in high-risk areas);
- structural details (floors, roofs, artifact supports, hardware);
- handling (crating, uncrating, moving in-house, isolation from public);
- shipment (shipping hazards); and
- long-term wear (cumulative forces in storage or from repeated handling).

Control of damaging force levels is possible by a variety of individual features at three different levels of implementation: buildings, hardware, and procedures. Building-level controls are the most expensive to achieve. Large institutions will incorporate many of their control features here. Effective control is also possible at a lower cost at the hardware and procedural levels. For any level of implementation, individual features will enable a sequence of control stages to avoid, block, detect, and respond to the action of force agents. Each stage in the control sequence comes into play whenever a preceding one is either not feasible, or not possible, or fails. This establishes an effective line of defense against physical forces or other agents of deterioration. A general summary of control features by level of implementation is provided below.

1. Basic (Control of major risks)

Buildings
- Earthquake-resistant buildings in zones of seismic activity.
- Consider all nonstructural hazards (including monumental items such as sculptures) in seismic zones and secure as necessary.
- Ensure seismic stability in the design of pedestals, hangers, and mounts for large objects in seismic zones.
- Good, structurally sound buildings with adequate floor strength. Ensure that the use of existing buildings is appropriate for museum application.
- Attention to basic building design features (halls, doorways) to promote good access.
- Avoid flat roofs.
- Relocate vibration-sensitive equipment to ground floors, near load-bearing walls, or near support columns on upper floors to avoid vibration problems.

Hardware
- Rigid shelving and stabilization of all objects in seismic areas.
- Provide moving equipment (e.g., dollies, carts, lifts, slings) for prompt evacuation of objects when necessary.
- Basic isolation between the public and objects on display (cases, barriers).
- Specialized packaging for highly fragile or vulnerable items.
- Select appropriate storage surfaces and mounts for specific items.
- Use specially designed (high mass) tables or vibration isolators for sensitive equipment.

Procedures
- Use specialized carriers for highly valuable or fragile items, appropriately crated.
- Primary packaging on a basic level to protect selected fragile items from punctures, dents, scratches, abrasions, and minor impacts. (Primary

protection refers to a basic packaging treatment that enables easy handling of a fragile item. Protecting the item during shipment normally requires additional packaging.)

- Identify and protect highly susceptible items from routine handling while in storage, during display, and in transit.
- Secure all objects or packages in vehicles during transport.
- Provide staff training on handling fragile objects.
- Provide staff training in machine operation and in handling objects (rigging) up to 2,300kg or hire experienced handlers (riggers) for loads greater than 2,300kg.
- Acquire training and expertise in packaging requirements for vulnerable items.
- Provide security staff in exhibition areas.
- Ensure that object surfaces are clean before packing to avoid abrasion or forcing dirt into object surfaces.

2. Medium (Control for moderate- to high-intensity forces)

Buildings
- Provide specialized loading bays and handling equipment such as smooth lifts, load levelers, smooth soft floors, and wall finishes.
- Provide impact-absorbing door perimeters.

Hardware
- Provide gantry cranes for moving or reorienting heavy objects.
- Ensure seismic stabilization of small-to-medium-size objects.
- Transit framework and modular systems for transporting and handling large objects that travel. This may take the form of incorporated features that enable easy movement of large, heavy items during a multivenue exhibition.
- Primary packaging with the basic benefits that it provides (as discussed above).
- Basic packaging—good crates with adequate (typically at least 50mm) thickness of cushioning material.
- Well-designed mounts for storage, transport, and display.

Procedures
- Staff training in object susceptibility, object handling, mount making, and packaging; and
- High-level isolation of fragile items from the public in display areas (effective barriers, cases, alarms).

3. High (Control of all perceived risks)

Requires all of the above control strategies plus implementation of collection-specific needs determined by a comprehensive collection survey. Rank order and implementation of relevant building hardware and procedural features for collection.[14]

Primary Rooms and Locations within the Internal Environment

The following information will be presented in three sections relative to the primary areas where collection objects reside and collection care activities are undertaken within the internal environment of the museum.

Section 1: Objects in Collection Storage

Storage rooms vary per institution as do the collection objects they contain. Unless storage rooms have been designed as such in the original plans of the building's construction, the chances are that the rooms now being used may have been designed for another purpose. The rooms now used for storage of collection objects may not be the best physical space, but were thought to be effective and efficient for other collection needs.

The museum building structure that protects collections in storage is multilayered. The outer layer is the protective shell of the building or other structure (which, for example, might be a disused coal mine or an underground bunker rather than a conventional building). Within the building are segregated storage areas or rooms, within which are additional protective layers in the form of shelving, racking, and cabinets, crates, boxes, trays, and packing media. Each of these layers affords additional physical protection and buffering from environmental conditions, if carefully planned with the optimal conditions for each object or collection in mind.[15]

Proper museum storage should be highlighted in the museum's mission as a top priority in preserving and protecting the collection, which is entrusted to the museum trustees, directors, curators, and collection care staff. The dedication to creating and maintaining these spaces should be an ongoing commitment of support for trained staff, quality equipment, environmental maintenance, and budgetary investment for the present as well as future collection needs.

As storage is a primary role of the museum in preserving and caring for the collection, it is often not as high on the management's priority list as it probably should be. This secondary focus of priorities presents a continual challenge for the collection care staff to create standards that are best for the objects in their arrangement and protective housings and for managing and monitoring the activities related to collection objects within storage. The location of these rooms is also a challenge for the facility's security and maintenance staff to maintain limited access and the specific environmental requirements of collections. As each collection varies in the type of objects and their specific preservation needs, the storerooms become individual puzzle pieces where they reside and the interlocking combinations of the relationships of the museum's mission and the staff responsible for maintaining the collection.

Storage Environmental Requirements

The environmental requirements of collection storerooms are comparable to the general levels required within the museum gallery spaces. The collection storerooms have additional advantages in that they can be a box within a box (room within a room). These highlights include:

- heightened security with restricted access for individuals;
- entrances to the storage room kept to a minimum;
- internal environment less susceptible to fluctuations in temperature and humidity;
- light levels reduced and maintained;
- air filtration that can be specific to the space and maintained to control airborne particulates;
- the mitigation and management of pests; and
- microclimates created within to establish specific conditions for object preservation.

A unique highlight is the capability to create and house objects in individual microclimates in the form of cabinets or other housing methods required for specific objects' care and preservation. Cabinets can eliminate exposure to the external elements by the use of closed doors and custom gasket seals around doors. This sealed closure greatly reduces temperature and humidity fluctuations, pollutants, and pest infiltrations. With the doors closed, levels of light and access can be better controlled.

Light levels in storerooms need to be kept to a minimum and lamps turned off when not in use. Though many objects are in cabinets or are covered, the lights left on in spaces that are not occupied by staff are damaging to exposed objects and a waste of energy. Light levels can be monitored by motion sensors, which need to cover large areas to prevent staff from being left in the dark and unable to access the sensor if the lights are turned off.

Exit pathway lights emitting low levels of light need to be installed and maintained to prevent total darkness when lights are turned off or if power to the room is lost. Emergency flashlights with glow-in-the-dark markings have been used in many storerooms just as a secondary precaution to prevent a total blackout. Objects in collection storage will need to be monitored and cleaned within the schedule created for the collection on display. Though many objects are kept within a cabinet, many are not. A routine of cleaning the objects and replacing or washing dust covers is essential for keeping the object itself and its surrounding environment clean. Monitoring the objects in storage cabinets will reduce the risk of the object being potentially affected by internal off-gassing of any construction materials or in reaction to the other objects' inherent material properties.

Routine scheduled monitoring for pests within a storeroom is an ongoing process that needs to be done in a focused, methodical manner. Traps and fumigants need to be placed at each entry point from the exterior spaces such as hallways as well as holes in walls where there are pipe and electrical entries. The number of objects within the storeroom can be quickly contaminated if pests infiltrate the space. As objects are accessed and moved, one should check for possible infestation of the object being handled or any objects in the surrounding location.

Interior collections storerooms have the great advantage of maintaining a heightened level of security, because access is limited by the number of entrances, with minimal or no light exposure. For museum staff, restricting levels of access based on collection responsibilities creates a defined policy and procedure to keep essential personnel accountable for working with collection objects.

Video surveillance within the room can be monitored directly by the security staff at a central control room, and environmental conditions can be monitored as well, which will assist in correcting any changes if needed when the room is not occupied during various times of the day, week, and month.

Managing Storage

Managing a museum storeroom is a group effort of the key personnel in collection care, security, and facilities maintenance. A specific manager should be designated within the collection care staff to manage all activities related to the storerooms and be assisted by dedicated staff if possible. The activities of managing and working in a storeroom are similar to assembling a picture puzzle.

The first part of the puzzle is developing ongoing maintenance in a storeroom, and any specific needs that the collection may require. Factors to consider are as follows:

• Inherent physical characteristics: (material makeup, size, weight, shape). Example: Shelf of unglazed ceramics of similar sizes and weights;

- Type of objects: (ceramic bowls and pots). Example: Native American unglazed ceramic bowls and pots;
- Objects of cultural relationships: (same type of objects, from same cultural background and time period). Example: Native American ceramic pots made by the Navajo tribe; 1800s–1900s; and
- Objects of the same type and physical characteristics in combination with similar type of objects with similar characteristics and cultural background (Native American Navajo ceramics with Native American baskets made by the Plains Indians).

The puzzle and the adjacent pieces continue to be constructed in a logical format to provide accurate documentation and accountability of location as collections are used. The locations of collection objects can change on a frequent, if not daily, basis, depending on the active use and programming requirements of the collection. The puzzle combinations rely on the knowledge of the collection care staff and curators to orchestrate the best and most efficient usage of space. The pieces may be restricted to the appropriate environmental and housing conditions that are available to them in the allotted location, and the budget restraints.

This puzzle approach will change as objects are rotated off and on display, lent for defined periods of time, or segregated for restoration or treatment, and as new collection objects are acquired by the museum. The luxury of having a permanent designated location or home for an object would be desirable, but in the majority of collection storage spaces, this is never practical because of the museum's mission to acquire objects. In planning new storage facilities, surveys and percentages are planned for collection growth, but again this is still a challenge to the puzzle.

When designing a space for a new building, it is common to estimate future growth by determining the size of the present collection and adding 60–70% more space. Any variation such as the size of a new object or an unplanned donation of a collection can quickly alter any preplanned assumptions regarding the use of the space.

Some objects require a specific separation from other collection objects or a specific environmental control to best preserve and protect them. Because of these distinct requirements, there are fewer alternatives for consideration. Locations may need to be constructed and designated specifically for these storage needs.

- Vault: Objects such as jewelry, decorative arts, coins, and firearms of high value are iconic in significance and may need to be locked and placed within a secure environment that can be monitored and maintained according to the conditions required.

- Temperature sensitive: Objects made of certain metals, films, and plastics will be better protected in a lower temperature environment as compared to general storage.
- Hazardous materials: Objects treated with arsenic or specimen collections sealed in formalin or alcohol require to be kept in a vented, low-temperature room. These objects, no matter how they are housed, require labels indicating their hazardous contents so that the staff who come into contact with these objects are aware of their harmful properties. Handling precautions, limited access, and trained personnel for proper handling of these objects are essential.
- Weight-load restrictions: The weight of objects and the equipment housing them and the location in which they are placed need to be considered. Packing too many objects together in order to optimize space can have ruinous consequences.
- A box or tray packed too heavily with objects will compromise the structural integrity of the housing, causing it to buckle or break.
- A shelf in a cabinet that has too many objects placed upon it may bend or flex, causing it to buckle or spring back when the weight is removed.
- Large, heavy objects or several heavy objects on a pallet placed on the floor next to each other or on pallet racking may cause distortion of the floor or compromise the supporting frame of the rack.

The following is an explanation of common components found within storerooms to support and house collection objects. The information presented will focus on two areas: collection equipment for storage and object housings, and staff workspaces within the storeroom. More detailed information will be provided in the chapter "Working with Materials and Equipment" and in the reference source lists.

Purchasing Storage Equipment

When buying new storage equipment, it pays to invest in the very best that is affordable, because it is a long-term capital asset. Collection storage equipment will see hard use for many decades, and the cost in labor and temporary housing when removing collections in order to repair or replace underperforming equipment can be considerable. Equipment that fails in use can cause damage to people as well as collections, creating an insurance and liability issue. It pays to do research, talk to at least three reputable dealers, and review their products.

Examine performance tests and specifications, and talk to at least three reference customers from each firm. One option is to buy a prototype unit and put it into use during the planning period so that the museum personnel can subject it to testing for capacity, adaptability, sturdiness, and quality finish. Future availability of the equipment and its parts is also an important criterion.[16]

The above approach to research and purchase of the best storage equipment for your needs is critical. Recognizing it as a long-term investment is the most efficient and cost-effective solution, and will ensure the best storage capabilities you can have to properly store and provide additional protective layers for your collection objects.

Do not look at, or make the mistake of approaching, this investment as a temporary or simple solution. Work with commercial vendors who specialize in storage housings and equipment. They can develop the best and the most logical space solution for the collections and the rooms where they will be housed and located. The U.S. National Park Service has created a few general guidelines for flexible, adaptable, and compatible storage cabinets, which work for a large variety of objects. These documents are basic in their presentation but have been developed over years of work within many locations, considering space restraints and budgetary restrictions, and provide some common general solutions for a variety of collection object types.

The documents are found online in the *Conserve-O-Grams* section of the NPS Website. I find that three of the leaflets of particular interest are 4/1,

Figure 6.7   Common Storage Housings. *Source:* Author.

Figure 6.8 **Common Storage Housings.** *Source*: Author.

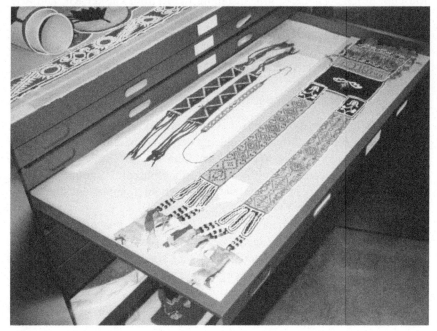

Figure 6.9 **Common Storage Housings.** *Source*: Author.

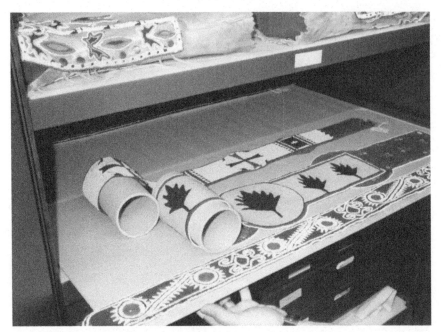

Figure 6.10   Common Storage Housings. *Source*: Author.

Museum Storage Cabinets; 4/3, Installing the Retrofit Gasket Kit; and 4/13 Modifying Museum Storage Cabinets. These leaflets may be somewhat dated in technical information but will give you an overarching picture of what type of cabinets and equipment can work in unison with other types to give the best solution. Understanding the big picture will ensure the best solution.

Storage Housings and Equipment Examples

- Common housings include boxes, trays, supports, mounts, frames, mats, and other specific enclosures for placing the object within to protect it from the elements and/or assist in ease of handling.
- Research can be conducted by observing other museums' storage housings, locations where they reside, and the combination of equipment support for the housed object.
- Archival material suppliers offer storage housings that are available in standardized sizes or can be customized to the particular needs of an object.
- Premade boxes that accommodate different sizes and weights of objects can be purchased in different strengths and archival grades.
- Standard materials can be purchased that collection care staff can design, and with which they can construct, a customized housing to fit the needs of a particular object.

- Nonarchival housings are extremely affordable but will require a barrier or buffer to reduce the transference of their acidic content.
- Considerations in using acidic materials need to balance the object's material makeup and the time it will reside in the storage housing.
- "Temporary" can quickly change to long term for any housing system and its contents. Be very wary of this!
- Investment in archival housing materials is the optimal solution to creating the best protective environment for any object.

In regard to investing in archival materials used in housing storage materials, the old truism prevails:

Better to have it and not need it, than to not have it and then need it.

Commercial General Warehousing Equipment

Commercial warehousing companies offer a variety of cost-effective, quality solutions for general equipment, sometimes termed "furniture" designs. Research the structural materials, paint qualities for off-gassing properties, and weight-load limitations by requesting material data sheets from the manufacturer. Basic cabinets, flat files, shelves, and pallet racking can be

Figure 6.11   Textile Flat Storage. *Source*: Author.

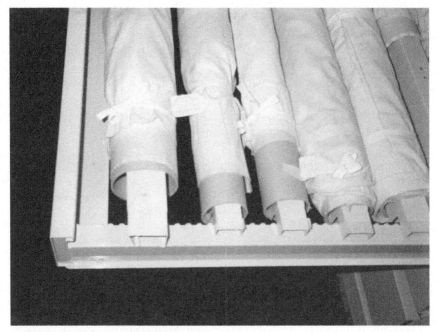

Figure 6.12   Rolled Textile Cabinet. *Source*: Author.

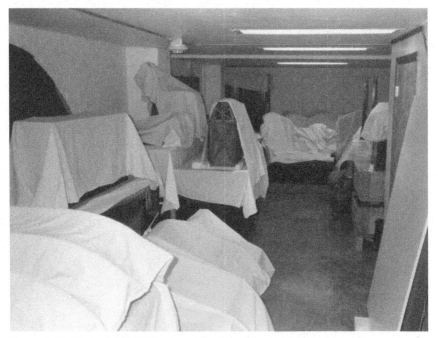

Figure 6.13   Dust and Light Covers on Furniture. *Source*: Author.

purchased and modified where needed to best fit the storage requirement of the object. Research what materials are best for archival barriers and supports, and are adaptable to the construction design of the base equipment. Commercial warehousing suppliers are also excellent resources for handling equipment that is compatible with the storage housing and equipment furniture.

Commercial Museum Specialty or Custom-Designed Equipment

Commercial museum storage companies specialize in providing the museum community with advanced material, technical research, and structural components built to a museum's particular collection needs or specifications. Over the last fifty years, the industry knowledge and professionalism these companies have acquired, working alongside private and museum conservators and multiple disciplines of collection care staff, have led to their becoming an excellent resource in planning for storage projects. The following is a list of products that these companies produce and a basic explanation of their design and function.

Figure 6.14 Large Open Shelving . *Source*: Fisher, NPS San Francisco.

Free-Standing Open Shelves

These shelving units follow a similar structural design to their counterparts in general warehousing companies. Customized versions may be created by building them to a specific size or strength of material. Customized features may include shelves with additional support for weight, perforations to allow water from fire suppression to penetrate lower levels in a greater flow pattern, and customized edges to allow barriers to be placed inside the shelf unit, which will retard slippage of the barrier material.

Pallet Racking

Pallet racking units follow a similar structural design to their counterparts in general warehousing companies. These units can be custom-made to fit various sizes and shapes, and access to objects per location. Access to equipment and object load must be accounted for in allowing efficient room to maneuver between shelving units.

Long-Span Shelving

Long-span shelving units follow a similar structural design to their counterparts in general warehousing companies. These units can be custom-made to fit various sizes and shapes, and provide access to objects per location. In many examples, these are designed to hold large, heavy, and awkward types of objects, which dictates that they be customized to a specific object in some instances. Access to equipment and object load must be accounted for in allowing efficient room to maneuver between shelving units.

Painting or 2-D Object Racks

These units are commonly designed for the storage of framed or unframed paintings, framed works on paper and other objects such as mirrors, architectural components, or sculptural objects in low relief. They can be customized to allow for specific depths between racks and made of heavy-gauged metal to accommodate large-size objects. These racks can be built to be accessed by pulling a unit out singly to an adjacent open floor space or by rolling the unit in a parallel fashion to each rack, as in to a modular storage cabinet.

Flat File Units

Flat file units are made to store flat works on paper or other materials such as textiles, which need to be kept in a horizontal position. These units can be made to store large-size works, and can take a considerable amount of weight per file drawer or tray load. The overall cabinet can be designed to be

Figure 6.15 Pallet Racking. *Source*: J. Carey, Artex FAS.

compatible with other flat file units so that they can be stacked to support the additional weight.

Custom Pallet or Support Units

Many objects may be unique in their size, weight, or fragility, which may require custom-made pallets or supports to be built. These custom-made units will allow the object to be handled and transported on the same unit so as not to be handled on and off a piece of transport equipment. Many of these supports can be designed in such a way that when the object is chosen for display, the display plinth or base can be built around it, and the object can remain on the original support.

Storage Cabinets

Cabinets within a storeroom can house a variety of objects and offer an additional layer of protection by creating the box-within-a-box approach to space. Their best attribute is that cabinets can be customized to create a controlled microclimate for specific objects. The following is a list of customized features that can be built into these cabinets:

- Windowed doors for viewing the objects within prevent unnecessary opening, thus maintaining the internal environmental conditions.
- Gaskets designed to create a seal around the door frame eliminate airflow and potential airborne pollutants filtering into the interior and onto the objects.
- Ventilation systems can be added to the doors that allow air to flow through a cabinet, but various forms of filtering pads are placed within these systems to capture any airborne pollutants.
- Ventilation systems can be built to extract air through and out of the cabinet for objects that continue to off-gas because of their inherent properties or materials that give off a high level of toxic fumes in their state of preservation. Example: Wet-tissue specimens and the chemicals in their container can often have an old seal which is compromised and eventually will leak.
- Drawers can be custom-built to accommodate size and weight specifications. The design must account for the type of track-slide that will support the overall weight of the loaded drawer.
- Drawer-tracking systems can be designed so that a drawer can slide out to a central balancing point to be accessed or easily detached from the track and fully removed from the cabinet, which then can act as a handling tray.
- Drawer-tracking systems can be designed where the track mechanism is a telescoping design, so the drawer can be pulled out and be supported securely without falling away from or off the track.

Figure 6.16   Standard Storage Cabinets. *Source*: 2015 Museum of Fine Arts, Boston.

- Tray-tracking systems can be designed that allow the tray to simply slide in and out of a track with minimal detachment of the track. Extra caution must be maintained when handling this design so that the tray does not tilt or fall away as it is being pulled out of the cabinet.

- Tracks for holding the drawers or trays can be made in such a way that they are easily removed and adjustable if changes are required for the configuration of the drawer spacing.
- Tracking systems can be designed to take extremely large objects and weight loads. Example: Systems where the textile is rolled on a tube and placed on an insert, which sits within the drawer framework that moves in and out of the cabinet. The rolled textile can be lifted on and off the framework with relative ease and safety.

Versatility within Cabinet Design

Versatility when designing custom cabinets should be a high priority. Consideration should be given to how compatible these cabinets would be if they were rearranged within a space or moved to another location in the future to accommodate these possible changes.

Due to economic constraints, many times the entire outfitting of the storeroom cannot be afforded at one time. Therefore, it is highly desirable to choose systems that will be compatibly expandable to the growing collection.

Cabinet interiors and the basic cabinet shell should be designed such that if the type, size, or weight of the contents needs to be changed, so too can the structural components within the cabinet, that is, shelves, trays or drawers.

The design of standard cabinet hardware is crucial as it must allow for different cabinets using the same hardware type as the others. If replacements or additional components are needed, they can be interchanged between cabinets and be compatible with one another. It is very important that when purchasing new cabinets, the additional hardware is supplied by the manufacturer or is purchased and kept as replacement stock. Designs in custom-made hardware change and can make the old system unavailable for replacement when needed.

Compactor High-Density Mobile Storage Cabinets

Compactor cabinet designs offer an excellent way to store a large number of objects in a small space by having the cabinets built on mobile carriages, which allow the space to be condensed or compacted, cabinet to cabinet. The average space gained is 50–70% more than the footprint of the same-sized cabinets being placed in the free-standing footprint.

The initial cost of compactor cabinets is high because of the mechanical components that are required for the cabinets to move in such a way that a compacted space arrangement is created. The initial expense of purchase quickly balances and becomes less with depreciation over a period of time. When factoring the basic facility maintenance costs per year (per square foot or square meter) and the factor of the additional amount of space gained for other storage needs, the investment turns out to be cost-effective.

The objects to be stored within the compactor cabinets need to be housed and padded to eliminate the shock and vibration created by the movement of the cabinets on the carriages. The manual or mechanical operation for moving the cabinets is designed for smooth movement and resistance to vibration and initial shock when carriage bumpers come in contact.

Depending on the type of objects being stored and the ease of accessibility, multiple levels of cabinets can be designed and they can still move efficiently on the mobile-track systems. Additional stabilizer supports can be added to the original design to prevent tipping or swaying motion.

Safeguards should be added in the form of sensor devices to stop motion if obstructed and alarms being activated when there is compaction of the cabinet. This is a primary safety precaution for staff working in the spaces between units and a secondary one for protecting the objects housed within.

The advances within the last twenty years in technical design and testing of the mechanical components to control movement, shock, and vibration and to reduce human error have made this type of storage cabinet a main feature in many new projects in renovation storage projects. Though it may not be advisable to store liquid containers of wet specimens on these systems, the continual advancements in technical design may soon offer a solution for storing more fragile objects in a compacted space to reduce their present free-standing storage footprint.

Other Components of Space Requirements in Storage

All storerooms need designated spaces other than locations to store objects, which are directly related to the activities that take place within a storeroom. Many of these rooms are essential while others need to be in close proximity to the storeroom. The following is a basic list of rooms that are essential or can be in close proximity.

Office: An office with a desk, phone, and computer is a bare minimum for the manager, or an additional space, if the manager has a separate office in another location.

Monitoring and Safety Spaces: Areas where environmental monitoring equipment and pest-management tools can be placed without obstruction should be designated. Fire alarms, fire extinguishers, protective gear, and first aid equipment should be kept in a visible area for easy access.

Equipment Space: Designated space must be allotted for handling equipment to be stored for use within the storeroom. When equipment is used, it must be marked to the storeroom it services and be returned to this location so as to make it available for the next individual who requires it.

Tool and Material Space: Space for general hand tools and handling materials needs to be allocated in a similar fashion as for equipment space. Areas can also be allocated throughout the storeroom where items such as protective gloves, tape measures, pencils, note pads, and so on are easily available.

Work tables or surfaces: Space should be allocated for tables or work surfaces where objects are placed for handling, general packing, treatment, or viewing. Cabinets themselves can sometimes be designed as a workspace, which will also assist in easily handling the objects in and out of the adjacent storage location.

Open Floor Space: These spaces need to be located around the storeroom. This will allow different storage activities to be undertaken, such as unpacking a crate, staging objects on carts waiting to go out of or come into storage, and basic general viewing of objects.

Pathways between storage furniture need to be designed so as to allow enough space for equipment to be maneuvered within the storeroom. Pathways should not be used for temporary storage at any time and must be left open and accessible for staff evacuation if required.

Photography, conservation treatment, and mount or exhibition preparation may be required at times, but these activities are better undertaken at another location in secure and close proximity to storage.

Section 2: Collection Objects in Galleries for Display

One of the primary missions of the museum is to interpret cultural heritage through the collection objects in its stewardship by placing them on public display. When on display, these objects require a unique approach for collection care as compared to when they are in storerooms and other rooms within the building where they may reside for related activities. The main difference is that the objects are available for viewing by the public and need to be cared for and monitored in a specific manner.

The following section will address the basic collection care needs that are encountered in the various spaces and how they are maintained and monitored. The best way to research is to contact or visit other museums to find out how they have accommodated these needs of collection care display within their buildings.

Temperature and Relative Humidity Levels

Obtaining additional support in maintaining temperature and relative humidity level requirements beyond the ambient levels within each gallery can be approached by creating the box within a box (room within a room) for specific object needs. The most common is the display case that is designed to prevent external fluctuations while covering the object with a vitrine so that it can be seen. The interior environment of the display case can be altered and maintained at a desired humidity level with the use of conditioned silica products or mechanical humidifiers, depending on the object's specific requirements. Extreme cases may require an entire room to be the display case, controlled and monitored to specific levels. The doorway and entrance to the room then becomes the access point to which the fluctuation effects are minimized.

Light Levels

Light levels will vary per object on display and will depend on the viewer's ability to see the object comfortably in balance with the light-level requirements for the object. The specific requirements are based on the individual object chosen, its inherent properties, and the length of time for which it is displayed. The method of display will also dictate how an object is viewed and the light levels needed to adequately view the object. As with any display, scheduled monitoring of the light level, especially on sensitive objects, is important.

Objects Monitored and Cleaned

Objects displayed in permanent gallery spaces will require a scheduled program of monitoring for their condition and the potential risks they are exposed to by being on public display. By conducting a regular cleaning program, the collection care staff can monitor the uncovered objects and assess the residual effect of airborne particulates combining with the moisture in the air, which in time can cause structural deterioration depending on the material makeup of the object. The objects in display cases should be monitored for internal off-gassing of construction materials that could affect the object's condition.

The added benefit of a scheduled cleaning program is that the objects and the display cases are at their best for the public's viewing pleasure. The internal benefit of the program is that curatorial and collection care staff and security and other departmental staff will be observant in maintaining this ongoing level of presentation. The benefits of a cleaning program and the preventive care measures need support within the overall preventive conservation and exhibition programming of an institution.

Depending on the size and material type of the object, the cleaning may be a complicated task to conduct on a regular basis without encroaching into public hours. Though this may seem awkward to the viewing public, it is an excellent time to educate them on the behind-the-scenes responsibilities that are undertaken to maintain the collection.

Special Security Requirements

Objects may require special security dictated by their physical characteristics, lender requirements stated in loan agreements, and the location where the object is being displayed within the exhibit space. Basic security protocol may require the object to be covered with a vitrine or, if uncovered, placed beyond the reach of the viewing public on a structural base or plinth. The most effective form of security is the physical presence of a security guard. The need to have a particular object viewed by a dedicated guard is expensive and may require other approaches to secure a specific object or area. Other approaches may be achieved by custom display cases with security measures such as locking devices of vitrine covers, alarms that produce an audio notification or that are transmitted in a direct notification to the main security office.

The Display Case within the Gallery Environment

The display case within the gallery environment acts as a box within a box (room within a room) for protecting the object as well as displaying it. As with storage cabinets, the microclimate environment created in a display case has many functions and can be designed for the many challenges in making a stable environment for the object. The advances made in research by companies manufacturing museum cases in conjunction with private and museum conservators continue to increase the levels of quality and standards. The effects of the microclimate, the materials used, the type of object or combinations of objects to be displayed create a similar puzzle as in the microclimate of storage cabinets. To properly display and protect the object within the display case, spend time observing different types of cases, and work directly with manufacturers who can assist with their knowledge of the current research, materials, and techniques.

A well-designed display case has two primary functions: to display the object in an aesthetic presentation, and to create a microclimate to protect the object from the external environmental elements within the gallery spaces. The following is a list of customized features which can be built into these display cases:

- To protect the object from being touched by the viewing public, the display case can offer a variety of clear protective glazing elements that will allow the viewer to see the object but not touch the object.
- The clear viewing panels can be made of glass or cast acrylic sheeting. Depending on the number of sides exposed for viewing and the weight of the glazing, a frame may be needed to support the glazing.
- Glazing can also be treated to block UV light, IR light, and reduce reflections, and to be shatterproof within limitations.

Figure 6.17   Gallery Exhibition Display Cases. *Source*: Author.

- A common display design is a case that allows the object to be seen in the round. Each side of the vitrine is constructed of cast acrylic panels, which when adhered and polished create a clear edge and leak-proof weld on five sides. The sixth side is open and attaches directly to the display base.
- At the point where the vitrine attaches to the base is an interlocking configuration. Often, this design is in the form of a rabbet (or slot), which is slightly bigger than the thickness of the glazing. The vitrine sits down within the rabbet of the case deck (1.5″ +) creating a depth so that the

Figure 6.18   Gallery Exhibition Display Cases. *Source*: Author.

hardware can then be attached through adjacent holes between the display case deck and the corresponding holes in the base of the vitrine glazing.
- A gasket is placed into the rabbet that will conform to the glazing edge to create a seal that eliminates any air exchange between the internal and external environments.
- Custom hardware can be used to attach the vitrine to the base to create the tight seal and, more importantly, to ensure a tamper-proof security system that cannot be easily accessed.
- Security hardware and locking devices can be hidden from the general viewing. The design of the hardware and the tools should be unique so that they cannot be opened with common tools but only by a specialized tool.
- Alarms can be installed that activate when motion is detected on the case, which can result in a direct audio alarm near the case or activation of a signal directly to the security control room for notification.
- The microclimate can be stabilized to control humidity levels within the space, which can be maintained for specific object requirements. Interior compartments are built within the case to allow humidity controls such as silica products or other systems to be added to assist in maintaining the RH levels at the specific percentage.
- The interior compartments can be designed to be accessible from the exterior of the case for changing control systems or monitoring devices without harming or handling the object while on display.
- These interior compartments can assist in air filtration by reducing the induction of dust and other pollutants through passive exchange or other mechanical means of positive pressure airflow.

- Other mechanical supports can be designed to assist humidity or temperature monitoring devices as required to control the desired microclimate environment.
- The construction materials used inside the case and those connected to the microclimate environment need to be inert or have an inert material, which will create an impermeable barrier so that no off-gassing or penetration of pollutants can occur.
- Poplar, a common wood known for its low-warping capabilities, is used in combination with a hardwood veneer plywood as a case wall or panel elements. Wood surfaces can be isolated from the display areas using polyethylene/aluminum laminate, with the generic name "Marvelseal," which creates an impermeable layer of protection.
- Certain types of water-based paints can be used, but all paints require drying and off-gassing periods of a minimum of three weeks, a time constraint that is to be reckoned with in the installation schedule during display changeovers.
- Fabric-lining materials need to be Oddy-tested to ensure that they pass a sodium azide test for sulfur.
- Some fabrics may require washing and cleaning to eliminate sizing additives or coloring agents coming into contact with the object.

Figure 6.19 Versatile Wall Cases. *Source*: Author.

Figure 6.20   Interchangeable Cabinets. *Source*: Author.

- Case decks for the interior buildup of the display are often constructed of acrylic expanded PVC or aluminum panels. Inserts, blocks, or mounts are commonly made of acrylic, aluminum, polyethylene foam, or brass supports.
- Cases need to be designed such that they can be attached to the floor, or to an adjacent plinth or wall, or if freestanding, there must be a way to add

weight to them to create a ballast to reduce or eliminate their possible tipping or toppling if hit.
- The display case also acts as a rigid line of defense against pests or rodents.

Versatility within Display Case Designs

- Versatility within display case design follows a similar approach as in the design of storage cabinets. Consider the other possibilities for which other types of objects could be displayed within the case.
- Many cases are designed to a specific style of object display, for example, table-top cases where only flat works can be laid for display and viewed from above. The table-top for larger objects will afford you a versatile footprint to arrange single large objects or multiples of small objects.
- Cases may be designed and used within a particular gallery or section of the museum. The case profiles should be uniform and consistent to other cases within the museum so that when interchanged they can be painted to match the new gallery and its color scheme where required.
- Internal space compartments for concealing microclimate components, and security and monitoring equipment should be a consistent part of the design to allow interchanging of components, which in turn, will service a variety of special requirements needed for display.
- The system design for attaching cases to the floor, wall, or plinths or for adding ballast needs to be versatile to accommodate a variety of sizes and weights of specific objects and the required space where they are located.
- Accounting for tipping or toppling of a case can vary according to the location in which it is placed. An example would be areas where there is heavy traffic flow, and the weight of the object makes the case extremely top heavy and easily vulnerable to impact.
- Cases should be designed in such a way that the staff can easily move and handle all components for security, microclimate, and monitoring devices. There should be uniformity in design for mechanisms among various case styles and components.
- Security hardware needs to be made of tamper-proof hardware, easily hidden and discreet but accessible and universal for the trained staff who will be working with the cases.

Permanent Galleries

The permanent galleries in a museum highlight examples of the collection and are commonly arranged by cultural relevance, chronological groupings, or by object type. Changing the displays in a scheduled rotation program requires staff, time, and resources in collection care. I will divide the explanation of these programming types and activities into three categories: short term, long term, and special exhibition display in the museum's permanent galleries.

Short-Term Programmed Displays

Short-term displays depend on the active participation of the curators and the collection care staff in changing the displays according to a scheduled rotation program. The opportunity to exhibit items on a more frequent schedule gives curators an opportunity to present the depth of their existing collection and in comparison with objects on loan to a new display.

The collection care activities involved in a short-term changeover can involve many hours of attention to documentation, inspection, treatment, preparation, and actual movement of the objects to the particular gallery space. Oftentimes, these objects may have never been displayed before, and the opportunity for display also becomes an opportunity for restoration if time, budgets, and staff commitment can be allocated.

Short-term display changeovers can become much like a small exhibition, depending on the number of objects and the amount of work needed to make it happen. Objects will first be handled in storage for documentation, initial inspection for condition, and final selection by the registrar, conservator, and curator. Once the final list of objects has been confirmed, preparation begins with the inspection by the designer, installers, and conservation staff to establish how the objects will be safely displayed.

The specific focus of preparation will then involve the possible restoration of the object by conservation, mounts fabricated to support and feature the object in a specific manner, and the technical requirements to meet the design of the display. The scheduling of all of this work will be based on the original concept by the curator in discussions with the conservators as to the condition of the objects and with the designer as to the space that they may require. Building from the initial estimation of time, this will establish the overall schedule and the allocation of time appropriate for all the combined collection care activities.

Other short-term changeovers are dictated by certain object types, usually those which are subject to limited exposure to light (works on paper, textiles, or organic material). Scheduled rotations for these objects are calculated by balancing time on display with time in storage, where the light-sensitive object "rests."

The objects requiring a short-term changeover will need to be combined with other objects included in the display. The workload of collection care activities will need to be adjusted to that of other activities that the collection care staff may be undertaking with other projects. The short-term changeover will involve attention to the environmental needs of the objects. The galleries should have an established existing temperature and humidity level, which is comparable to that in collection storage. If an object needs different temperature and humidity levels, then the design of display needs to accommodate this in the construction of specific cases, microclimate environments, and security devices.

Long-Term Programmed Displays

Long-term display is established when the galleries are first being designed and built or when a major renovation is undertaken to the overall museum or a section of a museum. Objects selected to be put on permanent display are deemed significant by the curator or director to represent the collections. These objects may or may not be of the highest quality because of the long-term exposure they will undergo. Though the objects may be of a lesser quality, they are chosen to represent the interpretive and study attributes for the education and interest of the viewing public.

The second criterion in the choice of objects for long-term display is that the object's inherent properties are stable enough to endure the long-term exposure to light, fluctuations in temperature and RH, and airborne pollutants, if placed on open display.

The selection process and collection care activities follow a similar path to that of the short-term display in selecting the objects, assessing conservation treatment, and designing the display, again with all related to the specifics of the individual object.

The planning process of new galleries being built or existing galleries being renovated creates the need for a project-based schedule, typically to be conducted over a long period of time and in relation to continuing other standard collection programming activities. Sometimes the capabilities of the staff and their schedule require that the museum postpone or suspend regular collection programming while the major project is being undertaken so as not to overload staff and facilities, which could lead to high costs.

Objects placed on long-term open display (as compared to a case or closed display) are subjected to all the potential changes of environmental conditions within the space they are displayed. These objects are also at risk through public contact. Whether the objects are displayed in a shared gallery space or are placed singly in open halls or courtyards, there are fewer protective measures that can be maintained in comparison to other forms of display.

The first line of defense is the display plinth, base, or pedestal on which the object is placed. The height and depth of this display design will prevent the object from being reached by the viewing public. Stanchions can also be placed around the object to create a barrier between the viewer and the object. In some settings, where a physical barrier could detract from the viewing pleasure, a line is placed on the floor, which passively indicates to the public that they should not cross that point. The same approach can be maintained with a security beam that is unseen, but when crossed activates an audio alarm.

Security staff cannot view all the objects at the same time that the public is viewing them. The museum guard, however, has the best opportunity to educate the public regarding the reasons for not touching the objects or displays, and this basic information should be a key component in the security staff's training. Appropriate signage located near the object can remind the viewer not to touch it, and explanations in the museum brochure given to the public at the admission desk can highlight the importance of these preventive measures.

Cleaning or monitoring of objects during public hours may be required because of the length of time it takes to work on a particular object. The benefit of doing this work in public hours is that the public will be educated regarding the preventive measures being undertaken by the museum staff responsible for collection care.

Visual Storage Display

This style of display gives the museum and its curators the opportunity to present to the public a large variety of objects of a similar type or relationship in their cultural background in proximity to each other. Although it is called "open" storage, this display showcases the objects behind a glass wall to create a view into an interior storeroom. The objects are displayed closely together in a similar fashion to that within the traditional storeroom. Creating this room as a complete display space affords environmental controls in a similar fashion as in a display case (box within a box and room within a room).

When displayed in a visual storage open display, objects can be placed in the round to create multiple viewing angles. The cleaning and monitoring of the open display becomes very difficult because many objects in close proximity to each other will require more handling and moving in order to reach certain objects.

This display style has also been designed in some gallery spaces in such a way that the glass wall for viewing the interior room allows the public to look directly into the adjacent working storeroom of the museum. This approach to the combination of spaces gives the public a unique opportunity to see and be educated about the work of collection care within an institution.

Special Exhibition Programmed Displays

Gallery spaces dedicated to special or traveling exhibitions are usually constructed in such a way as to give the museum the flexibility to take on a variety of display options. The versatility of these spaces is essential for exhibitions that have many object types, protective environments, and security and loan requirements that are contracted by lending institutions for their objects in these exhibitions.

Generally, many of the environmental features for monitoring and maintaining the conditions within these spaces are the same as within the other permanent gallery spaces in the building. The following is a list of some of the specific features that special exhibitions may have for the collection care needs.

The overall location of these rooms is primarily dedicated to giving easy access to the general public to enter. The spaces are commonly found on the ground floor in the vicinity of the public entrance to the building, with direct or close access to a large hall or open space to accommodate events and functions that are affiliated with official celebratory events, school and tour assemblies, educational programs, or the exhibition-related retail shop. These extra features emphasize the need to take into account the requirements for environmental and security measures that are unique to this space.

Placing the location of special exhibition spaces adjacent to other collection care areas and related activities is desirable. The proximity satisfies the need for easy access and compatibility to short handling routes, and the need for clear access to freight elevators, collection storerooms, and loading dock facilities. The primary importance of this compatibility of space is, first, for the safety of the objects to be transported and protected, and, second, for the efficiency of the staff and the related activities required during a special exhibition.

Large-scale objects must often be brought into these spaces by other routes, which can require removing doors and frameworks, windows or walls, and special equipment and trained staff to operate them. Depending on the object, the costs of hiring additional expertise, handling the logistics of the move, and the material and equipment for such display will dictate the feasibility of the object's actually being displayed.

The special exhibition rooms are designed specifically to be versatile and to accommodate different design formats on a continual basis. The interior walls are custom-built to a specific exhibition and are subsequently dismantled and destroyed, or refurbished and used again for other exhibitions. Similarly, display plinths and bases are designed and custom-built to accommodate the objects, but can also be refurbished for the next exhibition.

Interior walls, plinths, bases, display cases, and other peripheral components are subjected to change of paint color per exhibition. The type of paint to be used and the length of time the paint has to dry and off-gas are crucial factors that must be taken into account for scheduling between the changeovers.

Even within the special exhibition space, there may be exhibitions that require segregated areas to accommodate a specific environmental chamber.

If a display case cannot contain the object, then a separate room within a room needs to be designed and built. These separate spaces may require HVAC units to be designed into the space of the room and specifically monitored and maintained. Dust filtration units are sometimes added to a special exhibition space to reduce the dust or airborne particulates created by the larger number of individuals moving through the space.

Controlling lighting is a common cause for this design of a room within a room for a highly sensitive object to be displayed or a video to be projected in an appropriately darkened space. Motion-activated sensors can also be installed, so lights are turned on when a viewer is present and then turned off when no one is occupying the space.

Special exhibition display cases vary by object. The primary function of a case is to act as a microclimate to maintain a specific temperature and humidity as well as to reduce the levels of pollutants by creating a sealed environment. Interior compartments are built to be accessed from the exterior of the case without harming or handling the object on display. These compartments house silica packets and air filtration and monitoring devices which control the microclimate to create the desired environment. In some designs, the monitoring devices are incorporated as part of the display, so the readings can be easily seen. These cases should always be designed and constructed with materials that will not off-gas and potentially affect the object.

Security requirements for special exhibitions are heightened because of the object's value, lender requirements, and volume of visitor traffic, which increases in these spaces. Display cases are also designed to accommodate special security requirements such as customized hardware, tools, and alarms that sound off or send notification directly back to the security control rooms. Security staff are placed in strategic locations, and cameras are positioned to cover and record all areas where people can be seen in the room during and after hours.

Events associated with a special exhibition opening and ongoing educational and tour programs must be monitored to prevent food being served or consumed near the objects and their displays. Preparation for these events often takes place during the final days leading up to the opening of the exhibition. Collection activities are often compromised by those of the event planning, and conflicts can arise concerning access routes to freight elevators, hallways, and loading docks. Preplanning logistics of all events with the various groups involved is essential to protecting the objects being handled and displayed.

Display Spaces Other Than Permanent Galleries

Collection objects are often displayed in nonpublic areas in a museum. These spaces are often limited to noncollection care museum staff, with limited or no security present. The objects selected are from a secondary collection, are less valuable, very durable objects, and used more as decorative components than for interpretive display. Though these objects may be termed less valuable, equated to less important, they still need to be given the same attention and care as the rest of the collection and must be monitored and cleaned on a regular basis. A list of spaces where these types of objects are displayed and how the objects should be safely displayed is provided below.

Director's Office, Board or Conference Rooms

Generally, these rooms are where the collections should be represented and displayed because the business of the museum is conducted here and the congenial atmosphere is highlighted by collection objects being seen and even used. Because of the exposure and possible wear and tear on these objects, the selection should be made with the approval of the curator and conservator, in concert with the director. These decisions should be justified for such use and documented in the object's record. Handling and caring for these objects still needs to be done by collection care staff unless otherwise approved. Artworks on walls should be located in safe locations where they will not come into contact with people walking by, or have chairs and tables bumping against them, or be directly exposed to sunlight.

Patrons' Lounges and Private Outside Courtyards

These are locations where a select group of museum members are allowed access to meet and consume food and drink, as in the case of collection objects being displayed in nonpublic areas. These spaces are generally occupied by a larger number of people on a more frequent basis. In most instances, the objects displayed in these locations are two-dimensional framed works or small sculptures. Furniture and other decorative arts should be used as decorative elements only and not used in the manner for which they were originally constructed. An early twentieth-century Tiffany vase should not hold flowers, nor should a Sèvres teapot serve Darjeeling tea. Objects displayed in both the interior space or an open exterior courtyard must be able to withstand the rigors of their environments. Handling and caring for these objects must be done by collection care staff unless otherwise approved.

Staff Offices and Hallways

In many museums, staff offices, which have limited public access, generally have collection objects on display. There should be a policy outlining the specifics as to whose office and what objects can be used for display.

The reception area and the hallways to the conference rooms often have collection objects or decorative components. Framed exhibition posters or decorative elements from former exhibitions tend to decorate offices and hallways, where previously collection objects had been displayed.

As collection care has improved and the importance of how to preserve and care for objects has increased, so too have the restrictions placed on the use of collection objects increased. When I started my museum career, we were allowed to handle objects for many events in a variety of locations that would now not even be considered. Often, locations and objects were dictated by the politics of the event or the office or room in which the objects were to be displayed. In 1987, it was still common to smoke cigarettes in private offices, and during that time, curators and some other staff smoked even in storage!

Section 3: Other Locations Where Collection Objects Reside

There are many areas in an institution where collection objects reside for certain periods of time because of their particular needs such as size and condition, treatment, inspection, imaging, or temporary storage. These rooms need to have the same climate-controlled environment as found in collection storage or on display.

These rooms should have access to one another and to main storerooms so as to reduce movement between spaces. Sometimes, these rooms may have multiple collection activities taking place or are shared with other noncollection departments and their activities. Space in a museum is always a hot commodity, and allocating areas that are specifically outfitted for collection care is a challenge not easily met when programming and public spaces tend to be in the forefront of the museum's mission.

The following are examples of spaces in a museum where objects reside other than in storage or on display. These are just some of the basics, and further information and research is provided in the appendix of this book. The best research is to contact other museums in your region and take a tour to see how they configure collection care rooms within their building.

Conservation Labs

The conservation lab offers facilities that are found in no other collection area in the museum. Here one can find specialized equipment such as treatment lights, fumigation extraction systems for chemical use, specially designed work tables, and other specific equipment for treatment, research inspection, condition reporting, mount making and other related activities.

Conservation labs are secure areas with limited access. The activities undertaken in conservation require limited access because the objects placed in the lab can be in vulnerable states of disassembly, awaiting restoration or in the process of preparation for display.

Imaging Services Studio

The imaging services studio is a secured location with technical equipment such as cameras, lights, backdrops, filters, and power boxes to produce a range of images required of collection programming, publications, and marketing.

Objects are brought to this location for the purpose of imaging and should therefore be in this location for a minimum length of time. Objects are often handled only by designated handlers and are not touched by the photographer.

The object can be in a very vulnerable state in this location as the photographer's equipment and work environment is often cluttered, and it can be difficult to maneuver within. Power cords, light stands set at obscure angles, and some areas of the workspace are exposed to limited or reduced light while work is in progress.

Mount-Making Studio

The mount-making studio is best divided into two separate work areas. One is the clean room where the object can be fitted and materials stored. This room should be kept clean and not be used for other dust-producing activities related to the mount-fabrication process. The second room is adjacent to the clean room and is where the mount structure is fabricated. Depending on the type of material used to make the mount, equipment in this room is often used for metal or plastics fabrication. Common equipment includes grinders, drill presses, welders, and gas-powered torches as well as cutting tools and other tools needed to produce the mounts.

The object can be very vulnerable when being fitted as it may require being handled multiple times to make the accurate fit. When the object is in the clean room, it should be secured, or it should be taken to storage or the conservation lab until it is ready for its mount.

Preparation Shop

A dedicated preparation shop is a luxury in most museums. Most areas are designated on an ad hoc basis where all sorts of activities are conducted. Spaces used to conduct preparation work include an equipped woodshop, painting booth, temporary storerooms, or the actual gallery space before the object is installed. The majority of preparation work should not require the object's being present, but if so required, a secure location should be chosen. Any inspection or measurement of the object should be undertaken

Figure 6.21   Prepartor Carpenter Shop. *Source*: Author.

in a secure location such as storage or conservation lab, prior to display and movement to the display location.

Matting and Framing Room

The matting and framing room is a dedicated space where works on paper are mounted into a mat or display mount constructed in preparation for their being framed.

   Depending on the matting and framing methods, the workspace should have a minimum amount of equipment and tools, but it is necessary that the area be kept extremely clean and environmentally stable. Light levels should be monitored and access limited. Objects should be covered when not being worked on to reduce unnecessary exposure to light. Proper storage and locking cabinets such as flat files should be used for short-term storage when the object is not being handled.

Loading Dock

The loading dock is the first location where collection objects encounter the internal museum environment. Objects should be received and accounted for here but should not be left for any period of time because of the less favorable environmental conditions and security.

The best loading dock is one that will envelop the entire truck with the exterior door closed. If this kind of dock is not available, the next step is to have a covering which, when the truck is backed up to the door, can be extended to enclose the dock door and the opening of the truck to prevent the external weather from disturbing the unloading process.

To reduce external fluctuations to the internal environment at the entrance of the loading dock, many museums use a double seal to allow the transfer of items from outside to inside. The items are first placed into a dock area with a door open to the outside, and an interior door that accesses the adjacent interior room is closed. Once the truck is in the outer area, the outside door is closed, the interior door opened, and the items moved into the interior of the building. The process is then repeated until the unloading is complete.

Extra security staff should be present to assist with any external entry of people, and they should monitor the overall activities while the collection objects are being brought into the building. The ideal is to have a dock dedicated solely to receiving and releasing collection objects. Many museums are required to share a dock, which can compromise scheduling, security, and maintenance of cleanliness because of pests and other contaminants potentially coming into contact with the collection objects.

Shipping/Receiving Area

This area is where the shipments are unloaded immediately after they have been removed from the truck. This space should have a sealed door between it and the loading dock and another sealed door that is adjacent to the hallway or to the room dedicated for temporary storage or unpacking. This area should accommodate a workspace for registrars to document and record the shipment, sign documents, and receive couriers traveling with the shipment.

A security room or observation window should be situated in the receiving room or adjacent to the loading dock. This will allow security to observe the activity of the truck, drivers, and other personnel who are allowed only up to this point and need to be supervised by security.

Inspection/Isolation Room

The inspection/isolation room is a luxury in many museums. The space is dedicated to objects arriving at the museum for exhibition, loan, purchase, or other collection activities. This area is the first line of defense for inspecting incoming shipments that could be infested with pests or other types of pollutants before they enter into areas where collections are stored or handled. This room should be located near the loading dock and regularly monitored and secured through limited access. It should be used for temporary storage only.

Fumigation Room

A dedicated fumigation room is a luxury in most museums because it is a space that should not have to be used. If a room cannot be dedicated for this purpose, then alternative policy and procedures need to be in place should the need arise. This room should have limited access, and there should be signs posted when fumigation is being conducted, when hazardous materials are being used, and when dangerous conditions occur. This room should be located near the loading dock and regularly monitored and secured through limited access. It should be used for temporary storage of objects only.

Hallways and Corridors

Internal hallways or corridors are required for moving collection objects between secured rooms or display areas. These pathways need to have clutter removed prior to moving objects, and there should be notification of activities to other museum departments so as to reduce unnecessary traffic during movement. It is advisable that additional personnel act as spotters to avoid potential obstructions, and to assist with doors or elevator controls and to instruct other museum staff of the movement that is taking place. Because the environmental levels in these areas fluctuate greatly, are used by multiple museum staff, and are not secure, halls and corridors should never be used for storing objects.

Elevators/Lifts

Elevators and lifts are an extension to the pathway movement of objects between secured rooms and display areas. The same protocol as for hallways and corridors should be followed. The space between the hallway floor and the deck or floor of the elevator carriage is a vulnerable area for moving wheeled equipment. Depending on the type of door (potentially recessed door), the physical space between hallway and carriage makes this transitional area a hazard.

To reduce the shock and vibration of traversing the space between hallway and carriage floor, it is advisable to lay a sheeted material to bridge the area so wheels roll up and over the sheet displacing the unevenness of the area. Commercially made aluminum plates can be purchased, plates that have a T-plate welded on the bottom which fits in the empty space between components, reducing slippage of the sheet when a weight is placed over it. These plates can be heavy and awkward to use for many staff members.

Custom-made or basic bridge covers can be made of a thin (1/4" or 3/8") durable material such as Masonite, double-wall corrugated cardboard, or plastic sheeting. The sheets need to have edges angled, be light enough to be easily picked up and moved, and wide enough to reduce the potential trip hazard of the sheets sliding when wheels first come into contact with the material. This is an effective, inexpensive aid that can be easily replaced when needed.

Stairways

Stairways are not recommended for moving collection objects from one floor to another. With that said, most museums and historic houses will have some location where collections are stored or displayed to which the only access is by traversing the stairways.

Move small objects within a box or other handling device, which will be easy and safe to support during movement. Large objects may need to have a template made prior to the move to test the choreography of the movement. Make sure that there is adequate staff available because the movement may require handing the object from one individual to another to fit the restricted space.

CONCLUSION

The collection care activities conducted within the museum's internal environment can be compared to an interlocking puzzle. The problem solving and management of the overall picture can be worked out on paper in theory, but the actual pieces need to be researched, analyzed, tested, and fit together to ensure success and efficiency. As the museum continues to acquire objects that enter into the internal environment of the museum, the puzzle changes and the pieces of the puzzle must once again be rearranged.

FOCUS ON: LIGHTING IN THE MUSEUM

by Simm Steel

This article is an introduction to the practice of lighting artworks for those who are not lighting professionals and are not acquainted with museum lighting, and therefore it attempts to be as approachable as possible and excludes technical terms deemed unnecessary for communicating its concepts and advice. The care of collections, subjective analytical responses to artistic and curatorial intent, the fundamental principles behind the lighting of exhibition environments and artworks, and the visual comfort of the museum visitor are its main foci. Museum lighting design and new lighting technologies are only obliquely referenced.

FUNDAMENTAL PRINCIPLES BEHIND EXHIBITION LIGHTING DESIGN

The visual perception of all objects relies upon the relationship between light and dark, form through shading. The relationship of an object to its surroundings is therefore dependent upon relative lightness or color contrasts.

Museum and gallery lighting necessitates a lot of looking at the object from the perspective of the visitor. Lighting an artwork or exhibition is an intensely subjective process and involves making judgments about the overall feel of a space. This entails listening and learning from those who regularly immerse themselves, or are involved, in the creation of the museum and gallery experiences. Part of the skill is to interpret what you have done, learning from and improving upon good results and resolving issues before the doors open to the public.

Before choosing to adopt any recommended lighting technique, it is important to understand some basic principles and information regarding the requirements of the museum and gallery environment as well as the positives and negatives associated with the technical alternatives available. Being informed and forewarned will not only avoid costly mistakes but also provide valuable insights when communicating your needs to lighting consultants, technicians, and salespeople to help them help you achieve the desired outcomes.

LIGHT IN THE MUSEUM

The Light-Sensitive Environment

Conservation is a highly important and complex topic. It is commonly accepted that public, private, and commercial galleries should have tightly controlled climatic environments and that light is a necessary part of these conditions. Table 6.1 provides a simplified list of materials and their sensitivity to light and should be understood by everyone involved in lighting objects within museums. However, it must be noted that these are recommendations only, and extenuating circumstances that may require flexibility could arise

Table 6.1 CIE Classification of Materials According to Responsivity to Visible Light

Category	Description
1. Irresponsive	The object is composed entirely of materials that are permanent, in that they have no light responsivity.
	Examples: most metals, stone, most glass, genuine ceramic, enamel, most minerals.
2. Low Responsivity	The object includes materials that are slightly light responsive.
	Examples: oil and tempera painting, fresco, undyed leather and wood, horn, bone, ivory, lacquer, some plastics.
	Silver gelatin black-and-white prints, not RC paper.
3. Medium Responsivity	The object includes fugitive materials that are moderately light responsive.
	Examples: costumes, water colors, pastels, tapestries, prints and drawings, manuscripts, miniatures, paintings in distemper media, wallpaper, gouache, dyed leather and most natural history objects, including botanical specimens, fur, and feathers.
	Most photographic print papers with the word "chrome" in the name
4. High Responsivity	The object includes materials highly responsive to light.
	Examples: silk, colorants known to be highly fugitive, newspaper.
	Most color photographic print papers with the word "color" in the name.

from artists' requests for particular light conditions (permissible if the work is owned by the artist or the curator agrees to an insistence) or loan agreements that require lower levels than generally accepted.

The Dangers of Nonvisible Light

It is highly recommended that the nonvisible spectra of ultraviolet (UV) and infrared radiation (IR) from all natural and artificial sources be eliminated wherever possible from the museum environment. The display of artworks will require the use of low-damage light sources, filtration of the UV and IR spectrum, limitation of display hours, or removal of light-sensitive artworks from damaging environments altogether. Table 6.2. provides ballpark CCT and UV content of daylight conditions and artificial light sources.

The Qualities of Visible Light

Even after the damaging nonvisible spectra of light have been eliminated, museums' objects remain susceptible to high-energy wavelengths in the visible blue spectrum. Correlated Color Temperature (CCT) is a metric that

Table 6.2   UV Content in Light Sources*

Light Source	UV Content (µW/lm)
Daylight—direct skylight* 5000K-8000+K	350–1500
Tungsten incandescent 2700K	70–80
Tungsten halogen dichroic w/glass cover 3000K	36–170
Fluorescent lamps 3000K	30–100
Metal halide 3000K (museum quality)	36
LED (museum quality)	<5

*Daylight includes a range of conditions from overcast to clear with sunlight component. Skylight refers to clear with no direct sunlight component.
Source: Adapted from International Commission on Illuminations, Technical Report, Control of Damage to Museum Objects by Optical Radiation CIE157:2004, The Illuminating Engineers Society of North America Lighting Handbook 9th Ed. (Editor in Chief) Mark S. Rea, Ph.D., FIES, and supplemented with readings taken from Sydney sky conditions and a range of products released in 2013.

describes the color of light emitted by a source, and in museum display lighting this is usually 2700–3300K (warm white). It is therefore highly recommended that the International Commission on Illumination (CIE) recommendations of a maximum CCT of 4000K be adhered to, and only after safe light spectrum conditions have been achieved can the measurement of lux levels be considered relevant.

Pigments can also look different under diverse light sources. The effect of two colors looking the same under one source but different under another source is the result of metamerism. This is important for the correct rendering of artworks, but it is also the reason that choosing colors for display walls must always be done under the final lighting conditions. To ensure that all colors in an artwork are correctly represented, it is extremely important that a light source have a high Color Rendering Index (CRI), and a CRI of 95 (out of 100) is acceptable for the display of artworks. As the Correlated Color Temperature merely describes the color of emitted light, it does not guarantee the color-rendering quality of that source. For example, incandescent light sources are accepted as having 100 CRI but do not provide good color quality or contrast, especially when dimmed. Figure 6.22 clearly illustrates the dramatic difference between halogen light (right of frame) and high-quality LED light of the same CCT (center and beyond) used to light walls of the same color.

There is no doubt that LED light quality is ready for museum applications, but it is still advised that CCT, CRI, and CQS are sought from manufacturers and that only luminaires and lamps from reputable suppliers aware of museum sector requirements are accepted. Hand-held illuminance, UV, and IR meters, and spectrometers are available (refer to Equipment listing in chapter 8).

Recommended Lux Levels and Alternative Lux Hours.

Another way of looking at how much light an object is receiving is to calculate lux hours (200 lux × 10 hours = 2000 lux hours). Reducing the number of

Figure 6.22 Difference between Halogen Light and High-quality LED Light. *Source*: Simm Steel, AGNSW Sydney.

lighted hours per year can allow an increase in the amount of illuminance the object receives. Conversely, increasing the amount of light an object receives forces a reduction in the number of display hours per year. Calculation of lux hours must include extended daylight ingress, cleaning and maintenance hours, and regular viewing events, and may even have to include bright security night lights. Table 6.3. is an adaptation of the original CIE *Damage to Light Sensitive Materials by Optical Radiation* recommendations for lux levels and lux hours, extending it to a ten-hour day to include cleaning and maintenance hours, and an eleven-hour day to include an extension of opening hours to 10 p.m.

LIGHTING DESIGN AND THE MUSEUM

Light changes the way objects are seen and how form is interpreted, and good lighting should bring out the best in the artwork. There have been times when curators or conservators have found an exciting detail in a painting simply because it is being viewed under particular lighting conditions for the very first time. Lighting should also be able to unite or separate art from its surrounding environment or to enhance an environment.

Table 6.3 Extended List of the Original CIE Limiting Annual Exposure Recommendations

Material Classification	Lux Level	Max Lux Hours per Year	Display Days per Year (10 hrs/day)	Display Days per Year (11hrs/day to include 1 night viewing/week)
High Responsivity	25	15,000	60	55
	50	15,000	30	27
	100	15,000	15	14
	200	15,000	7.5	7
Medium Responsivity	41	150,000	365	333
	50	150,000	300	273
	100	150,000	150	136
	200	150,000	75	68
	300	150,000	50	34
	500	150,000	30	17
Low Responsivity	164	600,000	365	333
	200	600,000	300	272
	300	600,000	200	136
	500	600,000	120	68
Irresponsive	No limit	No limit	No limit	No limit

Approaching lighting design within museums can be thought of as encompassing three spheres of response. The largest sphere is the all-enveloping museum itself, its purpose, and how the institution wants to visually present itself to the public. Within this all-encompassing sphere are the smaller galleries and/or exhibitions, and within these spheres are the artworks themselves. Each sphere has its own requirements, but it is important to be aware of the ever-shifting compromises that must be made between a predetermined museum lighting concept and the flexibility dictated by a broadening museum mandate. Another consideration is how to maintain the usual balance between a lighting design response to content and an exhibition concept. The ability to adapt to new challenges demands a fundamental understanding of these three spheres of museum lighting.

The Museum

The body of the museum itself is the all-encompassing environment where a balance between highlighting the architectural features and the flexibility for the myriad display requirements is paramount. Display philosophies now merge in an amalgam of varying illuminances and multimedia installations conceived in ever-changing contemporary artistic practice and curatorial intent and across large sections of the museum footprint. Daylight is also playing an increasingly important role in the architectural statement of new buildings and refurbishments, forcing institutions and architects to find innovative ways to resolve issues of object conservation and exhibition design flexibility.

LIGHTING EXHIBITIONS

Forward Preparation Is Essential for Good Exhibition Lighting

The results of good exhibition lighting rely on being prepared and involved with the exhibition, and it will also help others understand your needs and limitations. Below is a guideline to better exhibition design through preparation.

- Be available for early stages of exhibition design, and respond to the curatorial and design objectives of the exhibition.
- Understand and work within limitations such as conservation requirements, available lighting equipment, and exhibition layouts.
- State potential issues early and clearly so that timely changes can be made to the layout, but be open to compromise and do not rule out possibilities without due consideration.
- Always work to the CIE guidelines and communicate any foreseeable issues to conservators and/or curators, but prepare to be flexible.
- Do not rely on assumptions unless you are extremely experienced.
- Mockups and trials are valuable for new museums, exhibitions, and showcase designs.
- Get ahead of the schedule whenever possible, as things do go wrong.
- Keep the syntax of the exhibition consistent where required, but know when and where it requires a shift in lighting style and development of the hierarchical relationships between exhibits.
- Always be on the lookout for ways to make the lighting better.

Responding to the Exhibition Space

Within the museum or individual gallery, there may be a multitude of differing needs. The next sphere of design involves a response to the overall exhibition design. The lighting of spaces and display objects may need to be broken down into a hierarchy of light levels to distinguish features, maintain subtle contours and modeling of objects, and lure the visitor from one space to the next, but before this can be done, some questions need to be asked: Will it require a dark theatrical space or a bright, crisp, contemporary feel? What are the primary objects in the space? What role does the secondary interior architecture (if any) play?

Lighting of Artworks

This next sphere of lighting covers the three subcategories of lighting two-dimensional artworks, three-dimensional objects, and showcases, each of which may require a cross-pollination of principles from the other two.

Two-Dimensional Artworks

One of the greatest issues when lighting artworks can be disabling specular glare from the light source reflected in the glossy surface of varnished paintings.

Altering the viewing angle or the height of the lighting is rarely easy, but the troubling angle of incidence can be easily translated to a horizontal perspective, as illustrated in Figure 6.23. Move the luminaire to the side to shift the glare from the center of the visual field to the painting's edge, allowing the viewer to move around the region of glare. Semigloss surfaces can be more problematic than high-gloss surfaces, acting as diffusers that break up the reflected light over a larger portion of the painted surface. Extreme strafing light can partly resolve diffuse disability glare, but it is necessary to be aware that deep surface textures will create shadows across the surface, and will alter the textural quality of the painting and increase the depth and breadth of distracting shadows within and beyond the picture frame.

Multilux-Level Displays

It has become a common practice to place highly sensitive artworks within a larger, less-light-sensitive group of artworks to construct vital curatorial connections. This can often look like it will conflict with the objects' conservation needs, but the lighting designer or technician should consider it as just another challenge.

There are often situations where the broad lighting of display objects is not appropriate. In situations like this, a framing projector can be used to frame the small objects, but special care needs to be taken to not create the unnatural "television screen" effect, which occurs when the objects stand out too strongly from the background. This can be resolved by softening the hard beam edge of light to bleed either across the matte or outside the frame or by reducing the light levels.

Three-Dimensional Forms

Shading and shadows enable us to perceive form. An understanding of how shading accentuates curvature and how shadow anchors an object to its environment will assist with better lighting of all artworks. Lighting

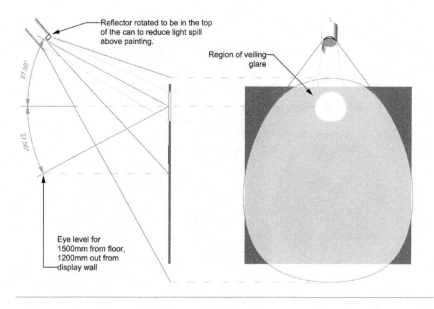

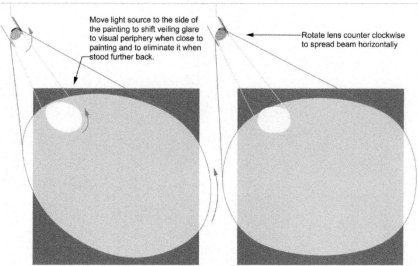

Figure 6.23 *Source:* Simm Steel, AGNSW Sydney.

three-dimensional forms properly is educating in that it demands a three-dimensional lighting response of a primary accenting source, a secondary source to bring shading into balance with the primary source (of which there can be more than one), and often a tertiary source as a specialized highlighter, extra fill light, theatrical backlight, or uplight.

Figure 6.24 Lighting Three-Dimensional Works. *Source*: Simm Steel, AGNSW Sydney.

Direct source glare must always be minimized wherever possible. This form of disability glare can linger on the retina for some time and greatly diminish the museum experience. Counterintuitively, glare can play a major role in the definition of form as can be seen in Figure 6.24. Framing projectors are often the best luminaires to use when lighting sculptures that are viewed from many angles as they allow the aperture of visible light to be reduced to tightly controlled shapes that may light a very small or a very large part of an object or an entire object from a very particular angle.

Shadows can play an important role in directing the viewer to features that can only be seen from a certain angle. They can entice the viewer around a space, connect one object to another, and act as isolating plinths. Or they can encroach upon neighboring objects creating a convoluted shadow-play that draws attention away from the artwork. Object lighting should be simplified by reducing the quantity but not the quality of light upon the contours of the object and avoiding distracting Christmas-tree-like arrays of lights. Where there are tight clusters of sculptures, a subtle shift of primary light flow can double as a secondary source and create a smooth transition from one object to the next.

Finally, lighting designers or technicians need to ask themselves the following questions: What are the requirements of the angles of light and the potential for disabling glare, or will specular glare be useful? What are the relationships between the objects, and what impact will the lighting of one object have on its neighbor?

Lighting for Showcases

Showcases are often difficult in that they have limited interior space and are often made of materials that create their own shadows or reflections, which impinge upon the object within. Knowing the exhibition space, the capabilities of the luminaires, the size of objects, and the showcases themselves at a very early stage in the design is invaluable. Advice regarding orientation or shifts in position can help curators or exhibition designers to get the best from their display, and if lighting an object from one important side cannot be achieved because of the nature of the space, it will be imperative that this information is made available so that adjustments can be made. There may

Figure 6.25   Lighting Showcases. *Source*: Simm Steel, AGNSW Sydney.

be situations where large, heavy objects simply cannot be moved, and compromises will have to be made if lighting cannot be resolved, Where there are unavoidable shadows, look at the form of the object to see if there are any positions within the object itself where shadows can be hidden. Folds or patterns in textiles can take shadows well or even have shadows fall into the dark interior of an object to give the impression that the shadow is part of the object.

SUMMARY

- Be prepared in advance, be involved in early stages of design, and remain flexible in your approach to every challenge.
- Eliminate the potential of nonvisible light and lux levels that may damage light-sensitive artifacts, and consider the effects of the quality of light on the visual outcome.
- Be aware of shadows, shading, glare, the needs of individual objects, how you might be able to guide the visitor through the space through biased lighting and transitions. Be aware of how varying gallery lighting can aid visual adaptation and the effect that the lighting has on the design concept and delivery outcome of the exhibition.
- Look for ways to do better, learn from mistakes, take pride in your achievements, and above all, enjoy the process.

Simm Steel
Senior Lighting Technician and Lighting Designer
Art Gallery of New South Wales
Sydney, Australia

NOTES

1. *Managing Collection Environments Initiative* (Los Angeles: The Getty Conservation Institute, 2014), accessed December 2015, http://www.getty.edu/conservation/our_projects/education/managing/overview.html.

2. "Trends in Environmental Management for Collection Storage," *Storage Management Working Group* (Melbourne, Victoria, Australia: National and State Libraries Australasia, 2014), accessed December 2015, http://www.nsla.org.au/publication/trends-environmental-management-collection-storage.

3. Genevieve Fisher, "Preventive Care: Relative Humidity," *Museum Registration Methods*, 5th ed. (Washington, DC: AAM Press, 2010): 288.

4. David Gratten and Stefan Michalski, "General Set Points," *Environmental Guidelines for Museums* (Ottawa, Ontario: Canadian Conservation Institute,

2013), accessed December 2015, http://www.cci-icc.gc.ca/resources-ressources/
carepreventivecons-soinsconspreventive/enviro-eng.aspx.

5. "An Introduction to Collections Preservation: Light" (St. Paul, MN: Northern States Conservation Center, 2014), accessed December 2014, http://www.collectioncare.org/light.

6. Barry Lord, Gail Dexter Lord, and Lindsay Martin, eds., "Visible Radiation—Recommended Light Levels," *Manual of Museum Planning: Sustainable Space, Facilities, and Operations*, 3rd ed. (Lanham, MD: Rowman & Littlefield, 2012): 316–17.

7. "Dust and Gaseous Air Pollution," *Museum Handbook Part 1999* (Washington, DC: Department of the Interior, National Park Service, 1999) 4:43.

8. Ibid.

9. Ibid.

10. Genevieve Fisher, "Preventive Care: Relative Humidity," *Museum Registration Methods*, 5th ed. (Washington, DC: AAM Press, 2010): 291.

11. Barry Lord, Gail Dexter Lord, and Lindsay Martin, eds.,"Particulate Filtration," *Manual of Museum Planning: Sustainable Space, Facilities, and Operations*, 3rd ed. (Lanham, MD: Rowman & Littlefield, 2012): 328.

12. "Preventive Conservation and Agents of Deterioration," *Caring for Objects and Collections* (Ottawa, Ontario: Canadian Conservation Institute, 2014), accessed December 2014, http://www.cci-icc.gc.ca/resources-ressources/agentsofdeterioration-agentsdedeterioration/index-eng.aspx.

13. "Damage Caused by Incorrect Temperature and RH," *Caring for Objects and Collections* (Ottawa, Ontario: Canadian Conservation Institute, 2014), accessed December 2014, http://www.cci-icc.gc.ca/resources-ressources/carepreventivecons-soinsconspreventive/damage-dommage-eng.aspx.

14. "Physical Forces. Control Strategies/Mitigating Shock and Vibration," *Caring for Objects and Collections* (Ottawa, Ontario: Canadian Conservation Institute, 2014), accessed December 2014, http://www.cci-icc.gc.ca/resources-ressources/carepreventivecons-soinsconspreventive/damage-dommage-eng.aspx.

15. Barry Lord, Gail Dexter Lord, and Lindsay Martin, eds., "The Collection Storage Facility," *Manual of Museum Planning: Sustainable Space, Facilities, and Operations*, 3rd ed. (Lanham, MD: Rowman & Littlefield, 2012): 251.

16. Barry Lord, Gail Dexter Lord, and Lindsay Martin, eds., "Materials and Construction of Storage Equipment," *Manual of Museum Planning: Sustainable Space, Facilities, and Operations*, 3rd ed. (Lanham, MD: Rowman & Littlefield, 2012): 268–69.

Chapter 7

Collection Care

The External Environment

INTRODUCTION

The preceding chapter explored the various locations and facilities (the internal environment) in which collection care practices are followed. This chapter, on the external environment, will approach collection care practices concerning packing and crating, transport, and off-site facilities for both storage and display. Information about commercial companies will address the services they provide to museums and other clients for their collections.

In the external environment, collection objects are subjected to conditions different from those that are encountered in the internal environment of the museum building. The primary differences are climatic conditions, display spaces, and the rigors of packing, crating, handling, and transport that the object may encounter.

Unlike the internal environment, where all aspects of collection care can be monitored, corrected, and maintained by designated staff with defined responsibilities, the external environment may not have the high level of accountability required for optimal collection care.

Risk assessment, as has been emphasized throughout the book, is paramount for maintaining best practices. In the external environment, the risks are much greater because the factors of environment and personnel are subject to changes that are beyond the control of the museum staff. Policies that dictate best practices for collection objects should outline the requirements for conditions when the objects are not physically in the museum and are in transit or off-site.

CONTROLLING AND MAINTAINING THE PHYSICAL CLIMATE CONDITIONS WITHIN THE ENVIRONMENTS

The same factors that affect objects in the internal environment must be considered in the external environment: temperature and humidity, light exposure, pollutants and pests, and security.

Temperature and Humidity

When an object is moved from one place to another, the goal is to maintain a consistent temperature and humidity throughout the transfer, from point A to point B. During the transition, temperature and humidity levels may change dramatically. To mitigate the damaging effects that could occur with the drastic fluctuations, the design of packing, crating, and method of transport should be carefully considered for reducing the levels of fluctuation that may occur in the changing climatic conditions.

A sealed environment should be provided by designing the crate and internal packing to eliminate humidity levels or moisture coming into direct contact with the object. Insulation within the packing and materials will mitigate the effects of fluctuations of temperature and humidity.

Transport options may require that a climate-controlled, air-ride truck is used to house and transport the object between locations. Allowing the packed objects to acclimate to the new environment for a period of time after arrival will reduce the impact of fluctuations in levels of temperature and humidity.

Light Levels

Light levels are to be maintained at required levels for the object when it is installed for display or when placed in storage.

Pollutants and Pests

Maintaining clean and pest-free conditions during the various phases of transition is extremely difficult. Shared loading docks are best known as a potential location of pests. The best way to reduce these risks is to create a sealed environment in the packing and crating. Monitoring conditions during and after the transport will mitigate risks to the object after it has been unpacked and placed into its new environment.

Security

Monitoring and maintaining levels of security become a greater risk to the object during the transport and in some final destinations as they may vary from the museum's policies.

Transport activities must be kept confidential, and drivers and related handling staff must understand the need for discretion and circumspection in their duties. Background checks and proper licensing for operating vehicles should be required of all drivers. Vehicles need to be compliant with government regulations, and drivers must follow transport laws to eliminate any subsequent issues with the vehicle and its cargo during the shipment. Commercial trucks can be fitted with alarms and should have GPS and satellite tracking on board.

Two individuals should accompany the cargo during transport to share driving responsibilities and to ensure that the vehicle and cargo are not left unattended at any time during the transit.

FACILITIES AND LOCATIONS OF THE EXTERNAL ENVIRONMENT

Long-Term Storage

As a museum's collection grows, space becomes a commodity that may no longer be adequate within the museum's internal environment. Policies and procedures similar to those for the internal collection care must be established, implemented, and maintained for the off-site storage. The museum must commit to staff and budgetary support for as long as the off-site space is leased.

Replicating the quality of space needed to store and protect the objects can be difficult and expensive. The risks of the off-site facility and the objects to be stored need to be assessed. Objects slated to go to off-site storage are those that are seldom used, stable, of lower insurance value, and easily transported between sites when required. Other factors include distance between the facilities, standard forms of transport, and dedicated staff needed to perform all related activities of moving objects between sites. Security at the off-site facility needs to be maintained and budgeted for round-the-clock surveillance with instant communication back to the museum's security staff or combined with a commercial security service provider.

Commercial storage can be a viable alternative because different levels of service can be offered, and often facilities are built, maintained, and monitored to state-of-the-art standards.

Short-Term Storage

Often, objects need to be handled outside of the museum and will require short-term storage arrangements. The storage needs will vary depending upon the object and the time needed for the particular activity undertaken. Some examples are the following:

- temporary storage for exhibition crates (both packed and empty) and display items traveling between venues;
- space to accommodate conservation treatment of large objects;
- space to assemble and create mounts and fit large-scale objects to display furniture or decorative components for exhibition use before installation in the museum; and
- fumigation may be required of incoming shipments or of objects that have been found to be infested with pests in the museum and need to be treated off-site.

MUSEUM OFF-SITE DISPLAY FACILITIES

A museum's mission may involve lending objects to other facilities—usually other museums or exhibition spaces. These facilities will have their own individual characteristics and capability to display objects, and the request for the loan should be accompanied by a facility report of the borrowing institution.

Satellite Display Facilities

Many museums have one or more buildings to display objects. These locations are a direct extension of their exhibition programming and are scheduled for changeovers in the similar cycles that are performed at the main facility. Adjacent buildings on a site are often acquired or built specifically and used for an extension of the main building. Because these spaces are usually under the jurisdiction of the main building, the policies and procedures governing these spaces are the same.

Institutions may have buildings within the same city that have been donated or acquired for the development of an extension of the main facility. These spaces are commonly developed to house a particular collection or have programming activities to interpret the collections displayed. Contemporary art collections are often displayed at another site while the main facility displays the broader encyclopedic collection. Some satellite facilities are built specifically to house a specific collection type or individual artist. Satellite facilities can be placed in highly visible, public locations. Airports often have site-specific artworks or objects on display as part of the historic heritage of the region.

Large city airports have developed spaces within the public areas of the terminal that offer the public a more traditional gallery setting in the display of the objects. This cultural experience is created by borrowing objects from collections of regional museums, giving the visitor a view of what they have to offer. An excellent example of this type of space and the lending program is the San Francisco International Airport in San Francisco, California.

Created in 1980, SFO Museum was the first cultural institution of its kind located in an international airport. An ever-changing schedule of exhibitions on a diverse range of subjects provides an educational and cultural experience for more than 44 million passengers who use the airport annually. SFO Museum has become an integral part of the San Francisco International Airport, and its exhibitions are an established tradition enjoyed by frequent visitors from the San Francisco Bay Area and travelers from all over the world.[1]

Historic collections can be displayed in multiple buildings that have a specific functional relationship to the overall site. These buildings have objects placed on display to reflect the historic aspects of the buildings. The relationship and display of objects within the overall site can be a challenge to maintaining the best standards and conditions for the objects. Each object chosen for display needs to be assessed for the risks that could be encountered. The collection care challenges are many, but each institution should have policies and procedures to accommodate care of the collection objects that are displayed.

An excellent example of this type of institution and collection display is Colonial Williamsburg in Williamsburg, Virginia. Colonial Williamsburg is a living-history museum and private foundation representing the historic district of the city of Williamsburg, Virginia. The 301-acre (122 ha) historic area includes buildings dating from 1699 to 1780 (during which the city was the capital of Colonial Virginia), as well as Colonial Revival and more recent reconstructions. The historic area is an interpretation of a Colonial American city, with exhibits including dozens of authentic or re-created buildings related to colonial and American Revolutionary War history.[2]

Internal Loan Programs

Many government-funded museums are required to lend objects to specific federal or state buildings. These objects are placed on display in various locations such as designated galleries, conference rooms, or politicians' offices. Often, these objects are those that are stable and of lesser value or importance to the overall collection type. Another example would be objects that reflect the cultural or historical heritage of the government or the specific building site.

Many state or regional museums or galleries may depend on the loans from the larger state museum. Single loans and full traveling exhibitions are created and shared among these museums, which support their ongoing programming activities. The money to support these activities is part of the taxpayer benefits and is an excellent way to share cultural objects.

In Australia, all public galleries (museums) are financed and maintained primarily by government support, and employees are considered part of the public service domain. The exchange programs that are developed and shared within the public galleries are an extraordinary example of how government support and sharing of cultural heritage can benefit all the citizens.

Public Sculpture

Large monumental sculptures are commonly placed outside of the museum in the external environment, whether on the grounds owned by the museum or in the public landscape of the city in which the museum is located. Caring for these objects requires specialized knowledge of the materials the

Figure 7.1 Deborah Halprin Sculpture Installation. *Source*: Author.

objects are made of and their durability against the risks to which they are exposed. These risks involve the seasonal climatic changes; animals interacting with the object; pollutants, both solid and airborne; and human interaction. Securing these objects can be achieved with minimal deterrents, but the 24/7 exposure to the external environment makes overall protection a challenge.

Depending on the medium, sculptures can be coated with a sealant to retard the immediate penetration of moisture, dirt, or acidic material. A common example is for a bronze sculpture to be cleaned and then have a coating of new wax applied to its surface. The wax coating, though not permanent, will buffer the surface for a period of time depending on the location or the sculpture in its exposed environment. In some harsh winter environments, some sculptures may be covered within a structure to protect them against the season's extreme conditions.

A cleaning program needs to be developed and implemented so that outdoor sculptures can be monitored on a frequent basis to ensure nothing has dramatically affected the object between routine cleanings. Because of the size of the object, the necessary equipment, and the need for securing the worksite from the public and climatic elements takes planning and implementation, and staff and budgetary support must be ensured for the continual care of these objects.

The least known and most difficult risk is animal or human interaction with the object in the public space. Animals can perch, climb, and make nests on the object and scratch, chew, tear, or defecate on the surface. The acidic reaction of animal waste can quickly stain, deteriorate, or destroy the patina of an object's surface.

Human interaction is the most damaging and the highest risk. Climbing on sculptures, adding other elements such as food, drink, or rubbish, and vandalizing the object—for example, spray painting, cutting, or gouging the surface damages the object, making it difficult or expensive to repair and in some cases there can be a permanent total loss. While substantial legal fines can be a deterrent to such behavior, identifying the culprit is unlikely to occur, given the nature of vandalism. Unintentional damage to an object is best deterred by educating the public about the care required for the preservation of art for future generations.

MUSEUM TRANSPORT OPTIONS

The risks involved in transporting objects between sites can be minimized if the museum owns and operates a vehicle or hires a commercial service company that specializes in handling art and artifacts. Depending on the needs of the institution, transport costs can be a substantial part of the operational budget.

In-House Vehicle Options

Using vehicles that are owned, maintained, and operated by a museum is an option for moving collection objects within a local or regional area. Such an option may or may not be cost-effective when compared to hiring a specialized transport company. Knowing and analyzing the risks will assist you in making a good decision regarding the best packing and handling methods for the type of transport vehicle you will use.

The collection care staff must work with senior management to support such transport activities by tracking related expenses and schedules throughout the fiscal year. Monitoring these activities will provide the budgetary information to cover the cost of purchase and ongoing maintenance of a vehicle, liability insurance for the vehicle and selected drivers, and insurance coverage for transporting objects. Most institutions acquire a vehicle for general use and divide the costs among the various departments' budgets.

As with any transport scenario, large or small, internal or commercial, two staff members must be delegated per shipment for managing, handling, and driving and for avoiding security risks.

Cars

Cars are a common vehicle used for small objects that can be packed into a box and secured in the passenger seat, the trunk, or the cargo compartment of the vehicle. The use of a personal car is not recommended as insurance options are limited and the risks are higher for the staff member and museum if an accident occurs.

Vans

Vans are the most common type of vehicle that a museum may own and operate. Depending on the interior of the cargo compartment, boxed objects can be tied to securing points and padded underneath with moving blankets or pads. Seats in the cargo area can be removed, and the floor attachments can be used as effective tie points. The cargo compartment can be fitted with additional tie points, support rails, and floor padding to accommodate various packing needs. The modifications need to meet safety and insurance standards and should not affect the vehicle's operation. Some vans, called standup box or sprinter vans, provide a greater height, which allows an individual to work upright in the cargo space.

Figure 7.2   Standard Profile of Sprinter Van. *Source*: Carey, Artex FAS.

Figure 7.3   Sprinter Van with Lift Gate. *Source*: Carey, Artex FAS.

Figure 7.4 Sprinter Van with Load. *Source*: Carey, Artex FAS.

Small Truck

Trucks come in various sizes; the "small truck" has a cargo compartment with an interior space of between 10′ and 18′ in length. This size of truck can be easily driven and parked and accommodates a large variety of transport options. Any size above 18′ can be too large for use on a regular basis. Depending on the size of truck and the cab configuration, many small trucks have a direct flow of heating and air conditioning, which can be used to climatize the cargo compartment. Trucks can be designed to have added features such as lift gates and ramps, which assist in handling and air-ride suspension to reduce shock and vibration.

Rental Vans and Trucks

Rental vans and trucks can be acquired for a specific one-time use and can be a cost-effective way to transport objects. The size and use of rental trucks follow the same description as given for small trucks. Many rental trucks are designed to have added features, which assist in handling. Insurance and rental agreements need to comply with the museums' policies regarding the drivers' operating the truck and the coverage for collection objects in a rental vehicle.

MUSEUM LOAN PROGRAMS

Loans are arranged between museums or with private individuals or commercial entities for a variety of purposes. The term "loan" covers a broad spectrum of categories for all works of art—owned or borrowed—under the museum's care. Loans for exhibition are the most common type. Objects are borrowed for a specific period of time for a specific purpose.

Loans for traveling exhibitions are similar to single-venue loans, but the issues are multiplied by the number of venues. Exchange loans are made for two reasons. They may be for mutual benefit of the museums, or an institution may request a loan to fill a gap in its permanent exhibition that occurs when another museum borrows an important work. Study loans are made between museums or between museums and individuals. The latter type of study loans are more common in science or archeology museums than in art or history museums.[3]

These three types of loans are the primary and most common reasons for taking objects out of their internal environment. When a museum receives a request for the loan of its objects, a detailed risk assessment must be undertaken before the decision to approve (or decline) the request can be made. The process to determine the decision varies from one museum to another, but there are certain basic and fundamental aspects that must be considered.

To explain all of the possible scenarios would be an endless task. For the purpose of this chapter, I will present examples of the policies and procedures for objects that are lent to traveling exhibitions.

Evaluation Process Prior to Lending Objects

In organizing a traveling exhibition, the initial phase is to identify the objects needed and the owners to be asked for the loan. The request is sent to the director, curator, or exhibition manager with whom the organizer of the exhibition has had previous discussions related to the concept of the exhibition, the overall content, and the prospective venues to which it will travel. When the formal loan request is received by the lending institution, procedures for dealing with such a request commence.

The director and curator in whose jurisdiction the object resides evaluate the benefits of lending the object for the proposed exhibition and how its absence, if it is currently on display, may affect the current programming. This is the primary key in the loan process and dictates the proposed period of the loan and benefits to be gained by making the object available for the exhibition. Once the director and curator have deemed the exhibition worthy of the request, the conservator and registrar should weigh in with their consideration and determination of the levels of care required based on the risks the object will be exposed to once it is outside the internal environment.

The object's inherent properties and condition for travel must be taken into consideration to determine who will care for the object, what its care requirements will be, where it is being lent, how it will be displayed, and the length of time the object will be on loan.

Analysis for Loan

Where the object is being lent is a major key factor as it dictates the other components of the activities of the loan and how they will be addressed. A facility report establishing the borrower's environmental and security conditions within its facility is required of the institution or location where the object will be sent, handled, and displayed. This is crucial in evaluating the lender's requirements of care for the object and the borrower's ability to meet those requirements. A facility report lists the environmental standards such as climate-control systems, security controls, emergency procedures, and the personnel who will monitor its procedures and protocols.

The conservator and registrar examine the object to ascertain the initial condition report of the object. This will list details of the object's overall physical condition and inherent properties that may dictate any additional requirements unique to handling of the object during the life of the loan. The conservator may require that the object be stabilized or restored in preparation for the loan approval. The time and associated costs (or shared costs) to perform these activities would need to be approved by the organizing institution and established as a part of the loan agreement.

Consideration of the fragility of the object in its handling and display may require special components, such as a specific display case or mounting system to be fabricated and sent with the object. Temperature, humidity, and light levels must be set and adhered to throughout the duration of the loan period. If these basic conditions cannot be met or agreed upon, then the object may not be eligible for loan.

The facility report should also include information such as size of the space where the object is to be displayed; specifications of door heights and widths through which the crated object will pass; elevator dimensions and weight capacity; smoke and fire detection and mitigation systems; and level of staff experience and expertise in dealing with the rigors of exhibition activities.

How the object is to be packed, crated, and transported during the exhibition are key considerations because the object will no longer be in the control of the lender. Packing and crating must be designed to be effective in controlling the fluctuation of the temperature and humidity changes and shock and vibration levels encountered during its physical handling and transport via truck, air, or sea freight. The type of truck and the associated equipment that will be needed to aid handling during the transport process should be assessed as well.

Other matters that determine the decision to lend an object are insurance and supervision during the time that the object is out of the jurisdiction of the lender. Who is responsible and what kind of insurance coverage needs to be in place to recover costs of repair of the object if damaged or the monetary recompense if destroyed must be determined. The extent to which supervision is required of the loan can vary depending on the stability of the object, the venue(s) for the exhibition, the complexity of installation, and the personnel who will be handling the object throughout the loan period.

Insurance policies and loan agreements need to be in place before the exhibition commences. Supervision for a shipment during the transport process or having a courier designated to travel with an exhibition to supervise transport and display needs to be determined as well. The costs entailed by these stipulations for the loan are borne by the organizer(s) of the exhibition.

Once the object has been assessed and any additional requirements that will need to be met by the organizing institution have been determined, the information is passed along for final review and approval by the director, curator, representatives of the board of trustees, and other assigned museum staff, based on the established policies and procedures developed by the museum. The policies to be adhered to exist in the documents describing outgoing loan conditions and the specifics of the outgoing loan agreement, which have been established to maintain the high standards of the museum.

The outgoing loan conditions document states in detail the specific standards of collection care that are to be maintained while the object is in the custody of the borrower(s), packing and transport and insurance being the main points. Other factors that should be included are rights and reproduction of images, budgetary confirmation, and potential changes to the existing period of the exhibition.

When lending objects internationally, even more stipulations are dictated according to government regulations for importing and exporting objects, obtaining permits for certain materials (ivory and endangered species), and passing muster with exhaustive provenance research on the object.

Monitoring the Object

The registrar assigned to supervise the loan is responsible for monitoring and managing the terms and conditions of the loan. This person is required to oversee and work with the staff of the lending and borrowing institutions, the service companies hired to pack and transport the object, and the insurers— whether the borrower's, the lender's, or in the case of international loans, the government indemnification program.

Any changes to an object's condition or alterations to the specific requirements of handling, packing, or display need to be referred to the registrar of the lending institution. The information will be conveyed to the appropriate individuals, addressed, documented, and then placed on the condition report for future reference and clarification. This position is essential for creating a bridge between the lender and the borrower. The registrar is the hub of the wheel; the spokes are the conduits of communication to the related entities, which are the rim of the wheel: borrower, transit companies, insurance policy holder, freight forwarder, and, of course, the lender's own cast of characters—director, curator, and conservator. A registrar's position is critical for vital communication and documentation.

Condition Report

Prior to the object's leaving the museum, a full condition report is prepared. This report, a collaboration between the registrar and the conservator, notes the object's tombstone information (maker, title, accession number, material composition, size, and weight), as well as a description of the inherent properties, existing damage, areas of treatment or repair (either past or recent), and the specific location of the anomalies. Color photographs with detailed markings are essential for reference when comparison with future condition reports may be required.

The condition report travels with the object and is referred to and documents the object's condition at each packing and unpacking stage at the venues of the exhibition. Any changes are noted and dated so as to document changes that may have occurred in the handling or transport between venues.

During the time that the object is on display, if there is a question regarding the object's condition, the incoming condition report can be referenced to see if there is an actual change or if the condition noted is an existing attribute of the object. The condition report is a continuous record of how the object is being handled and maintained according to the requirements stipulated in the original loan agreement.

Packing and Installation Manual

Each object will have specific requirements as to how it should be packed, handled, or installed for display. The explanations presented in the manual can add greater detail to the handling and display requirements, thus augmenting what is stated in the condition report.

Packing and crating details should also be well documented, and these step-by-step instructions should accompany the packet of paperwork that includes the loan agreement and condition report. When the object is packed for the initial outgoing transit, written instructions and illustrative pictures of the packing should be compiled. Photographs can be included, which may assist in clarification and act as a quick reference. This very important document will be used at each venue for unpacking/installation and de-installation/repacking.

Installation instructions and handling requirements need to be written in a step-by-step format starting from the unpacking stage, to the equipment required for the transfer, to the actual steps in the execution of the installation process. Notes need to be supplied for any specifics regarding preparing the object for display such as mounts, hardware, or material related to the object when placed on display. Once again, photographs should be included to provide a visual reference to how an object is to be handled, joined, or attached to other components and to the final display configuration.

Rigging may be required when handling heavy, large, or cumbersome objects. Proper handling procedures and techniques must be fully understood by the borrower as there can be no margin for error in preventing damage to the object and the safety of the staff performing the operation. In these instances, a courier from the lending institution, who is well versed in the complexities of the object and its handling, should be at the installation site.

Transport Options

There are three major types of transport vehicles used for transferring an object from one location to another: truck, airplane, and sea container. The type of transport is based on the number and type of object (size, weight, fragility), and the distance and potential obstacles between locations. The most common method of transport used on a daily basis is truck transport. Examples of the various truck types and their particular functions will be explained later in this chapter under the broader subject of commercial service companies and the type of truck options offered by them.

For an object traveling from point A to point B, truck services are chosen on the basis of the object type, size, weight, and its transit requirements. The organizing or borrowing institution will often work with companies with whom it is familiar and which offer routes between the destinations. The use of a particular company depends on the agreement between the lender and borrower.

The shortest route between two points and the least amount of time on the road is the best scenario, but is often the most expensive. As an **exclusive use** of the truck's availability, the route and timing are mapped so that the shipment will be handled the least and will arrive at the borrowing institution as soon as possible after its departure from the lending institution.

In terms of the costs, an exclusive-use transport may be too expensive for the organizer's budget. Another less costly alternative would be the object's being transported on a **shared truck** load with other objects going to the same destination, not necessarily the same exhibition. Because all the objects are not traveling to the same destination, the time on the road may be lengthier as a result of the number of stops to pick up the various objects, but the handling would be the same as when it is an exclusive use.

The third option is based on a shared truck scenario and is called a **shuttle transport**, which means that the object would be picked up from the lender, transferred to a location of the service company (usually its hub), and then the object would be off-loaded to await reloading onto a truck to then be transported to its final destination. This is often referred to as "cross-docking." This option is the least expensive but does require the most time for transport and will be subjected to more physical handling and potential environmental changes.

Controlling the internal environment of the truck cargo area is also important. Many of the larger specialized companies have a variety of trucks in their fleet, which are equipped with climate-controlled mechanisms that monitor and maintain the conditions to which the object is subjected. This service is more expensive than nonclimate-controlled truck service. Further explanation will be given under the broader subject of commercial service companies and the type of options they have to offer.

Loan Arrival after Transport

When the object arrives at the designated venue, it is handled in the following steps:

- Crated objects are unloaded at the loading dock, and recorded as received and placed into the current museum's care.
- The registrar assigned to the loan and a courier, if accompanying the shipment, will inspect the crate for any notations of mishandling or damage. Any notation will be discussed with the driver and noted on the transport bill-of-lading (receipt) and on the incoming institutional receipt to the shipment by the museum.
- The crated object will be placed in a receiving room or designated location and allowed to acclimatize for a minimum of twenty-four hours or until it is ready to be unpacked.
- When the object is ready to be unpacked, the process will be undertaken in a designated secure area such as storage, exhibition gallery, or conservation studio.
- Unpacking instructions will be reviewed if supplied by the lender. If no previous instructions are provided, new notations will be made as to how

the object was packed, so the object can be repacked in the same way as when it was sent.

- The condition assessment will be conducted by the assigned registrar and conservator. A courier traveling with the object will be present and discuss any previous condition notation and sign off indicating approval of the condition upon the shipment's arrival.
- Time is scheduled for the unpacking of the object so that it will coincide with its being installed directly in the exhibition space, thus minimizing unnecessary handling.
- The object will be installed according to the instructions supplied by the lending institution. If the object has insufficient hardware or needs modification to be safely installed in the gallery, then communication will be required between the courier, installation manager, and registrar to reach an agreed solution.
- Any microclimate controls such as a display case vitrine, products for RH controls, monitors, or security devices to be housed within a display case will need to be installed prior to or immediate following the final placement of the object in its display. The object once installed will be lighted to the designated light levels.
- A courier usually stays to see the object placed in its final location and that all requirements have been met for its care and display. The courier will sign off on all required paperwork.
- The unpacked crates with the interior packing materials will be taken and stored in a dry, pest-free, and, preferably, climate-controlled environment.
- All crates will need to be acclimatized to the gallery environmental levels before being repacked.

Loan Being Returned to the Lender

The returning of the loan to the lender will follow a similar sequence of events, but in the reverse order of process. This process will be dictated by the same factors established in the original loan agreement. If any changes have been made, for example, an extension of the loan dates, additional venues, or return to another location, all the changes should have been addressed and approved before the objects leave the museum.

- The level of care for the object's return remains at the same level of standards that was required for its handling and transport to the borrowing institution.
- The inspections and condition reporting will be performed and signed off, with a designated courier stating the object's condition upon departure.

- The materials used to pack and crate an object will be used again unless new, replacement materials are required to bring the packing standard up to the original or a better level.
- Transport options may be reflected in any changes of routing by time of year because of seasonal climatic conditions, if the shipment is not being transported by a climate-controlled truck to reduce the effects.
- The same standards within a controlled cargo space will be required as during its delivery.
- The purpose of the loan agreement and condition report is to keep the standards consistent and the communication levels open to make any changes effective and to focus on the proper care of the object.

Working extensively with objects being packed and transported for various loans and touring exhibitions, I have always admired the dedication and persistence of the collection care staff designated to overseeing these collection care activities. These individuals must maintain the focus and dedication to collection care as the risks to the object are always present. Often, when a loan or exhibition is first lent and then arrives at its destination, the attention to activities can be highlighted by the drama of the events surrounding the object and the overall program for which it was requested. After the loan has been completed, the exhibition is closed and the excitement diminished, that same focus and dedication to the object's departure must be maintained to the highest levels and standards as when it arrived.

I use the analogy of decorating the Christmas tree. Each year in the events surrounding the holiday season, people spend time decorating the house and placing their precious ornaments on the tree. When the tree is taken down, it is not as exciting, but still those precious ornaments need to be cared for, packed securely, and stored to survive for the next Christmas. Setting up for Christmas is much more exciting than taking down the decorations. Keeping the level of enthusiasm, dedication, and focus at the end of the program is just as important as at the beginning. The common remark often heard when the loan returns to the museum is "I forgot the object was still on loan or I thought that the exhibition was over ages ago." Collection care has no scheduled end date when an object is lent; it is a continual process until it returns.

Condition Reports

A condition report for an object being lent is specific to the details of the loan. This type of condition report varies considerably from a conservation condition report for history and treatment of the object, but it does include the object's primary physical composition and inherent properties. The complete conservation report can be referenced if past history or some discrepancies are in question.

A good condition report is an accurate and informative account of an object's state of preservation at a particular moment in time. It provides a verbal and visual description of the nature, location, and the extent of each defect in a clear, consistent manner. A condition report written by a registrar, curator, or collection manager is not the same as a condition report written by a conservator. The former aids collection management while the latter is intended for planning and performing object treatment.

A condition report can

- establish the exact condition of an object at the time of its departure or upon its return;
- benchmark the type and rate of deterioration;
- differentiate otherwise identical objects from one another;
- document an object's condition history, providing past evidence for future problems;
- set priorities for conservation care and treatment;
- suggest a default monetary value for an object in lieu of the actual value for insurance purposes; and
- make future handlers aware of seen and unseen problems.[4]

There is not much written regarding condition report descriptions. These reports vary per institution and the type of object. The primary notations of size, weight, title, ID tracking numbers, and so on will follow a similar path. The details and descriptions of the terms used vary tremendously and are specific to the object, the material it is made of, and the overarching type of collection to which it belongs. A condition report for a Chinese hand scroll differs tremendously from a condition report for a Native American headdress; possibly both could be found in the same exhibition as well.

For more information, a good source related to the various general activities involved in the preparation of a condition report is the following: Collection Management, Section 5 (d), Condition Reporting, Marie Demeroukas, *Museum Registration Methods*, 5th edition; 2010, pages 223–232. This MRM document includes a Condition Report Glossary of common terms used to describe conditions commonly found on objects (pages 227–230) and a sample Condition Report for two-dimensional works (pages 231–232).

Courier Responsibilities

A courier provides a chain of custody when an object is shipped from one institution to another. The courier is a representative of the owner of the work; she/he may be a staff member of the lending institution, an independent contractor, or a staff member of a sister institution sharing the task.

There are many good reasons for museums to send a courier along when an object travels locally, nationally, and internationally. Museums make the decision to have a courier accompanying a shipment when shipping is not direct, when an object has a high value or is very fragile, when customs have to be cleared, or when the object has special installation requirements. The destination could be down the block, or a trip could easily last thirty to forty hours with combined surface and air transportation. Couriered shipments may be soft-packed, crated, or placed in a special case for a hand-carry.[5]

Certain museum objects are of a fragile nature, whether by construction or formation, size, materials used, or deterioration by age or abuse, and may require special handling or installation techniques. Certain museum objects are irreplaceable, rare, and unique; politically or culturally sensitive; of extreme artistic, historical, or scientific worth; or of extreme value for other reasons.

Certain shipping routes may prove dangerous for fragile museum objects because such routes expose the object to careless handling, excessive movement, changing or extreme temperatures, and other human and/or natural hazards.

The courier must be a museum professional (who understands the condition of the object and its special requirements, is familiar with packing, trained in handling, and, as applicable, experienced in transport procedures) in whom the lending museum reposes complete trust for execution of all courier-related duties.[6]

PACKING AND CRATING OPTIONS

The purpose of packing and crating objects is to provide structural support for protecting the object when it is being handled or transported. The information provided here will present the various methods and methodologies that are commonly used and the levels of protection that can be provided against the risks encountered by the object in the external environment. Two primary options are soft packing and fully crated designs, which will be addressed in the following paragraphs, with various design options for each.

Each object is different in its size, weight, shape, and structural and material makeup. Each object has its specific inherent properties that dictate the individual treatment that will inform the packing design. Understanding the need for protecting the object during transport starts with the factor of the travel distance between the points of origin and destination and the potential risks the object may encounter. The analysis of the approach to designing the packing to avoid risks is the same as for the housing (box) to move an object within the museum as well as for moving the object in a fully crated state for a touring exhibition traveling to various venues around the world.

The analysis of design is to create the components required for "working from the object out." In this approach, the object is considered at every level of protection and that is added to the final design. The first consideration is for the packing materials that will come into direct contact with the object and how that will create the structural support for the object when it is placed into the structure of the box.

A basic analogy of this concept is putting an organic shape into a geometric shape while maintaining its support integrity. Once accomplished, it becomes a simple geometric shape to handle instead of an organic shape that can be awkward. The combination of using this geometric shape in the multiple facets of transport, ease in handling, equipment, and the choice of transport suitable for the traveling distance will offer countless solutions of risk protection as compared to handling the object in an organic configuration. The risks during the rigors of handling and transport in the external environment are similar to the ones found within the internal environment: temperature, relative humidity, shock and vibration, pests and pollutants. Though similar, these risk factors can vary tremendously in the levels involved . The packing design needs to anticipate these variations in relation to the time, distance, location, and environmental fluctuations it may encounter. The following are two types of packing designs and examples that will explain some of the common options that have been proved to be successful.

Soft-Packing Options

The term "soft packing" is defined as a design method of packing an object with materials that give the object structural support and protection without the solid, hard-shell structure offered by a crate.

- Soft packing can be an effective method of handling objects, but the risk factors must be considered and monitored at every step.
- Soft-packing methods employ materials that will be used once and then disposed.
- The decision to soft pack an object should take into account the distance it will be moved, the handling time, and the staff and equipment to accommodate it safely.

- The most common benefit is that if the risk can be mitigated in the soft packing, the expense of not building a fully crated object is economically viable. Budgetary concerns can often overshadow the analysis of risk to the object.
- Individuals who choose an insufficient level of soft packing design to save money are gambling with the risks that may be encountered in the overall transport.
- The steps in adding additional support and protection can easily provide the quality of protection needed and at little additional cost.
- The decision to fully crate the object in a hard shell may, in the end, be the best for the extra money, but again assessing the levels of risk in using soft packing designs must be fully understood.

Levels of Design Steps of Protection

The following paragraphs will give a basic explanation of the different levels of protection that can be easily offered by the soft-packing method. There are many technical and manufacturer names to describe materials. I will be using the most generic terms to give clarity to the function of the material. The example is of one type of object, a framed painting, that will give the reader a visual understanding of the steps. These same levels can be applied for other objects when the type and amount of protection is considered.

Wrapping Concepts

The first, most common step of protection is to wrap the painting in a barrier of plastic sheeting. Depending upon the painting and frame surface, an additional barrier of breathable or impermeable sheeting material may be provided to protect the surfaces from abrasion or adhesion, which sometimes occurs when plastic is directly applied to the object.

- Bubble wrap is the most common sheeting used because of its combination of air-cushioned pads with the sheeted plastic, which can create a sealed and padded surface.
- Cushioned paper wrap will need to be used with a barrier to protect the surface of the object from the abrasiveness of the paper.
- A removals or packing blanket can be used in combination with a barrier sheeting to protect the object against abrasion from plastic sheeting and to create a sealed environment.
- Additional padding can be provided to the corners and bottom of the frame of the wrapped package for additional protection from shock and vibration during handling and transport.

Housing Concepts

If additional protection is chosen, a more solid sheeted material can be added to create a simple housing that will add to the structural support and reduce the risk of puncture through the wrapping.

Corrugated sheeting (cardboard) is often placed on both sides of the painting, which creates a sandwich effect by placing a semisolid sheet of protection on the two main sides of the wrapped object. Corrugated sheeting can be increased in strength by using fully sheeted single, double-, or triple-thick corrugated sheets or by cross-corrugating sheets to increase the support dramatically. Corrugated plastic sheeting (similar structural design in fluting and sheeting combination) can also be used, but will require different construction techniques to provide a similar design to paper corrugate.

A fully corrugated box or housing can be purchased or built to house the painting. The level of interior padding can be increased to supply additional support and protection against shock and vibration to the object. A fully boxed, soft-packed object can be the next step to fully packing it in a hard-shell crate.

Creative Alternatives between Soft Packing and Fully Crated Objects

Because of their size, weight, and structural makeup, in combination with distant venues and transport distances, some objects may require an alternative level of protection that falls between soft packing and fully crated design.

An object can be placed on and supported by a pallet, which can then be moved. The object must be secured to the pallet, padded, and a barrier put on the bottom of the object to protect it from the pallet surface. The object can then be wrapped or covered to protect it against the elements. Extra support can be provided by attaching a slat or skeletal structure to the pallet base, rising above, and connecting around and over the object. Additional support bracing further secures the object and allows for protective coverings.

An extreme example is when an open-top or flat-bed truck is used for transporting a large object, with the object being placed on the truck bed in a similar fashion to that of the palletized surface. The object is rigged on/off the truck, and wrapping and securing is kept to a minimum.

The cargo section of the truck can be designed and used as a box or housing. The object is placed inside the cargo section and the padding, support, and bracing are attached directly to the interior walls and floor. This example would follow a similar structural support design as is found in a skeletal or possibly a fully crated structure.

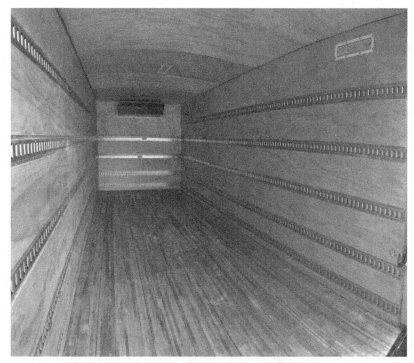

Figure 7.5 Truck Cargo Bay as the Box. *Source*: Carey, Artex FAS.

Figure 7.6 Air Cargo Container as the Box. *Source*: Author.

This same design is often used when packing an object into an air-freight container. The benefits of using this type of container is that it can be arranged to be brought to the museum or packing location where the object resides, and the packing can then be conducted with the essential materials available. If the packing can only be done at the airport cargo terminal, the freight forwarder must have the essential materials on site. The interior of these containers has strapping mechanisms inside to allow for multiple attachment options of straps and bracing.

Similar to the air-freight container is the sea container, which can be designed to be used as a housing or box. Additional support structure and dunnage (packing) need to be provided because of the extreme rigors of movement in all directions and the shock and vibration that occur in sea-freight transport. The packing of a sea container needs to be done on the site where the object resides and where the proper handling equipment and materials are.

Research has been conducted and evaluated on the benefits and risks involved in moving soft-packed objects. An excellent report to reference is titled *Soft Pack—The Soft Option?* written by David Saunders, Christine Leback Sitwell, and Sarah Staniforth for the 1991 *Art in Transit* publication and Conference Presentation. The National Trust throughout England, Wales, and Northern Ireland transports paintings using basic, soft-packed methods because it does not have the trained staff or budget to have its paintings fully crated. The research follows the standards of handling, transport, and packing commonly used in the soft-packing design which are compared with the standards for fully crated objects used by the National Gallery of London. The research procedures and the results are an excellent explanation of the risks encountered and the benefits derived from understanding and using the soft-packing design.

Fully Crated Options

To fully crate an object for transport is to make the commitment to design a secure protective structure in combination with the appropriate interior packing system to protect the object or objects within the crate shell. A similar design concept as for the storage cabinet or display case is used for the crate: the "box in the box" concept. The crate and its interior packing creates an effective microclimate in which the object can be protected against the various environmental effects and the handling of transport.

The Interior Packing Concepts

The interior packing is custom-built to house the object or objects that are to be transported. The primary function of interior packing is to make sure

Figure 7.7   Crate / Box Within Box Concept. *Source*: Carey, Artex FAS.

that the object rides "in tandem" with the packing material, in combination with the structural support of the external crate. The "in tandem" design minimizes or eliminates the constant levels of shock and vibration during transport, which is the primary risk that the object can encounter during all handling and transport. Packing the object in a crate-within-a-crate (box-within-a-box) disperses the shock and vibration that are transferred through to the interior box and its contents. Interior packing design protects the object by creating a microclimate to decrease fluctuations of temperature and humidity levels and forming a barrier to eliminate moisture penetration. The interior packing should be designed for simple understanding by the various individuals who will be unpacking and repacking the object. Packing designs should be easily understood as to how the object should be handled in relation to the materials, supports, or bracing that are required to properly protect the object during the transport. A good rule of thumb is to "pack the object so that the individual unpacking it can clearly understand how it is to be unpacked." To assist in the steps of unpacking and then repacking the object, there should be registration marks, a written explanation (in relation to the packing manual or condition report), spaces for hand access, and diagrams of hardware accessibility.

The Exterior Crate Concepts

The exterior crate shell supports the interior packing design. Crates can be custom-designed, or be retrofitted and recycled. The shell becomes a protective layer that retards the effects of moisture, temperature, and humidity fluctuations, and prevents possible puncture penetration into the interior packing. The crate can be outfitted to meet additional microclimate components that the object may need during its transport; for insulation against temperature fluctuations; for double-sealed housings; for components to maintain RH levels; and for monitoring equipment to track various effects of transport handling.

Moisture penetration can be eliminated by painting (sealing) the crate exterior, gluing or caulking (sealing) all joints, adding a barrier lining material to the interior crate shell, and by gasketing the lid or related access points to the crate interior.

The quality of the crate shell is assessed for its overall strength, weight, and costs to determine the best design to support the interior packing. The shell of the crate is commonly built by using sheets of plywood or other cross-composite material that is then attached to battens or wooden support structures to create each side. The sides are joined together in either a butt-joint or a cross-joint (lapped) configuration attached with glue and screws, except for the side that is to be opened (lid) to allow access.

Crates should be designed to accommodate the various individuals who will be moving the crate during all phases of transport; the more user friendly the crate, the more care will be given to handling the crate by the person moving it. Simple components such as lifting handles, handling markings, and structural support for equipment-lifting access points underneath the crate in the form of skids or feet will assist in the operation of mechanical handling devices, such as dollies, pallet jacks, case movers, and forklifts. Designing the crate so that it can accommodate one, or preferably all these equipment types, will ensure that the crate is handled smoothly and effectively.

The crate and objects are subjected to shock and vibration most when the crate is being physically handled in the museum, via transport equipment (dollies, pallet jacks, and forklifts) and moved into or out of the transport vehicle.

Figure 7.8 Crate / Fully Sealed Crate. *Source*: IAS Sydney, Australia.

Interior Packing Design Options

Designing an interior packing requires, first, the object's being assessed as to the various risks it will encounter in regard to its physical and inherent properties. An object can be wrapped and packed within the crate directly or it can be supported in the crate by an interior packing that will both structurally support the object during transport and double as an object handling device into and out of the crate.

The Object Alone/Basic Pack

The crate acts as the initial handling box with the object being packed directly into the crate. This basic packing is created by adding loose fill, padding, or bracing, which is fitted to the interior of the crate and which will support the object from shifting during transport movement. This is a common method for a small single shipment that will travel a short distance and is less fragile, but needs the structural support of a solid full crate rather than a cardboard box.

A crate-within-a-crate (box-within-a-box) design is the common approach to creating a second layer of structural protection within the crate. Dispersing shock and vibration is more easily achieved by the crate-within-a-crate design, and it is often used for very fragile objects such as pastels, glass, or objects with surfaces that are friable to touch or to shock and vibration.

This protective environment is best achieved by placing the object in "a-package-within-a-package" (box inside a box). In general terms, the object is packed in a primary container, and is then floated in shock-absorbent materials within a solid outer shell. Both stages of packing in this procedure— packing the object in the primary container and then into its outer shell—are governed by the same criteria for safety: there must be no movement in any direction, and the floated item should be a safe distance from the hard surfaces of its protective container. (Although such a design safeguards the object from all threats, it is particularly important in preventing shocks to the outer shell from being transmitted to the artwork.)[7]

Corrugated Box

Corrugated boxes can be purchased in standard sizes and thicknesses, composed of plastic or brown (acidic) or blue (archival) paper-based, fluted and sheeted material. This same corrugated material can be purchased in sheets to build a custom-sized box. Creating a template pattern on the sheet offers many different styles to be cut, scored, folded, and glued into the size, shape, and style of box desired. The added benefit of using plastic sheeting is that plastic creates an excellent seal against moisture and offers a stronger structural support.

Corrugated support dividers can be easily made from leftover material and fitted in the box for packing multiple objects. Doubling or cross-corrugating pieces of the sections will increase the structural support of the divider sections.

Foam Sheet Box

Boxes that can be built easily are those made from Foam-Cor or Gatorfoam. Foam-Cor is constructed from sheets of foam (of varying thicknesses) that are covered with paper on each full side. Gaterfoam is another type of sheeting composed of a denser, more rigid foam that is covered with a more durable paper. Both foam sheets can be easily cut and assembled by hot-gluing sections in a butt-joint formation. The edges can be taped to prevent foam dusting and can be used as a hinging system for lid attachments. The complete box can be wrapped in polyethylene (plastic) sheeting to create a sealed moisture barrier.

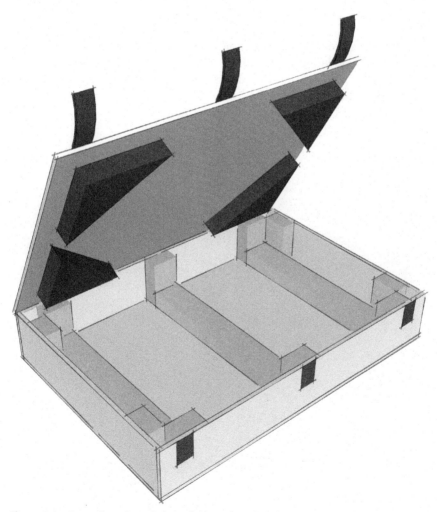

Figure 7.9   Foam Core Box. *Source*: Barber, Artex FAS.

Travel Frame

Travel frames are designed to act as a rigid support on which to attach a flat, low-relief object or a framed, two-dimensional object. The most common is a five-sided wooden structure to which the framed object can be attached. The sixth side is the opening into which the framed work, attached and then covered with a corrugated sheeting or plastic cover, is placed.

The flat or framed object can be attached to the travel frame with metal mending plates or Oz Clips, which are attached to the back of the frame, rotated out, extending past the edge of the frame to allow an attaching screw or bolt system, and attached directly to the support frame.

Brace Pack

Brace designs are the most common type of support within the crate. The braces that come into contact with the object are padded and attached to the wall of the crate or the inner crate. Braces must be marked and identified for the exact location where they should be placed and how they are to be attached. An effective method is to create guide blocks to ensure that they are located correctly.

Figure 7.10   Brace Pack Design. *Source*: IAS Sydney, Australia.

Contour Braces/Guillotines, Yokes

Contour bracing is created by cutting foam to the specific shape of an object that will support the object at its contact point and be braced to the wall of the crate or the interior box. The foam is cut and shaped to one half of the object, and the other half of the brace supports the other side of the object in the same level area. In combination, they support the object on each side in one corresponding unit of support. The back side of the brace is secured to the interior of the crate and acts as a receiving guide or lock. The front half of the brace can be removed so that the object can be lifted out or pulled from the crate. The packing design is used to brace the object in a horizontal fashion, but it can be used to pack an object vertically as well. The object must be able to withstand its sliding into and out of the bracing with ease. The guillotine or yoke is a good visual name to describe how the elements brace the object.

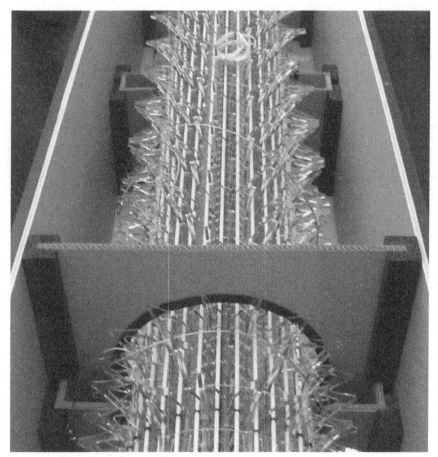

Figure 7.11   Guillotine / Yoke Pack Design. *Source:* IAS Sydney, Australia.

Multiple Object Interior Packing

Frame-Slot Design

A frame-slot design creates slots or openings into which a framed work can be packed and supported in a customized slot. The slot is lined with a nonabrasive material, which allows a compatible framed object or a plastic-wrapped frame to be slid directly into its designated slot. This is an extremely effective packing design, which allows a number of similarly sized objects to be transported in one crate and to be easily packed and unpacked.

Travel Frame Slots

A travel frame-slot design is similar to a frame-slot system. This design is used for large-sized works, which require the additional support of a travel frame. The travel frame slides into a custom slot, which is accessed through one end of the crate and allows the object to be packed directly into the crate. Depending on the size and weight of the object within the frame, this design may be able to accommodate only two or three travel frames for safe handling of the fully packed crate.

Drawer Packing

Drawers or boxes can be designed as drawers that can slide into a crate by following support tracks in a horizontal format. The drawers or boxes can be removed and used as a handling support until the object is unpacked. The top of the drawer is covered with a corrugated sheet to protect the contents of the drawer. Visually, it follows the same design as a travel frame slot, except that the drawer design travels in a horizontal instead of a vertical fashion.

Multiple Object Tray Dividers

The packing within a tray can be separated by dividers constructed to separate the tray or box into compartments. Objects can be wrapped or padded individually and placed into the compartments. The dividers can be constructed using corrugated sheeting or other appropriate sheeting material to create the support structure.

Cavity Pack

The cavity pack is a custom design that is tailored totally to the shape of the entire object. The interior of the drawer, box, or tray is first filled with layers of foam sheeting that will fill the entire interior space. The shape of the object is then assessed and measured, so that a cavity can be cut from the layers of foam that will accommodate the exact shape of the object. Depending on the

Figure 7.12 Slot Pack Design. *Source*: IAS Sydney, Australia.

object's size, shape, and fragility, additional space is allotted for extra packing to cushion or reduce abrasion from the foam cavity.

An effective cavity pack must be constructed by an experienced packer to make sure that the shape, support material, and layers of foam accommodate the object properly. The layers must be carved in steps to create the cavity—whether it is a single layer or multiple layers of foam. If layers must be removed to access the object, then related markings should be added to the registration marks so that it can be easily repacked in the same manner.

The author's noncollection example of a cavity pack: My mother-in-law, a gourmet cook, used to say I grew the best tomatoes. She lived across the country, so I would, in season, send her some ripe tomatoes packed in a cavity pack design via the postal service. It was assessed as extreme risk to a delicate object, but my knowledge of the design proved to be extremely cost efficient and effective. The Japanese are known to use similar methods for packing high-end, elegant produce that is ripe, flawless in appearance, and perfect for the consumer. This is not an endorsement for shipping valuable, fragile art, or artifacts in this manner, as the risk to irreplaceable objects is not as easy as it was for going to my garden for some more ripe tomatoes.

Multiple Packing Designs for Traveling Exhibitions

The designs for packing multiple objects should be used for traveling exhibitions. Drawers, trays, and boxes with interior dividers allow multiple objects to be packed safely into a single inner box, which can then be combined with

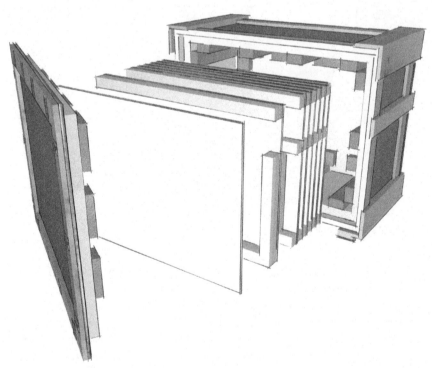

Figure 7.13   Multiple Pack Design. *Source*: Barber, Artex FAS.

other inner boxes that can then travel in a single crate. These multiple designs are extremely effective in reducing risks to an exhibition that has many objects that need to be transported. These designs must be undertaken by individuals who understand the risks in combining different objects within similar housings that are then placed into a single crate. The benefits are that fewer crates mean fewer handling risks and reduced expenses in the overall budget.

Crate Design Options

The crate is the protective exterior shell for which the interior packing has been designed to work in unison with the crate to protect the object during the rigors of transport. This shell protects its contents from the external environment's damaging conditions.

The crate itself is often underestimated in its importance in protecting its contents. Building the appropriate crate will ensure the safety of the interior packing required for protecting its contents. The climatic conditions and handling situations that an object faces during transport should be anticipated, and steps should be taken to afford the best care and protection within the budget constraints of the exhibition.

Single Shipment

A single shipment, also known as a one-time crate, can be as basic as a six-sided wooden box with no structural support battens. One side opens for accessing the interior, and the outside should have handles and skids to assist in movement. An example of a single-shipment crate would be housing for an object during transport from seller to buyer: one way; no return.

Multiple Shipment

A multiple shipment, also known as a two-way or return crate is a six-sided wooden box with structural support battens placed on all external edges. The battens act as additional support for the corners or edges of the crate and to which the side components can be joined more securely in construction. This fully battened crate is the best standard and from which all basic crate designs are developed for various transport requirements in both the museum and commercial crating scenarios.

2-D Side Loader

A 2-D side-loading crate offers access to the interior by removal of one of the two largest sides of the crate. The crate is laid down on one side and the opposite side is then removed. For an extremely large and heavy crate, the side can be removed with the crate in an upright position as long as the crate can be secured to a wall by tilting or tying off the main body so that it does not move as the lid is being removed. An example of a side loader would be one made for a large painting or framed work traveling as a single object to one or more venues.

End Loader

The end-loader crate allows one end of the crate to be removed for accessing the interior. This design is often used for large, heavy objects, which are slid into or out of the end of the crate, unlike the object being lifted up and out of a side-loading crate. Depending on the type and size of object, multiple objects can be transported in one crate, thus reducing the number of crates, cutting costs, and minimizing handling. An example of an end-loading crate would be one that is designed to transport paintings housed in travel frames.

Top Loading

The top-loading crate is basically just as it is called: the top of the crate is removed for accessing the interior. This design can be used for many

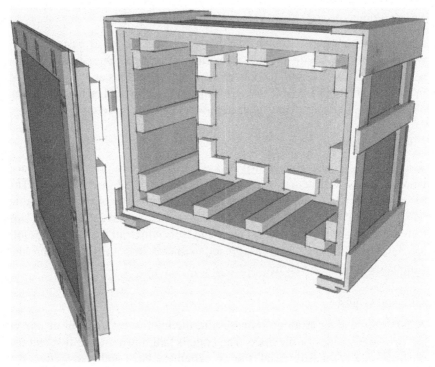

Figure 7.14   Crate / Side Loader Design. *Source:* Barber, Artex FAS.

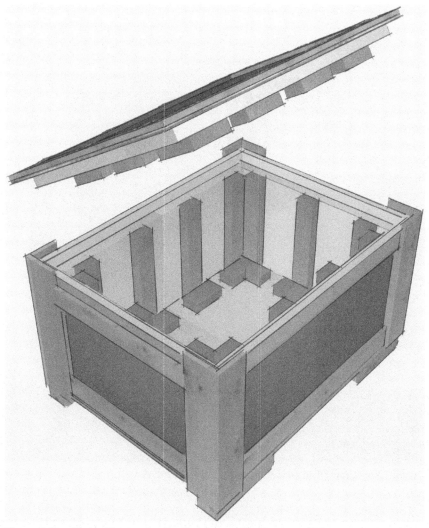

Figure 7.15 Crate / Top Loader Design. *Source*: Barber, Artex FAS.

types of objects and multiple objects as the interior can be adapted accordingly. Depending on the size and weight of the object, the major factor is how the object can be easily lifted up and out of the crate. The layers of support provided by the use of boxes or trays can make a top-loading crate a versatile transport container. The layers of support can be lifted out of the crate and used for housing and handling the object during its next use. An extremely heavy object can be rigged out of a top-loading crate if

Figure 7.16   Crate / End Loader. *Source*: Carey, Artex FAS.

adequate access is allowed for inserting lifting straps to be placed around the object.

3-D Side Loader

A 3-D side-loading crate offers the access to the interior of the crate by the removal of one of the larger sides of the crate. The crate remains in its upright position, with side or lid removed, and the objects contained within are removed. Depending on how the objects are packed, any internal bracing, boxes, trays, or drawers can be pulled or slid out of the crate. For heavy objects, often a floor plate or tray will support and slide the object into and out of the crate while the object remains in place on the plate, which can then be used to handle and transport the object to its destination.

Slot Crate

A slot crate often has its opening on either the top or side of the crate. When the lid is removed, the interior of the crate can be used to transport a series of framed objects, which can be slid into and out of the designated slot.

Touring Crate

A touring crate is built for repeated use and durability over a longer period of time, for example, the duration of a traveling exhibition with multiple venues. The crate must have reusable hardware, convenient handles, and components that allow staff and equipment to move the crate easily. The exterior should be sealed for moisture protection, and proper markings must be applied to make sure that handling is done in the correct manner throughout packing, unpacking, and transport.

Figure 7.17   Crate / Kiva Plastic Design. *Source*: Carey, Artex FAS.

Figure 7.18   Crate / Kiva Stacked Design. *Source*: Carey, Artex FAS.

Break-Away Crate

A break-away crate, also known as exploding crate, is designed so that the top and each side of the crate can be dismantled and removed to access the object within. The object can remain on the crate bottom or pallet and be moved to

Figure 7.19 Crate / Kiva Interior Design. *Source*: Carey, Artex FAS.

its next destination. This design is extremely effective for transporting large, heavy objects.

Composite Crate

A composite crate is built from a combination of materials: cardboard, corrugated plastic, composite or particle board, honeycomb aluminum panels, and aluminum or steel structural supports. An example of a composite crate is one that has been constructed from corrugated plastic on the sides instead of plywood, thus reducing the combined overall weight. The plastic sheeting offers structural strength and puncture protection comparable to those of plywood.

Figure 7.20   Crate / Barrel Design. *Source*: Carey, Artex FAS.

Corrugated Plastic Crates

Commercially viable crates are sometimes built totally of plastic materials: walls, lids, pallets, and locking devices. These crates can be adapted to meet many transport or storage needs. The combinations of parts and interchangeable parts can make this design an effective resource for multiple-use needs.

Barrel Design

Commercially viable barrel designs are available for a unique packing design. They are available in durable paper-based composition materials for the cylinder section and lined with an interior wax coating for a moisture barrier. The lid and base are commonly made of metal, with the lid having a metal clamping strap for securing it to the main body. This shape can be adapted for many interior shapes.

Slat Crate

A slat crate is often viewed as a hybrid between soft packing and fully crating an object. When assembled, the structural support can create effective protection without being completely sheeted between the slats or supports. This type of design can reduce weight and material costs and be effectively

Figure 7.21   Crate / Slat or Skeletal Design. *Source*: IAS Sydney, Australia.

used for large or awkwardly shaped objects. A protective cover from dust and moisture can be created by enveloping the structure in plastic sheeting or tarpaulins. It is a compatible and very effective design for noncollection objects that may need to travel with the object, such as display cases, pedestals, plinths, or decorative components involved in a touring exhibition.

COMMERCIAL SERVICE COMPANIES

Throughout this book, commercial companies that provide collection care services have been referenced and cited. In this section, I would like to focus on the collection care service that these companies offer and their relationships to museums. Collection care principles and methods and methodology continue to be the primary focus of these service companies as they rely on their professionalism to sustain their customer base and growth in the market. Their clients include museums, commercial galleries, corporate collections and private collectors.

Over the last thirty years, the level of training and communication between the staff of museums and the staff of the service providers has improved dramatically. Prior to the 1980s, the two groups were working for the same goal but from two different perspectives, and they often struggled to understand each other's concerns regarding the required needs of the object. Museum staff work within a single collection, within a limited location, and within a focused mission of preserving the object. Commercial staff work with multiple collections, in multiple locations, and with a mission of providing the customer with the best possible service. Good communication between the two groups is crucial because their levels of knowledge about the needs and standards that must be met for each activity vary. Each party has much to gain from the other: museums offer standards of best practice for the preservation and collection care of objects, and commercial providers offer multiple options, based on the diversity in their client base, for performing specific activities. Together, they can offer a broad range of solutions for collection care activities.

The type of service that these businesses offer varies and is dependent upon the market needs, staff expertise, facility structure, and level of growth and expansion that they can manage and maintain. The major difference between museums and the commercial company is that museums are, for the most part, nonprofit organizations, and commercial companies are for profit. The services offered by them must be profitable on an ongoing basis, which means that clients must use their services regularly for the companies to maintain the overhead costs to staff and facilitate that service. Other services require long-term investment in a building, infrastructure, and specialized vehicles.

A comparison that I have used over the years from my experience working on both sides of this industry is the following: a good idea in a museum can be researched and developed over a period of time both in staff commitment and in budget allocation to see the idea come to fruition. A good idea in the commercial sector can be researched and developed, but must be formulated within a shorter period of time so that it requires less staff time and a budget that must be supported for a quick return of profit and a future for its becoming a part of the service offerings. This is a comparison of a nonprofit and a for-profit perspective for seeing an idea put into practice.

Services primarily offered by companies typically include local, regional, and international transport, installation, packing and crating, and short- or long-term storage. Other services can be matting and framing, mount making, display-case production, photography, and documentation services.

Many larger companies have full-service offerings. These are activities related to their primary business of installation, packing, and transport. An example of full-service offerings can be managing communications between parties, packing and crating the object, transporting it to its destination, and following up with the installation of the object. They can also provide project management, national and international shipping, custom brokering, management of government regulations, courier services, airport supervision, insurance options, photography, and short- and long-term storage facilities.

The commercial services that will be highlighted in the following paragraphs include truck transport, international air and sea transport, customized storage, packing and crating, installation, and rigging. Many of the other service offerings may be referenced but will not be explained in great detail. To understand more of what a commercial service provider can offer, call or email to make an appointment to discuss your needs and interests and to learn the details of what they have to offer. Communication is the key in creating a sound working relationship between the museum and commercial service provider. Both parties need to discuss the collection care methods and methodology that the museum client needs and what the provider can offer.

Truck Transport Options

There are many varieties of specialized truck transport that are available on the market. If you own a classic car, there are trucks and trailers specially made to transport it. If you have a military airplane or tank in your collection to be moved, there is a transport company that offers that service. If you need a house moved (and not just the contents), then, yes, that can be done as well. The point of this introduction is to emphasize the need to find the specialist and type of truck to do the job in the best possible way.

The term common carrier is often used to refer to companies that transport a variety of freight and mixed shipments, have minimal suspension and no climate controls, and may load and reload shipments at one warehouse hub, then load them onto another truck several times during the transit. The latter is called "cross-docking" and is a standard practice with such carriers as UPS (United Parcel Service) and FedEx. The costs are less, but the risks are higher for the object.

A common carrier can be a good solution for transporting less fragile, large, and stable objects or display elements from one location to another if it guarantees that the objects will not be taken off and reloaded. Some common carriers that transport delicate objects such as computers have air-ride suspension and climate control for their cargo box. Objects that have restrictive or hazardous materials, such as wet tissue specimens, may require a specific licensed "hazardous materials or waste" carrier that can be employed to transport these objects legally. Common carrier transport can be a viable alternative if you can be guaranteed that your shipment will not be cross-docked or that it will only require minimum handling during the shipment.

We will focus on companies that specialize in shipping art and artifacts and use trucks that have enclosed cargo boxes and are equipped with specialized features to provide safe and reliable transport to nearly any location.

Exclusive Use

This service deals with one institution's cargo, with all stops and deliveries defined by the institution. This is door-to-door delivery service. Exclusive use affords maximum control in timing and security. The registrar chooses the day, time, and route and can make arrangements for special guards or museum couriers to accompany the shipment. This, naturally, is the most expensive service.

Last On, First Off (LOFO)

Other freight may be on the truck, but the LOFO shipment is guaranteed to be the last freight loaded and the first unloaded. There is slightly less control of the time and slightly less cost than with exclusive use. This is a uniquely American service, not available in Europe.

Expedited Use

With this service, the shipper indicates a certain finite range of dates during which your shipment as well as other freight will be loaded on the vehicle. Each shipment has a reserved space. This service is less expensive than exclusive-use service.

Shuttle Service

This service is defined as "less than truckload lots" (LTL) or smaller "space reservation" with no special time or route restrictions. Shuttle service is the least expensive method and can be safe, but in some cases it may be more time consuming. Ask for details of the route and whether your cargo will be off-loaded or "cross-docked."[8]

Figure 7.22   Regional Support. *Source*: Carey, Artex FAS.

Figure 7.23   Long Distance Shuttle. *Source*: Carey, Artex FAS.

Figure 7.24   Tractor Trailer, Interstate. *Source*: Carey, Artex FAS.

Figure 7.25   Truck Fleet Sizes and Styles. *Source*: Carey, Artex FAS.

Specialized Transport Equipment

Trucks vary in size and the type of equipment they have to provide specialized protection during the transport. The following are highlights of available
truck types and the type of equipment that offer the best standards of collection care for transporting art and artifacts:

Figure 7.26 Trailer Interior Cargo. *Source*: Carey, Artex FAS.

- Air-ride suspension is available on all sizes of trucks, from vans to the long-distance tractor trailer. This suspension is designed to give the truck a smoother ride with varying load capacities.
- Climate-controlled cargo spaces are equipped to cool and heat the environment to maintain temperature and relative humidity levels during transport. Digital monitors within the cab provide the driver and occupants with the current temperature and RH levels within the cargo space. All information is recorded for the duration of the transport. The shell or body of the cargo space of the truck can be insulated as well so as to help in maintaining the interior environment created by the climate controls.
- Some climate controls have been designed and developed to supply and remove humidity whereas standard units can only take humidity out, but cannot supply additional humidity. See the Climate Control Transport/Australian Case Study in chapter 8.
- The cargo space is commonly equipped with tie rails for attaching straps to objects and to secure them to the walls or floors. Various other tie points can be made to accommodate various objects and load structures as they occur.
- Aluminum customized support or stabilizing bars can supply cross-bracing from side to side within the box, which provides options for securing loads. Some interiors will also accept vertical bars, attached to floor and ceiling, which also aid in support.

Figure 7.27   Staff Loading Cargo into a Truck. *Source*: Carey, Artex FAS.

Figure 7.28 Truck and Trailer Docked. *Source*: Carey, Artex FAS.

- Trucks and trailers of all sizes are equipped with hydraulic lift gates that come in various sizes and platform types. When loading crates or pallets on the lifting platform, caution needs to be maintained in that the load is secure and will not be subjected to toppling off the platform when it is lifted or lowered during operation.
- Staff should support the load by riding on the platform if physical space allows them to be stable in their supportive stance. Staff must be cautious when climbing on and off the platform at any level of operations, and the only safety barrier is their attention to the actions being performed.
- Loading ramps or dock plates can be used to ease the transition of loads from dock to cargo floor. These ramps and plates reduce the sudden shock and vibration that can be encountered in varying levels at these transition points.
- Standard equipment travels with the trucks to assist in handling the objects: dollies, pallet jack, J-bars, moving blankets, and padding of various sorts. Specialized equipment such as forklifts and rigging tools, if required, may need to be contracted.
- Satellite tracking is most common on long-distance transport but is a developing feature on local and regional transport. Cellular phones and other

communication devices are supplied for drivers, allowing contact at all times during transport.

- Two drivers should be required for all transport activities to assist in driving as well as security in case of an accident or during times of layovers. Drivers are cross-trained in company practices for handling, packing, and installation, which benefits the client in terms of the quality of handling throughout the transport.
- Additional space in most regional or long-distance vehicles has accommodation for the driver to sleep or relax between shifts. These spaces can also be used to accommodate a courier, if required to travel with a shipment.
- Many commercial vans now are standup box vans, which allow staff to stand upright in the space and to which taller objects can be secured. These vans are very advantageous in moving small, single shipments in the "exclusive use" format.
- Standard local or regional trucks are often referred to as straight trucks. These smaller-sized trucks come in cargo sizes of 10' to 26'. The cargo height can vary depending on the type of truck.
- Tractor-trailers are the largest commercial vehicles and have a cargo capacity of 30' to 54'. Trailer doors vary in height from 105" to 117". High-cube trailers can be as tall as 125" in height.

Commercial Storage/General and Climate-Controlled

All commercial service companies offer some level of storage for collection objects on a temporary or long-term rental basis. The two main types of storage offered are general storage and climate-controlled storage, with one distinct difference. General storage has only the basic interior environmental levels regarding temperature and humidity controls. Climate-controlled storage has specific controls to maintain and monitor temperature and humidity levels to museum industry standards. Each company can offer several options for storage equipment, handling expertise, environmental protection, and security, depending upon its investment and client needs.

For museums, commercial storage can be a viable alternative to building or refitting an existing building to meet the growing needs of storing their collections. These spaces can be an excellent solution for short-term storage such as housing traveling exhibitions between transport, storing empty exhibition crates, or holding incoming or outgoing shipments before transport.

For long-term storage, a museum may consider the cost of renting a space in comparison to the investment it would take to develop and manage a space of its own. A contract between the museum and commercial storage facility can be negotiated to accommodate various types of objects and multiple levels of access, and for varying time periods.

A commercial service company has the advantage of having its own facility or refitting a building to meet the needs of the client. This approach requires a large investment of time and money; this can then be supported by having multiple clients rent the spaces, which will ensure the continued income required to maintain and to provide profit margins to make it a viable business opportunity. Some spaces, when being developed, can be designed to a specific client's collection; however, a contract with the client should be negotiated before the investment is undertaken. The following are equipment and related services that can be available for housing museum or private collections:

- creating and maintaining a building that is up to museum standards for environmental conditions with controlled temperature and humidity, and providing 24/7 monitoring and recording of internal conditions and the mechanisms to alert the client to any changes or fluctuations;
- having light levels that are easily controlled within storage rooms by having no access to external windows, and using motion activation or independent switches when accessing the space;
- monitoring spaces for tracking pests and eliminating infestation of insects and rodents;
- providing round-the-clock security with on-site personnel or external security providers and supplying cameras positioned at access points and interiors that will record and track activities related to the space;
- offering individual suites that allow access to museum staff only. If shared spaces are offered (for reduced costs), items will need to have additional packing or crating to ensure that they are not handled by nonmuseum staff;
- applying barcodes or RFID tags to objects in order to track any movement of the object while in storage;
- developing documentation procedures similar to those of the museum's accession files, photography, and provenance;
- many larger companies offer viewing space where clients can have an object installed and lit for viewing or conservation inspection. These viewing rooms are often set up for photography of objects by the client's private photographer, or photographic services can be provided by in-house staff;
- many companies have conservators on contract who can conduct minor treatment on a client's objects. Some may offer conservation treatments by their staff of full-time, trained conservators in laboratory spaces dedicated and equipped for undertaking various types of object treatment;
- all commercial companies can insure objects while in storage through an array of options, depending on the requirements of the client, or the clients can insure them through their existing collection policy.

Commercial Storage Room Examples

Figure 7.29   Pallet Racking and Stairs. *Source*: Carey, Artex FAS.

Figure 7.30   Separate Room Arrangements. *Source*: Carey, Artex FAS.

Figure 7.31 Pallet Racking and Stairs. *Source*: IAS Sydney, Australia.

Transit Storage Facilities

Figure 7.32 Transit Storage. *Source*: IAS Sydney, Australia.

Figure 7.33   Rolling Transit Crate. *Source*: IAS Sydney, Australia.

Packing and Crating Services

Packing and crating services provided by commercial companies correlate to museum standards for those clients who can afford the service. Over the last thirty-plus years, service providers have worked closely with museum conservators and packing technicians in researching the risk to objects while being transported. These studies are continually being tested and assessed to find better techniques and materials to improve the standards and to reduce the risks of damage or deterioration.

Many larger museums have in-house staff who specialize in packing and crating for loans and traveling exhibitions. These staff members have

Figure 7.34   Rolling Transit Crates. *Source*: IAS Sydney, Australia.

developed their expertise through packing many objects and by studying the different designs and styles of packing and crates that arrive at the museum from other institutions for loans and exhibitions. A commercial packer creates new packing and crating for objects, which are then shipped, and the packer seldom sees other institutions' designs or has the experience of unpacking and repacking. A museum packer in a large museum also has the advantage of working directly with in-house conservators who often have knowledge of and ideas for better packing methods.

Commercial packers follow the lead of museum conservators and packers in establishing and developing the designs according to museum standards. The volume of work they execute and the variety of objects they encounter give the commercial packer an opportunity to acquire a broad range of experience and technical knowledge of different methods and materials. Smaller museums offer commercial providers the opportunity to build exclusively for one client and to a prescribed design to which they agree.

Usually the commercial provider will offer set levels of packing, which are either soft packing or custom interior packing that would be supported by a crate shell. Soft-packing options include wrapping, cushioning, and structural support, so the customer can obtain a level of protection for the cost it can afford.

The commercial provider must explain the different levels of risks involved and the benefits of protection that are available in accordance with cost. Custom packing may require a hard-shell crate to be built to give support to the internal packing. The levels of crates that are offered are recommended, first, for the protection of the object; second, for the time that the object will be in transport; and, third, for the cost of the crate itself. Generally, three levels of crates, and sometimes more, will be offered by the provider. Each represents the type of service levels it will provide to the type of interior packing it can support.

Economy Crate or One-Way Crate

An economy, sometimes called a "one way," crate is designed to offer good protection for a reasonable cost. This style of crate is a six-sided box with no additional battens for support. These types of crates will meet the basic requirements for standard freight systems, especially FFA airline regulations.

Standard/Returnable/Multiple-Use Crates

The primary function of this type of crate is to offer additional structural support to the six-sided box by the addition of battens and other supports such as handles, skids, and hardware. These crates are strong enough to be reusable several times.

Museum Standard Crates

These crates offer the premium structural support and options for interior packing protection that can be built by the service provider. These crates follow the same designs that are built or required by museum packers and conservators. These options offer additional structural support, quality handles, hardware and mechanical access for transport, and sealed exteriors and are reusable even for multiple venue exhibitions. These crates are premium in their protection and are premium in their costs. For further information regarding types of packing and crating designs refer to the section titled "Packing and Crating Options" in this chapter and other links available in the reference section of this book.

Handling and Installation Services

Handling and installation services offered by commercial companies vary depending upon the client market and the in-house staff who can perform the specific service. Training within the company is the primary key to ensuring that the staff have the latest knowledge of the methods and methodology required to handle collection objects. Museum clients require that a provider's staff work with them in the best practices of collection care at all levels. The museum client must also understand that the provider has other clients, and a request for service or schedule needs to be submitted early, remain flexible, and be thoroughly understood as to its specifics.

Handling of art and artifacts by commercial companies is undertaken in a variety of locations: museums, private collectors' residences, commercial galleries, business or corporate offices, trade fairs and auctions, and public and private outdoor sculpture parks. Each situation requires that staff have a wide range of technical skills, and the equipment and hardware to properly handle and install the object.

Museums

Depending on the size of the museum and the level of expertise of staff dedicated to collection care programing, the need to use a commercial service company on a contractual basis may arise if the work cannot be done in-house. The types of collection care activities that the commercial service providers offer have been described in this section. In the United States, most ongoing collection care work is done by in-house staff. Smaller museums, because of their fewer collection care staff and their overhead costs to maintain staff and facilities, may require the use of commercial services to a greater degree to fill the gap. The level of commitment in using a commercial service provider will depend on the services required, the expertise of staff, and the budgetary considerations.

Private Collectors' Residences

Residences are a challenge for the installer because access and maneuverability within the property can be difficult. The obstacles range from access to the site with a truck, pathways for moving the object to and through the grounds or house, sidewalks, doors, stairs, furniture, floors, and the many pathways or items that need to be covered, moved, or avoided to execute the work.

A site visit to a residence is often required to make sure that the staff are properly prepared, and the extent of the activities that need to be undertaken must be understood and agreed to by the client. Coordination of schedules, security access, and any building maintenance issues must be addressed by both parties before the work begins.

Depending on the type of object, its size, and weight, further discussion and explanation regarding wall types, floor coverings, and floor load-bearing specifications of the residence may need to be undertaken so as to prevent any possible damage.

An active collector may require that a rehang or changeover be conducted within the residence. These activities are similar to a small exhibition changeover where objects are removed, walls patched and painted, and objects brought to the residence, and then the installation of the next group of objects is designed and arranged. Coordination between all parties and schedules is crucial, and the safety of the objects is at a higher risk because of the multiple handling and work activities that may surround them.

Commercial Galleries

Commercial galleries tend to operate with a small staff, so installation and rotation of objects often require outside installation expertise. As in a museum exhibition, the changeover requires multiple movements of the objects and removal, rebuilding, and painting of exhibition furnishings before the objects can be installed. Some companies offer full service to perform all of these activities. Galleries are very dependent on commercial providers for handling and transporting objects that are used for exhibition, for viewing at collectors' homes, or for displaying in trade fairs, or objects that have to be packed and crated after being sold.

Business and Corporate Offices

Many businesses acquire objects as an investment and place them on display in offices throughout their corporate network. The handling and installation of these objects follow similar patterns as handling in the private collector's residence, but on a much larger scale, primarily because of location and public exposure while on display.

Except in restricted areas, objects are usually displayed in a public setting. The service provider should give advice regarding collection care concerns because often the office staff see the objects only as decorations, and not as part of the company's investment. As collection objects, they are purchased, transported, and stored, and can be lent to exhibitions.

Corporate collections need to be maintained and monitored in similar ways as a collection on public display in a museum. Glazing 2-D objects in frames or 3-D objects with vitrines assists in reducing dust and human interaction with the object. An ongoing cleaning program is an important part of caring for the collection of the business investment. Many commercial providers offer services that are extensions of their general handling and installation services.

Trade Fairs and Auctions

Commercial galleries actively attend and market their work at art fairs. Auction houses specialize in and are dedicated to displaying and selling art and artifacts of various collection types and for different levels of collectors. Objects handled in these situations are at a much greater risk with regard to handling, installing, packing, and transporting because of the sheer volume of objects used in short periods of time. Commercial service providers offer numerous levels of services for these activities, which have demanding schedules and deadlines with the high volume of objects being handled and transported.

Art fairs have become an effective marketing event for commercial art and antique galleries. These events are generally located in large metropolitan areas and can attract galleries seeking exposure worldwide. The time periods of these events are short and require that the exhibitors have their works transported to the location and ready for display in an expedited manner. Service providers excel in this business by collecting, transporting, and installing the exhibitors' objects within the short timeframe. To safely move objects, the providers must be efficient and punctual. Attention to the details of all phases of these operations is required to safely handle the objects. Specialized equipment and handling techniques have been developed by the service providers to ensure protection of the objects and to increase efficiency in working within a hectic environment.

Auction houses schedule events that are targeted to selling certain collection types on a specific day or range of days. The objects to be sold are brought to the auction location from the seller and then prepared in storage to await the preview display and auction. Service providers often collect, handle, and transport these objects to the auction location. Depending on the size and staff at the auction house, the providers may assist in the other handling requirements of the auction. The volume of objects and the short period of time in which they are handled, as in the art fairs, create an atmosphere with an exceptional level of risk to the object. Using trained handlers and coordinating all handling activities will reduce potential risks.

Some large contemporary art exhibitions are held around the world in different locations on an every-other-year basis, termed biennales. These events are focused on displaying the artwork and giving exposure to the artist. Objects travel from many locations around the world, in all forms of transport, and are displayed in specific spaces in the host city. The coordination between and expertise for all phases of these biennales require multiple service providers working with the organizer and artists to create the exhibition.

Outdoor Sculpture

Many service providers offer the expertise and equipment to transport and install outdoor sculptures on museum, municipal, or private property. Planning for handling and moving large sculptures requires time to review techniques and equipment needed for a successful execution, and is invaluable in preventing risk of damage to the object or injury to the handlers. With the scale of the project, time for planning is vital because the object will be moved and placed just once. Do-overs are not an option.

The expertise of museum or company staff comes from a very specialized level of individuals who have been trained and have gained on-the-job experience. Most large museums have staff who are trained, dedicated to, and proficient in doing this work, but not on a regular basis. Mentoring or apprenticeship among rigging staff is a viable legacy, but only if the lead staff make the time to teach and younger staff are willing to learn.

Larger commercial service companies have staff who are trained and do rigging work on a regular basis, depending on the quality of their experience and the ongoing client needs. Depending on details regarding locations and equipment required, these service providers will work directly with cartage companies to perform the work.

Cartage companies can assist when needed to transport and rig large objects. Their professional background and equipment are based in the construction industry, and by working with them directly, museum staff can bring their standards of care required to handle the object in line with the technical knowledge and equipment that these companies have to offer.

A few companies have evolved and specialize in transporting and rigging large sculptural objects. Their combined knowledge of equipment and the intricacies involved in handling artworks of this scale are invaluable. The advantage in contacting these companies and working with them is that the levels of risk can be reduced. The care and skills required in moving large sculptural objects cannot be underestimated when analyzing the cost of performing the work required.

Some conservators specialize in handling and treatment of monumental sculptures. Like specialized handling companies, these individuals and their expertise is invaluable for ensuring that the work is handled properly. A trained conservation specialist can assist in analyzing the current condition of the object and determine if it needs cleaning, treatment, or display mounts before it is relocated to a site.

Europe and the United States/Transport Differences

Europe and the United States have been actively involved in managing and transporting exhibitions over the last century as museums have become more active in their approach to lending and borrowing objects for exhibition. The differences between the two have developed out of the investment of the commercial service providers building their companies around the management of required standards and methodologies to perform the service required. In Europe, transport distances between venues are shorter but involve crossing borders and require that management deal with the various government regulations. In the United States, the distances are farther between major venues, but federal and interstate regulations do not affect the shipments.

The following is an excerpt, which though dated in its writing, gives a good overview of the difference between European and U.S. transport services for moving exhibitions. Michael Scott's presentation for the 1991 *Art in Transit*;

Studies in the Transport of Paintings publication and conference is titled "The Relationship between Shipping Agents."

A question that has been posed many times, each time receiving different answers, is "How do European fine art transport agents differ from their U.S. Counterparts?" Fundamentally there is no difference in respect to the care and responsibility to ensure that the items placed in their individual care are dispatched efficiently and safely. However, it is the service they provide that differs, with each adopting its own systems.

The European fine-art transport agent is contracted to organize the dispatch of an exhibition, and supplies his/her own work force to complete the packing, necessary trucking, forwarding, and customs clearances. This results in the overall control of all matters relating to shipment, which is contained within one management team. For an international shipment to and from the United States, however, the services listed above are brought together by using a freight forwarder/customs broker (agent), who will draw together the independent services of the specialist trucking companies and specialist packing art handling companies to form a combined service.

Both systems have enormous advantages in performance; the European agent is able to keep the management control within a close environment that normally allows the direct personal supervision of each specific aspect of the exhibition movement. The U.S. system allows that agent (sometimes under the guidance of the museum registrar) the freedom of greater diversification enabling the services of numerous specialist trucking and packing companies to best complement the needs and requirements of the exhibitions.

These systems have been developed over many years and while both have advantages and disadvantages, the primary factor is to know what to expect from the agent responsible for dispatching an exhibition.[9]

CONCLUSION

The external environment and the challenges of caring for objects are tremendously different from the challenges found within the internal environment. The same risks have to be assessed, but the variables of the risks in the majority of cases of the external environment can only be anticipated. Anticipating these risks requires the process of thinking outside of the box, asking the next question, and creating the protection scenarios for the object to balance potential scenarios. The external environment scenario is a combination of known situations that can only be anticipated but not controlled as in the internal environment scenarios of the building envelope.

FOCUS ON: INTERNATIONAL SHIPPING BY AIR AND SEA

by Kim Powell

Choosing a method of transport for international shipments requires serious consideration and understanding of the options available. It is important to ensure that the chosen method holds the safety of the object paramount. This is best achieved by very careful planning and opting for the solution that provides the highest level of control and certainty.

In international shipping, you should consider the two main options:

Air Freight

You can choose to send the shipment either:

- on dedicated (sole use) airline pallets, or
- as general cargo on a mixed-use (shared) pallet

Sea Freight

As with air freight, there are again two main options:

- full container load (FCL) where the container is dedicated to your use, or
- less than a container load (LCL) where your shipment is included in a mixed-use (shared) container.

There is a third option—the international courier (FedEx or DHL)-type service—which should only be considered in the most dire circumstances, as these services provide even less handling, routing, and scheduling control than sea freight. You've seen how airlines handle your luggage. Consider that the international courier services use a similar conveyor system and that your package will transfer through numerous vehicles and hubs en route to its final destination.

It is critical that you apply standard risk management principles when deciding whether to send a loan or exhibition via air or sea freight.

Air freight, given its very nature, is, in most instances, the more expensive option, while sea freight presents a more cost-effective solution, but there are many more factors of risk to consider.

Here are some things to think about when making your decision.

Air Freight

- Is there a direct flight from location of origin to destination?
- If not, how many times will my shipment transfer at intermediate airports?

- Is the entire journey completed on an aircraft? Or are there some Road Feeder Service (RFS—airline truck) legs?
- What is the best routing? Consider transhipment time, airline reputation, local agent knowledge and experience, weather, political situation at transhipment point/s and so on.
- Can the shipment be completed during normal working hours?
- Can the shipment be completed during the course of a normal working week (Monday to Friday or as dictated by local custom)?
- Are there any local holidays or religious events during the proposed shipping dates?
- Can the local logistics agents (origin, transhipment, and destination) get tarmac access to perform palletization and loading/unloading supervision?
- Is there access to climate-control storage at the transhipment airport?
- Will the crates fit into a passenger aircraft (under 160 cm. high)? Or do they require main deck (freighter) service?
- Do the aircraft on the selected route/flights have the capacity for palletized cargo?
- Is it a dedicated pallet? Or is it a shared pallet with other (unknown) cargo? (Dedicated pallets with a confirmed booking through to destination will always get priority at transhipment airports over shipments sent as general cargo on shared pallets, which may require re-palletization at the transhipment point.)
- Can crates be stacked to minimize the number of pallets required?
- Can pallet load plans be prepared ahead of time? Will they be followed by the airline staff?
- Will a courier be sent with the shipment?
- If it is a main deck shipment, will the airline allow a courier on board their freighter aircraft?

Sea Freight

- What is the best routing and how many ports will the vessel stop at?
- How many times will the container move from one vessel to another?
- How long will the shipment take port-to-port?
- How far is it from the arrival port to the ultimate destination?
- How many days before departure does the container need to be delivered?
- How much time will it take after arrival for the container to be delivered?
- What type of a container do I need
  - 20′.
  - 40′.
  - Refrigerated (reefer)
  - Insulated (a decommissioned or nonoperating reefer)
  - Hi Cube (for very tall crates)

- Can the crates be stacked or can the crates be turned?
- Is it possible to have someone present at the port to supervise the container being loaded/unloaded? (Usually not.)
- Is it possible to send a Courier on the ship? (Usually not.)
- Shipping schedules are much less reliable than airline schedules, mainly because of weather conditions, tides, etc., so the likelihood of missing the connecting vessel is higher. What steps can you take if this happens? When is the next available connecting vessel?
- Can my container be stowed below deck (a requirement of many insurance policies)?
- Will the shipping line allow an operating reefer to be stowed below deck?
- If customs or quarantine inspection is required at the destination, can I have a representative present to ensure correct handling?

Customs and Quarantine

Your international logistics agent will ensure that all documentation is in order at both origin and destination prior to the shipment proceeding.

If special licences or permits are required (CITES, Export/Import licences, Firearms licences, Belle Arte, etc.) are required, ensure that there is sufficient time for processing.

Once shipment is completed, obtain copies of documentation from your logistics agent (air way bills/bills of lading; import clearance; export clearance; permits; etc.). Having these documents on file will allow you to produce proof of export/import for the return shipment(s). This is particularly useful in the event that a different logistics agent is used on subsequent shipments.

Beware of artists or lenders offering to "bring it in my suitcase," as this bypasses the export and import customs formalities and will present real problems on the return journey. If there is no proof of export, then the return shipment will be considered a definitive import and the local duty and tax rates will apply. Some countries, including China, impose serious financial penalties for illegally exported goods as well as extremely high import taxes when such goods are returned.

The same caution should be applied to the offers to send it via the postal service.

Kim Powell
Project Manager
Crozier Fine Arts
New York, New York

FOCUS ON: ART PACKING AND TRANSPORT: CUSHIONING FOAM SELECTION AND APPLICATION

by Geoff Browne

When I began working in the field of fine art and artifact packing and crating in 1990, the information available regarding the correct application of packing foams—taking into consideration object fragility, weight, load-bearing surface, and the likely drop-height of a given package—existed almost entirely in books in libraries or in corporate literature intended for industrial users, and it was difficult to acquire, even for those who knew exactly what they were looking for.

While most, if not all, of that same information can now be found online, the search can still be daunting because of the proliferation of vendor websites for packing materials that do not have the application information on their sites or links to it.

In addition, much of that information, even if found, represents only the data specific to a commercial product or is exclusively geared for packaging engineers and technicians who already understand its application. Some of the few exceptions to this are the publications that derived from the Art in Transit Workshops organized by the Canadian Conservation Institute, The Smithsonian Institution, The National Gallery, and the Tate Gallery in 1991, and even those publications can overwhelm many employed in the field who are not as well grounded in the sciences as conservators.

When I was invited to give a presentation at the Campbell Center for the Packing and Crating Information Network of the American Association of Museums in September 2013 on the subject of my choice, the decision was easy, as I am almost daily presented with either packaging specifications or actual packaging examples that do not take correct foam-loading principles into account.

The following paper is a more fluid and self-explanatory version of my presentation for PACCIN in 2013, and something that I personally would have really appreciated when I started working in this profession.

The fragility of objects, shock levels, and cushioning values are expressed in G forces or "Gs." Fragility is expressed in terms of how many G forces an object can withstand before damage occurs.

Shock levels are expressed in terms of how many G forces are applied to an object upon impact with an immovable surface given a specific drop height.

- In common usage, the term "G forces" is most often applied to the acceleration of racing cars, high-performance aircraft, and spacecraft, forces that however rapid and potentially dangerous to living things they may be, are nonetheless applied relatively gradually and are mild, typically in single digits, as compared to G forces measuring shock values, which represent the force applied to a free-falling *and constantly accelerating object* at the instant it impacts an immovable surface such as a concrete floor, which if dropped from a height of only 12″ can be 50 Gs.

- G forces times the weight of the object at rest equals the force applied to the overall object upon impact expressed in pounds.
- Dividing overall force by the area of the object actually making contact with the "floor" upon impact equals "point loading" force in pounds per square inch. Example:

If a 10 lb. object is dropped from a height of 12″ onto a concrete floor, yielding a 50 G shock, the overall pressure applied to the object upon impact is 500 lbs. If the object is a 10″ cube that happens to land perfectly on one of its flat sides, the surface area of the object actually making contact with the floor upon impact is 100 sq. inches, and the locally applied pressure is only 5 pounds per square inch. If, however, the cube landed on a slightly rounded corner with a contact area of 1/10 sq. inch, the locally applied pressure would increase to 5,000 psi.

Cushioning values are expressed in terms of the extent to which a properly loaded material can limit the G forces experienced by an object dropped from a given height onto an unyielding surface.

REFERENCE TABLES

Object fragility ratings:
(U.S. Dept. of Defense MIL-HDBK-304c & Dow Ethafoam Guide)

Table 7.1   Browne

Extremely fragile	15–25 Gs	Altimeters, hard drives, missile guidance systems, precision aligned test equipment, gyroscopes, inertial guidance systems
Very delicate	25–40 Gs	Altimeters, digital electronics equipment (hard drives), medical diagnostic apparatus, X-ray equipment, mechanically shock mounted instruments
Delicate	40–60 Gs	Computer display terminals and printers, electric typewriters, cash registers, aircraft accessories; Typical Paintings – 50 Gs; Glass Bottle – 60 Gs (*Art in Transit*)
Moderately delicate	60–85 Gs	Stereos and television receivers, floppy disc drives, aircraft accessories
Moderately rugged	85–115 Gs	Major appliances and furniture, electromechanical equipment
Rugged	115+ Gs	Table saws, sewing machines, machine tools, aircraft structural parts such as landing gear, control surfaces, hydraulic equipment

Shock levels experienced on various modes of transportation, with sensors secured to vehicle:
(American Association of Railroads Intermodal Environment Study & MIL-HDBK-304c)

Table 7.2

45′ Nonair-ride trailer, 1900 miles on highways, 1400 miles on urban streets	Vertical shock: 95% < 4 Gs; Longitudinal shock: 95% < 1 G; Lateral shock: 95% < 2 Gs;
Nonair-ride trailer, semiloaded, composite	Vertical shock: 99.5% < 4 Gs, 1 – 300 Hz
Air-ride suspension trailer, measured on floor	Vertical shock: < 1 G peak, 2 – 500 Hz
Jet aircraft, vertical shock and vibration composite	Vertical shock: 3 G peak, 1 – 2000 Hz

Shock levels for perspective, from crude testing:

Table 7.3

Rapping a pen (accelerometer) on a desk	20 Gs
Dropping a slab of wood 12″ onto concrete	50 Gs

Probable Drop Heights of Packages by Weight:
(US Dept. of Defense MIL-HDBK-304c & Dow Ethafoam Guide)

Table 7.4

Package Size	Handling	Probable Drop Height
0–10 lbs.	1 person throwing	42 inches
10–20 lbs.	1 person carrying	36 inches
20–50 lbs.	1 person carrying	30 inches
50–100 lbs.	2 people carrying	24 inches
100–250 lbs.	light equipment	18 inches
250+ lbs.	heavy equipment	12 inches 6 inches if palletized

Incredible as it may seem when considering the very low shock levels experienced on air-ride trailers, consider the fact that ripe tomatoes are routinely successfully shipped to market in refrigerated air-ride trucks over thousands of miles, with the tomatoes stacked atop each other in packaging rarely exceeding simple wooden slat crates—a 2 G shock, effectively double the weight of a tomato, could easily rupture its skin.

Please note that the shock levels provided for vehicles alone were necessarily measured against the structure of the vehicle, as if the sensors were secured like cargo—this is crucial.

In American Society for Testing & Materials (ASTM) protocols for package testing, one of the test regimens is referred to as a "loose load" test, where the cargo is totally unsecured in the vehicle, as is commonly the case with express package carriers and some common carriers—in that case, individual G forces of shock could easily exceed the 50 G level, and the cargo could also be subjected to repeated shocks, resulting in cumulative damage that isolated events might otherwise not cause.

PRINCIPAL CAUSE OF DAMAGE DUE TO SHOCK

If one is shipping via modes of transportation where cargo is secured, especially if the carrier vehicle is an air-ride trailer, the inescapable conclusion one may derive from the foregoing tables is that carrier vehicles are not, in and of themselves, the major source of potential damage, but rather that *the handling of the objects in transitional stages is the likely source of damage in any transport sequence.*

CUSHIONING MATERIAL SELECTION AND APPLICATION

Cushioning foams act as shock absorbers, returning to shape slowly after impact, as opposed to upholstery foams, which act like springs, bouncing back quickly, and resulting in significant rebound shock and vibration.

Upholstery foams are additionally, in most cases, polyurethane compounded with ether, whose solvent properties are, of course, hazardous to most materials, *including the foam itself, making it prone to rapid breakdown.*

Open-celled foams (typically polyurethane, as is sound-proofing foam) are inherently better at damping vibration than closed-celled foams (typically polyethylene foams, which are also "harder").

Both of the most common varieties of packing foams are available in military grades which reputedly employ better chemical compounds and use better controlled processes to lessen any chemical reaction with items to be packed. Unfortunately, in the case of Ethafoam, the blowing agent (which

Table 7.5

Foam Type	Thickness	Static Loading—object lbs. per sq.in. foam (psi)	Static Loading—sq. in. foam required per object lbs.	G force limited to:
Polyester Urethane	2″	.375 psi.	2.67 sq.in./lb.	37 Gs
Polyester Urethane	4″	.375 psi.	2.67 sq.in./lb.	14 Gs
Ethafoam 220	2″	.67 psi.	1.67 sq.in./lb.	46 Gs
Ethafoam 220	4″	.85 psi.	1.17 sq.in./lb.	24 Gs
Plastazote LD24	2″	~ .5 psi.	~ 2 sq.in./lb.	60 Gs
Ethafoam HS 45	2″	.75 psi.	1.33 sq.in./lb.	54 Gs
Ethafoam HS 600	2″	1.2 psi.	.833 sq.in./lb.	45 Gs
Ethafoam HS 900	2″	2.2 psi.	.454 sq.in./lb.	53 Gs

inflates the foam cells during manufacturing) used in the military grade is proprietary.

Zote foams (Plastazote) are cross-linked polyethylene, their cells being filled with nitrogen while the polyethylene is subjected to strong vacuum.

Packaging Foam Comparison and Static Loading tables:

All figures shown are based on a 30″ drop, considered the maximum likely drop in truck shipments. Static loading values shown are from manufacturers' cushioning curves based on multiple impacts to allow for hard usage. These static loading values will yield optimum protection/lowest possible G forces for that type and thickness of foam, as shown in the right-hand column.

To pack a modern painting in a simple rectilinear frame measuring 30″ × 36″ × 2″, weighing approximately 10 lbs., with a nominal fragility rating of 50 Gs, for truck shipment, the use of either 2″ thick Polyester urethane foam or 2″ thick Ethafoam 220, correctly loaded, would provide adequate protection, at 37 Gs and 46 Gs, respectively. Using 2″ Polyester urethane foam, a total of 26.7 sq. inches of foam in contact with the frame would be required (2.67 sq. in. foam per pound x 10 lbs.). Given the 2″ depth/width of the frame, a theoretical single cushion would thus need to be 13.35″ long × 2″ wide—in actual practice, two cushions, one at each corner, would each need to be 6.68″ long × 2″ wide, typically with additional width extending to back and lid of crate to prevent buckling of foam at its edges or knifing between layers of foam—see *Additional Considerations in Cushioning Material Usage.*

Other cushioning materials frequently employed in tandem with foregoing foams.

Table 7.6

Fiberfill	100% Polyester, low-melt heat fused vs. resin bonded—cushioning for extremely lightweight and/or irregular artifacts, relatively inert, easily worked
Ethafoam 222 (1/2″)	large cell, low density polyethylene foam, good soft initial surface for heavier objects when applied over harder grades of Ethafoam
Volara (1/8″)	Cross-linked polyethylene, good soft initial surface for heavier objects when applied over Ethafoam, but crushes and tears easily, should only be presented directly to object surfaces, not slid against

ADDITIONAL CONSIDERATIONS IN CUSHIONING MATERIAL USAGE

Double Packing

When an object requires rigid support so that the components do not move relative to one another, or when a work that is structurally weak because of its media needs to be supported, an inner case should be made to provide that rigid support, and the inner case is then cushioned by foam elements within the outer crate shell.

Small lightweight/low mass objects extremely sensitive to vibration, such as a pastel, can also benefit from the added mass of an inner case, as the overall resonant frequency is lowered. An inner case also provides a greater and safer surface for application of cushioning foam.

Fit/Clearance

Ideal Clearance = 0, with/if Friction also = 0—is perhaps most nearly achieved with foam and object both wrapped in slippery material. An object should easily lower into place within foam cushioning elements under its own weight.

Excess clearance allows rebound, thereby *adding* to total shock and vibration. Excess tightness promotes abrasion of object on insertion/removal, or possible damage, and can interfere with cushioning (e.g., if side foam is too tight, bottom foam cushioning is diminished or negated).

Handling Cutouts

Finger- or hand-width gaps to lift out or load objects must be provided, and should be in proportion to weight of object as object size increases. Allow access for two hands per 50 lbs. of object. Handling cutouts also provide positive identification of correct handling areas for future handlers.

Air Traps

Air traps occur most often with large flat works, trays, or inner cases with tightly fitted cushioning, having few or small gaps between cushioning blocks, and thus little or no means for air movement around inner case or object. Vacuum or air pressure created by air traps diminishes or negates cushioning. To minimize this, allow larger gaps between cushions, which may require use of foam with higher load-bearing capacity; trays may have corners cut off to allow greater flow of air.

Foam Placement in Package/Relative Object Form

Foam should be placed at points where the structure of the object can safely support its own mass under stress, for example, at the corners of a frame or stretcher rather than in the middle where no bracing may exist.

NOTE: When more than one grade of foam can be properly loaded and applied in the cushioning of an object, the foam requiring the greatest area will provide the most even support and likely the best cushioning value as well.

TOPPLING

Toppling is a rotational drop, such as a painting crate falling over on its face or back. Toppling is equivalent to a flat drop from 2/3 the height of the crate. To best address this issue, the use of 4″ foam on front and back faces is recommended both for its greater cushioning value, and because the additional depth of the crate will decrease the likelihood of toppling.

TRAVEL BEYOND STATIC POSITIONING, LAYOUT

Foam applied in a single container should not only extend the entire depth of the face against which it bears, but also beyond that face by the thickness of the cushioning material on the adjacent sides; for example, floor foam for a painting crate should generally extend from the full depth of the crate, so that if the adjacent side cushioning bottoms out under severe impact, the object does not drop off the floor cushioning.

Buckling

Buckling is the result of high loading at or near the edge of the foam cushioning. If the object has a narrow load-bearing surface, such as a painting with a shallow-frame profile, the bottom foam should extend from front to back of crate.

If a foam element is proportionately taller than wide, buckling becomes likely—the use of foam elements at least one-and-one-third times as wide as thick/tall is recommended.

If voids exist in the corners of the package or between the floor and side foam elements, a corner drop may cause buckling because of the angle of impact. Additional foam should be added to the floor foam to fill corner voids.

Fatigue/Compressive Creep

Foam fatigue results from continuous object static load on foam and from repeated shock or severe environmental conditions, and may be offset by the addition of about 10% load-bearing foam area.

Platens (Load Spreaders)

Platens are rigid flat plates that increase the load-bearing surface of an object to permit correct cushioning of heavy objects; in the case of hollow-metal castings, they also prevent excessive point loading and knifing of media through foam cushion; they are also useful in facilitating lateral transfer of an object into its container if it has a slippery surface. Platens also allow better cushioning of lightweight objects while evenly distributing the load.

Progressive Cushioning

Progressive cushioning may be achieved by the mixing of cushioning materials or densities of foam, such as by placing fiberfill pads atop Urethane foam, or Volara or Ethafoam 222 atop other grades of Ethafoam. Care must be taken, particularly with fiberfill, to limit the thickness of the innermost/softest material to avoid rebound, as with excessive clearance.

Progressive cushioning may also be achieved via the use of trapezoidal cushioning elements, which upon compression not only become denser, but also engage more surface area as they compress.

Usage of Foam as Insulation

While Urethane foams, in particular, have R values nearly equivalent to high-density polystyrene such as Dow Blueboard, USG Pinkboard, and so on, the usage of foam as insulation can easily result in overfoaming if the insulation layer/lining is also the cushioning layer and no consideration is given to correct loading.

Cavity packs/full encapsulation of objects in foam naturally creates insulated packaging.

CONCLUSION

As I was gathering reference material for my presentation for PACCIN in 2013 and this paper, I was reminded that far and away the greatest risk to any item in the shipping process is from handling, NOT from the mode of transportation itself, except in the case of a "loose load," which explains how soft-packed artwork can be transported on air-ride trucks IF properly secured and handled.

The one consideration that is not addressed in this paper is cost analysis, which tends to be a lesser consideration for institutions whose mission stresses preservation. For those interested in further exploration of these topics, I strongly suggest that they acquire copies of "Art in Transit: Studies in the Transport of Paintings" ISBN 0-89468-163-X, the "Art in Transit Handbook" ISBN 0-89468-165-6, and the U.S. Department of Defense publication, MIL-HDBK-304c, which can be downloaded for free online. It is very thorough, over 100 pages long, and includes free software as well, if desired.

Geoff Browne
Crating Shop Manager and Senior Project Manager
Terry Dowd, Inc.
Chicago, Illinois

NOTES

1. *About SFO Museum*, assessed February 2015, http://www.flysfo.com/museum/about#sthash.CtprZGUk.dpuf.
2. *Wikipedia*, s.v. "Colonial Williamsburg," accessed February 2015, http://en.wikipedia.org/wiki/Colonial_Williamsburg.
3. Sally Freitag and Judy Cline, "Loans," in *Museum Registration Methods*, 5th ed. (Washington, DC: AAM Press, 2010): 120.
4. Marie Demeroukas, "Condition Reporting," in *Museum Registration Methods*, 5th ed. (Washington, DC: AAM Press, 2010): 223.
5. Cherie Summers, "Couriering," in *Museum Registration Methods*, 5th ed. (Washington, DC: AAM Press, 2010): 342.
6. "RC-AAM Courier Policy Statement," in *Museum Registration Methods*, 5th ed. (Washington, DC: AAM Press, 2010): 346.

7. Stephen Horne, "Crating General Principles," in *Way to Go! Crating Artwork for Transit* (New York: Gallery Association of New York State, 1985): 10.

8. Irene Taurins, "Shipping by Land, Air and Sea," in *Museum Registration Methods*, 5th ed. (Washington, DC: AAM Press, 2010): 332.

9. Michael Scott, "The Relationship between Shipping Agents," in *Art in Transit: Studies in the Transport of Paintings* (Washington, DC: National Gallery of Art, 1991): 331.

Chapter 8

Working with Materials and Equipment

Temporary in the real world can mean a few days or weeks; temporary in the museum world can mean a few days or possibly many years, choose your materials wisely.

—Unknown Author

INTRODUCTION

Throughout this book, material and equipment types have been listed as part of the explanations for the topic being presented. In this chapter, the focus will be on the presentation and listing of materials and equipment commonly found within collection care techniques and practices. The list will not be a comprehensive summary of collection care relationships per type of object and the scenario one may find the object subjected to. The list will be supportive of the common examples that exist and the context in which one would find them in relation to the collection care activities. To explain and list the best support for each object according to the correct material or piece of equipment to use would be impossible. One must understand the relationships of the object, material, and equipment type that best fit the scenario that the object being accessed will encounter.

In my research, over my career, there have been numerous lists I have referenced, used in teaching, and passed along to colleagues on the topic of material or equipment. In the research for this book, I referenced some of the old lists for examples that are still relevant and new examples that are beneficial additions to the list. Among the old lists, as in recent ones, there is no one comprehensive list that can be created, maintained, and updated with recent testing results of material or equipment per scenario of object within its collection care use.

As Mervin Richard states in his foreword of this book, "There are many books that address collection care, but they tend to be written by specialists for specialists. Thus, they are inclined to be narrowly focused and too often beyond the grasp of a generalist seeking a broad understanding of collection care."[1]

These lists are created as a compilation developed from numerous resources and reviewed by other colleagues. The examples selected were determined to give the readers a broad reference for their research and assessment as to what is viable or as a link to direct them to further research. At the end of this chapter will be a reference list to the sources used for this compilation. In the reference section of the entire book, more information on additional research can be found as well.

Educated Consumer

No one person can say that he knows everything about any one type of material or piece of equipment, but he may know enough to ask the next question to find an answer or to reference another source to repeat the question. No question is unworthy of being asked; until it is asked, there will never be an answer. The cycle of assessment is a give-and-take exchange within one's own thinking process but crucial for communicating with others. Becoming an educated consumer is essential in searching for the best solution to your collection care needs.

Regarding what material or equipment solutions are best, one of the best sources of information I have used within my career has been networking with other colleagues in museums, commercial providers and technical companies that have similar needs or examples. The discussion of the subject of a specific material or equipment type can easily be developed and continued by asking the question to another professional. Almost all professionals are usually excited to be asked for their opinion on a specific subject. "No one lays bricks like a bricklayer" is a comment my father-in-law, who is a furniture maker, always makes about finding the correct answer.

In my career I have been fortunate on occasion to have someone I respected, whose opinion I sought, made available to me to establish the opportunity to ask the question. Giving oneself a push to start the conversation, one quickly discovers that those same individuals also learned in the same fashion and are willing to help. Paying it forward, returning the favor, or basic good karma should be approached in networking in any educational experience. We are all interested in the same subject, and networking is similar to public speaking: you must not be afraid to open your mouth.

Internet research and networking in today's profession is an amazing tool to find the information you are seeking. In the research for this book, I spent many hours searching for new information and confirming my own beliefs and expertise. For materials and equipment, conservation websites offer endless information and research on specialized topics. On websites, commercial companies may not explain their product or service in great detail, but can give you examples of information for which you can either contact them directly or find additional information from client references. There are specialty websites that are created for sharing of technical information and provide quality reference listings. The various groups and sites are cited in different sections and at the end of this chapter. In the world of social media, even if you are shy and introverted, asking a question has become so much easier.

Summary of intent: The information listed in this chapter has been compiled from current research, from information collected during my career, and from personal knowledge and expertise gained by working within the institutional and commercial sectors of the industry. The examples selected have been chosen to support the readers with information from which they can learn and which can assist in directing them to the next level of information. The attempt may appear to some as not providing enough information on a particular subject and they might think that it should have been more inclusive. The viability of these examples being available, affordable, or applicable in every workplace or of personal preference was the obstacle in creating a more inclusive list. The common denominator is for the examples to act as a source or link based on commonly known scenarios in the continuing research and growth within collection care programing.

COLLECTION CARE MATERIALS

Material Testing

Testing of materials used within collection care activities is crucial. Researching materials that have been tested and approved will reduce the risk of the object being affected by unsafe materials it may come in contact with. If a material has never been used before, research to find test results or have the material in question tested, must be undertaken.

The materials used regularly can change in their overall composition unbeknownst to the user. The manufacturer can change the base formula of ingredients composing the material or the actual production process for the product, all of which can change its chemical and functional properties. Often, the reactions to these changes are not immediately obvious; retesting of the materials on a scheduled basis can assist in alerting the user regarding any changes. Common variants within materials include the type of chemical used as the binding agent of the product, barrier release products placed on materials during the production process or for long shelf life, basic coloring agents added, which can migrate to the object, or off gassing as the material reacts with the environment, which starts the decomposing process.

Material testing is part of all manufacturers' processes that is undertaken and the results are made available by the material supplier. The suppliers, as part of their professionalism in promoting and selling a material, should be aware of the testing methods to which their products have been subjected and the results of the tests. Often the analysis is best resourced by working directly with the manufacturer; the supplier can promote the product but may not know the specific details you may require.

Materials are often not directly developed for the museum industry but are commonly used within collection care activities. An example of this use of similar materials can be seen in the comparison of the medical industry and the museum industry. Many medical supplies are developed to be totally inert and free of static, and are produced without transferable residues. There are many examples of sheeting materials and the most common among them are handling gloves, which both industries use, but it was for the medical industry that they were originally developed. Other industrial manufacturers of delicate objects such as electronic equipment use cushioning foam, and the material and technical approaches have been modified and used in the transport of art and artifacts.

The International Organization for Standardization (ISO) specifies the physical and chemical requirements for many materials used in relation to collection care activities, especially for enclosure formats. As an educated consumer in your research of materials, ask the supplier if they have any material data sheets that specify IOS Standards or if they have had these materials Oddy tested. Other standard organizations are listed in the reference section of this book.

A material safety data sheet (MSDS), safety data sheet (SDS), or product safety data sheet (PSDS) is an important component of product steward-ship and occupational safety and health. It is intended to provide workers and emergency personnel with procedures for handling or working with that particular substance in a safe manner, and includes information such as physical data (melting point, boiling point, flash point, etc.), toxicity, health effects, first aid, reactivity, storage, disposal, protective equipment, and spill-handling procedures. MSDS formats can vary from source to source within a country depending on national requirements.[2]

Operational manuals for equipment and tools supplied by the manufacturer will list safety precautions and correct operation procedures to protect the individual operator. This information should be kept in the manual in an eas-ily accessed location for reference when questions arise. In many scenarios, the infrequency of operation of an equipment or a tool may require review as the particular individual may not be well versed in a procedure. Working with the institution's or company's Occupational Health and Safety manager will assist in developing appropriate reviews and training for individuals on a reccurring basis. This information can also be incorporated in your workplace Occupational Health and Safety manuals and training programs.

Oddy testing: The Oddy test is a procedure created at the British Museum by conservation scientist Andrew Oddy in 1973, to test materials for safety in and around art objects. Often, materials for construction are evaluated for safety. However, though materials may be safe for building purposes, they may emit small amounts of chemicals that can harm art objects over time. Acids, formaldehydes, and other fumes can damage and even destroy delicate artifacts if placed too close to them.

This test calls for a sample of the material in question to be placed in a con-tainer with three coupons of different metals—silver, lead, and copper. The container is sealed with a small amount of water to maintain a high humidity level, then heated at 60 degrees Celsius for 28 days. An identical container with three metal coupons acts as a control.

If the metal coupons show no signs of corrosion, then the material is deemed suitable to be placed in and around art objects. The Oddy test is not a contact test, but it is for testing off-gassing. Each metal detects a different set of corrosive agents:

- The silver is for detecting reduced sulfur compounds and carbonyl sulfides.
- The lead is for detecting organic acids, aldehyde, and acidic gases.
- The copper is for detecting chloride, oxide, and sulfur compounds.

There are many types of materials testing for other purposes, including chemical testing and physical testing.

Members of AIC have begun an Oddy Test Materials Database on the AIC wiki and believe that even though the test may be subjective, by sharing protocols and images of results, conservators can consider the results themselves for their own purposes. Results have been organized into four pages:

- Exhibition Fabrics
- Case Construction Materials
- Exhibition Adhesives and Tapes
- Exhibition Paints and Sealants

More information on how to use the data and participate in creating additional entries in the Conservation Materials database is given on the Oddy Tests: AIC Materials Databases.

Oddy testing information is provided for informational purposes only. Neither AIC nor participating institutions endorse particular products, businesses, or services. It is recommended that all materials be retested before use as proprietary formulas as manufacturing processes can change without notice. Photographs of test results are included where possible for users to make their own assessments of the materials tested.

References

Studies in Conservation, Vol. 44, No. 2 (1999), pp. 86–90.
Studies in Conservation, Vol. 48, No. 4 (2003), pp. 263–68.
http://www.vam.ac.uk/content/journals/conservation-journal/issue-43/standard-materials-for-corrosiveness-testing/.
http://www.britishmuseum.org/pdf/OP_111%20selection_of_materials_for_the_storage_or_display_of_museum_obj.

Material Lists

The following is a list of commonly used materials found within collection care activities in the museum industry. The list is compiled from various references found in professional books and conservation, collection care, and commercial material suppliers' websites. It is not intended to be a comprehensive or complete list of all the materials that are available in the market today. It is intended as an overarching list of specific categories and types of materials commonly used and has been compiled from various resource lists.

Boards

The category of boards covers materials constructed from a corrugated or other composite material in structured flat formats for boxes, supportive panels, and so forth. Boards come in different thicknesses, lengths, and widths and, depending on material composition, are rated as acidic or archival.

- Matt board: Paper material boards of different strengths and thicknesses for use in card stock, matting, barrier and support structures may or may not be acid-free or buffered.
- Corrugated board/paper: A corrugated board is a combination of two flat paperboard sheets with an interior layer of fluted paper corrugated in structure. This material comes in different thicknesses and different layers of corrugate structures termed single-, double-, or tri-wall.
- Corrugated board/plastic, commonly called by brand names Coroplast, Coreflute, or Corex, is a combination of two flat plastic sheets with an interior layer of fluted corrugated plastic that is rigid, inert, and chemically stable. It is manufactured in many shapes of flutes and thicknesses of sheets and is used in structural scenarios.
- Foam board: Foam board, commonly termed Foam-Cor, is a combination polystyrene foam core, laminated on both outer sides with heavy-duty paper sheets.
- Gatorfoam: Commonly called Gator Board, Gatorfoam is a lightweight, rigid display board with a dense polystyrene core and a surface sheeting that is fiber composed with a resin-based veneer.
- Honeycomb panels: Honeycomb core panels have geometric interior structures made of hexagonal shapes and are commonly made of aluminum, plastic, or paper. They are lightweight, strong, durable, and rigid.

Sheeting

Paper sheeting product basics: Purchased by stock weights, acidic or archival, various sizes, in rolls or individual sheets.

- Kraft or butcher paper: Standard name for common acidic paper used as a basic wrapping material or covering. Commonly purchased in brown (Kraft) or white (butcher) color and in different stock thicknesses.
- Newsprint: Standard name for common acidic paper, which is lighter in stock weight and is used for wrapping or crumpled and wadded to create fill for packing voids and minor cushioning.

- Acid-free paper: Commonly made of a combination of 25% rag and 75% wood fiber. Used for printing and drawing, and as a barrier paper, or folded into shelves to act as a sleeve or envelope.
- Glassine paper: Glassine, a paper-based sheeting commonly used as an interleaving material in matted or loose works on paper. It is semitranslucent and is easily torn, folded and/or creased, creating an abrasive edge. The flat surface also has a tooth which can be abrasive.
- Silicone release paper: It is a higher quality paper than glassine and works well as a covering, liner, or interleaving with less adhesion capabilities. Like glassine, it can easily be torn, folded, and/or creased, creating an abrasive edge.

Plastic sheeting product basics: Purchased by thickness strength, translucency, static properties, nonbarrier residues, sizes, rolls or individual sheets.

- Polyethylene sheeting (HDPE): High-density polyethylene is a common inexpensive wrapping material used to create a vapor barrier or cover for protecting objects. It comes in different thicknesses and levels of translucency that allow the wrapped or covered object to be seen. FDA-approved "Virgin" polyethylene may be considered functionally inert.
- Clear archival polyester: This sheeting is clear, inert, and commonly used as a liner or barrier. It can be used as a wrap, but is more expensive than other alternatives.
- Stretch wrap (LLDPE): Linear low-density polyethylene is an extremely flexible material used to wrap boxes, seal packages, and secure packing material to the object or to a packing structural system. Recent reports indicate that this material is typically functionally inert.
- Tyvek: Tyvek is spun bound from 100% high-density polyethylene fibers. It is very strong and resists tearing, and the hard variety creates a strong, clean surface for workspaces and a strong covering for frame backings. The soft variety is thinner, and is used as a pliable wrapping material for shape contours; it acts as a smooth contact barrier between brace and objects, and is waterproof and breathable.
- Dartek: Dartek is a soft, transparent nylon film with no plasticizers, additives, or surface coatings. The film does not tear easily, conforms to a surface to create a smooth barrier, and is an excellent covering as it does not stick to the majority of dry material surfaces. It makes an excellent wrap for paintings as it is transparent and breathable as well an excellent dust cover for various objects.
- Marvelseal: This sheeting material is a combination of aluminized polyethylene and a nylon barrier film. It creates a moisture and vapor barrier, which is suitable for crate linings, display case linings, and storage barriers

that require an impermeable barrier between acidic structural materials and the object. It is widely used with wooden construction materials for storage and display of furniture.

Tissues

Tissues often vary in brand and reference name from source to source, in chemical makeup, and in structural strength, and by users and locations where they are manufactured. The primary difference is in the acidic content and buffering capabilities of the tissue in relation to the object and other structural materials used for handling, packing, and storage. Mistakes are commonly made in proper selection per use because of its visual appearance. When unsure as to which type of tissue to use for collection activities, choose an unbuffered one if the material content is mixed or unknown.

- Unbuffered tissue: Used with protein-based materials (wool, silk, leather, fur) and other materials sensitive to alkali (silver, color photos).
- Buffered tissue: Standard tissue that has a component added to push the pH to a neutral or alkaline range, which can help scavenge acidic pollutants. Commonly used for noncollection objects.
- Acid-free tissue: Made from high-quality pulp that does not contain lignin.

Polyester Felts and Batting

These materials can be purchased in both archival and nonarchival quality and thickness. Often used as a basic barrier or cushioning for display and storage, and as a protective barrier on supports for mounts and packing applications.

- Polyfelt: This 100% polyester felt material is a pliable, lightweight cushioning material that can be used as a liner for drawers and boxes, but as with all felts, it has a tooth that can damage delicate or flaking surfaces placed against it. This felt is inert and has no coloring agents as compared to common felts on the market.
- Fosshape: This is a specially engineered polyester material that is similar to a thick felt. It can be used in combination with wet or dry heating by shrinking it to the shape of an object support to which it adheres when dried. It is an excellent material for covering of mounts or other padding structures.
- Nomex: This product is made of spun woven aramid (aromatic polyamide) fiber commonly used as an extremely soft, pliable wrap for lining material in support cavity packing or storage mounts.
- Polyester Batting: It is an 100% polyester material, which is produced in layered unwoven rolls or sheets—the best versions are not bonded at all, or

are heat-fused low-melt polyester, and functionally inert materials—resin bonded varieties should be avoided. It is commonly used as support in cavity packing or for storage mounts as it fills to object contours or packing voids. It must have a barrier covering to keep it from coming in contact with the object and transferring its fibers. It can act as a cushioning material for light fragile objects, but has minimum compression strength.

Foam Sheet and Plank

Foams are manufactured by a variety of processes, come in different sizes and thicknesses, and are produced in sheets, rolls, and planks. Their cellular composition mandates cushioning levels of support in relationship to the footprint weight (PSI) placed upon the foam structure. Reference links listed will provide a more detailed explanation.

- Expanded polystyrene: The Styrofoam brand is a rigid, lightweight material most commonly used as a thermal insulation in crating, but provides very minimal support as a cushioning material. Often used as a covered support for nonenclosed display of lightweight objects or decorative elements. Typically Blue (Dow) or pink (USG) in color and not to be confused with the more friable white version that is commonly found within the general packing industry.
- Volara: It is the brand name of a polyolefin-based polyethylene foam. In the production process, the irradiation crosslinking creates a closed-cell foam with microscopic cells and an extremely smooth surface finish. It is highly versatile and is used widely as a surface covering for packing and mount making design techniques and as a padded support barrier for storage shelves. It functions best when presented directly to the object surface, but can easily be snagged and torn if hard object edges and corners are slid across its surface, which may be prevented by lining with Tyvek, Nomex, or the like.
- Ethafoam: Ethafoam is the common name used for the closed-cell, polyethylene foam base material. It is functionally inert for most purposes and is widely used throughout the museum industry. Ethafoam adheres to itself and other polyethylene-based materials with direct heat or to most other surfaces with industrial-grade hot glue. This foam comes in various compression ratings, sizes, and thicknesses, and is produced in sheets, rolls, and planks. The overall archival qualities of the material make it very versatile, and it is used in numerous scenarios in relation to other structural materials. It is recommended that the material be described as "functionally inert for most purposes"; ostensibly more pure versions are available in military grades.

- PolyPlank: PolyPlank is the common reference term used for this version of closed-cell, polyethylene foam formulated differently and having a larger cell structure on average compared to Ethafoam. It is softer in density; produced in planks; is easily cut, shaped, and glued; and has numerous uses for packing, storage, and display.
- Polyurethane-ester: This foam is an open-cell foam with responsive memory and very soft compression characteristics. Being an open-celled foam, it provides an inherently better vibration mitigation than closed celled foams. It has a fairly high tensile strength for a polyurethane, but cannot be compared to standard polyethylene. It is commonly found within the commercial shipping and furniture industry as an inexpensive packing and support material.
- Polyethylene shapes: Commonly termed backer rods, this is a polyethylene foam, which is extruded and produced most commonly in a rod shape, but also in other shapes and sizes nowadays. The shapes can be easily cut, glued, and shaped to create custom supports for objects for packing and display, and for storage support mounts.

Padded Sheeting

Padded sheeting is a commercially viable and inexpensive wrapping and padding material used in soft packing transport scenarios, but it is not beneficial or safe for long-term storage of objects.

- Bubble Wrap: Bubble Wrap is a trade name that has grown and remained as a description of a material more than as a known brand. Polyethylene or polyvinyl chloride films are sandwiched to create air-capsulated compartments of similar sizes per sheet. The size of bubbles and the variants of sheeting thicknesses and styles can offer a wide selection for various uses.

  The proper use of the way to pack an object with bubble wrap is an ongoing question: bubble in or bubble out? Objects wrapped with bubbles facing inward can leave distinctive surface marks echoing the bubble pattern, especially if no interim barrier is used. Bubbles facing out are more prone to breakage and the material is hard to tape in wrapping scenarios. Bubble wrap is available double-faced, which avoids this issue, for about a 10% higher cost. Bubble wrap is not an all-in-one packing solution, so it must be considered along with using a barrier material against the object and not be depended upon for total structural or cushioned support.
- Quilted or paper padding: There are many types and brand names related to this common commercial padded wrapping. Often, it is made of two layers of heavier stock paper with internal layers made of softer or expanded layers of paper. It is commonly sold in rolls, which are perforated in repeated

lengths and widths to allow easy use in creating sizes and shapes. Manufactured combinations with paper and plastic bubble can often be found. Some of the all-paper versions have very abrasive surfaces and are very acidic, and should not be used in direct contact with objects

• Moving blankets: Blankets are quilted with a batting filling or made of a composite recycled cloth in a pliable thickness and are commonly used in museums and commercial transport companies. These blankets are used for wrapping and cushioning and can provide effective protection when handling or transporting objects. When they are used as a wrapping material, objects must be covered with an interim barrier to protect the object from the blankets' abrasive surface. They are often used to cover or to protect and cushion an object placed on a surface, such as a lifting fork or the floor of a room or for securing and padding objects in for transport.

Fabric Sheeting

Fabric sheeting is often used for covering and for structural support, and as a barrier, especially within textile collections, because of the compatibility in inherent characteristics and structural handling support. Fabric should be Oddy tested for fiber composition, coloring pigments, and manufacturers' sizing for potential off gassing pollutants coming into contact with objects.

• Muslin: Muslin, if composed of 100% cotton muslin, is unbleached, unsized, is the most common fabric used for collection care and is most often used for textile mounts, for covering mannequins, to support handling slings and for other purposes.
• Polyester sheeting: This sheeting makes a quality alternative to muslin if is made of 100% polyester, has been washed, and is of a flexible thread count.
• Linen and Silks: These fabrics are also used in combination with material types that best suit the object. Some linens and silks are also used for repairs on torn textiles and paper stocks.

Fillers

These examples are of basic materials that are used to fill voids in soft packing scenarios and/or to create a soft support when handling objects in short-distance collection care activities.

• Extruded Styrofoam shapes: This material is commonly made of polystyrene foam in different shapes and different sizes. Commonly named after its extruded shapes, which are small balls, peanuts, or bowl shapes that, when used as pieces, settle and lock together to create structural support. In collection care uses, these shapes are often put into semifilled plastic bags that can be shaped to support an object or used as a packing fill to support a wrapped object in a soft packed scenario. The foam pieces are extremely static, messy to use, and not recyclable. Some types are made of a biodegradable starch and are readily disposable, but easily attract pests.

- Wadding: Wadding is more a term for shaping a material to fill a void or create cushioning than an actual material name. Tissue, newsprint, bubble wrap, and polyester batting are commonly used in soft packing scenarios and in cushioned handling and storage support.

Wood & Plywood

- Lumber: Dimensional lumber should be selected according to purpose, and if used in display casework, care must be taken to use varieties that do not present the risk of off-gassing. For crating purposes, grade 2 or a better pine is a typical choice—lower construction grades frequently have knot holes, bark, and so on, which can easily present issues in fabrication that more than offset their lower cost. Higher grades such as clear wood tend to be more true and may provide a more visually pleasing product, but are generally unnecessary for crating. If crates are being produced for export, the lumber must be kiln dried and heat treated (KDHT), which should be clearly stamped on the ends of the boards—please note, however, that production of crates for export using pine and other wood varieties requires a special license, and periodic inspection of purchasing records, inventory, and crates, and a "bug stamp" with the license number provided by an authorized agency must be applied on the visible sides of a given crate, or else the crate and its contents can be impounded by the receiving country.
- Plywood grades: AA, AB, AC codes refer to the quality of finish of the faces: A means the face has had any knot holes plugged, filled, and sanded, C means the face is neither plugged, nor filled or sanded, and B falls somewhere in between —plugged but not filled or sanded. An AC grade means that one side is totally finished, while the other side is unfinished.
- Interior grade plywood: Interior grades of plywood should generally NOT be used in proximity to artwork or artifacts, and particularly not in enclosures such as crates unless there is an impermeable barrier in between— interior plywood uses urea formaldehyde-based glues, which break down easily in heat and high humidity, releasing formaldehyde, which is a solvent and a carcinogen, and is known to cause migraines.
- Exterior grades of plywood use phenol formaldehyde-based glues, which are far more stable than those used in interior applications, and present a far lesser risk of off-gassing.
- Medium density overlay (MDO) plywood is an exterior grade plywood originally made for painted highway signs, and which has an outer layer

of phenolic plastic with a skin akin to Kraft paper on one or both faces. It is an excellent choice if the casework is to be painted, and, particularly, if double sided, can be the basis of a highly water-resistant crate—the layer of phenolic plastic prevents penetration by moisture and the off-gassing of any components in the core. So long as all joints of a crate made with MDO are well sealed with a good silicone, and the lid-to-side mating surfaces employ a good gasketing material, the crate will resist even water under pressure, as if it were actually submerged.

Metals

Metals are used within many collection care activities to supply different levels of structural strength and support. Display and mount-making activities commonly have metals used in the structural support. These metals are shaped, padded, and/or coated to create a barrier to protect the object from the metal surface. Some metals such as aluminum and stainless steel can be uncoated and used in direct contact with the object, but it is ultimately more protective to add a barrier between the metal and object to prevent abrasion or corrosion.

- The most commonly used metals are brass, aluminum, iron, stainless steel, and copper. Manufactured metals are produced in the form of sheets, tubes, wires, screws, pins, rivets, and nails.
- The metals can be altered by cutting or shaping with varying levels of heat to manipulate their molecular structure. Metals can be attached to each other by applying heat with a flux to compatible solders that create a weld when combined with the specific level of heat to two compatible metal surfaces.

There are two categories of solders: soft and hard.

- Soft solder contains soft alloys (mostly tin) that have low melting points. It can be done with an electrically heated soldering iron, and is suitable for low-load-bearing joints in brass.
- Hard or silver solder contains hard alloys of silver, copper, and certain other metals at higher temperatures than those in soft solder. Several grades are available, depending upon melting temperatures; the easy and medium grades are most useful for mount- making applications. Because of its high melting temperature, hard soldering requires the use of a gas torch (propane, butane, MPG, or acetylene). Hard solder creates stronger joints than soft solder, and is therefore the preferred choice for most applications in steel and brass.[4]
- Electronic welding: Welding metals of similar composition and thickness can be done with an ARC or MIG-type machine. The combination of the

flux and soldering material in relation to the heat applied by the electronics of the machine creates the desired fusion process of the two pieces of metal.

Plastics

Many plastic-based products are used as materials for building displays, mounting and packing supports, and protective glazing for framed objects. The following are some common types of plastic material used.

Acrylic: Acrylic sheets are widely used for case vitrines, two-dimensional object framing, mount-making supports, handling supports, and other structural designs for display or storage supports. Sheets are produced in two types of processes: cell cast (stronger) and extruded (softer, more easily manipulated), which come in different sizes and thicknesses and can be adhered to each other with specific adhesives. Acrylic can be purchased in different colors; the commonly used and desired version is the transparent one, which allows clarity for seeing through or assists in reducing its physical appearance. For use as a transparent covering, acrylic sheeting with protective fluttering agents can be purchased for reducing light effects and reflective glare. Acrylic sheets can be cleaned to maintain appearance, but are easily scratched or crack with improper handling.

- Extruded shape acrylic: Acrylic can be purchased in extruded shapes and sizes such as cylinders, rods, and square or angular stock and in different sizes, thicknesses, and finish.
- Polycarbonate sheeting: Polycarbonate is a transparent plastic sheeting that is much stronger and more resistant to shattering compared to acrylic sheeting. The advantage of this material is that it can be used for impact-proofing cases or glazing for security protection where needed.
- Teflon: Teflon (DuPont brand name for Polytetrafluoroethylene (PTFE)), is a synthetic fluoropolymer of tetrafluoroethylene and is produced for different applications. Its hardness and surface abrasion-resistant qualities make it an excellent aid for support of movement of heavy objects on display or in different phases of handling and transport in the form of sliding sheets or strips.
- PVC plastics: Polyvinyl chloride, commonly abbreviated as PVC, comes in both hard and soft versions of manufacture, in many shapes and sizes for a multitude of commercial construction uses. The economics of using this material as a support material is very tempting, but the chemical agents and off-gassing capabilities make it a high risk for material use onto or near objects. PVC tubing is often used in the form of tube support for transporting rolled objects. If this method of transport is considered, the object must

be covered with an impenetrable barrier to protect it against off gassing and stored on the tube as a temporary solution.

Tapes and Adhesives

A large variety of tapes and adhesive are used for collection care activities. The following section will focus on the most common types used. With the multitude of different materials and applications available, often an object's needs may require a specific product to be used. The acid levels in adhesive materials are of primary concern for use within the vicinity of or directly on an object. Many archival products are available, tested, and sold as per their performance application and material composition (MSDA reports). The advancement in quality and application process of materials is in constant evolution, but many are tried, true, and economically efficient.

Adhesives should never be used directly on artifacts as a method of attaching a material to a display or to a mount for support. Adhesives used in conservation repair are selected for the material type and reversing nature for future removal.

Archival-tested adhesives should be used in most scenarios. Acidic adhesive materials are used within the museum but must be used in combination with the material used to reduce or eliminate the risk of the adhesive off gassing next to the object or in the microclimate where the object is housed or displayed.

For further research, go to conservation websites and archival material suppliers to seek the best product for your needs. Networking with other colleagues is essential as the discussion can follow multiple tracks and the industry is in constant advancement for new products.

- Masking tape: Standard paper tape, beige in color, and has excessive adhesive properties for general use. It will tear most delicate wrapping and can leave residue and dry if left for long periods of time on a surface.
- Glass tape: Paper tape backed with extremely low-tack adhesive permitting easy removal. Some varieties are approved for use on coated glass. Static electric charges may be avoided during removal by moistening the tape with a damp cloth before removal.
- Blue tape: Commonly called painter's tape, it has less adhesive properties and is preferred for use in display marking on paint or floor surfaces as it is easily removed with less residue remaining. It works better than most tapes for securing covering wraps of paper.
- Duct tape: Strong, durable, highly versatile tape for general use in holding items or sheeting material together. It is highly acidic and recommended for temporary use only.

- Packing tape: PVC tape (brown or clear) used for adhering plastic sheeting and other materials, but it tears easily when severed, and the adhesive is very acidic and off-gasses near objects.
- Packing tape: Other plastic-based tapes are backed with polypropylene with an acrylic adhesive, a better choice for reducing off-gassing.
- Tabs: Tape strips should be cut, then shaped to a folded tab at the end of the strip. This is an effective method for locating where the tape strip ends, which assists in removing tape for package. Clear tapes require being tabbed as the tape is so transparent that it become impossible to find the end or edge of the tape strip.
- Nylon filament tape: Plastic tape that is constructed with nylon fibers embedded in the plastic. Very durable but has a strong adhesive, is highly acidic, recommended for temporary wrapping use only.
- Reinforced paper tape: Like filament tape, it has nylon fibers embedded in the paper tape to give it strength. The adhesive is a water-based emulsion that when dampened will adhere to other paper surfaces.
- Double-sided tape: This tape is used as it has adhesive on each side and can bind two sheets of like materials. Comes in different adhesive strengths but when used near an object within a matt, the archival version should be used.
- Tyvek tape: This pressure-sensitive tape has an acrylic-based adhesive with a Tyvek-based backing. It is very versatile and archival compatible with artworks such as book repair or hinging of mats.
- Velcro tape: Velcro tape is composed of Velcro strips with an adhesive backing placed on both the hook and loop sections of the strips. This adhesive is very strong in attaching to wood, paper, painted surfaces, or other materials commonly used in creating closures for storage boxes and in some display techniques. It works effectively in combination when one nonadhesive-backed strip needs to be attached in another method to the actual object and then attached with the adhesive-backed strip to the support material. Velcro when used needs to be accessed for the risk of the physical motion and pressure that is required to separate the two combing strips in relation to the pressure that may be transferred to the object.
- Cotton twill tape: Quality archival use twill tape is composed of a non-adhesive, unbleached, unsized 100% cotton. It comes in rolls of different lengths and widths and is a common and versatile material to tie support objects in different scenarios. Twill tape is also available in high-strength low-stretch nylon and other synthetic versions.
- Hot melt glue: These adhesives melt in the combination of different levels of heat applied by a heating tool of gun application. The main component of these glues is an ethylene vinyl acetate copolymer base. Glues are manufactured in both acidic and archival applications in a multitude of sizes and shapes specific to the gun construction. FDA-approved and noncorrosive

versions may have a polypropylene base and, in addition to better chemical properties, promise to adhere better to plastics. 3M and Bostik are two commonly purchased brand names of archival-based glues.

- Hot glue guns: These application tools are made to different styles, for the hobbyist to industrial use, varying levels of heat controls, melting processes and manual operation comfort. Risks of the molten glue must be managed for the protection of both the operator and the object. 3M and Bostik manufacture different glue guns that are directly compatible with the glue styles they supply.
- Wood glue: Polyvinyl acetate (PVA), commonly called carpenter's glue, is designed and used on wood or in combination with other related construction materials. Formaldehyde (a carcinogen) is a byproduct in the off gassing of this commonly used adhesive. Polyurethane glue can be used on wood and can bond with multiple other types of materials.
- Museum wax: Museum wax, commonly called sticky wax, is used to create a light adhesion to assist in securing an object for display to its support surface. Museum wax can leave a residue on porous objects. Silicone adhesive should not be used for these same scenarios as residue is irremovable from almost all material surfaces.

Paints and Varnishes

Using paint and varnishes within collection care activities is a critical concern because of the risks that are created within an enclosed microclimate environment such as a storage cabinet, display case, or shipping crate. The rule commonly stated is to use only acrylic, water-based coatings and never use oil and alkyd-based coatings as their vapors can harm the objects in the confines of that environment.

The overarching rule is to always allow all coatings sufficient time (two to three weeks) to dry and the coating material to off-gas before placing the object within the confined space created. Of course, these are only basic rules, and the composition of the material used and the risks to the object must be accessed and analyzed before the construction materials and coating are chosen.

The following introduction is an excerpt from a CCI Technical Bulletin titled Coatings for Display and Storage in Museums; Technical Bulletin #21 by Jean T'etreault of the Canadian Conservation Institute. The entire document is an excellent explanation detailing the issues of risks in choosing the correct coating to use in relationship structures and the protective care of the object.

Coatings such as paints and varnishes are often used in museums for aesthetic reasons as well as for the protection of buildings and display cases, cabinets, or transportation cases. The requirements for coatings used for preservation purposes differ from those used for domestic and industrial purposes. Coating the interior of a display case is one example of a challenging situation that museums face regularly: coatings usually emit a large range of volatile compounds, and there is often a very short drying period available before the installation of objects, so emissions from a coating can create a harmful environment for objects in a display case.

The goal of this document is to alert architects, designers, contractors, fabricators, project managers, and museum staff to the damage that coatings might cause to objects, and to provide guidelines for the selection of coatings that will help minimize this risk. A list of coatings is provided for many different situations and, when possible, alternative materials and procedures are given. Recommendations are based on the various classes of coatings and resins; trade names are not specified because there is a large variety of coatings on the market and their formulations may change in the future. Tests that will verify coating specifications or monitor the emission of volatile compounds are described, and information on substrate surface preparation is also provided.[5]

COMMON EQUIPMENT TYPES

In compiling the following list of equipment found and used in collection care activities, I have categorized the individual equipment described by the similar functions they perform. The list will be supportive of various examples that exist and the context in relation to the collections care activity for which they may be used. To describe each object to an exact piece of equipment would be impossible. One must understand the relationships of the object, protective material, and equipment type that best fit the scenario that the object will encounter.

Equipment types that perform the same function may be different in manufacturers' design, quality of construction, brand name, or terminology in regard to its physical function. For example, a vertical platform lifter indicates the function of equipment that operates in a vertical motion; it has a platform that lifts the payload vertically up or down. The next context is the specific types of vertical platform lifters, hydraulic or geared mechanics. The hydraulic mechanism can be operated by an electrically or manually operated control. Geared mechanisms commonly are operated by a manual control, but some manufacturers offer the operation to be done with an electrical control. The point of this example is that depending on manufacturers and the equipment they produce, each offers specific operational functions with various options to choose from to manipulate those functions.

The various functions a piece of equipment can offer dictate how an object can be moved in regards to its physical support and safety. An electronic control on the vertical platform lift may be a great option as it moves the object with no human physical requirement for its operation. The problem with using the electronic control is that the platform may move with a quick jerk when the lifting mechanism is first engaged or at the end of the lifting motion, causing shock and vibration being transferred to the object being lifted. Often, depending on the manufacturer and, of course, the price, the electronic controls may be designed to have an extra-sensitive control that may be adjusted to regulate its operation. This is a common complication of larger hydraulic lifting devices such as forklifts and elevators but is not common in smaller pieces of equipment. Researching and testing the equipment before purchase can provide the excellent benefit of being an educated consumer.

Specialized equipment can be developed and built to a specific need.

Many handling requirements cannot be met sufficiently with standard designed equipment. The concept of what you want the new equipment to achieve or be as an adaption to an existing piece of equipment must first be visualized and drafted. The draft of the equipment must then be presented to a supplier, manufacturer, or engineer to get constructive criticism as to the idea being feasible. Having the confirmation of your design being viable, approved, and stated it can meet all safety standards of a piece of equipment is crucial, and then the actual build can begin.

Mark Slattery from the National Gallery of London addresses these specifics in his article titled "Specialized Art Handling Equipment, When Is It Necessary and How to Develop It," at the end of this chapter.

Building accessories, attachments, extensions, and so on to adapt existing equipment is often done but can be extremely hazardous to both the operator and the object. Understanding the risks of how this adaption may impact on the operation is the question. Take the time to discuss the idea with the institution's safety officer, engineer, and building facilities staff to get other opinions regarding the effectiveness of your idea. Unless you are a certified engineer or have been educated in structural dynamics of material and equipment, you are taking a risk. Overbuilding something can be as dangerous as underbuilding it when adapting a tool or piece of equipment. Common sense will lead you in the right direction in your planning if caution and risks are key words in the assessment process.

Describing equipment types can be confusing with the different names for pieces of equipment or the words commonly used to describe the function of the equipment in regard to the location in the world and the terminology used. Another point of confusion is when the equipment is often referred to by the brand name and not by a commonly termed function or generic name.

Communication to describe a particular piece of equipment to someone from another institution or country can be accompanied by a photograph or illustration. The use of photographs to visualize each piece of equipment is not possible in this book, though many good images have been supplied. The information here should be used as reference in conjunction with commercial equipment websites to visually see the examples stated. The following is a list of equipment types placed in categories according to the function types they support.

Hand Tools and Tool Carts

The actual hand tools of the collection care activities vary tremendously and many of the basics such as hammers, screwdrivers, knives, and drills really need little explanation. The biggest issue with the difference in choice of tools is the technical use per a specific activity and, more importantly, personal preference. In my career, I have heard, and been a part of, numerous conversations regarding the types of tools commonly found within the toolboxes of any museum and commercial service provider. The conversation never ceases to end, and it can reach different levels at any point of time and over many years. These conversations all have valid points but never reach a commonly agreeable one tool result. The new tools found on the market today may be the next additions to the continually developing conservation toolkit.

A good example of a tool commonly discussed is the knife. The knife and its purpose generally center on its effectiveness in the cutting of foam, and in other relationships it can be used to manipulate related materials in the workplace. Do you use a retractable knife with replaceable tips per blade as they stay sharp, or a common produce knife with a long thin blade that needs to be sharpened, or a Japanese saw that remains sharp and has great flexibility? This is just to show three different varieties, and as the reader you may have just added a couple more as examples.

Your choice—though all three knives can be used and each may be better for a certain application. For years I preferred a knife with a serrated edge for cutting foam but could not sharpen it when it dulled. We purchased an electric knife sharpener for the workspace and a group of common produce knives of different lengths and thicknesses. This approach and idea seemed to greatly suffice until a crew member found another example of an interesting style of knife, and then we tried and adopted it into our knife selection in our tool box.

The point is there are a variety of tools on the market from various trades and industries that can be adapted for use in working with materials for collection care activities. Always be open to trying new tools, but choose quality tools that will last longer and not be disposable. The use of disposable tools soon turns the local hardware store into the immediate toolbox for your working environment, effectively inefficient and cost prohibitive.

Tools vary from country to country where you may be required to work or ask someone to do the work required in a certain way, for example, the correct tool needed for a crate closure system or for attaching hardware on a specific mount. Never assume that everyone has the same tool, and in the case of specialized hardware it may be advisable to send the tool and extra hardware along as part of the exhibition. A common example of this is for security case hardware when an exhibition travels with its display furniture or certain mounts. It is best to know and ask other individuals if they have the tools required for the actual design. When determining the design, one can make the hardware or system common to ensure the versatility of possible tools required. Coordinating the discussion of tool and hardware compatibility is important; communicating with images will save a thousand words.

The last discussion regarding tools in this chapter is to focus on the toolbox, tool cart, or tool cabinet you keep to secure your tools within. Hand tools are designed for the ergonomics of your hand and body. Human nature is such that the hand becomes an extension to pick up the tool, borrow it, or simply move it to another location. Finding the tool when you need it may be a harder task than anticipated because the tool has left the confines of the

Figure 8.1   Custom Designed Tool Cart. *Source*: Author.

container you store it in. Not having your tool when you need it impacts on the time it takes to do the work and potentially the money you have budgeted for tools in your workplace. The most effective method to avoid tools being misplaced or taken is to mark them in some fashion with a recognizable mark; engraving or painting are the most common.

I have managed several large museum relocations and at multiple sites. Tools and tool carts were always purchased in quantity and fitted out with similar tools and hardware. The best solution to keep them organized was for each cart to have a colored marking, which related to the designated group and their particular set of tools and cart. This way each group could track their tools if borrowed or misplaced, to be returned to the specific cart. In an ongoing workspace in any collection care department, this same approach of marking is important, as different departments share these workspaces and at times will use each other's tools. The time spent marking will tremendously outweigh the time spent searching when tools are missing. The other benefit is that it creates a sense of ownership and pride in keeping your tools organized.

The tool cart, toolbox, or cabinet should also be lockable to maintain control and assist in monitoring your tools. If someone needs to borrow a tool, it is often basic human nature to borrow the tool but not return it. For some, the borrowing may extend to the home for use over a weekend, but then that tool may never be returned. Never accusing someone of stealing, but this does happen when anyone leaves tools near a common public space or near exits, which makes the tool an easy morsel to taste. Budgeting for loss of tools is expensive, and by using simple identification and marking systems and locking them away, the tools can be easily retained in greater numbers. In the construction trade, it is most common to be required to personally supply all your hand tools to the worksite. In this requirement, the personal pride and expense of managing the care of your tools is self-evident.

To identify and create a list of tools found within all collection care activities would be difficult. The many common tools can create crossovers in the many versions of each, such as the knife, for example. The specialty tools that a conservator uses can in themselves make a daunting list as the various technical examples would be ongoing, and new tools would continually need to be added after the list was completed. In conducting the research for this topic, I found that the lists were often small or included no explanation. The following is a list of hardware and tools commonly found in collection care activities.

Hardware

Hardware like tools make an endless list because of the varieties of the types of hardware made for a specific use, quality, size, limitation, availability, and personal preference. All manufacturers will supply specifications such as weight load limitations and instructions for properly mounting hardware to the designed surfaces. Altering specifications increases the risk of the hardware failing. Research should be undertaken by contacting colleagues in other museums, and networking through collection care networks and museum suppliers to find out what hardware is specially made to assist in your collection care needs. The following list will only focus on hanging hardware and some most common hardware examples used for display.

Installation Hanging Hardware

- Security hardware: Security screws are a basic hardware example that have been made to have a unique head design that requires a specialized driver to tighten or remove it from its mounting use. Two common designs are spanner and pinhead (snake eyes) designs.
- Security hardware: Lock-in or "T" screw security hardware is a brand of security hardware that is often used and considered a versatile hanger by museums; it comes in adjustable designs and various sizes for different weight limits. The basics are a "T screw" mounted to the wall that when turned will lock in the slotted receiving plate hardware that acts as the mount to the framed object.
- Security hardware: The Ryman brand hanger is a good choice for artwork with a structurally flat back to hang securely and tightly on the wall. It comes in different sizes for various weights. A slide spring keeper attaches the two receiving plates together and is adjustable.
- Common hardware: D-ring, a single or strap hardware that is made to be mounted on the back of wooden frames; also available for metal frames, with a single hole for small frames or multiple-hole attachments for heavier frames. Accommodates individual wall hooks in compatible hook size and weight specifications. Hanging from a two-point design is more secure, but often the two D-rings used are connected with hanging wire as a secondary solution for hanging artwork.
- Common hardware: Floreat hangers are high-quality, versatile, standard wall hangers that are sold in different sizes and weight load capacities. Large versions have holed centers for use with a wall anchor, and other varieties have flexible clips to prevent artwork from lifting off the wall. It is a standard hanging for framed works hung from a wire hanging system or individual D-rings.
- Common hardware: The adjustable J-hook design is adaptable to multiple attachment hardware and different wall types. It is a single-variety heavy-duty picture hook that allows for height and level adjustments. Good choice

Figure 8.2 Ryman Security Hardware. *Source*: Author.

for earthquake-prone areas, as it allows works to swivel with the movement of the earth and minimizes damage from vibrations.
- Speciality hardware: Magnets are used to hang lightweight paper or fabric sheeting for display. The advantages of magnets are that they offer a support handing system without a physical alteration to the object. The use of magnets continues to develop as different sizes and methods of contact to the object are tried and tested.
- Speciality hardware: A cleat wall hanger is designed for heavy and oversized frames. The design can handle a broader weight load while offering stable attachment to the wall by multiple points of mounting. Commonly made of aluminum or wood with an interlocking "Z" design or bevelled at 45°; suitable for many different wall and frame types.
- Speciality hardware: Picture rail and track hanging systems are installed with the support rail or track mounted parallel to the ceiling with cables, chains, or rods for hanging down to receive the hanging hardware of the object. The speciality designed hardware creates a secure support system for various weights of object in the specified deign of the track and cable hardware mechanisms. The hangers slide on the vertical support cables,

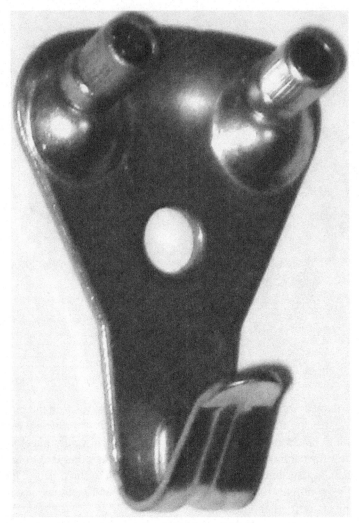

Figure 8.3   Floreat Hanger / Common Style. *Source*: Author.

which allows for ease in adjustment and reduces damage and repair to wall surfaces.

• Speciality hardware: Custom-made hanging hardware systems are best for complex, heavy works of contemporary art and old, heavy, century frames with deep frame structures or lavish ornamentation. There are endless options, but common designs are constructed of flat strap steel, which can be shaped to suit hanging or mounting hardware. Hanging weight tests should be conducted or in standard use settings be manufactured and tested by a steel engineer.

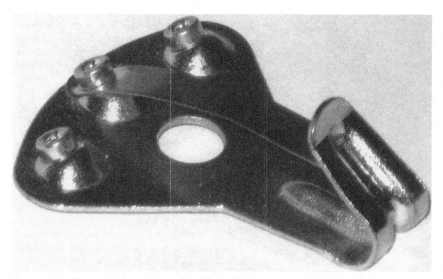

Figure 8.4 **Floreat Hanger / Security Clip Style.** *Source*: Author.

- Speciality hardware: Oz Clips, brand name, are multipurpose hanging hardware attached to framed artworks and compatible for both a hanging device and security attachment. Commonly used to mount artworks within handling frames or collars for storage or transport as the frame does not need to be directly padded. The hardware is constructed of heavy-gauge brass with a steel pivot pin; it secures the object's frame to the handling frame or collar by one bar attaching directly to the frame, and the other extended out past the edge of the frame and screwed to the travel frame. The object then appears to be floating, not touching on the surface or frame. When placing the object on display, the hardware's outer bar can be swiveled, placed behind the frame, and hidden while the whole clip still remains attached to the object's frame. Some designs include a hanging hook loop to be turned outward to receive the wall hook for installation.
- Speciality hardware: Closure plates are a hardware design usually used to secure the lid of a crate to the main body of the crate shell. The system consists of two metal plates with a threaded hole on the bottom plate and a corresponding receiving hole on the top plate. Each plate is screwed to the wooden framework; the top plate has a corresponding hole drilled through the framework, so the threaded bolt connects the two metal plates. When tightened, the framework sections close and remain secure until the bolt is unscrewed and removed allowing the lid to be separated from the crate body. This same design can be used in multiple attaching methods for securing two wooden structural components together.

Figure 8.5   Oz Clips Components. *Source*: Carey, Artex FAS.

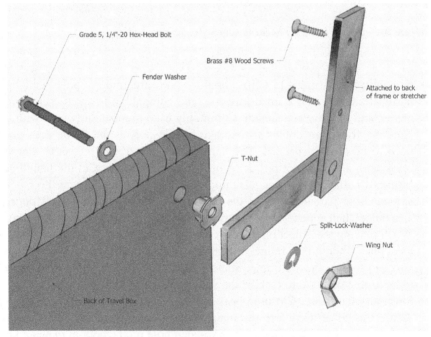

Figure 8.6   Oz Clips Installation Diagram. *Source*: Barber, Artex FAS.

- Draw latches, cam locks: Closure plates using flip levers, butterfly/hand operable wings, or 1/4-turn nuts, which cannot be opened using power drills, avoiding potential vibration issues; invaluable when used with pastels or other friable materials. May be sprung to maintain a given pressure, particularly good for use with gaskets.

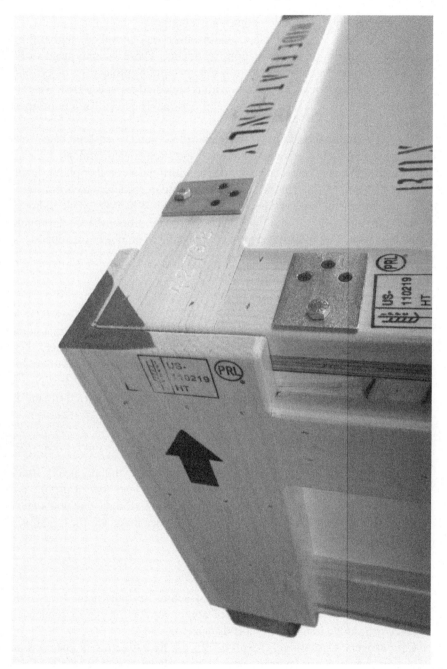

Figure 8.7 Crating Closure Plates. *Source*: Carey, Artex FAS.

- Support weights: Support weights are commonly used for holding flat objects such as paper in place while observing, unrolling, and rolling works or performing conservation treatments. These weights need to be uniform in weight and covered in a soft material to protect the object and to be easily kept clean. Glass bars with rounded edges make great weights as they are easily cleaned, durable, and reasonably priced for a number of different sizes.
- Support bags: Support bags, sometimes called "sand or cushion bags," are used to support objects in the daily work and storage environment. A clean, washed sand bag is best to use within a flexible tight-weaved or plastic-lined, cloth bag. Other fill materials include Styrofoam beads, which are light-weight and easily manipulated within the bag. Most bags are made in-house and commonly shaped into long snake- or square pillow-shapes to provide the best variety in versatile adaption for shaping to an object for support.

Rolling Support Equipment

Rolling Bars

- Steel rolling bars of the same diameter, same length, and in multiple numbers can be placed under the flat underside of a box or object and then rolled on top of it in a singular direction. This is a basic method of equipment moving dating back to the ancient Egyptian and other cultures. Nylon and other synthetic rod stock is also available, has lower friction, and is kinder both to object and floor surfaces.

Skates

- Skates or rolling platforms are commonly used for extremely heavy structures with flat bottoms. These rolling devices are very low in profile, are designated by weight capacity, and come in both straight line and swivel directional rollers. The most common skate types made are for a platform or corner, or for barrel-rolling support.

Mechanical Jacks

- These devices assist in lifting a boxed structure from the floor. Jacks slide under objects to allow placement of corner movers or can in sequenced placement move items for a short distance.
- Case Movers: Case movers / Roll-a-Lifts are hydraulic lifters that work in tandem, one each on opposing sides, base forks placed under the load, the ratchet strapped together. When manually pumped up, the weight moves on the rollers with little physical effort.

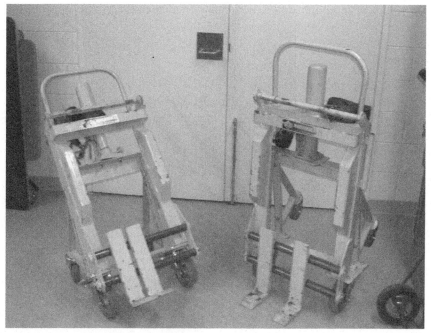

Figure 8.8   Case / Crate Dual Movers. *Source*: Author.

Casters

- Casters are the wheeled mechanism attached to a support structure allowing it to roll in the required directional movement. Casters are the foundation of the quality of any rolling equipment's structure.
- Casters come in a variety of sizes to support various loads in both size and weight. The directional movement of the wheel is commonly structured of encased bearings. The caster can be selected to operate for straight line, swivel, locking, or for adapting to combination movements when a specific directional use is needed. Casters may also be equipped with brakes, pivot locks, and levelers.
- The caster wheel coverings come in a variety and range of material quality. The differences are specified for the type of load being supported, for shock absorption, and for transferring of material to a floor surface. Common wheel types come in solid steel, plastic, nylon, or rubber, or are pneumatic.
- Casters can be purchased for numerous specialty uses. When purchasing or building equipment, the investment in quality and repairable casters is essential. Casters take the brunt of the load weight during movement over the variety of surface obstacles they encounter. Speak to a caster company

or with your equipment representative to understand the best selection for your specific location and needs.

Dollies

- Dollies are the most commonly used pieces of equipment found within the museum industry; they offer a diversity of uses, are available for purchase at different costs, and provide ease in storing and handling to make them a viable solution for many handling requirements.
- The main aspect of selecting the right dollies for use is the type of deck or support structure in combination with the quality of casters attached to the deck for movement.
- Decks come in different designs to accommodate different load shapes and weights placed upon them: flat top, open top, custom fit form such as to a rectangular box or a round support to accommodate a cylindrical shape.
- Casters used on dollies come in a variety of styles and are selected to be used for directional movement, weight support, and surface protection.
- Dollies can be easily custom-built to fit a specific need of movement. Combining the proper structural support with the correct amount of casters can offer a quick, effective solution to moving a specific shape or size of object.

Hand Trucks

- Hand trucks are an upgrade to the common dolly and like the dollies are a commonly used equipment found within the museum industry. The basic premise of a hand truck is that it has a platform that slides under a load and a vertical support attached to two wheels that allows load to be tilted and rolled.
- Compared with dollies, only loads of a certain size can be placed on the platform adjoining the vertical support. Common loads handled are boxes more easily moved than by the carrying motion of the operator. Many attachments can be made or purchased to add additional size and support to the platform section.
- Hand trucks are custom designed to be used for a variety of loads and for use in a particular location. Two common examples include the stair climber and the appliance hand truck. The stair climber has a duel set of three wheels which rotate and move to support the load as it is transverses each level of steps. The appliance hand truck has straps to be placed around the appliance or load and rigged by a tightening mechanism to secure it to the vertical support; it often also has a secondary set of swing-out legs with wheels enabling tall objects to be leaned back while safely supported when passing through low doorways.

Figure 8.9 Dollie under Crate. *Source*: Carey, Artex FAS.

Platform Trolleys

Sometimes termed warehouse trucks, platform trolleys are commonly used and found within the museum industry. The basic premise is that the trolley is built to have a larger platform on which to secure and move items compatible with the structural and caster load restrictions.

Figure 8.10   Flat Top Dollie. *Source*: IAS Sydney, Australia.

- Their additional platform size and structure in comparison to a dolly makes them highly versatile for moving objects. Trolleys come with single, dual, or removable handles to accommodate the size of loads and to provide ease in controlling the movement.
- Platform decks are commonly made of solid metal, wood, or open mesh, which are rated for load weights and are all compatible to strapping and securing a load to the deck. Casters are rated for load restrictions, accommodate the directional movement, and are recommended for being lockable for securing the load.
- Panel carts are types of platform trolleys commonly found within the museum industry and were initially designed to move sheeting materials such as plywood and plasterboard cardboard. Both single and multiple vertical supports on these carts can be padded and adapted for moving delicate two-dimensional objects.
- Specialized carts made for woodworkers can be had with hydraulics to elevate stacks of material up to 4' × 10' and rotate them from flat to vertical and vice versa—invaluable not only for material handling, but also for items such as large bas reliefs.

Painting or Framed Carts

- These carts are designed to handle two-dimensional objects such as framed paintings and drawings. They are based on a panel cart design, but in most collection care workplaces, they are custom-built to meet the size and needs of the objects within the collection.
- Painting carts are often designed to an "A" shaped vertical support on which the objects will be placed to lean into the "A" support angle. Each side of the bottom portion of the "A" shape allows space for the object to

Figure 8.11 Standard and Stair Hand Trucks. *Source*: Author.

be set up on the cart's base. The angle of the vertical shape is not a dramatic angle, so it does not allow the object to slide away from the vertical support structure. Objects can be tied directly to the "A" shape if the need to secure them is required.

- Another common design is a straight vertical support in the center of the base of the cart, which also allows objects to be leaned against the vertical support. This design offers the option of the object being tied directly to the support in a vertical fashion, if required, for safe transport of the object. Examples of this support would be for sheets of marble, stained glass, or Asian folding screens, and other objects.
- These types of carts can be designed to have support extensions incorporated in the structural design to be accessed and locked into place if

Figure 8.12   Painting / Frame Cart. *Source*: Author.

required for oversized objects. Common extensions are made for both the vertical and horizontal adaptions for large objects.

- Other support adaptions can be easily and safely designed by attaching extra wooden or metal extensions directly to the main vertical structure to assist with oversized objects. Securing the extension to the cart is essential so that the support maintains its structural stability during the movement.

Figure 8.13   Painting / Frame Cart. *Source*: IAS Sydney, Australia.

- Frame carts are designed to support smaller framed objects by allowing them to be placed into the central vertical support of the cart. The vertical support has open spaces in the bottom section, so the object can sit on and across the cart base and lean into the vertical support. These carts allow for multiple framed objects to be moved at a time.

Figure 8.14   Small A Frame Cart. *Source*: Author.

Figure 8.15 Small A-Frame Cart Bottom View. *Source*: Author.

- All of these types of carts need to have tying points designed into the structure so that securing the objects to the carts can be easily executed. Casters are rated for load restrictions and for accommodating the directional movement, and it is advisable to make them lockable for securing the load.

Object Carts

- Object carts are designed to move small three-dimensional objects and can be found in various sizes; they provide structural support and can be built to meet the specific needs of a specific collection.
- Many commercially made carts can be purchased and easily adapted by padding and covering the surface of the cart with foam and a fabric sheeting.
- Any custom padding and covering needs to be designed to be easily replaced and/or cleaned because with repeated use, these carts do become dirty.
- Additional drawers or spaces for specific tools within the cart design assist in avoiding placing the object and the tools together on the main support surface of the cart.

Ramps or Plates

- Ramps or plates are made to assist in bridging and traversing an unleveled surface such as in loading docks, truck cargo decks, elevator carriages, and sea containers. These should be used and stored near locations where loads will be moved over unleveled surfaces most frequently.
- Bridging ramps or plates can be purchased or made to meet specific weight restrictions and equipped with handling adaption such as fork-lift guides and/or hinged handles for manual handling.

Ladders

Ladders found within the workplace are commonly represented in three groups: step ladders, extension ladders, and rolling platform ladders. Each ladder is designed to reach a specific height with weight limits on the user climbing on the steps or platform. Manufacturer safeguards are designed into the ladders' structural design, but proper training in the use of this basic tool is important.

- Step and extension ladders are most commonly manufactured out of aluminum or fiberglass. The fiberglass ladders are more expensive but have a more durable structure than aluminum ladders and do not conduct electricity.
- Some ladders are designed with telescoping supports, so the ladder can be adjusted when placed on an unleveled surface making it sturdy and secure before climbing. Examples are step ladders with a telescoping front support, which can be adjusted to be placed upon stairs.
- Multipurpose ladders of aluminum construction have capabilities to convert from a-frame support to an uneven a-frame for support on unleveled ground and use on stairs. The multipurpose ladder can also be conformed into a straight ladder support.
- Extension ladder bases can be designed with an angled support bracing to provide greater vertical structural support. Ladder standoffs are an accessory that can be attached to the top of an extension ladder to assist in stabilizing sideways motion and allow the individual to be positioned away from the wall surface when working at the ladder's top.
- Platform ladders are designed such that the individual can ascend the steps and stand on a flat platform to perform the work at that height. The platform has a guard rail that surrounds the platform on three sides. These ladders are heavier in structural weight and are equipped with rolling, locking wheels to aid in maneuvering them into the desired location.

Lifting Equipment

Johnson Bar or J-Bar

- The Johnson or J-bar is the basic tool for applying leverage under the edge of an object and lifting it to access the underside for adding rolling support equipment. The lip of the bar is a small platform that slides under the box. The long bar or handle to which the platform is attached swivels on two wheels to tilt and lift the box by physical leverage.

Pallet Jacks

- Pallet jacks are commonly used within the museum industry for moving not only palletized objects but also crates and storage housings that have been built with access points to access its lifting fork capabilities. They are sometimes termed pallet trucks.
- Pallet jacks come in different styles, primarily in load-lifting restrictions and the width and length of the lifting forks. The majority of the lifting mechanisms are controlled by a manual hydraulic pumping movement created within the handle. More industrial pallet jacks have electrical hydraulics for controlling their lift and motion.
- One version of the pallet jack is designed with digital scales for measuring the weight of loads placed on forks through the use of the pallet, the crate, or storage support. Scaled pallet jacks may be expensive in terms of the initial investment, but buying quality equipment is essential. It is an invaluable tool for weighing objects for general documentation to be used in accessing collection care activity in regard to choosing proper handling techniques and structural supports.

Platform or Stacker Lifters

Platform or stacker lifters come in various designs of mechanized operating systems and structural support. The basic function of the platform lifter is to move a load from a low height to a taller height to access the location where the load is being moved. The structural components of the lifter will dictate the lifting capabilities and maneuverability of the lifter to access loading of objects or in specific locations when positioning a load into place.

In researching which design to purchase, it is advisable to seek information from other colleagues about what they use and prefer within its lifting capabilities. Working with the supplier and possible trial use of the lifters is a viable approach to test its capabilities.

Figure 8.16   J-Bar / Leverage Bar. *Source*: Author.

Figure 8.17   Pallet Jack with Digital Scales. *Source*: Author.

Manual Operation Lifters

- Lifters designed to handle smaller and lighter loads are often operated by a manual operating mechanism. There are two common mechanisms: one is operated by a hand crank in a revolving motion in relation to a cable or chain, which raises or lowers the platform. The second operates the lifting motion by using a hydraulic design for the platform's movement by a foot pedal or a combination of the pump and the operating handle, similar to a pallet jack.
- The overall weight of these lifters has many advantages: they are easy to maneuver and can operate in tight places. The manual lifting controls offer the advantage of slowly moving the platform into position, thereby avoiding additional shock and vibration, in comparison to electrical control mechanisms.

Figure 8.18   Manual Hand Crank / Platform Lifter. *Source*: Author.

Electrical Operation Lifters

- Lifters that use an electrical mechanism for operating the hydraulics of the lifting platform are generally for lifting larger and heavier load capacities. The electronics and battery support for operating this equipment must be maintained and monitored to ensure long and effective operations.
- On newer lifts, the charger may be a part of the battery power system enclosed within the machine's housing. Chargers for larger machines, and traditionally for all machines, are separate units to which the machine is taken for a recharge when needed.

- The vertical structural components often include the ability to lift the platform to taller heights with a telescoping extension. This design can be advantageous for use in collection storerooms to access high shelves or racking units.
- The overall weight of the machine offers the advantage of a good counter balancing structure when lifting heavy objects. The disadvantage is that the equipment is harder to move into locations because of the overall weight and the potential point load damage to floor surfaces.
- The majority of the mid- or large-size machines use electrical power to operate the wheels to move the machine, in combination with the steering handle. Power controls are placed in the handle, which provide adjustable levels of speed of movement, braking capabilities, and safety power release to stop movement.
- Lifting motion for the platform or forks of the lifter is operated by a separate set of controls, so the two actions are not mistaken or operated at the same time.
- Controlling the movement is conducted by walking behind the machine while operating the controls. Caution must be taken when moving the machine because of the visual field of the operator being restricted by the vertical mast and structural components. Controlling the rate of speed of the movement is hazardous. It is advisable to have another staff member act as a spotter when maneuvering these machines in any location or in levels of movement.
- Moving heavy electrical lifts on a slope is not advisable. If required, it should only be done with the operator on the upper side of the slope with the machine moving down the slope. This control should be used in combination with the movement and braking system to avoid the momentum of the machine's weight becoming uncontrollable. Staff in assistance should not be positioned on the lower side during movement.
- Training programs must be mandated for the staff who will be operating this equipment, conducted by a licensed trainer. The training should be an essential requirement for all staff working within and around these machines, whether they are operating them on a regular basis or assisting in the activity of the operation.

Versatile Lifting Designs

Lifters, both manual and electric, can be purchased that fulfill specific lifting requirements, to aid in the work in specific locations.

- Hydraulic table lifters offer the option, when objects are being lifted directly to a prescribed height, of providing access to staff from all sides of the lifting platform. Table lifters come in different size platforms (tops) and lifting weight capabilities. They can create an excellent work surface for many stationary work activities as different heights can be achieved for different purposes. These tables also come in a rolling design so as to access numerous locations and allow clearer access to the object when moving it from the table to a prescribed location.

- Broad-base stackers have additional support through the placement of front wheels in the extended outriggers to give stability and support to the forward weight load as it is lifted. The width between the outriggers allows the forks or platform of the lifter to still pick up the load next to the vertical lifting structure and center the load weight in the overall footprint of the machine.
- Board-base stackers are excellent for lifting heavy pallets onto racks to support the balance of the forward weight being placed on extended outrigger rolling supports. The racking system will need to have the bottom rail placed high enough for the support outriggers to move under the rail to the back of the rack to access the load on the rack.
- Lifters can be designed to have front extensions of their platform or forks to assist in extending the load into a location. This design offers the versatility of lifting as well as placing the load onto a location. The balance of weight at the center must be assessed properly to avoid off-balancing the lifter.
- Lifters can also be designed to have a side-shift motion in the lifting forks. This allows the load to be shifted from side to side when placing the load

Figure 8.19   Hydraulic Lifting Table. *Source*: Author.

into the prescribed location. The combination of the side-shifting motion and the forward extension creates a very versatile machine for moving objects in storage or display.

Forklifts

The history of the forklift as a machine to move and lift things dates back to the late 1800s when it was used in the transport and construction industry. The forklift has been developed over the years to be an extremely useful and compatible piece of equipment in a museum for operating around and with collection care objects. Forklift designs have features that allow a traditionally large cumbersome machine to be operated in tight, close quarters, and in a pollutant-free environment.

Basic forklift specifications: Forklifts are rated for loads at a specified maximum weight and a specified forward center of gravity. This information is located on a nameplate provided by the manufacturer, and loads must not exceed these specifications. In many jurisdictions, it is illegal to remove or tamper with the nameplate without the permission of the forklift manufacturer.

Another critical characteristic of the forklift is its instability. The forklift and load must be considered a unit with a continually varying center of gravity with every movement of the load. A forklift must never negotiate a turn at high speed with a raised load, because centrifugal and gravitational forces may combine to cause a disastrous tip-over accident. The forklifts are designed with a load limit for the forks, which is decreased with fork elevation and undercutting of the load (i.e., when a load does not butt against the fork "L"). A loading plate for loading reference is usually located on the forklift. A forklift should not be used as a personnel lift without the fitting of specific safety equipment, such as a "cherry picker" or "cage."[6]

A good publication for referencing operational protocols for staff operating or working near forklifts is the National Institute for Occupational Safety and Health (NIOSH) publication titled "Preventing Injuries and Deaths of Workers Who Operate or Work Near Forklifts"; DHHS (NIOSH) Publication Number 2001-109 by http://www.cdc.gov/niosh/docs/2001-109/

The following is a descriptive list of highlights and protocols regarding the operation of forklifts commonly used within the museum industry and the internal environment where collections reside:

- Forklifts are a large initial investment for a museum of any size, but they can be an extremely beneficial piece of equipment for numerous collection and noncollection activities. These machines can be rented but often do not have all of the features required to operate within a museum.

- Electrically powered forklifts are the best for operating within the internal environments of a museum's galleries, storerooms, or loading docks because of the fact that they do not emit damaging exhaust fumes. Depending on the location and contents within a building, a natural gas (LP) forklift may be suitable because of its exhaust levels as compared to a gasoline or diesel lift, which is not appropriate at any time. The risks need to be thoroughly analyzed and understood before this option is used.
- Training for staff must be conducted by a licensed trainer. Staff will need to be certified and have their certification updated on a required basis. Staff who are most efficient in the operation of forklifts should be assigned first for operating the machine when needed. Staff who are uncomfortable in using the machine need to be trained to understand the operations and working conditions of the forklift for safety reasons.
- The forklift's driving mechanism is most commonly based in a rear power wheel and the two front wheels directly under the lifting mast. This allows the machine to make short turns and maneuver in tight places effectively. The operator must be well trained and comfortable with this method of movement as it is not a common steering sense found in most equipment-operating movement.
- When these machines are used within galleries or on delicate floor surfaces, floor protection should be laid to reduce wheel markings. Special rubber tires can be put on the three wheels, which will assist in avoiding wheel markings, but the rotating rear drive wheel can easily mark any type of surface because of its weight and its powered motion. Keeping the tires clean and free of debris is a common practice when operating the machine on delicate surfaces.
- Weight restrictions of both the machine and its potential load need to be understood and accessed, in comparison to the load-bearing restriction of any floor surface the machine may be operated upon. This is especially crucial in elevator carriages for the type of floor and the carriage's overall weight-lifting capacity. When in operation for lifting, a load sheeting material may need to be laid to assist in dispersing the point load of the wheels, especially under the front two wheels, which directly support the mast of the forklift. Seeking advice regarding floor load capacities and dispersing weight is crucial in the preplanning of any movement.
- Masts on forklifts come in a variety of types and with different heights and tilting capabilities. Mast height when lowered must be compatible with door heights within the building for access. Masts should always be in the lowest and most level position before moving the machine within a room or building to prevent damage to the building components. Telescoping masts are an excellent option for reaching prescribed heights within a location but need to be observed at all times when the load is being lifted as it

is often being watched at the lower end rather than at the top of the mast in its extension.

- Lifting forks (blades or tines) are used to lift the load into position. The forks are made to fit pallets or other lifting platforms depending on the size and use needed. The forks can also have various accessories added to them such as extensions (slippers), cages, hoists, and lifting jibs to increase the lifting options. These accessories should be purchased and certified to be compatible to work on your style of forklift.
- Additional options to the lifting forks are the adaption of the side shift and the extending lift. The side-shifter option allows the forks to move from side to side, which aids in placing the load. The extending lifter option of the forks allows the load to be placed into a location by gaining extra measure to a location. Both of these options are excellent features when placing objects in storage and especially when installing an object for display.
- Power controls when handling objects need to be sensitive to the reaction of the movement of the lifting action as well as the movement of the machine

Figure 8.20   Forklift / LP Warehouse. *Source*: IAS Sydney, Australia.

Figure 8.21   Forklift / Controls Panel. *Source*: IAS Sydney, Australia.

within space. Over the last twenty years, the sensitivity of operation mechanisms has improved dramatically. The hydraulic pressure valves or electrically controlled actuators that operate the movement have been designed
to react in a slower progression of motion. This aids in reducing the abrupt
motion that results in shock and vibration being transferred to the load. This
feature may be more costly when purchasing a forklift, but it is a priority
for safer operating conditions for both the operator and the object.

Personnel Lifts

Personnel lifts, commonly termed scissor lifts, are used within museums to
lift personnel to heights in a more secure and safe fashion than by the use of
ladders. The lifts are electric powered and have similar control mechanisms
to forklifts in driving and operating the lifting platform. The size of the lift
will dictate its height and stability in securing the vertical lifting action. Standard equipment types found in museums are for single or dual operation and
working on the lift.

 Scissor lifts in their design have the limitation of two individuals as the
standard number of personnel permitted to ride on and operate the machine.
The operator must be trained and certified in all aspects of operation and
safety precautions of the machine. A safety guard rail surrounding the platform protects the individuals moving and working on the platform. Any

leaning over to reach a location requires that the individual be wearing an appropriate safety harness.

These machines are not to be used as lifting devices for moving objects. Often, objects will be placed in the platform area, then lifted, with the individual riding in the lift, then placed on a wall or pedestal. The risk is if the weight is too heavy for that individual to safely lift over the guard rail and place into the location. The more common daily use of scissor lifts is for staff members changing lights and fixtures on the ceiling of a room.

Lifting Heavy Objects

Lifting heavy objects can be accomplished by various types of equipment. The main factor in working with this type of equipment is having the correct knowledge, training, and certification required to operate the specific machines. The knowledge of the mechanics and physics of lifting large amounts of weight to specific shapes of objects is crucial and should not be attempted on a casual basis. The best thing to do to know which type of equipment is best for a specific task is to ask for the assistance of a professional rigger to execute or supervise this work. The risks of using heavy rigging equipment with semi- or nonexperienced staff dramatically outweigh the costs of hiring an experienced rigger to avoid potential personal injury or damage to the object while being lifted.

Kevin Marshall's article titled "Rigging Safety Is No Accident" at the end of chapter 5 titled "Three-Dimensional Objects: Procedures and Practices" is an excellent explanation of the knowledge, concepts, and equipment needed to understand the importance of protocols used for safely rigging large objects. In his article, he describes the specific equipment used for lifting heavy objects and commonly found in the industry.

The following are some basic examples of common lifting equipment types used in rigging and moving large objects.

- Slings: Rigging has many accessories that are made specifically for lifting heavy weights. Slings are the most important tool as they are secured to the shape of the object and then connected to the lifting fork of a jib to support the object's structure while lifting. Synthetic round or continuous loop slings are made of polyester core yarn covered by a seamless, tubular polyester or nylon cover. These slings are the most common sling style used as they are very pliable and conform firmly to uneven organic shapes. Synthetic nylon web flat slings are available in a variety of eye-to-eye and continuous loop configurations and work well on flat geometric shapes.
- Small extension jib lifts: A small but common piece of equipment that can be used for lifting heavy objects of smaller sizes with an extension jib,

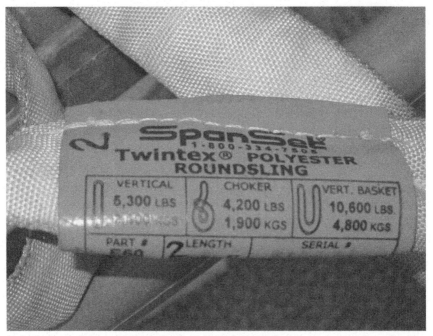

Figure 8.22 Sling Load Rating Tag. *Source*: Author.

commonly known as an engine jack. The lifting jib or extension can be angled to different degrees and to limited heights. These smaller lifts have angled, outrigging supports to surround and support the object in a central counter balanced manner. These lifts have limited capabilities but can be effective for lifting an object in certain scenarios.

- Gantry crane: Gantry cranes, with fixed or portable positioning in structure design, are highly versatile in lifting loads of different load capacities to different levels of heights. The horizontal lifting beam can have rolling chainfall hoists attached to lift and move the object within the set limits of space. The gantry crane offers lifting capabilities in locations where a forklift cannot fit and with the removal of the forklift's substantial weight on the floor loading limitations.
- Forklifts: Forklifts and platform lifts are commonly used to lift and move heavy objects to a place at a specific location. As previously cited in this chapter, there are many advantages to using this equipment in various scenarios. The weight capacities this equipment can lift will accommodate many objects found within the museum's collection. The physical size and maneuverability of this equipment in the small, tight spaces of the internal museum environment aids in handling large objects in storerooms and display areas.

Figure 8.23   Gantry Crane. *Source*: Carey, Artex FAS.

Figure 8.24   Chainfall Hoist. *Source*: Author.

- Mobile cranes: Commercial cartage or specialized rigging companies offer a large variety of mobile cranes that can lift extremely large amounts of weight in unique locations. These machines offer a diverse range of capabilities to move heavy weights, in extreme locations, and to unique heights. Having a good relationship with a professional rigging

Figure 8.25 Chainfall Hosit Hook. *Source*: Carey, Artex FAS.

company will ensure that your rigging scenario will be set up properly and safely for the location where it needs to be conducted within any environment.

- Most people have seen these large cranes on building sites and observed how they lift items to extreme heights from the street level of operation. Seldom do individuals observe the public installation of a sculpture or statue in a garden or in a courtyard. The next time you are observing a sculpture in its outdoor setting, look around and ask yourself how this large object got placed in this location. The actual scenarios often include moving over trees or buildings and working in locations where it is highly unmanageable to create a level area to set a machine. The versatile capabilities of the large mobile cranes and the talent of the operating staff are marvelous to witness for their ability to overcome many obstacles typically not encountered in the general construction sites.

ENVIRONMENTAL MONITORING EQUIPMENT

- Light: Illuminance meter—The illuminance (lux) meter is used to record the visible light levels.
  Measurement must be taken on the same plane as the object. Record the levels from the brightest part of the artwork. Ensure you are out of the path of all light, by crouching below the meter.
- Light: Ultraviolet infrared meter—The UV/IR meter is used to record the amount of damaging nonvisible light reaching an object. Operation of the UV/IR meter requires several readings pointed in the direction/s of the light source to ensure that all incidents of IR and UV are being covered.
- Light: Hand-held spectrometer—It is best used in conjunction with lux and UV/IR meters to assess the damage potential of luminaires, lamps, and neon or other sources integrated into artworks, as well as the maintained effectiveness of UV/IR reductive glazing films. Like the UV/IR meter, the best recordings are made by aiming the sensor directly at the source/s to be measured.
- Temperature and RH: A thermo-hygrograph is a chart recorder that measures and records both temperature and humidity (or dew point). Sensors record the humidity and temperature levels by being calibrated using a psychrometer reading of the interior temperature and moisture levels of the space. Charts are mounted to a cylinder that rotates to a scheduled movement with the recording levels being marked on the chart by felt tips to the designated level, time, and date. Charts are retrieved, the machine recalibrated, and a new chart installed per the scheduled period of the chart. These machines are commonly used within the display areas and

storerooms of the museum and can be visually monitored on a daily basis as the chart is visible through the case.

- Temperature and RH: A psychrometer is a measuring device used to determine the relative humidity levels within an environment. The data recorded is used to further calibrate a thermo-hygrograph recording equipment. These recorders are made in both the traditional hand-operated sling style and the newer digital style and can be used in both internal and external environments.

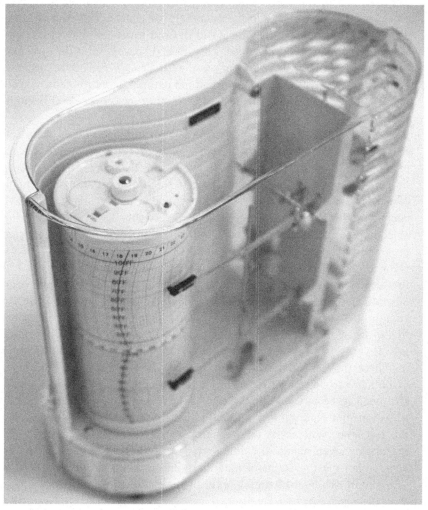

Figure 8.26   Hygrothermograph Chart Reader. *Source:* Carey, Artex FAS.

- Temperature and RH: Small digital display recorders are available to be placed inside a vitrine display case, on storage shelves, or other desired locations to monitor temperature and RH within a specific location. Some units are very small and become unobtrusive when placed within a vitrine space on a storage shelf. The data can be retrieved and analyzed using compatible software. Some units are designed to include the reading and recording of light levels as well.
- Humidity: Silica gel is an amorphous form of silicon dioxide, which is synthetically produced in the form of hard crystalized or beaded shapes that, when used in an enclosed environment, can assist in maintaining the desired level of humidity. The silica can be purchased loose, and then placed into containers, or in premade bags or panels. The silica is conditioned through a heating process to desired levels of absorption. The contained silica is then placed in a ventilated space within the structure of the case, cabinet, or box to allow the air flow of the entire space to come in contact with the silica. Silica gel can be reconditioned by heating to remove moisture to the desired level of dryness for new absorption levels.
- Shock and vibration: Data sensor recorders are designed to be placed on equipment, inside a truck or within the crated object to record the effects of shock and vibration levels transmitted to objects during different stages of handling and transport. The results give the user a better understanding of the levels of risks as well as of where and when an object may have encountered high levels of transmission. The results assist in redesigning of equipment and packing or handling procedures within collection care programing.
- Data recording/RFID and barcodes: A recent development over the last few decades, radio frequency identification devices (RFID) have been developed to be efficient tracking and documenting systems, which, supported by various software programs, have improved the capabilities of museum and commercial providers in collection care programing. Inventory barcoding of objects or their containers to the location of where they are stored or displayed has greatly decreased the level of human error in basic recording and documentation sharing. Objects still need to be physically marked with a registration number for identification, but barcoding the actual object if possible or accompanying the container will assist in the quick and efficient documentation of the object when handled. Commercial transport and storage providers have found these systems of barcoding and tracking an invaluable tool to maintain the ever-changing level of the movement of objects within their care.

Figure 8.27   RFID Barccode Reader. *Source*: Carey, Artex FAS.

Climate Control Transport/Australian Case Study

In Australia, the fine-art-transporting industry faces many challenges because of the size of the continent, the extreme distances between population centers, and the uniqueness of the natural environmental conditions year round. The fine-art-transport industry has developed systems to fully climate control cargo spaces, which assists in maintaining temperature and humidity levels where moisture can be added to, or removed from within, the controlled cargo environment. Most standard climate control systems can only remove humidity in its relationship to conditioning temperature levels.

The following is a summary presented to me by Kingsley Mundey, managing director and owner of IAS Fine Arts Logistics, which over the years has developed this system and has the largest fleet of fully climate controlled trucks in Australia.

Some of the key issues in being able to create a fully operational design are ambient weather conditions and water conditions for which Australia is perfect. Australia doesn't experience the incredible temperature extremes that much of the Northern Hemisphere experiences, such as −25°C thru + 40°C with frigid arctic wind, snow, and ice. Australian weather can vary in the range of −5°C for short periods to + 40°C for extended periods.

The drinking water throughout Australia is very pure and comes directly from the faucet, but more importantly, it is fluoridated. This means that the calcium has already been extracted from the water at its source. The IAS system design uses venturi's, and calcium buildup from the water would clog them very quickly—for this design the water is not a problem.

The original idea for the specific humidity control system was developed outside the business of transporting art. The original designs were developed and designed for IAS by a petrochemical engineer who was used to managing temperature and humidity under very strict and controlled conditions when transporting oil and gas through pipes in the refining process.

The cargo area design of the IAS truck is thermally insulated, including the roof, walls, and floor, in order to reduce the impact of the external ambient climate conditions. After the load is secured and the doors are closed, it takes twenty minutes for the climate to stabilize (21°C & 50% RH) inside the Pantech (cargo area), and then it is maintained this way for the entire journey. Readouts of the temperature and humidity can be monitored and recorded in the cabin of the truck for reference by the driver or the courier and they can monitor this throughout the journey.

Figure 8.28   U.S. Transport Climate Unit. *Source*: Carey, Artex FAS.

CONCLUSION

The materials and equipment listed in this chapter will hopefully give the readers the reference to assist them and direct them in further research on the best choice of equipment for the collection care activities. Being an educated consumer is an ongoing process of analyzing the risk-assessment levels for selecting the best material and correct piece of equipment to protect the object placed in your care.

REFERENCES

AIC: American Institute of Conservation; http://www.conservation-us.org. Resource and publications section excellent source for reference links and networking leads.

AICCM: Australian Institute for the Conservation of Cultural Materials; AICCM Visual Glossary has a helpful resource of a visual glossary of common reactions of objects to the damage they encounter. Excellent source for other links to materials and equipment resources. http://www.aiccm.org.au/

CCI: The Canadian Conservation Institute is a Special Operating Agency of the Department of Canadian Heritage. CCI offers a wide range of technical papers with excellent explanation to materials and equipment. The publications and networking links to quality resource connections. www.cci-icc.gc.ca

CCI: *Mountmaking for Museum Objects;* 2nd Edition, Canadian Conservation Institute; Robert Barclay, André Bergeron and Carole Dignard 1998. An excellent resource for information on material, equipment, and tools commonly used in mount-making techniques.

NPS: National Park Service; *Conserve-O-Grams* is a viable resource for listing a multitude of information on materials and equipment regarding a vast array of applications. http://cr.nps.gov/museum/publications/conserveogram/conserv.html

PACCIN: Packing Art Handling Collection Care Information Network. This website is valuable for finding links to other technical information regarding tools, materials, and equipment and collection care practices. It also offers unique articles, a forum networking page, and a listserve. http://www.paccin.org

FOCUS ON: SPECIALIZED ART HANDLING EQUIPMENT: WHEN IT IS NECESSARY AND HOW TO DEVELOP IT

by Mark Slattery

Working with a large and diverse museum collection over a number of years inevitably presents numerous technical challenges for the art handler. There is no shortage of tools and equipment that can be used to solve many of these object-handling issues, but sometimes the only approach is to look at the problem as a whole and create new solutions with specific objects or areas of the collection. This article looks at the reasons that we need to create specialized equipment and illustrates the practical steps to ensure success.

There can be a number of factors regarding the object, staff, and work environment, and why we need to review how objects or areas in a collection are dealt with from a handling perspective. Any one of the following aspects can direct a move or an enquiry toward the development of a specialized handling solution:

- the demands that a particular object or class of objects places on the expertise of the team;
- significant additions to the collection, which fall outside the existing skill set of the technicians and how they must learn to properly handle and care for this new object;
- a goal set by managers to develop the skills of their staff and to mentor them in the latest techniques and best practices currently employed within the industry;
- collaborations with other institutions that have higher standards than your own, which will bring in new knowledge and a fresh approach to improving one's workplace and procedures; and
- an expansion of museum facilities, which may demand modification and adaption of equipment to meet these changes.

Change may occur as current practices grow outdated because of new techniques' becoming widely adopted elsewhere, or are eclipsed by events such as the rapid expansion of a museum facility and its collection, or as changes to health and safety legislation are mandated. Expanding the handling team may be insufficient to keep up with the scale of moves planned for the future without first conducting a review of how the collection is currently being handled.

Good managers will recognize the need to categorize the types of objects in their museum to create an overview of the collection and its requirements for handling. Part of the documentation should be detailed descriptions of how to move and handle specific objects, with recommendations for the use of mechanical equipment in certain cases. Where special tools or equipment are in place, there is a requirement for staff to be properly trained in the use of that equipment and an up-to-date record maintained of when and to whom the training has been delivered.

If a museum collection contains a number of large and complex objects, like heavy sculptures, for example, this class of object is likely to be moved infrequently. There may be documentation with detailed descriptions of how those objects have been moved in the past, but it is possible that no documentation exists and the institutional memory of the last move has been lost. The current team will have to draw on its expertise and ideas to devise a plan. Old method statements might get dusted off and implemented, or the museum may decide to contract the move to a rigging company. Either outcome will provide a valuable lesson for the team in analyzing technical considerations before the move.

In the case of the professional advice and assistance being brought in, working with experts may provide insight into how best to execute this particular move. For similar moves in the future, the latest equipment and techniques might be demonstrated by these professionals, and the team should be made familiar with the current museum environment and the sensitivities surrounding fine art and cultural artifacts.

Sometimes it is sufficient to hire a single expert who will direct the team of in-house technicians and ensure the safe and correct use of specialized handling equipment, such as lifting gantries and other mechanically assisted devices. Relationships with these individuals are often fruitful from a logistical angle and in getting the job done efficiently, but it is also a way of challenging and invigorating the daily working practices of the in-house team. Fresh challenges are the life-blood of any art-handling team and should be grasped at every opportunity. The confidence gained through seeking expert advice and assistance should inspire managers in mentoring staff to rewrite old method statements and consider training their own teams to take on these tasks in the future.

Skill and experience gained by working with a particular collection will produce the most successful and enduring solutions to any art logistics problem. Recognizing that there are practical technology-based steps that you can take to streamline the effort of the art handler is the first step in the process of equipping the technical team with the tools it needs to do the best job possible.

Safety legislation may creep up on former working practices and render them untenable. What was once considered standard practice may be outlawed and viewed as unsafe. For example, the Working at Height Legislation in Europe, introduced in 2005, hastened the introduction of the mobile elevating work platforms, typically the Genie platform. The extendable and folding ladders, previously the mainstay of gallery installation work, were immediately consigned to the "emergency use only" register of equipment.

Along with the Working at Height Legislation comes the requirement to minimize the lifting effort of individual team members while at work. In recognizing this as an achievable aim, dual goals may be achieved. Inexperienced personnel who are inadequately trained in lifting techniques are more likely to injure themselves when performing a move. Assessing what is a safe manual move and what requires mechanical assistance, and proper training and good sense on the part of everyone involved is the responsibility of the manager.

Uncoordinated moves risk damaging the object and harming the staff. The increase in control afforded by mechanical lifting machinery reduces the risk of accidental damage and increases the predictability and precision of the move. Ensuring that the object is placed exactly where it is required with minimal impact of shock to and physical contact with the art should be among the principal aims of the exercise performed by the technicians.

No responsible museum will lend an object unless it is confident that the receiving institution is going to be able to handle it appropriately. A technical team may be dispatched along with the loan object to take charge of the installation or supervise and advise the borrower's team. Looking to other institutions for inspiration can be the first step when searching for innovative handling solutions. The arrival of an exhibit that is outside the norm for a particular collection and beyond the realm of experience of the team tasked to deal with it can sometimes provide the impetus to search for alternative handling solutions.

Within each handling team, there will be individuals who, by disposition, will always seek to push the boundaries of what is achievable with the resources available to them. A natural curiosity and an ambition to improve working practices are the precursor to exploring the development of specialized handling equipment. Allied to this is the support of the institution, both financial and technical, in a joint effort to drive forward best practices. These are the key aims of developing specialized pieces of equipment.

- Human interaction with objects can prove injurious to both the handler and the artifact.
- Using specialized equipment keeps the operator away from the object and allows for a more predictable and controlled approach.
- In the case of large and heavy objects with parts that could fall, trap fingers, or crush feet, a mechanized approach to handling and moving these works will go a long way toward minimizing these risks.
- Any physical intervention with an art object will leave a legacy, often incorporated into the surface or structure of the object itself. This is why we wear gloves and take other precautions not to leave our traces on the objects in our care.
- Palletization and other techniques for remote handling and isolating the object from human contact will help preserve its condition and facilitate ease of storage.
- Tools and techniques that allow indirect handling allow the operation to be broken down to clear and predictable elements, which, most importantly,

creates the opportunity to pause the action and allow time for refining the move.

Many pieces of equipment used for safe handling practices can be purchased from warehousing supply companies. It is only through working with off-the-shelf tools like these that some of their shortcomings are revealed, and a desire to adopt or modify them grows within the team. Ingenious adaptions can be devised to facilitate the safe use of certain types of equipment with many different types of objects.

Why just adapt or modify, when you can re-design and fabricate the correct tool for the job? As the custodians of the collection, you are best informed to understand what is required for the protection of the work. Taking as your inspiration the types of equipment that suggest themselves as appropriate for the task in hand, a more refined and adaptable tool might emerge from the drawing board instead.

In these exploratory stages, it is good to consider the use of prototypes, which can be subjected to testing with facsimiles that safely stand in for the objects. In this way, the principles can be thoroughly examined and any apparent shortcomings in the design addressed, ahead of the equipment's being fabricated. Only when this first step has been taken and a specific tool has been produced can a proper assessment be made of its effectiveness.

Changes to working practices may become necessary when introducing new equipment and this may highlight issues that were not present under the former protocols. A thorough review of the relevant method statements should be undertaken as part of updating working practices when introducing new equipment. Be aware that there may be resistance among the technicians on the team in adopting the new tool, especially those well practiced in previous ways of doing things. Take time during these developmental stages, especially if this is your first step into the area of engineering and fabrication. Rushing to produce and introduce a new tool for the museum may result in a tool not fit for the purpose and with which no one will be happy.

Depending on the type and scale of the collection, there will be objects that, for whatever reason, get moved on a more frequent basis than others. For collections comprising primarily framed, two-dimensional works, the single most obvious piece of specialized handling equipment is the picture cart.

Picture carts are often built by the in-house team in the woodworking shop and are viewed as a cheap and effective means of supporting framed works in transit. These carts tend to grow organically, often incorporating quirky features, and can become cumbersome and heavy, mainly because of the composite timber-based materials that are used in their construction. Investing time in examining exactly the way the piece of equipment like this is used, and the many different uses that it can be put to, makes all the difference between an amateurish, homespun effort and something that technicians take pride and pleasure in using.

In considering the various different uses a picture cart can be put to, we need to look at the range of frame sizes and styles of frames that are supported. A double-sided design will maximize the number of works that can be transported in one move. It may also offer greater stability when larger, heavier works are being transported.

A simple, wheeled frame sitting on a platform, with tie-off points, protected surfaces, and storage for fixings and tools on board can increase the flexibility of the handling team to move quickly and effectively throughout its working environment. This flexibility can extend to the cart's being used for temporary storage and also as part of a lifting frame, integrating with lifting trolleys or forklifts, thus making it possible to transfer the work from its location in storage, directly to its position on the gallery wall, with just one handling input.

Figure 8.29   National Gallery Double-Sided Picture Cart. *Source*: The National Gallery London.

Figure 8.30 National Gallery Mini Stacker Trolley. *Source*: The National Gallery London.

Removing the need to transfer the object from one mode of conveyance to another reduces the effort of the technicians and minimizes their intervention with the object.

Where there are multiple objects of a similar size, weight, and general construction, it may be possible to design and develop a handling frame, which by means of mechanical adjustment, can safely mount and transport all the objects within this category. A modest investment in time and money may alleviate hours of technicians' time and hands-on contact with the objects.

As the custodians of cultural artifacts and art objects, we are responsible for ensuring that risk of harm to these objects is minimized. Museum best practices require a multidisciplinary input from professionals and technologists working in related fields of collection care across the museum spectrum. The role of the art logistician is as significant as that of the conservator or curator in the safe and sustainable handling of art objects.

Active collaboration with partners, such as registrars, trucking companies, conservators, scientists, and engineers, will inform the design and commissioning of specialized equipment to assist in the movement and storage of art objects and cultural artifacts. We must never assume that empirical knowledge gained in the field can always be relied upon to deliver the correct solutions. Simplicity and efficiency are keywords when considering your special equipment project.

Over-elaborate equipment can become unpopular with the crew required to use it. Consequently, there is a much greater chance for overlooking or missing crucial steps, which can lead to a failure at a critical stage. It can be prone to niggling problems, leading to its becoming unserviceable and being consigned to the workshop for long periods, precisely when it is required out on the floor. It is vitally necessary to consult widely with all the users before any changes are made. If there is a requirement to produce further tools, then the preproduction exploratory stage offers the ideal opportunity to re-visit the drawing board and incorporate those refinements.

Finding the right fabricator is the next most important step in the process of commissioning new equipment. The fabricator should be able to give advice on the most appropriate materials to use and should have access to expert subcontractors who can supply the components that they cannot manufacture. They may be competent to venture some of their own suggestions on the suitability of your proposal to achieve the aims you have in mind for the equipment.

Frequent contact with and visits to the fabricator while the job is underway are essential. As the commissioner of this special equipment, you are best informed about what you and your crew will need. Avoid making assumptions on behalf of the fabricators that they know precisely how this piece of equipment is going to be used or how it is designed to perform.

Go ahead and design your dream machine, with all the bells and whistles that can be thought of, then get the eraser and slim it back down to the essentials. If you really cannot do without that marvelous refinement, look at how it can be accommodated within the overall structure at minimal cost.

Finally, view any specialized equipment project as a step toward your and your team's professional career development. You will be striving to enhance your working practices, furthering the reputation of your institution as a center of excellence, and, most important of all, protecting the future of its collection.

NATIONAL GALLERY, PRIMARY
LIFTING FRAME: A CASE STUDY

The National Gallery has an extensive collection of altarpieces, which were painted for Italian churches during the fourteenth, fifteenth, and sixteenth centuries. The panels were constructed from vertically jointed wooden planks and inserted within elaborately carved and decorated wooden frames, many of which were built in the nineteenth century as a means of enabling these church paintings to be displayed in an appropriate way.

These altarpieces are often multilayered, the bottom of which is a base section, or *predella*. This typically is surmounted by the main panels of the altarpiece. Sometimes there is a single, large panel, or it can comprise several separate panels arranged side by side, often of varying sizes. The altarpiece may be topped by yet another piece of wood of a decorative nature. The entire ensemble is usually sitting on top of a large, mountable plinth, which allows access for lifting equipment.

Because altarpieces are large, multifaceted, and heavy, they present the art handler with the type of challenge that requires a significant amount of time, concentrated effort, and several people to execute the move. A specialized handling approach lends itself well to this type of museum object.

Structures have been used over the years to support the altarpieces and provide access for the handling teams. While invaluable in conquering many of the difficulties encountered in moving these objects, none adequately covered the full scope of the separate operations involved in relocating these large pieces. The challenge was to incorporate both lifting and access capacity in one piece of machinery, with minimal mechanical parts for reliability and simplicity, but which was also safe to operate and provided access for crews working at higher levels above the gallery floor.

A design that provides flexibility and access for the crew was adopted. The device is versatile and can be used as a stand-alone structure or in association with detachable access towers, which provide additional forward stability in one of the two mounting configurations. The lifting element is provided by a proprietary hydraulic forklift/pallet stacker, and it is completely separate from the main structure. There is a docking position configured in the design for the stacker device. This aspect allows interchangeability in lifters while

Figure 8.31 National Gallery Primary Lifting Frame. *Source*: The National Gallery London.

removing the requirement for specific safety and maintenance inspections of the lifting element of the framework, as this falls within the separate inspection routine of the stackers and similar equipment.

The design incorporates a rolling bed as part of the lifting table. This permits the table to be moved forward to place it under the object to be raised, and then withdrawn once the object has been lifted clear of the plinth or support structure. Vertical support for the object is provided by personnel standing on top of the access towers on either side of the lifting frame.

The towers, when attached in their forward position, form a U-shape along with the lifting frame and wrap around the plinth, moving the footprint of the lifting structure forward, providing greater stability. This device is a good example of specialized handling equipment which has been designed specifically for use with the National Gallery collection. It was designed by the in-house team and built by a variety of fabricators and industrial finishers. Upon delivery, it was commissioned and completed by the art handling team. Safety inspection and certification for insurance purposes was provided by the Gallery's mechanical engineering contractors.

Mark Slattery
Senior Art Handler
The National Gallery, London

For further information regarding the process of developing, designing, and engineering specialized equipment, read an additional article written by Mark Slattery on other equipment development at the National Gallery of London titled "The Genesis of the National Gallery Case Roller."

Slattery, Mark. "The Genesis of the National Gallery Case Roller." Preparation, Art Handling, and Collections Care Information Network Case Studies, 2010. http://www.paccin.org/content.php?25-The-Genesis-of-the-National-Gallery-Case-Roller

NOTES

1. Mervin Richard, foreword to *Collection Care: An Illustrated Handbook* (Lanham, MD: Rowman & Littlefield, 2015).
2. *Wikipedia*, s.v. "Material Safety Data Sheet," accessed February 2015, http://en.wikipedia.org/wiki/Material_safety_data_sheet.
3. AIC Materials Databases, "Oddy Tests," American Institute of Conservation, accessed February 2015, http://www.conservation-wiki.com/wiki/Oddy_Tests:_Materials_Databases.
4. Robert Barclay, André Bergeron and Carole Dignard, "Solders," Materials for Mounting Artifacts; Mountmaking for Museum Objects, 2nd ed. (Ottawa, Ontario: Canadian Conservation Institute, 1998): 21–22.
5. Jean Tetrault, "Coatings for Display and Storage in Museums," *Technical Bulletin #21* (Ottawa, Ontario: Canadian Conservation Institute, 1999).
6. *Wikipedia*, s.v. "Forklift truck," accessed February 2015, http://en.wikipedia.org/w/index.php?title=Forklift_truck&redirect=no

Bibliography

Bachmann, Konstanze. *Conservation Concerns: A Guide for Collectors and Curators.* New York: Cooper-Hewitt National Museum of Design and Washington, DC: Smithsonian Institution Press, 1992.

Barclay, Robert, André Bergeron, and Carole Dignard. *Mountmaking for Museum Objects*, 2nd ed. Ottawa, Ontario, Canada: Canadian Conservation Institute, 1998.

Buck, Rebecca, and Jean Allman Gilmore. *Museum Registration Methods.* 5th ed. Washington, DC: American Association of Museums, 2010.

———. *On the Road Again: Developing and Managing Traveling Exhibitions.* Washington, DC: American Association of Museums, 2003.

Carliner, Saul. *Training Design Basics.* Alexandria, VA: ASTD Press, 2003.

Case, Mary, ed. *Registrars on Record: Essays on Museum Collections Management.* Washington, DC: American Association of Museums, 1988.

Considine, Brian, Julie Wolfe, Katrina Posner, Michael Bouchard, *Conserving Outdoor Sculpture; the Stark Collection at The Getty Center.* Los Angeles, CA: The Getty Conservation Institute, 2010.

Demakouras, Marie, ed. *Basic Condition Reporting: A Handbook.* 3rd ed. Florida: South-eastern Registrars Association, 1998.

Ellis, Margaret Holben. *The Care of Prints and Drawings.* New York: AltaMira Press, 1995.

Frey, Franziska, Dawn Heller, Dan Kushel, Timothy Vitale, Jeffrey Warda, and Gawain Weaver. *The AIC Guide to Digital Photograph and Conservation Documentation.* Washington, DC: American Institute for Conservation of Historic and Artistic Works, 2008.

Gardner, James, and Elizabeth Merrit. *AAM Guide to Collections Planning.* Washington, DC: American Association of Museums, 2004.

Hatchfield, Pamela. *Pollutants in the Museum Environment: Practical Strategies for Problem Solving in Design, Exhibition and Storage.* London: Archetype Books, 2007.

Hawks, Catherine, Michal McCann, Kathryn A. Makos, Lisa Goldberg, David Hinkamp, Dennis C. Ertel, and Patricia Silence. *Health and Safety for Museum Professionals.* Washington, DC: Society for the Preservation of Natural History Collections, 2010.

Lord, Allyn. *Steal This Handbook! A Template for Creating a Museum's Emergency Preparedness Plan.* [Florida?]: South-eastern Registrars Association, 1994.

Lord, Barry, and Gail Dexter Lord. *The Manual of Museum Exhibitions.* Walnut Creek, CA: Altra Mira Press, 2001.

Lord, Barry, Gail Dexter Lord, and Lindsay Martin. *Manual of Museum Planning: Sustainable Space, Facilities, and Operations.* Lanham, MD: Alta Mira Press, 2012.

Mayer, Ralph. *The Artist's Handbook of Materials and Techniques.* 5th ed. New York: Viking, 1991.

Mecklenburg, Marion. *Art in Transit: Studies in the Transport of Paintings.* Washington, DC: National Gallery of Art, Division of Conservation, 1991.

Merritt, Elizabeth. *National Standards and Best Practices for US Museums.* Washington, DC: American Association of Museums, 2008.

National Parks Service. *NPS Museum Handbook, Part I: Museum Collections.* Washington, DC: National Park Service, 2007.

———. *NPS Museum Handbook, Part II: Museum Records.* Washington, DC: National Park Service, 2000.

———. *NPS Museum Handbook, Part III: Museum Collection Use.* Washington, DC: National Park Service, 1998.

National Trust. *The National Trust Manual for Housekeeping: The Care of Collections in Historic Houses Open to the Public.* Amsterdam: Elsevier, 2006.

Rose, Cordelia. *Courierspeak.* Washington, DC: Smithsonian Institution Press, 1993.

Saitzyk, Steven L. *Art Hardware: the Definitive Guide to Artists' Materials.* New York: Waston-Guptill, 1987.

Shelly, Marjorie. *The Care and Handling of Art Objects: Practices in The Metropolitan Museum of Art.* New York: The Metropolitan Museum of Art, 1987.

Snyder, Jill. *Caring for Your Art: A Guide for Artists, Collectors, Galleries and Art Institutions.* 3rd ed. New York: Allworth Press, 2001.

Williams, S. L, and C. Hawks, eds. *Museum Studies: Perspectives & Innovations.* Washington, DC: Society for the Preservation of Natural History Collections, 2006.

ADDITIONAL READINGS

Cato, Paisley S., R. Robert Waller, Llyn Sharp, John Simmons, and Stephen L. Williams, eds., *Developing Staff Resources for Managing Collections.* Ottawa, Ontario: The Canadian Museum of Nature and the Virginia Museum of Natural History, 1996.

Creaser, Claire. 2011. "Measurement and Using Evidence." Paper presented at Impact: Redefining the Measurement of Collection Care at the British Library,

15 February 2011, accessed 11/18/2014, http://www.webarchive.org.uk/wayback/archive/20140326155230/http://www.bl.uk/blpac/pdf/impactcreaser.pdf.

Dawson, Alex, Susanna Hillhouse, and Natasha Hutcheson. *Practical Collections Care: A Syllabus*. Norfolk, England: Norfolk Museums and Archaeology Service, 2012.

Hebra, Alex. *Measure for Measure*. Baltimore, MD: Johns Hopkins University Press, 2003.

Heritage Collection Council. *Caring for Collections Across Australia: Handling, Transportation, Storage and Display*. Canberra ACT, Australia: Commonwealth of Australia, 1998.

Lewis, Geoffrey. "The History of Museums." In *Encyclopedia Britannica Online*. Accessed April 2, 2015. http://www.britannica.com/EBchecked/topic/398827/history-of-museums.

Lithgow, Katy. "Assessing Conservation State in the National Trust." Paper presented at Impact: Redefining the Measurement of Collection Care at the British Library, 15 February 2011, accessed 11/18/2014, http://www.webarchive.org.uk/wayback/archive/20140326155231/http://www.bl.uk/blpac/pdf/impactlithgow.pdf.

Lloyd, Helen, P. Brimblecombe, and Katy Lithgow. "Economics of Dust," *Studies in Conservation* 52, no. 2 (2007): 135–146.

Knole House Conservation Team Blog, National Trust. http://knoleconservationteam.wordpress.com.

Norris, Linda, and J. Rainey Tisdale. *Creativity in Museum Practice*. Walnut Creek, CA: Left Coast Press, 2014.

Söderlund Consulting Party Ltd. *Be Prepared: Guidelines for Small Museums for Writing a Disaster Preparedness Plan*. Canberra ACT, Australia: Department of Communications, Information Technology and the Arts, 2000.

Waller, R. Robert. "Cultural Property Risk Analysis Model: Development and Application to Preventive Conservation at the Canadian Museum of Nature." PhD diss., Göteborg Acta Universitatis Gothoburgensis, 2003.

Waller, R. Robert and Stefan Michalski. "Effective Preservation: From Reaction to Prevention," *The Getty Conservation Institute Newsletter* 19.1 (Spring 2004), http://www.getty.edu/conservation/publications_resources/newsletters/19_1/feature.html.

References and Resources

COLLECTION CARE NETWORKS

American Institute for Conservation of Historic & Artistic Works (AIC)
http://www.conservation-us.org/about-us
   The AIC is the national membership organization supporting conservation professionals in preserving cultural heritage.

- Conservation OnLine (CoOL) is a freely accessible platform to generate and disseminate vital resources for those working to preserve cultural heritage worldwide. http://cool.conservation-us.org/
- Journal of the American Institute for Conservation (JAIC, or the Journal) is the primary vehicle for the publication of peer-reviewed technical studies, research papers, treatment case studies, and ethics and standards relating to the broad field of conservation and preservation of historic and cultural works. http://cool.conservation-us.org/jaic/about.html
- Collection Care Network (CCN) was created in recognition of "the critical importance of preventive conservation as the most effective means of promoting the long-term preservation of cultural property" (from Guidelines for Practice of the American Institute for Conservation of Historic & Artistic Works, #20) and to support the growing number of conservators and collection care professionals with strong preventive responsibilities and interests. http://www.conservation-us.org/publications-resources/collection-care#.
- CCN Collection Care Staff Survey results http://www.academia.edu/5127749/Collection_Care_Staff_Survey_Reports:

Association of Registrars and Collection Specialists (ARCS) http://www.arcsinfo.org/home

The mission of ARCS is to represent and promote registrars and collections specialists, nationally and internationally, to educate them in the professional best practices of registration and collections care, and to facilitate communication and networking.

- ARCS Collection Care Resource links http://www.arcsinfo.org/programs/resources/links
- ARCS Collection Care Resource videos http://www.arcsinfo.org/programs/resources/videos

Australian Institute for the Conservation of Cultural Materials http://aiccm.org.au/

AICCM is the professional organization for conservators in Australia. Membership is made up of professional conservators, conservation students, and cultural heritage member organizations. Membership also includes people who work in related professions, such as archivists, architects, curators, and librarians, as well as volunteers and those with a general interest in cultural heritage.

- AICCM Visual Glossary (image-based glossary and terminology) http://www.aiccm.org.au/resources/visual-glossary
- AICCM: *The AICCM Bulletin* publishes original and quality papers, including research reports, discussion papers, literature surveys, thematic bibliographies, summaries of research papers, and dissertations.
- AICCM Collection Care: *Remedies Gone Wrong* http://aiccm.org.au/resources/collection-care/remedies-gone-wrong

Canadian Conservation Institute http://www.cci-icc.gc.ca/index-eng.aspx

The Canadian Conservation Institute provides guidelines and information on general care for heritage collections based on the principles of preventive conservation and risk management.

- Technical Bulletins: CCI has published more than thirty technical bulletins to assist heritage professionals and institutions in the care and preservation of their objects and collections. http://www.cci-icc.gc.ca/resources-ressources/publications/category-categorie-eng.aspx?id=18
- Types of Objects and Collections: CCCI provides information on understanding and caring for objects and materials commonly found in heritage

collections. These resources are based on the principles of preventive conservation and risk management. http://www.cci-icc.gc.ca/resources-ressources/objectscollectionsobjets/objects-objets-eng.aspx

- CCI Notes: CCI notes deal with topics of interest to those who care for cultural objects. Intended for a broad audience, CCI Notes offer practical advice about issues and questions related to the care, handling, and storage of cultural objects. Many Notes are illustrated and provide bibliographies as well as suggestions for contacting suppliers. Written by CCI staff, there are currently over 100 notes in this ever-expanding series. http://www.cci-icc.gc.ca/resources-ressources/ccinotesicc/index-eng.aspx

The Image Permanence Institute https://www.imagepermanenceinstitute.org/

IPI is part of Rochester Institute of Technology's College of Imaging Arts and Sciences and is a recognized world leader in the development and deployment of sustainable practices for the preservation of images and cultural property.

- IPI Webinars: *Sustainable Preservation Practices*. This series of free webinars provides practical guidelines for the implementation of sustainable energy management practices in collecting institutions.
- eClimateNotebook®: web-based environmental data analysis https://www.eclimatenotebook.com/plans

The Institute of Conservation (ICON) http://www.icon.org.uk/

ICON is a voice for the conservation of cultural heritage in the UK. Its membership embraces the wider conservation community, incorporating not only professional conservators in all disciplines, but all others who share a commitment to improving understanding of and access to our cultural heritage.

- How to Care For. http://www.icon.org.uk/index.php?option=com_content&view=article&id=9&Itemid=22

Northeast Documentation Conservation Center (NEDCC) https://www.nedcc.org/

- *NEDCC Preservation Leaflets*. NEDCC's Preservation Services department provides free preservation advice to institutions and individuals worldwide. These leaflets provide information on a wide variety of preservation topics and links to additional resources. https://www.nedcc.org/free-resources/preservation-leaflets/overview

- *NEDCC Preservation Training.* https://www.nedcc.org/preservation-training/training-programlist

Northern States Conservation Center http://www.collectioncare.org/home

This organization provides training, collection care, preservation, and conservation treatment services to collections worldwide.

- Publications http://www.collectioncare.org/catalog/collections-management-care
- Online Classes http://museumclasses.org/
- Web Links http://www.collectioncare.org/web-links

Preparation, Art Handling, and Collections Care Information Network (PAC-CIN) http://www.paccin.org/content.php.

PACCIN is dedicated to building a museum industry network of information and resources for the educational dialogue of professionals interested in the high standards of art and artifact handling. The focus of these standards includes packing, crating, shipping, installation, mount making, rigging, exhibition fabrication, educational and employment opportunities, as well as ongoing industry updates of current technical and material usage.

- Materials www.pacin.org/content.php?62
- Resources www.pacin.org/content.php?140
- Training http://www.paccin.org/content.php?9-Workshops-and-Conferences

Smithsonian Museum Conservation Institute (MCI) http://www.si.edu/mci/

The MCI is the center for specialized technical collection research and conservation for all Smithsonian museums and collections.

- Taking Care: Technical information for collection care per object type http://www.si.edu/mci/english/learn_more/taking_care/index.html
- Web Links: http://www.si.edu/mci/english/learn_more/taking_care/interesting_links.html
- U.S. National Park Service http://www.nps.gov/history/
- *Conserve-O-Grams* are short, focused leaflets about caring for museum objects, published in loose-leaf format. New topics are added as needed and out-of-date issues are revised or deleted. Semi-annual supplements will be issued for an indeterminate period. http://www.nps.gov/museum/publications/conserveogram/cons_toc.html

- NPS Museum Handbook: http://www.nps.gov/museum/publications/ handbook.html. This is a reference guide on how to manage, preserve, document, access, and use museum collections; *Part I, Museum Collections; Part II, Museum Records; Part III, Museum Collections Use.*
- *NPS Museum Handbook with Quick Reference.* PDF includes all three parts of the *Museum Handbook* and can be downloaded for free.

ENVIRONMENTAL TOPICS

American Institute for Conservation. "Museum Climate in a Changing World." *Environmental Guidelines*; AIC Wiki. http://www.conservation-wiki.com/wiki/ Environmental_Guidelines

Boersma, Foekje, Kathleen Dardes, and James Druzik. "Precaution, Proof, and Pragmatism: Evolving Perspectives on the Museum Environment." *Conservation Perspectives*. The Getty Conservation Institute, Fall 2014. http://www.getty. edu/conservation/publications_resources/newsletters/29_2/evolving_perspectives. html

The Getty Conservation Institute. Pollutants in the Museum Environment (1985– 1998). *Our Projects*. The Getty Conservation Institute, 1998. http://www.getty. edu/conservation/our_projects/science/pollutants/index.html

Hatchfield, Pamela. *Pollutants in the Museum Environment:* Practical Strategies for Problem Solving in Design, Exhibition and Storage. Western Association for Art Conservation (WAAC) *Newsletter* 26, no. 2 (2004).

Image Permanence Institute. *IPI's Guide to Sustainable Preservation Practices for Managing Storage Environments*. Version 2.0—July 2012. Rochester, NY: RIT Image Permanence Institute.

Nishimura, Doug. *Understanding Preservation Metrics*. Rochester, NY: RIT Image Permanence Institute. https://www.imagepermanenceinstitute.org/webfm_ send/316.

Perkins-Arenstein, Rachael. "Choosing the Datalogger That Is Right for You." *Connecting to Collections Online Community* (webinar). March 6, 2012.

Roy, Ashok, and Perry Smith, eds. *IIC 1994 Ottawa Congress: Preventive Conservation Practice, Theory and Research*. Preprints of the Contributions to the Ottawa Congress, 12–16 September 1994. London: Archetype Books, 1994.

Tumosa, Charles S., Marion F. Mecklenburg, David Erhardt, and Mark H. McCormick-Goodhart. "A Discussion of Research on the Effects of Temperature and Relative Humidity on Museum Objects." Western Association for Art Conservation (WAAC) *Newsletter* 18, no. 3 (1996). http://www.cool.conservation-us.org/ waac/wn/wn18/wn18-3/.

Van Duin, Paul. "Climate Effects on Museum Objects: The Need for Monitoring and Analysis." *Conservation Perspectives*. The Getty Conservation Institute, Fall 2014. http://www.getty.edu/conservation/publications_resources/newsletters/29_2/climate_effects.html

Weintraub, Steven. "The Museum Environment: Transforming the Solution into a Problem." *Collections: A Journal for Museum and Archives Professionals* 2, no. 3 (2006): 195–218.

TECHNICAL TOPICS

Many all-encompassing technical links are previously cited under the Collection Care Networks. References listed here are topic-based introductions to the literature. Sites provide an overarching list of valuable information links to many technical topics that focus on museum applications, which have other links or technical examples to offer.

American Alliance of Museums, Registrars Committee. *Form and Policy Swap.* Washington, DC: American Alliance of Museums, 2015. http://www.rcaam.org/resources/sample_documents

American Institute for Conservation. *AIC Mount-Making Forum.* http://www.conservation-wiki.com/wiki/Mountmaking

———. *Caring for Your Treasures: Guides for Taking Care of Your Personal Heritage.* http://www.conservation-us.org/about-conservation/caring-for-your-treasures

Ballard, Mary. *Gently Vacuumed: A Term Widely Used, but Rarely Measured!* Smithsonian Museum Conservation Institute; Washington, DC: 2003; http://www.si.edu/mci/english/research/technical_studies/gently_vacuumed.html

Barber, Chris. "RFID–Radio Frequency Identification." PACCIN, 2010. http://www.paccin.org/content.php?107-RFID.

Dawson, Alex, Susanna Hillhouse, and Natasha Hutcheson. *Practical Collections Care: A Syllabus.* Norfolk, England: Norfolk Museums and Archaeology Service, 2012.

Fifield, Rebecca. "Museum Monday: Get Rid of Those White Cotton Gloves: Time for Nitrile." *The Still Room* (blog). http://thestillroomblog.com.

Kelly, Wayne. "Security Hardware and Security System Planning for Museums." *Technical Bulletin* no. 19. Ottawa, Ontario, Canada: Canadian Conservation Institute, 1998.

National Park Service. *How to Select Gloves: An Overview for Collections Staff.* Conserve O Gram 1, no. 12. (September 2010). www.nps.gov/museum/publications/conserveogram/01-12.pdf.

Ogden, Sherelyn. *Caring for American Indian Objects: A Practical and Cultural Guide.* St. Paul, MN: Minnesota Historical Society Press, 2004.

Preparation, Art Handling, and Collections Care Information Network (PACCIN). PACCIN is a technical-based site with collection care resources to numerous networking opportunities regarding many technical subjects. http://www.paccin.org/content.php.

Saitzyk, Steven L. *Art Hardware: The Definitive Guide to Artists' Materials.* New York: Waston-Guptill, 1987.

Smithsonian Museum Conservation Institute, 2003. http://www.si.edu/mci/english/research/technical_studies/gently_vacuumed.html

Söderlund Consulting Party Ltd. *Be Prepared: Guidelines for Small Museums for Writing a Disaster Preparedness Plan.* Canberra ACT, Australia: Department of Communications, Information Technology and the Arts, 2000.

The National Museum of the American Indian. *Moving the Collections* (videos). Washington, DC: Smithsonian Institution NMAI, 2015. http://nmai.si.edu/explore/collections/moving/

Thickett, D., and L. R. Lee. *Selection of Materials for the Storage of Display of Museum Objects (Oddy test).* Occasional Paper No. 111, rev. ed. London: The British Museum, 2004.

Tremain, David. "Agents of Deterioration: Thieves and Vandals." *Conservation Resources.* Ottawa, Ontario, Canada: Canadian Conservation Institute, 2013.

PACKING AND CRATING

Canadian Conservation Institute. "PadCAD Version 3.0." *Conservation Resources.* Ottawa, Ontario, Canada: Canadian Conservation Institute, 2014. https://www.cci-icc.gc.ca/resources-ressources/tools-outils/padcad-index-eng.aspx.

———. *Preventive Conservation and Agents of Deterioration, Step 4. Recognize the Benefits of Primary Packaging (e.g. mounts, protective wrapping). Conservation Resources.* Ottawa, Ontario, Canada: Canadian Conservation Institute, 2014. http://www.cci-icc.gc.ca/resources-ressources/carepreventivecons-soinsconspreventive/step4-etape4-eng.aspx.

Heritage Collection Council. *Caring for Collections Across Australia: Handling, Transportation, Storage and Display.* Canberra ACT, Australia: Commonwealth of Australia, 1998.

ICEFAT: International Convention of Exhibition Fine Art Transporters. *Technical Case Studies.* http://www.icefat.org/newsletter2-14/technotes.htm.

Ingram, Patricia. "Two Housings Modifying a Standard Box and Constructing an Oversize Sink Mat." *Journal of the American Institute for Conservation* 36, no. 3: 253–261. http://cool.conservation-us.org/jaic/articles/jaic36-03-008.html.

Marcon, Paul. "A Circular Slide Rule for Protective Package Design." In Mecklenburg, Marion. *Art in Transit: Studies in the Transport of Paintings.* Washington, DC: National Gallery of Art, Division of Conservation, 1991: 93–106.

———. "Agents of Deterioration: Physical Forces." *Conservation Resources.* Ottawa, Ontario, Canada: Canadian Conservation Institute, 2014. http://www.cci-icc.gc.ca/resources-ressources/agentsofdeterioration-agentsdedeterioration/chap01-eng.aspx.

———. "Six Steps to Safe Shipment." *Conservation Resources.* Ottawa, Ontario, Canada: Canadian Conservation Institute, 2014. http://www.cci-icc.gc.ca/resources-ressources/carepreventivecons-soinsconspreventive/step3-etape3-eng.aspx.

McGrew, Ashley. *Lightweight Recyclable Hybrid Container.* Preparation, Art Handling, and Collections Care Information Network Case Studies, 2010. http://www.paccin.org/content.php?129-Light-weight-recyclable-hybrid-crate

Mickletz, Matthew. *The Sprinter.* Preparation, Art Handling, and Collections Care Information Network Case Studies, 2010. http://www.paccin.org/list.php?category/4-Shipping&page=2.

Molini, John. *Crate Packing* (video). PACCIN Preparator Conference 2, J Paul Getty Villa, Los Angeles, 2012. http://www.paccin.org/showthread.php?489-John-Molini-crate-packing-video.

Schlichting, Carl. "Working with Polyethylene Foam and Fluted Plastic Sheet." *Technical Bulletin* no. 14. Ottawa, Ontario, Canada: Canadian Conservation Institute, 1994.

Slattery, Mark. *The Genesis of the National Gallery Case Roller.* Preparation, Art Handling, and Collections Care Information Network Case Studies, 2010. http://www.paccin.org/content.php?25-The-Genesis-of-the-National-Gallery-Case-Roller

Smithsonian Museum Conservation Institute. *Preventive Conservation: For Paintings on Canvas in Storage and in Exhibitions.* Washington, DC: Smithsonian Institution. http://www.si.edu/mci/english/research/TravelBox.html.

DISPLAY

American Institute for Conservation. *Conservation Standards & Guidelines for Exhibitions Utilizing Museum Collections.* AIC Wiki. http://www.conservation-wiki.com/wiki/Exhibition_Standards_%26_Guidelines.

Avalos, Vincent. *The Science behind the Art of Making Mounts for Antiquities and other Objects in Earthquake Country.* San Francisco: The Asian Art Museum, 2014. http://www.conservation-wiki.com/wiki/4th_International_Mountmakers_Forum

Brooke Craddock, Ann. *Construction Materials for Storage and Exhibition: A Guide for Collectors and Curators.* New York: Cooper-Hewitt Museum and Washington, DC: Smithsonian Institution, 1992: 23–28.

Caliper Testing (Lighting) http://energy.gov/eere/ssl/caliper-testing.

Cuttle, Christopher. "Control of Damage to Museum Objects by Optical Radiation." *International Commission on Illumination* CIE 157, 2004. Vienna, Austria: Commission Internationale de L'Eclairage. http://www.cie.co.at/index.php/index.php?i_ca_id=433

———. *Light for Art's Sake: Lighting for* Department of Energy Gateway Demonstrations http://energy.gov/eere/ssl/gateway-demonstrations *Artworks and Museum Displays.* Oxford, England: Elsevier Linacre House, 2007.

DiLaura, David L. *The Lighting Handbook: Reference & Application,* 10th ed. New York: Illuminating Engineering Society of North America, 2011.

LED Lighting Facts http://www.lightingfacts.com

Illuminating Engineers Society of North America (IESNA) http://www.ies.org/.

Illumni—The World of Creative Design http://www.illumni.co/.

International Association of Lighting Designers (IALD) http://www.iald.org/.

The Institute of Conservation (ICON). *Guidelines for Conservation Mounting & Framing of Works of Art on Paper.* London: The Institute of Conservation, 2006. http://www.conservationregister.com/PIcon-Mounting.asp.

Jones, Scott. *Basics: Brass Mounts - Making a Simple Coin Mount.* Preparation, Art Handling, and Collections Care Information Network Case Studies, 2011. http://www.paccin.org/content.php?218-BASICS-Brass-Mounts-Making-a-Simple-Coin-Mount.

Julian, Warren G., and University of Sydney Department of Architectural and Design Science. *Lighting: Basic Concepts,* 6th ed. Sydney, Australia: Department of Architectural and Design Science, 2006.

Keynan, Daria, Julie Barten, and Elizabeth Estabrook. "Installation Methods for Robert Ryman's Wall-mounted Works." *The Paper Conservator* 31, 2007: 7–15.

Northeast Documentation Conservation Center. "NEDCC and the Nishio Conservation Studio (NCS) partner to conserve Asian artwork." *About Asian Art Conservation,* 2014. https://www.nedcc.org/asian-art.

Pullen, Derek, and Jackie Heuman. "Modern and Contemporary Outdoor Sculpture Conservation: Challenges and Advances." *Getty Conservation Institute Newsletter* no. 22.2, 2007.

San Francisco Asian Art Museum. "Fosshape to the Rescue." *Art Conservation,* 2014. http://www.asianart.org/collections/fosshape-mounts.

———. "Preventive Conservation: Magnet Mounts." *Art Conservation,* 2014. http://www.asianart.org/collections/magnet-mounts.

Smithsonian Museum Conservation Institute. *Furniture Care and Handling.* Washington, DC: Smithsonian Institution, 2014. http://www.si.edu/mci/english/learn_more/taking_care/index.html.

Tétreault, Jean. "Coatings for Display and Storage in Museums." *Technical Bulletin* no. 21. Ottawa, Ontario, Canada: Canadian Conservation Institute, 1999.

———. "Display Materials: The Good, The Bad and The Ugly." *Exhibitions and Conservation. Pre-prints of the Conference Held at The Royal College of Physicians, Edinburg.* Edited by. J. Sage. Edinburg, Scotland: The Scottish Society for Conservation & Restoration (SSCR), 1994: 79–87.

STAFF TRAINING

AICCM Visual Glossary http://www.aiccm.org.au/resources/visual-glossary.

Alten, Helen. "It Takes a Staff to Care for a Collection." *Northern States Conservation Center Collections Caretaker* 1, no. 1 (Summer 1997). http://www.collectioncare.org/pubs/v1n1p1.html.

ARCS Collection Care Resource videos http://www.arcsinfo.org/programs/resources/videos.

Association of Registrars and Collection Specialists (ARCS) http://www.arcsinfo.org/home

Australian Institute for the Conservation of Cultural Materials http://aiccm.org.au/.

Bergman, Carol. "Making It Work: No Klutzes Need Apply." *New York Times,* August 22, 1999.

Campbell Center for Historic Preservation Studies http://www.campbellcenter.org/

The Campbell Center provides interdisciplinary and continuing education to meet the evolving training needs of individuals who work to preserve historic landscapes and cultural, historic, and artistic properties. The Campbell Center offers over seventy courses on historic preservation and collection care techniques.

Canadian Conservation Institute http://www.cci-icc.gc.ca/training-formation/list-liste/index-eng.aspx.

Cato, P. S., R. R. Waller, et. al. *Developing Staff Resources for Managing Collections: An Initiative Cosponsored by The Canadian Museum of Nature and The Virginia Museum of Natural History.* Martinsville, VA: Virginia Museum of Natural History Special Publication 4, 1996.

Collection Resource for Museums Training http://www.museumcollectionmgmt.com/4436.html

Fifield, Rebecca. "Museum Monday: Who Makes Collections Care Happen?" *The Still Room* (blog). http://thestillroomblog.com.

Freer | Sacker. *Safe Handling Practice for Chinese and Japanese Scrolls and Screens* (video). Washington, DC: Smithsonian Institution, 2015. http://www.asia.si.edu/research/dcsr/safeHandlingDemo.asp.

McGrew, Ashley. *4th International Mountmakers Forum*, Preparation, Art Handling, and Collections Care Information Network Case Studies, Videos. 2013. http://www.paccin.org/content.php?260-4th-International-Mountmakers-Forum

Methods and Materials, Inc. Fine Art Rigging and Installation. Chicago, Illinois. www.methodsandmaterials.com.

Museum Study Online courses http://www.museumstudy.com/about-us/.

The National Institute for Occupational Safety and Health (NIOSH). *Preventing Injuries and Deaths of Workers Who Operate or Work Near Forklifts.* http://www.cdc.gov/niosh/docs/2001-109/.

The National Museum of the American Indian. *Moving the Collections* (video). Washington, DC: Smithsonian Institution NMAI, 2015. http://nmai.si.edu/explore/collections/moving/.

Northeast Document Conservation Center Preservation Training https://www.nedcc.org/preservation-training/training-programlist. https://www.nedcc.org/free-resources/.

Northern States Conservation Center provides training, collection care, preservation, and conservation treatment services to collections worldwide. http://www.collectioncare.org/home.

Online Classes http://museumclasses.org/.

Occupational Health and Safety Administration (OSHA). Safety & Health Training Resources. https://www.osha.gov/dte/library/index.html.

Pellow Engineering Services, Inc. *Rigging Training Handbook: Bob's Rigging and Crane Handbook.* Kansas City, MO: Pellow Engineering Services. http://www.donpellow.com/.

Preparation, Art Handling, and Collections Care Information Network (PACCIN) http://www.paccin.org/content.php. http://www.paccin.org/content.php?9-Workshops-and-Conferences.

Smithsonian Institution. Conservation Programs and other Training Opportunities http://www.si.edu/mci/english/learn_more/taking_care/conservation_training.html.

————. Museum Studies Programs and other Training Opportunities http://museumstudies.si.edu/training.html.

Wei, William (Bill). "Teaching the Concepts of the Mechanical Properties of Materials in Conservation." *Conservation, Exposition, Restauration d'Objets d'Art*, 2014. http://ceroart.revues.org/4215#tocto2n1.

Williams, S. L., and C. Hawks, eds. *Museum Studies: Perspectives & Innovations*. Washington, DC: Society for the Preservation of Natural History Collections, 2006.

Index

AAM. *See* American Association of Museums

acquisitions, 22

acrylic sheets and shapes, 323

adhesives, tapes and, 324–26

AIC. *See* American Institute for Conservation

AICCM. *See* Australian Institute for the Conservation of Cultural Material

air filtration, 172, 210

airplane, moving military, 277

airplane transport, 152, 246; air freight, 296–97; air-freight container, 256, *255*; FFA airline regulations for, 290

airports, as satellite display facilities, 236

air traps, 305

alarms: for compactor high-density mobile storage cabinets, 197; fire alarms and extinguishers, 68, 197; for long-term programmed display, 208; for special exhibitions, 210; for trucks, 234

album leaves, 93–94

alcohol, as preservative, 10

altarpieces, 377

American Association of Museums (AAM), 102, 107, 299

American Institute for Conservation (AIC), xxi, 73, 162, 314

American Society for Testing & Materials (ASTM), 302

analog thermohygrometer, 164

animals, sculptures and, 238

Anselm Kiefer exhibition, 150

appendices, 44

archeology museums, 242

Art Handling Manual (Tate Gallery, London), 34

Art Handling Workshop Wadsworth Athenaeum (PACCIN), *39*

Art in Transit (1991), 256, 294, 299, 307

art logistician, 376

art museums: collection manager of, 22–23; commercial service companies and, 27–30; conservation department of, 21, 24–25; grants for, 24; internships at, 25; management structures, 18–26; preparation department of, 23, 25–26; registration department of, 21–22, 25; small, 24–26; staff at, 20–23; staff at small, 24–26; training at, 24, 26; transport agent case study, 32–36; volunteers at, 24

and, 128; pests and, 128; plywood,
321–22; three-dimensional objects,
126–32. *See also* furniture
working from object out, 114, 150, 251
working with building envelope, 158, 177
workshops: Art Handling Workshop
Wadsworth Athenaeum, *39*; training,
56–57, 59
work tables or surfaces, 198
Wormius, Olaus, 6

wrap and wrapping: artworks, 63;
Bubble Wrap, 319; concepts,
252–53; "soft wrap," 35; stretch
wrap, 316
Wunderkammer (cabinets of
curiosities), 6

Yellowstone National Park, 102
yokes, guillotines, 263, *263*
Yosemite National Park, 102, *104*

About the Contributors

Geoff Browne has been crating shop manager and senior project manager at Terry Dowd, Inc., since 1990 and has designed packaging solutions for literally thousands of crates, for entire traveling exhibits, and individual artworks and artifacts, ranging from dinosaur bones and anthropological and historical artifacts to all types of fine artwork, both ancient and contemporary. He has conducted numerous workshops for PACCIN [Preparation, Art Handling, Collection Care Information Network] and provided illustrations and papers for its website, has produced software applications for the design of crates, and is author and illustrator of the Terry Dowd, Inc. "Services Guide Best Practices for Packing and Crating." He has a BFA from the School of The Art Institute of Chicago and lab experience in the R & D division of Celanese Hoescht Chemical Company.

Kurt Christian is the chief preparator and head of the Art Preparation and Installation Department at the Carnegie Museum of Art in Pittsburgh, PA. He manages a team that is responsible for the installation, packing, and crating of permanent collection and traveling exhibitions, and he is part of the museum's collections division. Kurt has over twenty years of experience working with teams at museums throughout the country, including the Whitney Museum of American Art and the Saint Louis Art Museum. He is the membership chairman for PACCIN [Preparation, Art Handling, Collection Care Information Network], to which he is a contributor.

Rebecca Fifield is a collections management consultant focusing on emergency preparedness and preventive conservation. She has over twenty years' experience working with art and history collections including the Metropolitan Museum of Art, where she provided leadership for the collections emergency program for seven years. Becky is chairwoman of the American Institute for Conservation of Historic and Artistic Works (AIC) Collection Care Network and sits on the Advisory Council of the Association of Registrars and Collections Specialists. She is author of "Emergency Management" in the upcoming *Collection Storage: Preventive Conservation Approaches*, published by AIC, SPNHC, and the Smithsonian Institution. She holds an MA in Museum Studies from the George Washington University.

Dr. Abby Sue Fisher has been a collection care consultant throughout her career. She specializes in preventive conservation, creative storage solutions, and collection planning. Abby Sue currently manages the Division of Cultural Resources for the United States National Park Service at Golden Gate National Recreation Area in San Francisco, California. Abby Sue's academic work in textiles and clothing focused on the sociocultural aspects of dress and adornment. She is widely published, and has conducted numerous workshops and presented talks on a variety of preservation topics. She earned her PhD from the University of Minnesota in 1992.

Jim Grundy is director of art operations at Gander & White Shipping in London. In addition to managing museum projects, he is responsible for the development of museum standard warehousing and procedures within the organization. He previously worked for over twenty years at the Tate Gallery, London, where as head of art handling, he managed the installation of many groundbreaking exhibitions. He steered the department through the unprecedented changes and expansion created by the opening of Tate Modern in 2000. He graduated from Maidstone College of Art in 1979 and continues to paint and exhibit his own work.

Kevin Marshall is the head of the preparations department at the J. Paul Getty Museum at the Getty Center and the Getty Villa. He started his career at the Getty in 1995 as the lead preparator for the packing and moving of the permanent collections and their installation. Prior to joining the Getty, Kevin was a special services supervisor at Fine Arts Express in Fort Worth, Texas, for ten years. He has presented talks on collection handling topics for a variety of workshops and conferences. Kevin is currently the program chairman for PACCIN [Preparation Art Handling Collection Care Information Network]. He holds an MFA degree from Texas Christian University, Fort Worth, Texas.

John Molini is the manager of packing and crating at The Art Institute of Chicago where he has worked since 1985. John established the packing and crating department, which services the extensive exhibition, traveling exhibitions, and loan programs of the AIC. John developed staff programs for students in the School of The Art Institute of Chicago for training students in museum practices. He has been an innovator in the research and development of hybrid crate designs for transporting highly sensitive exhibitions of pastel works on paper. A former chairman of PACIN, he has conducted numerous workshops and has been teaching at the Campbell Center for Historic Preservation Studies in Mount Carroll, Illinois, since 1994 on the subject of packing and crating objects for transport.

Kim Powell has worked in the art logistics industry since 1987. Like many others in art logistics in Australia, Kim got her start at Grace Fine Art. At the time she left Grace, after ten years of service, she was national manager of the Fine Art group. As an owner and director of IAS Fine Art Logistics in Australia from 1997 through 2007, Kim managed its international division. In 2002 she opened the Melbourne branch of IAS, and in 2007, she moved to the United States where she opened the San Francisco branch of a UK-based art logistics company. Kim has over twenty-five years of experience in the application of museum care standards and risk mitigation practices when managing international loan and exhibition logistics. In 2013 she returned to IAS to establish its Museum Services division. She has recently left IAS to pursue other opportunities.

Mervin Richard is chief of conservation at the National Gallery of Art, Washington, where he has worked since 1984. He completed his graduate studies in conservation at Oberlin College in 1978 and went on to be a painting conservator at the Intermuseum Laboratory, Philadelphia Museum of Art, and Winterthur Museum; he is an adjunct professor of painting conservation in the graduate program at the University of Delaware/Winterthur Museum. Mervin served as co-chairman of the ICOM Working Group for Preventive Conservation and co-chairman of the ICOM Working Group for Works of Art in Transit. From 1998 to 2013, he was a member of the board of directors of Heritage Preservation: The National Institute for Conservation. He is currently the co-principal investigator for ConservationSpace, an initiative supported by the Andrew W. Mellon Foundation.

Mark Slattery is a senior art handler at the National Gallery, London. He has spent over thirty years working in the art logistics industry. He joined the Gallery in 1992 after working for six years in the commercial world in a variety of roles. At the National Gallery, he has devoted much of his time working as lead technician on the gallery's extensive exhibition program. He has worked on hundreds of shows ranging from contemporary artists to Old Masters. Over the years, he has contributed to the design of many pieces of handling equipment for use with the collection as well as numerous items of specialized hanging hardware. Throughout his career, he has taken a keen interest in developing the professional standing of the art handler, and he has contributed talks and papers on the subject in the United Kingdom, Italy, and the United States.

Simm Steel is the senior lighting technician and lighting designer at the Art Gallery of New South Wales and lighting design consultant to public museums and private galleries. He has worked on numerous major international exhibitions and with acclaimed international artists and leading architects. Steel has a master's degree in lighting, is the recipient of several IESANZ lighting awards and works as a lecturer at the University of Sydney.

Nicole Bouchard Tejeiro is a director at Crozier where she manages corporate strategic projects. She started her career at Crozier managing international shipments, then led a team of project managers before she was promoted to her current position. She has been a contributor to the *L Magazine* and to the ICEFAT newsletter, and has presented international art logistics topics to students and professionals within the industry. Her undergraduate studies in art history were completed at Brandeis University, with a thesis on technological motifs in nineteenth- and twentieth-century American art. She also holds an MBA from NYU's Stern School of Business.

About the Author

Brent Powell has been involved in the collection care profession since 1984. Outside of his employment career, he has been active since 1990 in the professional development aspects of the industry. Brent was the chairman of PACCIN [Preparation, Art Handling, Collection Care Information Network] from 1991 to 1999 and from 2008 to 2013. He has co-organized three preparator conferences and numerous single-day workshops, and presented sessions at national and regional museum conferences and webinars on various collection care subjects in the United States and Australia. Brent has coauthored three publications and contributed to numerous professional collection care publications and newsletters. In his employment positions, he has coauthored two working staff manuals, and designed and structured training programs for new and full-time staff in the museum in commercial roles of his employment.

Brent has conducted private collection care courses at the Campbell Center for Historic Preservation Studies and Midwest Conservation Studies, and at Housatonic Community College, for individual collectors' staff and artists' groups in the United States and Australia, and in Malaysia, at the University of Malaysia in Kuala Lumpur.

Brent has been employed extensively: (2013–present) as a principal of Museum Collection Care, Consultancy and Management in Melbourne, Australia; (2011–2013) as a senior project manager at Artex Fine Arts for the National Museum of Health and Medicine relocation at Walter Reed Army Base in Washington, DC; (2007–2011) as the head of preparation at Asian Art Museum in San Francisco; (2002–2007) as the manager of art services at National Gallery of Victoria in Melbourne, Australia; (2000–2002) as the director of museum services at International Art Services in Sydney,

Australia; (1999–2000) as the director of special projects at Fortress FAE in Baltimore, MD; (1986–1999) as the chief preparator at The Nelson-Atkins Museum of Art in Kansas City, MO; (1984–1986) as the production manager at Smith Kramer Fine Art Services in Kansas City, MO. Brent also holds an MFA in painting from the University of Arizona, Tucson, AZ (1983).

Lightning Source UK Ltd.
Milton Keynes UK
UKOW01f1715140218
317887UK00001B/335/P